AF835990

PLACE OF PERFORMANCE

This book provides an unprecedented analysis on the place of performance. The central theme is that the place of performance is of considerable significance as a connecting factor in international commercial contracts. This book challenges and questions the approach of the European legislator for not explicitly giving special significance to the place of performance in determining the applicable law in the absence of choice for commercial contracts. It also contains, inter alia, an analogy to matters of foreign country mandatory rules, and the coherence between jurisdiction and choice of law. It concludes by proposing a revised Article 4 of Rome I Regulation, which could be used as an international solution by legislators, judges, arbitrators and other stakeholders who wish to reform their choice of law rules.

Volume 27 in the series Studies in Private International Law

Studies in Private International Law

Recent titles in the series

Interregional Recognition and Enforcement of Civil and Commercial Judgments: Lessons for China from the US and EU Law
Jie Huang

The Recovery of Maintenance in the EU and Worldwide
Paul Beaumont, Burkhard Hess, Lara Walker and Stefanie Spancken

Australian Private International Law for the 21st Century: Facing Outwards
Edited by Andrew Dickinson, Thomas John and Mary Keyes

Maintenance and Child Support in Private International Law
Lara Walker

The Choice of Law Contract
Maria Hook

The Nature and Enforcement of Choice of Court Agreements: A Comparative Study
Mukarrum Ahmed

Cross-Border Litigation in Europe
Edited by Paul Beaumont, Mihail Danov, Katarina Trimmings and Burcu Yuksel

Forum (Non) Conveniens in England: Past, Present, and Future
Ardavan Arzandeh

Commercial Issues in Private International Law: A Common Law Perspective
Edited by Vivienne Bath, Andrew Dickinson, Michael Douglas and Mary Keyes

Jurisdiction and Cross-Border Collective Redress: A European Private International Law Perspective
Alexia Pato

Rethinking Judicial Jurisdiction in Private International Law
Milana Karayanidi

Economic Sanctions in EU Private International Law
Tamás Szabados

Clawback Law in the Context of Succession
Jayne Holliday

Private International Law in Nigeria
Chukwuma Samuel Adesina Okoli and Richard Frimpong Oppong

Place of Performance

A Comparative Analysis

Chukwuma Samuel Adesina Okoli

• HART •
OXFORD • LONDON • NEW YORK • NEW DELHI • SYDNEY

HART PUBLISHING
Bloomsbury Publishing Plc
Kemp House, Chawley Park, Cumnor Hill, Oxford, OX2 9PH, UK
1385 Broadway, New York, NY 10018, USA

HART PUBLISHING, the Hart/Stag logo, BLOOMSBURY and the Diana logo are trademarks of Bloomsbury Publishing Plc

First published in Great Britain 2020

Copyright © Chukwuma Samuel Adesina Okoli, 2020

Chukwuma Samuel Adesina Okoli has asserted his right under the Copyright, Designs and Patents Act 1988 to be identified as Author of this work.

All rights reserved. No part of this publication may be reproduced or transmitted in any form or by any means, electronic or mechanical, including photocopying, recording, or any information storage or retrieval system, without prior permission in writing from the publishers.

While every care has been taken to ensure the accuracy of this work, no responsibility for loss or damage occasioned to any person acting or refraining from action as a result of any statement in it can be accepted by the authors, editors or publishers.

All UK Government legislation and other public sector information used in the work is Crown Copyright ©. All House of Lords and House of Commons information used in the work is Parliamentary Copyright ©. This information is reused under the terms of the Open Government Licence v3.0 (http://www.nationalarchives.gov.uk/doc/open-government-licence/version/3) except where otherwise stated.

All Eur-lex material used in the work is © European Union, http://eur-lex.europa.eu/, 1998–2020.

A catalogue record for this book is available from the British Library.

Library of Congress Cataloging-in-Publication data

Names: Okoli, Chukwuma Samuel Adesina author.

Title: Place of performance : a comparative analysis / Chukwuma Okoli.

Description: Oxford ; New York Hart, 2020. | Based on author's thesis (doctoral - Université de Luxembourg, 2018) issued under title: The significance of the place of performance in commercial contracts under the European Union choice of law rules | Includes bibliographical references and index.

Identifiers: LCCN 2020002165 (print) | LCCN 2020002166 (ebook) | ISBN 9781509936205 (hardcover) | ISBN 9781509936212 (Epub)

Subjects: LCSH: Conflict of laws—Contracts—European Union countries. | European Parliament. Regulation (EC) No 593/2008 of the European Parliament and of the Council of 17 June 2008 on the law applicable to contractual obligations (Rome I)

Classification: LCC KJE983.C66 O39 2020 (print) | LCC KJE983.C66 (ebook) | DDC 346.2402/2—dc23

LC record available at https://lccn.loc.gov/2020002165

LC ebook record available at https://lccn.loc.gov/2020002166

ISBN: HB: 978-1-50993-620-5
ePDF: 978-1-50993-622-9
ePub: 978-1-50993-621-2

Typeset by Compuscript Ltd, Shannon
Printed and bound in Great Britain by CPI Group (UK) Ltd, Croydon CR0 4YY

MIX
Paper from responsible sources
FSC® C013604
www.fsc.org

To find out more about our authors and books visit www.hartpublishing.co.uk. Here you will find extracts, author information, details of forthcoming events and the option to sign up for our newsletters.

To my parents: Professor (Dr) Simon Chukwuma Okoli, and
Mrs Felicia Nwakaego Okoli

SERIES EDITOR'S PREFACE

This book is the first book in the Hart Studies in Private International Law Series to focus on the applicable law rules for commercial contracts in the absence of party autonomy. Therefore, it is an excellent complement to Maria Hook's book on *The Choice of Law Contract* and to Sophia Tang's book on *Electronic Consumer Contracts in the Conflict of Laws*.

This book begins with a very enlightening and thorough historical introduction to the history of the applicable law rules in contract in the absence of party autonomy in Europe (including the UK). In a cogent and interesting way, the author promotes the place of performance of the "characteristic" obligation as the best main connecting factor for a revised Article 4 of the Rome I Regulation. This would replace the "habitual residence" of the performer of the "characteristic" obligation as the main connecting factor. The writer makes a strong case based on pragmatism. The place of performance of the characteristic obligation is much more in keeping with the idea of "proximity" than the current rule which, in relation to legal persons, focuses on the place of central administration of the performer of the characteristic obligation (in simplistic terms the non-payment obligation). The place of central administration (where the key decisions for a company are taken) might have nothing to do with the place where the particular obligation in dispute was performed.

Dr Okoli has a back-up proposal. If the relevant legislator is not persuaded to change the main connecting factor away from the habitual residence of the performer of the characteristic obligation, he proposes it should make specific mention of the place of performance of the characteristic obligation as a relevant factor in applying the escape clause that gives priority to the law of a country which is more closely connected to the contract (Article 4(3) of Rome I). This would make it easier for the decision maker to find that the law of the place of characteristic performance is "manifestly" more closely connected to the contract than the place of habitual residence of the characteristic performer.

On the other hand, the author carefully defends the general reference to the "place of performance" in Article 9(3) of Rome I as a basis for the decision maker applying the overriding mandatory provisions of that law even when it is not the applicable law or the law of the forum. His analysis takes full account of the negotiating history of Article 9(3), of its predecessor Article 7(1) of the Rome Convention and of the case law on public policy or overriding mandatory rules justifying protecting a contracting party who has failed to perform the contract because it is "unlawful" in the place of performance. In this context a focus on where the contested performance is required makes more sense than focusing on the place of performance of the characteristic obligation.

Furthermore, Chukwuma Okoli provides some very original analysis on the concept of "coherence of interpretation" of connecting factors when the same ones are used for jurisdiction and applicable law. His promotion of the place of performance of the characteristic obligation in a contract is nuanced to mean the "main" place of performance of the characteristic obligation (eg the main place of delivery of the goods in a sale of goods contract where the goods are delivered in more than one country). In this regard he gets the idea from Article 7(1)(b) of Brussels Ia and uses it in his suggested reform of Article 4 of Rome I for applicable law. To take coherence of interpretation further he then advocates a wide construction to be given to the scope of Article 7(1)(b) of Brussels Ia so that the forum ends up applying its own law more often. Once again, his theoretical motivation is pragmatism – reducing costs for parties and making it more likely that judges will give the correct judgment because they are applying their own law, while respecting the conflicts justice notion of proximity.

The book is a very thorough analysis of English language sources across this broad ranging enquiry as to how "place of performance" is and should be dealt with in applicable law and to a lesser extent in jurisdiction. Not unreasonably, recognition and enforcement of judgments is not covered. So, the recent indirect rule of jurisdiction on contract in the Hague Judgments Convention 2019 is not analysed. It utilises the place of performance of the contractual obligation adjudicated upon in the judgment (not the place of performance of the characteristic obligation). Doubtless this is something the learned author will turn his mind to in due course.

Okoli offers a model statute for the applicable law rule in international commercial contracts in the absence of the parties choosing the law to govern their contract. It is presented as amendments to Rome I but could, as Okoli claims, be adapted by other legislators or even by the Hague Conference on Private International Law as part of a widening of the Hague Principles on International Commercial Contracts which at present only cover cases where the parties have chosen the law to govern their contract. Since the UK will retain the Rome I Regulation as part of retained EU law after the end of the implementation period (ie after 31 December 2020) it is possible that in due course the UK legislator could take up some or all of Okoli's suggested amendments to Rome I whether or not the EU does. Hopefully Okoli's book will help to stimulate a debate globally, in the EU and in the UK about the objective applicable law rules for international commercial contracts.

Professor Paul Beaumont,
Professor of Private International Law,
University of Stirling

ACKNOWLEDGEMENTS

This book is based on a PhD thesis I submitted at the University of Luxembourg, and published as 'The Significance of the Place of Performance in Commercial Contracts under the European Union Choice of Law Rules'.

When one undertakes a big academic project such as writing a book, one runs into a debt of gratitude. During the course of writing this book, I am in debt of gratitude to many people.

I thank Professor Paul Beaumont, who was my LLM dissertation (on which this book radically develops) supervisor at the University of Aberdeen, for playing a significant role in initiating me into the field of European Union private international law. I also thank him for the careful editing of an earlier draft of this book

I thank my PhD supervisor, Professor (Dr) Gilles Cuniberti for the service, and thorough job rendered in supervising my PhD thesis – such as providing a vigorous critique, and very constructive feedback on the draft works, throughout the period of my PhD programme at the University of Luxembourg. I am also grateful to him for teaching me how to significantly improve my writing and presentation skills as an academic, and exposing me to continental or civil law perspectives.

I am grateful to the editors and peer reviewers of both the *Journal of Private International Law*, and *Lloyds Maritime and Commercial Law Quarterly* for their comments and criticisms on the choice of law articles I submitted to their journal, which helped in improving the quality of the content of this book.

I am grateful to Professors (Dr) Patrick Kinsch and David Hiez who were members of my PhD committee ('CET') that provided advisory opinions to my supervisor on the progress of my work. In particular, I thank them for the honest and vigorous critique they offered on the methodological approach I took in my PhD thesis, and providing me with the opportunity to see the law through the eyes of continental scholars.

I am grateful to Professors (Dr) Adrain Briggs, Olivera Boskovic, Stephanie Francq, and Matthew Happold for their comments and criticisms on some aspects of this book.

I thank Associate Professor (Dr) Richard Frimpong Oppong for reading some draft aspects of this book, and providing me with an outsider's feedback. I am also profoundly grateful to him for the informal mentorship he has provided me in the field of private international law.

I am grateful to the Luxembourg National Research Fund and the TMC Asser Institute for supporting this project.

I am grateful to the University of Aberdeen for organising a conference based on the EUPILLAR (European Private International Law in Reality) project, which improved the framework of my research ideas in this book. I am grateful to the University of Cambridge for hosting the conference on the *Journal of Private International Law*, and inviting me to speak in that conference. The knowledge I gained at the conference at the University of Cambridge improved the framework of my research ideas in this book. I am also grateful to Sciences Po Paris for inviting me to participate in their Intensive Doctoral Week. I learnt a lot about improving my writing skills at Sciences Po Paris.

I am grateful to the students I taught at the University of Luxembourg, some of whom I learnt from as well.

I wish to thank my colleagues at the University of Luxembourg, who I enjoyed interacting with – many of whom were from a different legal background. In particular, I am very grateful to Dr Fatima Chaouche and Dr Johannes Hendrik Fahner, who were PhD representatives during the course of my programme. It is worthy of mention that they did a fantastic job in providing me with the needed support during the period of my PhD programme.

I also wish to thank the non-academic staff at the University of Luxembourg, who were helpful to me during my programme. In particular, I am grateful to Miss Monique Roulling for her support during my PhD programme.

I thank many of the presenters at the EUPILLAR project, led by the University of Aberdeen for responding to my enquiries, as it relates to this book. In particular, I thank Miss Celine Camara for providing me with many of the materials (including Member States' case law) that were presented at the EUPILLAR project.

I thank Mr Felix Mgbekonye, Dr Roger Tafotie and Dr Athanase Popov for assisting me with translation of some of the works in French language utilised in this book.

I am indebted to my friends Mr Oluwaseyi Arigbabowo, Dr Eghosa Ekhator and Mr Osamede Osamede who played a supportive role during my PhD programme.

I thank Dr Jorge Toro-Pozo, Mr Amin Sleimi and Dr Huizhu Sun, who were patient enough to discuss some aspects of this book with me, and offer a non-professional's perspective on it.

I thank the staff of Hart Publishing (especially Tom Adams, Sasha Jawed and Emma Platt) for their work in making this book ready and accessible to the world. It has been a very pleasant experience working with Hart.

I cannot end without thanking my family in Nigeria who were supportive to me. I am eternally grateful to my father (Professor SC Okoli), and my mother (Mrs FN Okoli) for the endless support and encouragement they provided me during my PhD programme. I am grateful to my brother, Dr Chukwuemeka Okoli, who was supportive to me during my PhD programme in many ways one can imagine.

Finally, I am grateful to my wife, Mrs Uchechi Chiazokam Okoli (*nee* Ibekwe) for her continuous show of love, encouragement and patience.

Dr Chukwuma Samuel Adesina Okoli
21 October 2019

TABLE OF CONTENTS

TABLE OF CASES

Arbitral Decisions

Australia

Austria

Canada

Court of Justice of the European Union

Denmark

France

Germany

Hong Kong

Ireland

Netherlands

Opinions of Advocate Generals

Singapore

Spain

Switzerland

United Kingdom

United States of America

TABLE OF LEGISLATION, INTERNATIONAL CONVENTIONS AND POLICY DOCUMENTS

Australia

Canada

European Union

International

Switzerland

United States of America

1

Introduction

I. Background

This book is particularly concerned with the significance of the place of performance in the European Union (EU) choice of law rules in determining the applicable law in the absence of choice for international commercial contracts.[1]

At first sight, one may wonder why this study is important. Are matters of choice of law of any practical significance when compared to issues of jurisdiction, and recognition and enforcement of foreign judgments? If matters of choice of law are so significant, can the parties not always choose the applicable law, so that issues relating to the applicable law in the absence of choice, such as the significance of the place of performance as a connecting factor in choice of law for international commercial contracts, becomes otiose?

It is true that in private international law, matters of jurisdiction and recognition and enforcement of foreign judgments raise issues of considerable practical significance for litigants in cross-border transactions. Thus it might be argued that litigants are not really bothered with choice of law theories. In this connection, some scholars have submitted that litigants are not

> concerned about the principles of law to be used to adjudicate their dispute. Nor are they too concerned by the fact that those principles may become relevant to deciding disputes between other persons in the future. To a large extent, they are pragmatist and parochial actors; they are more concerned with the judgment as a remedy and the material consequence of being granted such remedy.[2]

In addition, some scholars argue that, while choice of law has traditionally dominated conflicts scholarship, there was a shift a few decades ago towards jurisdiction and recognition and enforcement of foreign judgments.[3]

[1] Rome I Regulation (Regulation (EC) No. 593/2008 of the European Parliament and of the Council of 17 June 2008 on the Law Applicable to Contractual Obligations [2008] OJ L177/6). Rome I replaces the Rome Convention (OJ 1980 L266).

[2] RF Oppong and LC Niro, 'Enforcing Judgments of International Courts in National Courts' (2014) 5 *Journal of International Dispute Settlement* 344, 346. However the authors rightly concede that their submission 'is not meant to underrate the importance of choice of law in many cross-border disputes. This is especially so in the area of remedies where there are significant differences between national laws … the applicable law also remains significant.' (ibid, 346).

[3] A Briggs, 'Essay in International Litigation and the Conflict of Laws' (1995) 111 *Law Quarterly Review* 159, 160–61.

However, it is opined here that the practical significance of the law that applies to an international commercial contract must not be underestimated. The law that applies to an international commercial contract in cross-border transactions is one of considerable significance. Where parties, through their lawyers, are engaged in the determination of the applicable law in the absence of choice, it usually serves one main purpose – the difference in the application of one of those laws usually provides a more favourable outcome for one of the parties.[4] This is usually significant from the perspective of the remedies the parties are seeking to obtain from the decision maker. In particular, some scholars submit that:

> Different legal systems provide different solutions to different legal problems. The following are just a few examples where the law may differ from State to State: whether or not commercial parties owe good faith obligations; the availability of specific performance as a contractual remedy; the enforceability of agreed sums for breach; and the length of time permitted to bring proceedings under relevant statutes of limitations.[5]

Parties, through their lawyers, do not debate the determination of the applicable law for the fun of it. Where the parties can reasonably predict in advance what law governs their international commercial contract, this is likely to facilitate a settlement of the dispute between the parties and avoid litigation, arbitration proceedings or any other means of dispute resolution. In addition, it is not uncommon for the parties to settle once the decision maker has made a finding on the applicable law.[6]

In the EU choice of law rules, the law that applies to an international commercial contract is very important because Article 12(1) of Rome I provides that it governs the interpretation, the performance, the consequences of a breach of obligations such as assessment of damages, the various ways of extinguishing obligations and prescription and limitation of actions, and the consequences of nullity of a contract. This is a significant point that will be returned to in this chapter.[7]

In addition, the EU choice of law rules can determine the allocation of EU jurisdiction for commercial contracts that are not contracts of sale and provision of services.[8] In effect, EU choice of law for commercial contracts can play a decisive role in the allocation of jurisdiction for some international commercial contracts.

[4] In other words, where there is no material difference in the applicable law, parties hardly ever waste time and costs in debating it, nor is it useful for the court to invite the parties to debate the point or make a decision on it. See also *PC Express AB v Columbus It Partner A/S (Denmark)* [2001] ILPr 22 (Eastern Appellate Court of Copenhagen); *VTB Capital Plc v Nutritek International Corp* [2013] 1 CLC 153 [46]–[49].

[5] B Hayward, 'Is Arbitral Justice Blind? The Conflict of Law and International Commercial Arbitration' available at http://afia.asia/2017/03/is-arbitral-justice-blind-the-conflict-of-law-and-international-commercial-arbitration/.

[6] See also P Rogerson, 'Problems of the Applicable Law of the Contract in the English Common Law Jurisdiction Rules: The Good Arguable Case' (2013) 9 *Journal of Private International Law* 387, 393; B Hayward, *Conflict of Laws and Arbitral Discretion – The Closest Connection Test* (Oxford, Oxford University Press, 2017) 38–39, [1.78]–[1.79].

[7] See Section II of this chapter.

[8] See generally C-12/76, *Tessili v Dunlop*, EU:C:1976:133.

In England, although the applicable law (as currently determined by the EU choice of law rules) does not automatically determine the existence or exercise of a court's jurisdiction, the applicable law of a contract is very important because it is a significant factor (and it *could be* decisive as well where it is an express choice of law) that an English court takes into account at the interlocutory stage to determine the existence or exercise of its traditional jurisdiction common law rules[9] where there is a foreign element.[10] Thus, based on an empirical and statistical study of the English Court's application of Article 4 of the Rome Convention (now Article 4 of Rome I),[11] it is observed that English practice is consistent to the effect that in all the cases where English law is held to be the applicable law, English courts exercised or assumed jurisdiction under the principle of *forum non conveniens*.[12] On the other hand, in all the cases (except one) under Article 4 of

[9] This is where the Brussels Ia (Council Regulation (EU) No 1215/2012 of the European Parliament and of the Council of 12 December 2012 [2012] OJ L351/1), Lugano Convention (Council Regulation (EC) L 339/3 of 21 December 2007 on Convention on Jurisdiction and the Recognition and Enforcement of Judgments in Civil and Commercial Matters), and intra-UK jurisdiction (Civil Jurisdiction and Judgments Act 1982 (1982 Act)) scheme are inapplicable. cf Article 33 of Brussels Ia which introduces some discretion to decline jurisdiction for third (or Non-Member) state cases.

[10] *BP Expoloration Co (Libya) v Hunt* [1976] 3 All ER, 879, 893 (Ker J); *The Hollandia* [1983] 1 AC 565; *Britannia Steamship Insurance Association Ltd & Ors v Ausonia Assicurazioni SPA* [1984] 2 Lloyd's Rep 98; *Spiliada Maritime Corporation v Cansulex Ltd* [1987] AC 460, 481 (Lord Goff); *Charm Maritime Inc v Kyriakou* [1987] 1 Lloyd's Rep 433; *Seashell Shipping Corp v Mutualidad de Seguros De Instituto Nacional De Industria ('Musini') ('Magnum) ex. 'Tarraco Augusta'* [1989] 1 Lloyd's Law Rep 47; *Irish Shipping Ltd v Commercial Union Assurance Co Plc and Another* [1990] 2 WLR117, 229 (Staughton LJ); *The Nile Rhapsody* [1992] 2 LLR 399, [1994] 1 LLR 382 (CA); *Macsteel Commercial Holdings (Pty) Ltd v Thermasteel v (Canada) Inc* [1996] CLC 1403, 1407 (Sir Thomas Bingham MR), 1408 (Millet LJ); *Tiernan v Magen Insurance Co Ltd* [2000] ILPr 517 (Com Ct) [18]; *BFC Aircraft Sales and Leasing Ltd v Ages Group Plc* Unreported, December 14, 2001 [10] (Morison J); *Lincoln National Life Insurance Co v Employers Reinsurance Corp* [2002] EWHC 28 (Comm) [25]; *Navigators Insurance Co & Ors v Atlantic Methanol Production Company* LLC [2004] Lloyd's Rep IR 418; *Tryg Baltica International (UK) Ltd v Boston Compania De Seguros SA & Ors* [2004] EWHC 1186 [42–49]; *Sawyer v Atari Interactive Inc* [2005] EWHC 2351 [57]; *Dornoch Ltd v Mauritius Union Assurance Co Ltd* [2005] EWHC 1887 [72], [86] (approved on appeal in *Dornoch Ltd v Mauritius Union Assurance Co* [2006] EWCA Civ 389); *Stonebridge Underwriting Ltd v Ontario Municipal Insurance Exchange* [2010] 2 CLC 349; *Novus Aviation Limited v Onur Air Tasimaciik AS* [2009] EWCA Civ. 122 [77]; *Golden Ocean Group Ltd v Salgaocar Mining Industries Pvt Ltd, Mr Anil V Salgaocar* [2011] EWHC 56 (Comm.) [139]; *Wright v Deccan Chargers Sporting Ventures Ltd* [2011] ILPr 37 [29] (report of the Master's decision at para 85 in the lower court which was approved); *Mujur Bakat Sdn Bdh v Uni Asia General Insurance Bhd* [2011] EWHC 643 [19]–[20]; *VTB Capital* (n 4) [46]; *Caresse Navigation Ltd v Office National de l'Electricite & Ors* [2013] EWHC 3081 (Comm.) [61]; *Navig8 Pte Ltd v Al-Riyadh Co ('The Lucky Lady')* [2013] EWHC 328; *Vizcaya Partners Ltd v Picard* [2016] 3 All ER 181. See also L Collins et al, *Dicey, Morris & Collins, The Conflict of Laws* 15th edn (London, Sweet and Maxwell, 2012) [12–055]; Rogerson (n 6). cf M Hook 'The Choice of Law Agreement as a Reason for Exercising Jurisdiction' (2014) 63 *International & Comparative Law Quarterly* 963, 968.

[11] For a detailed empirical study on the concept of implied choice and escape clause in the European Union choice of law rules for commercial contracts see MP Fons, 'Commercial Choice of Law in Context: Looking beyond Rome' (2015) 78 *Modern Law Review* 241–95.

[12] *Bank of Baroda v Vysya Bank Ltd* [1994] CLC 41; *Hogg Insurance Brokers Ltd v Guardian Insurance Co Inc* [1997] 1 Lloyd's Rep 412; *Gan Insurance Co Ltd v Tai Ping Insurance Co. Ltd* [1999] 2 All ER (Comm) 54; *Tiernan* (n 10); *Samcrete Egypt Engineers & Contractors SAE v Land Rover Exports Ltd* [2001] EWCA Civ 2019; *CGU International Insurance Plc v Szabo* [2002] 1 All ER (Comm) 83 (QB); *Latchin (t/a Dinkha Latchin Associates) v General Mediterranean Holdings SA* [2002] CLC 330 (QB);

the Rome Convention, where the law of another country is held to be applicable, English courts stayed proceedings or declined jurisdiction in favour of another country.[13]

Since the applicable law is very important in international commercial contracts, the significance of this is that it is very attractive and desirable for parties to choose the law that governs their international commercial contract. This saves time, and litigation and transaction costs, in determining what law should apply to an international commercial contract in the event of a dispute. The parties can also choose a law that is not hostile to their interests or the efficacy of the international commercial transaction. Perhaps, this explains why the principle of party autonomy is widespread internationally and has gained acceptance in some international statutes.[14]

The EU legislator had this in mind, and gave the parties to an international commercial contract the freedom to choose the applicable law that governs their contract.[15] The parties can either choose the applicable law in advance by a standard choice of law clause, or choose the applicable law during judicial proceedings.[16] The principle of party autonomy is so important in choice of law for contractual obligations in the context of the EU, that the EU legislator regards it as one of 'the cornerstones of the system of conflict-of-law rules in matters of contractual obligations'.[17]

As a starting point, the significance of this book must be viewed through the lens of party autonomy. This is because if the principle of party autonomy is always effectively and validly utilised in international commercial contracts, this book would not be worth writing. In reality, this book is worth writing because despite

The Lincoln (n 10); *Staines v Walsh* [2003] EWHC 458 (Ch); *Apple Corps Ltd v Apple Computers Inc* [2004] EWHC 768 (Ch); *Tonicstar Ltd (t/a Lloyds Syndicate 1861) v American Home Assurance Co* [2004] EWHC 1234 (Comm.); *Tryg* (n 10); *Marconi Communications International Ltd v PT Pan Indonesia Bank TBK* [2005] EWCA Civ 422; *Ark Therapeutics plc v True North Capital Ltd* [2005] EWHC 1585 (Comm); *Dornoch* (n 10); *Albon (t/a NA Carriage Co) v Naza Motor Trading Sdn Bhd* [2007] EWHC 9; *Pablo Star Ltd v Emirates Integrated Telecommunications Co PJSC (t/a Du)* [2009] All ER (D) 143 (Oct); *Cecil v Bayat* [2010] EWHC 641 (Comm); *BAT Industries Plc v Windward Prospects Ltd* [2013] EWHC 4087 (Comm.). See also *Scott v West & Mackie v Baxter* [2012] EWHC 1890 (CH).

[13] *Mirchandani v Somaia* [2001] All ER (D) 311; *American Motorists Insurance Co (AMICO) v Cellstar Corp* [2003] EWCA Civ 206; *Armstrong International Ltd v Deutsche Bank Securities Inc* [2003] All ER (D) 195; *Ophthalmic Innovations International (UK) Ltd v Ophthalmic Innovations International Inc* [2004] EWHC 2948 Ch; *Sax v Tchernoy* [2014] EWHC 795 (Comm). cf *Sharab v Prince Al-Waleed Bin Tala Bin Abdal-Aziz-Al-Saud* (Ch), [2008] All ER (D) 16. A major reason for this approach might also be that given that the concept of natural forum is a factor which is highly relevant in the *forum non conveniens* analysis, the implication of the foregoing is that the principle of closest connection in the EU choice of law rules usually leads the English court to determining whether or not it is the natural forum for resolving the parties' dispute.

[14] See for example Article 3 of Rome I; Article 1.3 of The Hague Principles on Choice of Law for International Commercial Contracts, 2015; Inter-American Convention on Law Applicable to Contracts, March 17, 1994. See Hayward (n 6) 10–15, [1.18]–[1.27].

[15] Article 3 of Rome I.

[16] In the latter case, it is the law of the forum that is usually chosen, where the parties do not make a choice of law in advance.

[17] Recital 11 to Rome I.

the significance of party autonomy in international commercial contracts, it is not always effectively and validly utilised.

In international commercial contracts, the parties (and/or the lawyers who act on their behalf) may be unable to make a choice of law for at least three reasons. First, they may be unable to reach an agreement on the applicable law due to conflicting interests – such that a choice of the applicable law in favour of one of the parties may be viewed as being a legal and commercial disadvantage to the other party.[18] Second, the parties may overlook the possibility of making a choice of law – this could be as a result of the haste in which the transaction is concluded; or the international commercial transaction is scattered in various jurisdictions such as in cases of back-to-back contracts like letters of credit; or the significance of making an express choice of law is simply not appreciated. Third, the choice of law may be regarded by the court as invalid or ineffective.

The law that applies in the absence of a choice of law thus becomes an important consideration. The approach of the EU legislator is to give principal significance to the habitual residence of the characteristic performer in determining the applicable law for most international commercial contracts.[19] In this connection, this book challenges the approach of the EU legislator which does not explicitly give the place of performance special significance in the EU choice of law rules for determining the applicable law in the absence of choice, and accordingly proposes a reform of the existing law. The key proposal in this book is that the place of performance is of considerable significance in international commercial contracts and thus deserves to be explicitly given special significance under a revised Article 4 of Rome I.

II. Scope of the Applicable Law: Place of Performance

It is opined here that in international commercial contracts, where the parties do not make a choice of law, the law of the place of performance should be applied as much as possible, so that it coincides with the law governing matters of performance as well. Given that it has been demonstrated above that the applicable law is one of considerable significance in international commercial contracts, the opinion here is a starting point for supporting the central claim in this book, and it would not be further discussed in other chapters of this book.

In an international commercial contract, the performance is a key element of the contract. For example the primary concern of the seller is to receive payment for goods delivered to the buyer, while the primary concern for the buyer is to receive the goods from the seller. If the obligations of the parties are not fulfilled, there is a failure.

[18] *Apple* (n 12) [5] (Mann J).
[19] Article 4(1)(a)(b)(e) and (f) and Article 4(2) of Rome I.

Given the considerable importance of the performance in international commercial contracts, the questions arising are: should the law of the place of performance always govern an international commercial contract? In the alternative, should the law of the place of performance always govern matters of performance? These questions are the starting point for a further elaborate discussion in this book on why the place of performance should be given special significance under a revised Article 4 of Rome I.

Ideally, it might be argued that given the importance of the place of performance, the parties should always choose the law of the place of performance to govern their international commercial contracts. Empirical studies that have been conducted on why the parties choose a particular law to govern their international commercial contract have not identified the significance of one connecting factor over another, as one of the reasons why the parties might opt for the law of the place of performance.[20] The parties in choosing a particular law might be more concerned with a law that suits their interest in the contract, and one that is not hostile to the international commercial transaction they are entering into. In effect, in international commercial contracts, the significance of the place of performance or indeed any other connecting factor might not be a decisive or strong reason why the parties would decide whether or not to choose a particular law. Moreover, under the EU choice of law rules, generally, the chosen law does not need to have a significant or relevant connection to the dispute.[21]

Given that the interests of the parties are paramount in exercising party autonomy, this book does not argue in favour of the European legislator compelling the parties to choose the law of the place of performance to govern their international commercial contract. In effect, the rule of party autonomy that the parties should be allowed to choose the law that best favours their interest should not be discarded by the European legislator.[22]

If the parties exercise party autonomy and choose a law that is not the place of performance, it may be argued that the law of the place of performance should regulate matters of performance. Article 12(1)(b) of Rome I works against such a situation by providing that the *lex causae* also governs matters of performance. In effect, generally, if the law of the place of performance is not the law chosen by the parties, it (the law of the place of performance) cannot be applied separately to matters of performance.

[20] G Cuniberti, 'The International Market for Contracts – The Most Attractive Contract Laws' (2014) 34 *Northwestern Journal of International and Business* Law 455; G Cuniberti, 'The Laws of Asian International Business Transactions' (2016) 25 *Washington International Law* Journal 35.

[21] Article 3 of Rome I. See also C-54/16, *Vinyls Italia SpA v Mediterranea di Navigazione SpA*, EU:C:2017:433.

[22] However, party autonomy is not always a good rule in international commercial contracts. It is not uncommon that the stronger party would have the upper hand in foisting a standard choice of law clause that suits its interest more.

The logic of Article 12(1)(b) of Rome I can be defended as being sound. The provision of Article 12(1)(b) was enacted in order to avoid or forestall the conflict or inconsistent results that may arise where for example the *lex causae* regards an international commercial contract as valid, but the law of the place of performance validly excuses the performance. This scenario arose in the English case of *Jacobs, Marcus & Co v Crèdit Lyonnais*.[23] In that case the plaintiffs brought an action against the defendant for non-delivery of goods in relation to a contract of sale that was governed by English law. The goods were to be delivered from Algeria. The defendants in their statement of defence admitted the non-delivery complained of, but alleged that the insurrection in Algeria and the military operations connected with it had rendered the performance of the contract impossible; and that the French Civil Code which was then in force throughout Algeria, recognised this situation as *force majeure* which was an excuse for non-performance. The English Court of Appeal held that according to English law non-performance of the contract could not be excused, and since the contract was governed by English law, the French Civil Code could not be applied to this case to excuse the performance of the defendant. If the French Civil Code had been applied in relation to the performance contrary to the decision of the English Court of Appeal, there would have been a logically inconsistent decision that would have excused the performance of the defendants contrary to what obtains under English law.[24]

However, Article 12(2) of Rome I provides that in relation to the manner of performance and the steps to be taken in the event of defective performance, regard shall be had to the law of the country in which performance takes place.[25] Article 12(2) of Rome I underscores the importance that is placed on the law of the place of performance.[26] Article 12(2) honours the view that in commercial transactions international businesspersons sometimes expect that the law of the country or legal system where the contract was performed would govern their commercial transactions.[27] Thus, if the *lex causae* does not coincide with the place of performance regard shall be had for the law of the country where performance takes place.

[23] *Jacobs, Marcus & Co v Crèdit Lyonnais* [1884] 12 QBD 589.

[24] See also *Auckland Corp v Alliance Ass'ce Co*, [1937] AC 587 (PC) at 606 (Lord Wright MR); *Mount Albert Borough Council v Australasian Temperance & General Mutual Life Ass'ce Society Ltd* [1938] AC 224, 241 (Lord Wright). cf *Adelaide Electric Supply Co v Prudential Ass'ce Co.* [1934] AC 122, 151 (Lord Wright).

[25] See generally F Ferrari, 'Article 12 of Rome I Regulation' in U Magnus and P Mankowski (eds), *European Commentaries on Private International Law* vol II (Munich, Sellier European Law Publishers, 2017) 735–37, [18–41]; M McParland, *The Rome I Regulation on the Law Applicable to Contractual Obligations* (Oxford, Oxford University Press, 2015) 750–54, [17.27]–[17.43]. See also A Chong, 'The Public Policy and Mandatory Rules of Third Countries in International Contracts' (2006) 2 *Journal of Private International Law* 27, 54–56 for a commentary on Article 12(2) of Rome I.

[26] cf Section 206 of the Restatement (Second) Conflict of Laws, 1971 provides that 'the local law of the place of performance will be applied to govern all questions relating to details of performance'.

[27] See also R Fentiman, *International Commercial Litigation* (Oxford, Oxford University Press, 2015) 210–12 on the issue of commercial expectations.

It is not clear what is meant by 'manner of performance'[28] and 'steps to be taken in the event of defective performance'.[29] It is suggested that 'manner of performance' includes currency of payment, time of delivery and method of examining the quality of goods, public holidays, manner or method in which services are to be provided.[30] It is suggested that 'steps to be taken in the event of defective performance' includes steps to be taken if goods are rejected, and form and time within which goods may be rejected for defective performance.[31]

Article 12(2) could lead to a split in the applicable law, given that it appears to create a distinction between the substance of the obligation which is governed by the *lex causae*, and the mode (or manner and method) of performance which is governed by the law of the place of performance.[32] Moreover, as the Giuliano-Lagarde report submits, it

> means that the court may consider whether such law has any relevance to the manner in which the contract should be performed and has a discretion whether to apply it in whole or in part so as to do justice between the parties.[33]

If this is the case, it is possible that there might be conflicting results where the *lex causae* is not the same as the law of the place of performance.[34] Assume Party A, habitually resident in Country X, and Party B, habitually resident in Country Y, enters into a contract for Party A to deliver goods to Party B in Country Y within a period of one month. Under the law of Country X failure to deliver the goods within 30 days releases Party B from his obligation to pay (Party A) under the contract, while under Country Y goods should only be delivered within a reasonable time. The place of agreed delivery is the country of destination, which is Country Y. Assume Party A fails to deliver the goods to Party B in Country Y within 30 days, but delivers it on the 35th day and Party B rejects the goods. Assuming the court decides Country X to be the governing law, Party B could argue that the applicable law is the law of Country X, so that Party B is released from his obligations to pay

[28] 'What is meant, however, by "manner of performance" of an obligation? It does not seem that any precise and uniform meaning is given to this concept in the various laws and in the different views of learned writers. The Group did not for its part wish to give a strict definition of this concept. It will consequently be the *lex fori* to determine what is meant by "manner of performance".' – M Giuliano and P Lagarde, *Report on the Convention on the Law Applicable to Contractual Obligations* ('Giuliano-Lagarde Report') [1980] OJ C282, 33.

[29] See BV Hoffmann, 'General Report on Contractual Obligations' in O Lando et al (eds), *European Private International Law of Obligations Acts and Documents of an Internat Colloquim on the European Preliminary Draft Convention on the Law Applicable to Contractual and Non-Contractual Obligation* 1st edn (Tubingen, Mohr, 1975) 1, 26–27; P Largarde, 'The Scope of the Applicable Law in the EEC Convention' in P North (ed), *Contract Conflicts: The EEC Convention on the Law Applicable to Contractual Obligations: A Comparative Study* 1st edn (Amsterdam, North-Holland Publishing Co, 1982) 49, 55; Giuliano-Largarde Report (n 28).

[30] ibid (all).

[31] ibid (all).

[32] *East West Corporation v DKBS AF 1912* & *Ors* [2002] EWHC 83 (Comm) [64].

[33] Giuliano-Largarde Report (n 28) 33. The interpretation concerned Article 10(2) of the Rome Convention, which is equivalent to Article 12(2) of Rome I.

[34] cf McParland (n 25) 750–54, [17.27]–[17.43].

for the goods which were delivered after 30 days. Party A could on the contrary argue that the court is concerned with the manner of performance and steps to be taken in the event of defective performance so that regard should be had to the law of Country Y. The court in having regard to the law of Country Y might actually follow the requirements of Article 12(2). The application of the law of the place of performance in this case is actually inconsistent with the *lex causae* (Country X).

This type of splitting of the applicable law and inconsistent solution described above could be reduced, if the principal connecting factor in determining the applicable law in the absence of choice was the place of performance, rather than the habitual residence of the characteristic performer.

In summation, the opinion here is that in situations where the parties do not make a choice of law, as much as possible, the place of performance should be applied. Where the applicable law is in issue, it is quite often concerned with matters of performance. The performance of an international commercial contract is usually a key issue for the parties in the event of a dispute. In addition, matters of interpretation, consequences of breach of obligations and extinguishing obligations provided for under Article 12(1)(a)(c) and (d) of Rome I would also be connected to performance.

III. Originality

The key contribution of this book to knowledge is that it proposes that the place of performance should be explicitly given special significance under a revised Article 4 of Rome I. To the best of my knowledge this is the first book or academic study *dedicated* to advancing the view that the place of performance should be explicitly given special significance under the EU choice of law for international commercial contracts. For the purpose of demonstrating the originality of this book, I would briefly consider other related academic publications and books (or PhD theses) separately.

In this connection, most academic publications focus mainly on the applicable law in the absence of choice for commercial contracts in the EU choice of law rules.[35] The discussion usually focuses on the law applicable in the absence

[35] G Güneysu-Güngör, 'Article 4 of Rome I Regulation on the Applicable Law in the Absence of Choice – Methodological Analysis, Considerations' in P Stone and Y Farah (eds), *Research Handbook on EU Private International Law* (Cheltenham, Edward Elgar Publishing, 2015) 170; A Arzandeh, 'The Law Governing International Contractual Disputes in the Absence of Express Choice by the Parties' (2015) *Lloyd's Maritime and Commercial Law Quarterly* 525; A Dickinson, 'Rebuttable Assumptions (*ICF* v *Balkenende*)' (2010) *Lloyd's Maritime and Commercial Law Quarterly* 27; G O'Connor, 'When in Rome: An Examination of Article 4 of the Rome Regime on the Governing Law of International Contracts' (2010) 9 *Hibernian Law Journal* 39–54; F Ferrari, 'Quelques remarques sur le droit applicable aux obligations contractuelles en l'absence de choix des parties – Art 4 du Règlement Rome I' (2009) 3 *Revue critique de droit international privé* 459; Z Tang, 'Law Applicable in the Absence of Choice – The New Article 4 of the Rome I Regulation' (2008) 71 *Modern Law Review* 785; S Atrill, 'Choice of Law

of choice without a detailed analysis of how potential connecting factors might operate.

Generally, the trend in academic publications is not to specifically focus in detail on how connecting factors might be significant or operate in the context of the EU choice of law rules for commercial contracts.[36] Thus, there are very few publications dedicated to the principle of accessory allocation or doctrine of infection[37] as a connecting factor in the context of the EU choice of law rules.[38] The only real exception in the context of the EU choice of law rules is the connecting factor of the habitual residence of the characteristic performer, which has attracted a detailed and focused analysis by some scholars in the past.[39]

This trend might be understandable on the basis that it is the habitual residence of the characteristic performer that is given principal significance in determining the applicable law in the absence of choice for most international commercial

in Contract: the Missing Pieces of the Article 4 Jigsaw' (2004) 53 *International and Comparative Law Quarterly* 549–77; W O' Brian, 'Choice of Law under the Rome Convention: the Dancer or the Dance' (2004) *Lloyd's Maritime and Commercial Law Quarterly* 375; J Hill, 'Choice of Law in Contract under the Rome Convention: The Approach of the UK Courts' (2004) 53 *International and Comparative Law Quarterly* 325.

[36] cf U Magnus, 'Article 4 of Rome I Regulation' in U Magnus and P Mankowski (eds), *European Commentaries on Private International Law* vol. II (Munich, Sellier European Law Publishers, 2017) 263.

[37] It refers to a situation where the court uses a law governing one or more contracts to govern another closely related contract(s), where the parties have not made an express choice of law to govern all the contracts they have entered into in an international commercial transaction. See Recitals 20 and 21 to Rome I.

[38] CSA Okoli, 'The Significance of the Doctrine of Accessory Allocation as a Connecting Factor under Article 4 of Rome I Regulation' (2013) 9 *Journal of Private International Law* 449; S Corneloup, 'Choix de loi et contrats lies' in S Corneloup and N Joubert (eds), *Le reglèment communautaire 'Rome I' et le choix de loi dans les contrats internationaux* (Paris, Lexis Nexis, 2011) coll.du CREDIMI spec 285. See also V Parisot, 'Note sous Civ 1ère 12 octobre 2011, no 10-19517' (2012) *Journal de Droit International*, Comm 20, 1335 (Convention de Rome du 19 juin 1980 sur la loi applicable aux obligations contractuelles – loi applicable au cautionnement); N Enonchong, 'The Law Applicable to Demand Guarantees and Counter-Guarantees' (2015) *Lloyd's Maritime and Commercial Law Quarterly* 194–215.

[39] HUJ d'Oliviera, '"Characteristic Obligation" in the Draft EEC Obligation Convention' (1977) 25 *American Journal of Comparative Law* 303; K Lipstein, 'Characteristic Performance – A New Concept in the Conflict of Laws in Matters of Contract for the EEC' (1981) 3 *Northwestern Journal of International and Business* 402; F Vischer, 'The Principle of the Typical Performance in International Contracts and the Draft Convention' in P North (ed), *Contract Conflicts, The E.E.C. Convention on the Law Applicable to Contractual Obligations: A Comparative Study* (Amsterdam, North-Holland Company, 1982) 25, 27; N Richardson, 'The Concept of Characteristic Performance and the Proper Law Doctrine' (1989) 1 *Bond Law Review* 284; G Kaufmann-Kohler, 'La prestation caractéristique en droit international privé et l'influence de la Suisse' (1989) XLV *Annuaire suisse de droit international* 195; PM Patocchi, 'Characteristic Performance: A New Myth in the Conflict of Laws? Some Comments on a Recent Concept in Swiss and European Private International Law', in *Études de droit international en l'honneur de Pierre Lalive* (Bâle/Francfort sur-le-Main, Éditions Helbing & Lichtenhahn, 1993) 113; LF Carillo, *Contratos internacionales: la prestación caracteristica* (unpublished PhD thesis, Bologne, 1994); F Vischer, 'The Concept of the Characteristic Performance Reviewed' in *E Pluribus Unum, Liber Amicorum G. Droz*, (Martinus Nijhoff Publishers, 1996) 499; P Mankowski, 'The Principle of Characteristic Performance Visited Yet Again' in K Boele-Woelki et al (eds), *Convergence and Divergence in Private International Law:Liber Amicorum Kurt Siehr* (The Hague, Schultess and Eleven International Publishing, 2010) 433. The non-English language sources are cited in C Robitaille, 'La doctrine de la prestation caractéristique en droit international privé des contrats' available at www.memoireonline.com/a/fr/cart/download/t1TQK3lCZSqh.

contracts in the EU choice of law rules. Dedicated attention by very few scholars to the doctrine of infection or accessory allocation might also be justified on the basis that such a connecting factor is explicitly given special significance under the current Article 4 of Rome I.[40] In effect, some scholars may not have been attracted to give a detailed study to the significance of the place of performance or other connecting factors, in the context of the EU choice of law rules for determining the applicable law in the absence of choice, because it is the connecting factor of the habitual residence of the characteristic performer, and doctrine of infection or accessory allocation that are explicitly given special significance by the European legislator, and thus worthy of attention and further study.

The only academic publication which I have come across that comes close to my work is Cuniberti's article.[41] It is a short article dedicated to the discussion of the place of performance in the context of the relationship between Article 4(2) and 4(5) of the Rome Convention. In that article, Cuniberti was puzzled as to why the place of performance which is of considerable significance in international commercial contracts is not the principal connecting factor in determining closest connection, whereas the habitual residence of the characteristic performer, which he regarded as a weak connecting factor (but not irrelevant) in determining closest connection was the presumptive connecting factor under Article 4(2) of the Rome Convention. Though Cuniberti's article argued for a reform in the logic of the EU choice of law rules in determining the applicable law in the absence of choice, he did not go as far as explicitly proposing that the place of performance should be given special significance, or inter alia contain some of the additional arguments (relying on Article 9(3) of Rome I and Article 7(1) of Brussels Ia) contained in this book on why the place of performance is a connecting factor that has considerable significance in international commercial contracts. Moreover, Cuniberti's article is a very short piece: not more than seven pages long. At best, like other academic works and authorities utilised in this book, it sowed the seeds for a reform of the law in the context of giving special significance to the place of performance in determining the applicable law in the absence of choice in the EU choice of law rules. In effect, Cuniberti's article does not rob this book of its originality.

In the context of PhD theses (or books), there are scant works dedicated to the determination of the applicable law in the absence of choice in the EU choice of law rules.[42] In particular, these PhD works are not dedicated to a study of the significance of place of performance in commercial contracts in the EU choice of law rules.

However, Hayward's book is worthy of attention as it appears inter alia to be concerned with the reform of Article 4 of the Rome Convention.[43] In reality, his

[40] Recitals 20 and 21 to Rome I.

[41] G Cuniberti, 'L'incertitude du lieu d'exécution sur la loi applicable au contrat. La difficile cohabitation des articles 4-2 et 4-5 de la Convention de Rome du 19 juin 1980' (2003) *Juris-Classeur Pèriodique* (general edition) 153.

[42] G Passarelli, *Contract Law in Contemporary International Commerce* (Munich, Nomos, 2019).

[43] Hayward (n 6).

book is mainly focused on international commercial arbitration, and in particular, the uncertainties arising from giving too much discretion to arbitrators in determining the applicable law in the absence of the choice. The key contribution of Hayward's book is that it proposes a modified form of Article 4 of the Rome Convention in determining the applicable law in the absence of choice for international commercial arbitration. More importantly, his book does not explicitly propose that the place of performance should be given special significance under his model Article 4 of the Rome Convention.

The only book I have come across that is dedicated to a study of a connecting factor in the EU choice of law rules is that of Ancel, which is focused on the concept of characteristic performance.[44] True to continental traditions, Ancel inter alia makes a theoretical analysis of the concept of characteristic performance, and how it applies in a variety of contractual obligations. However, Ancel's book is not focused on the central theme contained in this book that the place of performance should be explicitly given special significance under the EU choice of law rules in determining the applicable law in the absence of choice.

In summation, one does not wish to be misunderstood as submitting that the proposal in this book does not draw inspiration from other scholarly works and authorities. In fact, to the best of one's ability, one has cited and built on other scholarly works that either explicitly or implicitly support or contrast with the proposal or opinions in this book.

IV. Methodology

Given that methodology is an important criteria for assessing the quality of an academic work, this section is devoted to the methodology utilised in writing this book. It discusses how the research was conducted, and why this book adopts more of a pragmatic than theoretical approach.

A. How the Research was Conducted

This book radically develops my LLM dissertation undertaken at the University of Aberdeen, and my other publications on choice of law.[45] This book also follows the approach of making a dedicated study to a connecting factor in the EU choice of law rules for determining the applicable law in the absence of choice, other

[44] M-E Ancel, *La prestation caractéristique du contrat* (Paris, Economica, 2002).

[45] CSA Okoli and GO Arishe, 'The Operation of the Escape Clauses in the Rome Convention, Rome I Regulation and Rome II Regulation' (2012) 8 *Journal of Private International Law* 513–45; Okoli (n 38). See also CSA Okoli, 'Choice of law for Contract of Carriage of Goods in the European Union' (2015) 4 *Lloyds Maritime and Commercial Law Quarterly* 512–25.

than the habitual residence of the characteristic performer. In particular, I once undertook a detailed study on the significance of the connecting factor of the doctrine of infection or accessory allocation in the context of the EU choice of law rules.[46] In effect, this book now makes a detailed study of the significance of the place of performance in international commercial contracts in the EU choice of law rules.

The research is largely library based. Primary emphasis has been placed on the EU private international instruments focused on choice of law and jurisdiction for international commercial contracts. Also, the decisions the Court of Justice of the European Union (CJEU), Opinion of Advocate Generals (AGs), decisions of Member State courts, existing academic authorities and the historical and legislative background of the EU private international instruments on choice of law and jurisdiction for commercial contracts have also been utilised.

B. Adopting a Pragmatic Approach

At the outset of this book, one is well aware that there is a conflict between common law approaches and continental approaches in EU private international law.[47] This is really not the business of this book. What is of concern is that given that this book has adopted more of a pragmatic than a theoretical approach, one might be accused of favouring the common law approach that prizes pragmatic solutions over theoretical analysis, conceptualism and European continental style abstraction. Thus, it might be useful to clarify and justify why this book adopts more of a pragmatic approach than one of theory.[48]

This book is normative since it argues for a reform of the existing law. However, the methodology deployed is more pragmatic than theoretical. First, this book presents most of the relevant case law from the CJEU, Member State courts and the Opinions of AGs elaborately. The book has presented case law in-depth by providing the facts of most of the cases, and quotes extensively the ratio decidendi of the court and relevant Opinions of AGs. The reason for this is that it should be possible to read the description of these relevant case laws in this book without having to look at the law report. The practical significance of this is that it saves time and costs for the reader. It also makes the law more concrete in the mind of the reader.

[46] Okoli (n 38).

[47] TC Hartley, 'The European Union and the Systematic Dismantling of the Common law of Conflict Laws' (2005) 54 *International and Comparative Law Quarterly* 813–28; J Mance, 'Is Europe Aiming to Civilise the Common Law?' (2007) 18 *European Business Law Review* 77–99; J Harris, 'The Brussels I Regulation and the Re-emergence of the English Common Law' (2008) 4 *European Legal Forum* 181; J Harris, 'Understanding the English Approach to the Europeanisation of Private International Law' (2008) 4 *Journal of Private International Law* 347–95.

[48] For a similar methodological approach see also L Walker, *Maitenenance and Child Support in Private International Law* (Oxford, Hart Publishing, 2015) 6–8 (citing others).

As Lando, a respected European private international law continental scholar once observed when writing on a topic of choice of law for contractual obligations:

> As a law student I was once reading in a Swedish law library. At that time law bored me. The textbooks I was to read had abstract and stale principles and rules. They told me about law, not about life.
>
> … reported cases have been a constant source of knowledge and inspiration.[49]

Also, this book where necessary uses hypothetical examples to elaborate a point being made so it is made clearer to the reader.

Second, this book does not argue for a better choice of law rule, or compare Article 4 of Rome I with other choice of law rules, such as some of the choice of law approaches utilised in the United States.[50] In effect, this book is not a comparative analysis of different choice of law rules around the world in order to ascertain whether there is a better choice of law rule than that utilised under the current Article 4 of Rome I.[51] If one is looking for a book or monograph on comparative analysis of choice of law methodologies around the world, this book does not serve that purpose.[52]

In effect, this book does not challenge or question the methodological approach of the EU choice of law rules in determining the applicable law in the absence of choice, which is mainly based on conflicts-justice and territorial connections. It does not challenge the fact that generally speaking Article 4 of Rome I is blind to the substance or outcome of a case. Whether or not the application of the rules under Article 4 leads to substantive justice for the parties is really not the focus of this book. In this connection, some American scholars are very critical about the EU traditional choice of law rules in the absence of choice for being blind to substantive justice principles.[53] Perhaps, such scholars might argue that, inter alia, it is an important issue that should have been discussed or addressed in this book, or that one is not courageous enough to confront the methodology utilised by the EU legislator that is blind to substantive justice principles.

In this short introduction, I cannot really go into detail on why I do not agree with scholars who are critical of the methodology deployed in the EU choice of law rules.[54] Suffice it to say that the response to such scholars is that one does not see

[49] O Lando, 'Some Issues Relating to the Law Applicable to Contractual Obligations' (1996–97) *Kings College Law Journal* 55.

[50] SC Symeonides, *An Outsider's View of the American Approach to Choice of Law: Comparative Observations on Current American and Continental Conflicts Doctrine* (Doctoral Dissertation, Harvard Law School, 1980).

[51] See generally SC Symeonides, *Codifying Choice of Law Around the World: An International Comparative Analysis* (Oxford, Oxford University Press, 2017).

[52] ibid.

[53] FK Juenger, 'Two European Conflicts Conventions' (1998) 28 *Victoria University of Wellington Law Review* 527, 542; SC Symeonides, 'Rome II and Tort Conflicts: A Missed Opportunity' (2008) 56 *American Journal of Comparative Law* 173.

[54] This might be a limitation in the study undertaken in this book.

anything wrong with applying the conflicts-justice system at least in international commercial contracts. It leads to legal and commercial certainty for the parties. The EU is strongly focused on economic integration, so that uniformity in the determination of the applicable law is a good thing for international commercial actors connected with the EU internal market.[55]

This book is confined within the EU choice of law methodology. Thus some European doctrines relating to the contest between the goal of certainty and flexibility in conflicts-justice, what connecting factor best satisfies the requirement of proximity for international commercial contracts, avoidance of splitting the applicable law to govern a contract and the coherence between matters of jurisdiction and choice of law in civil and commercial matters, are some of the underlying themes that motivate this book.

In effect this book is restricted to one normative goal – that place of performance deserves a special place in the methodology of the EU choice of law rules for determining the applicable law in the absence of choice for international commercial contracts. While it is conceded that the focus of this book is somewhat narrow, the subject matter of this book is addressed in-depth. Indeed, this book provides the first detailed study of the significance of the place of performance as a connecting factor in international commercial contracts.

Another reason why this book could be considered as pragmatic is that it discusses the reality of existing case law, statutes and other academic authorities in the context of the EU as a basis for supporting the central theme. In particular, in this book, emphasis is placed on the practical implications of the proposal. This book does not unduly dwell on theories or concepts, which might not be very useful in real life adjudication issues. This is not to say this book is not conceptual at all, as it incorporates and engages some of the ideas and thinking of scholars, especially in the European continent (such as civil law and common law scholars).

In effect, what is being said is that this book tilts more towards practice than theory, which makes it pragmatic. Moreover, as a lawyer and academic, one does not subscribe to the methodology of absolute conceptualism and theory.

Finally, one might argue that the pragmatic approach taken in this book is influenced by my common law background. It is conceded that as a lawyer and academic with a common law background, one might not be completely insulated from the common law bias of adopting a pragmatic approach in this book. As Briggs aptly remarks:

> No doubt there are those who will say pragmatism is not a principle. Too bad: a principle it most certainly is. Pragmatism makes a powerful, if unstated, contribution to the force that drives the common law and its rules of private international law. A judge made the point in a telling way when he said: 'Academic writers of distinction concern themselves with Conflict, not surprisingly since it is a subject of great intellectual interest.

[55] See generally R Fentiman, 'Choice of Law in Europe: Uniformity and Integration' (2007–08) 82 *Tulane Law Review* 2021.

> We must do our best to arrive at a sensible and practical result'[56] Academic writers, few in number though they are, evidently do find the subject a stimulating one, but it is a different duty of the court to find sensible answers to practical questions. A surprisingly large part of the way in which they do that is by the application of the homespun wisdom of common law.[57]

This book does not suggest or think that the common law approach is superior to the continental approach (and vice versa). It also does not think that Briggs in this quotation suggests that the common law methodology of pragmatism is superior to any other methodology. It is just that the common law approach is very pragmatic, and that pragmatism is reflected in this book.

V. Structure and Summary of the Book

This book contains seven chapters, including the introduction and conclusion.

Chapter two contains the history relating to the significance of the place of performance as a choice of law rule. First, it discusses early scholarly opinion and case law from both the nineteenth and twentieth centuries, prior to the existence of the Rome Convention. It also discusses the history of the concept of habitual residence of the characteristic performer as a choice of law rule in determining the applicable law in the absence of choice. Second, it discusses the operation of Article 4 of the Rome Convention with a special focus on how some Member State courts and scholars viewed the significance of the place of performance in the context of utilising the escape clause. Third, it discusses Article 4 of the Rome I Regulation Proposal with a special focus on the issues related to whether or not the place of performance was to be given special significance. The importance and key contribution of this chapter is that it uses a historical approach to assess the significance of the place of performance as a connecting factor in determining the applicable law in the absence of choice in the EU choice of law rules.

Chapter three contains the central proposal of this book. First, it critically analyses why the concept of habitual residence of the characteristic performer, rather than the place of performance, was made the principal connecting factor for most commercial contracts in the EU choice of law rules. It considers these reasons to include the problems of classifying and identifying the place of performance, triumph of the law of the professional and country-of-origin principle. It is then opined that these reasons are not justifiable to expressly strip the place

[56] Citing *Macmillan Inc v Bishopsgate Investment Trust plc (No 3)* [1996] 1 WLR 387 Staughton LJ. Mance LJ in *Raiffeisen Zentralbank Osterrieich Ag v Five Star Trading LLD* [2001] 1 QB 825 [29] also submits that 'the conflict of laws does not depend (like a game or even an election) upon the application of rigid rules but upon a search for appropriate principles to meet particular situations'.

[57] A Briggs, *Private International Law in English Courts* 1st edn (Oxford, Oxford University Press, 2014) 7–8, [1.16].

of performance of special significance. Second, the significance of the escape clause is considered in the context of Article 4(3) of Rome I. It is then opined that despite the proposal that the place of performance should be given principal significance in a revised Article 4 of Rome I, the escape clause is a necessity in a conflicts-justice system and should not be dispensed with. In the alternative, it is opined that the current rules could be retained, and the European legislator should expressly give special significance to the place of performance in interpreting a revised Article 4(3) of Rome I. Third, a critical analysis is made on the determination of the place of performance in practice, given that it is proposed that it should be the principal connecting factor under a revised Article 4 of Rome I. The importance and key contribution of this chapter is that it considers the pros and cons of the place of performance in the context of determining the applicable law in the absence of choice, and justifies why it should be given special significance under a revised Article 4 of Rome I.

Chapter four contains the argument that the place of performance under Article 9(3) of Rome I is an expression of the principle of proximity, and this is a good reason why the place of performance should be explicitly given special significance under a revised Article 4 of Rome I. First, the significance of the place of performance pre-Rome Convention is critically analysed, and it is opined that one of the reasons why the place of performance was considerably utilised in regulating foreign illegality was because the place of performance satisfied the principle of proximity when compared to other connecting factors. Second, it is argued that though the place of performance was not explicitly given special significance under Article 7 of the Rome Convention, there was a wide consensus among scholars that the place of performance best satisfied the principle of 'close connection'. Third, it is opined that during the negotiations on Article 8(3) of Rome I Regulation Proposal, the key element that was in the heart of the negotiation process was the determination of how to make the concept of 'close connection' more precise. It is then opined that there was a consensus among scholars and Member States that the place of performance would best satisfy the test of 'close connection'. Fourth, it is then opined that based on the history that led to Article 9(3) of Rome I, the place of performance under Article 9(3) of Rome I is an expression of the principle of proximity. The importance and key contribution of this chapter is that it uses the place of performance, which is an absolute connecting factor in determining foreign country overriding mandatory rules in the current EU choice of law rules, as a basis to support the central claim in this book.

Chapter five contains the argument that based on the coherence between jurisdiction and choice of law in the EU rules for civil and commercial matters, the place of performance should be explicitly given special significance under a revised Article 4 of Rome I. First, it discusses the types of coherence between jurisdiction and choice of law in the EU. This includes coherence of principles, coherence of connecting factors and coherence of interpretation. Second, it critically analyses the historical connection between the European regimes for jurisdiction and choice of law rules for international commercial contracts. Third, it opines that in the context of the central argument in the chapter, there is already a form of coherence between jurisdiction and choice of law for the place of performance in commercial contracts, so that the central proposal in the chapter should not be considered as too radical or revolutionary. Fifth, it concedes that there are differences between jurisdiction and choice of law rules in the context of the EU, but concludes that such differences would not significantly compromise the proposal in this book. Sixth, it is then opined that based on the coherence of principles, coherence of connecting factors and coherence of interpretation, the place of performance should be given special significance under a revised Article 4 of Rome I. The importance and key contribution of this chapter is that it uses the coherence between jurisdiction and choice of law in civil and commercial matters as a basis for supporting the central claim in this book.

Chapter six contains a synopsis of the legislative proposal in the book. The importance and key contribution of this chapter is that it serves as a form of explanatory memorandum to the model statute proposed in this book.

Chapter seven summarises the research findings of this book. It also proposes the transmission of the proposed model statute (revised Article 4 of Rome I) as one that could be utilised as an international solution by legislators, judges, arbitrators and other decision makers in reforming choice of law rules. The importance and key contribution of this chapter is to justify why the proposed model statute could be utilised by other countries or legal systems outside the EU, as an international solution for the determination of the applicable law in the absence of choice for international commercial contracts.

VI. Some Observations on Terminology

Finally, it is necessary to make a few observations on the terminology used in this book.

Rome I Regulation is concerned with the law that governs contractual obligations in the EU. It replaces the Rome Convention, which came into force 1 April 1991. Rome I Regulation came into force 17 December 2009.

'Place of performance' could also mean '*lex loci solutionis*'.

'International commercial contracts' in this study excludes contracts of carriage of goods and persons, which are governed by Article 5 of Rome I. It also excludes contracts for consumers, insurance and employment, which are based on protection of weaker parties, and governed respectively by Article 5, 6 and 7 of Rome I.[58]

In this book, a lot of reference will made to 'private international law'. This could also mean inter alia 'conflict of laws' or 'international private law'.

The reference to 'country' could also mean 'legal system'.

[58] See also Recital 23 to Rome I.

A lot of reference is also made to 'courts', particularly in the context of applying the EU choice of law rules. The EU choice of law rules could also be applied by arbitral tribunals.[59]

The reference to 'Brussels Ia' could also mean 'Brussels I Recast' and 'Brussels Ibis'. Brussels Ia replaces Brussels I Regulation.[60]

The reference to 'escape clause' could also mean 'exception clause'.

The reference to 'professional' could also mean 'the party who is required to effect the characteristic performance'.

'Commonwealth countries' is defined here to mean countries that apply the domestic English common law private international law methodology, without European influences.

'He' is used as a generic term to describe persons in this book.

[59] Hayward (n 6).

[60] (Council Regulation (EC) 44/2001 of 22 December 2000 on Jurisdiction and the Recognition and Enforcement of Judgments in Civil and Commercial Matters [2001] OJ L12/1). Brssels I replaced the Brussels Convention (Convention of 27 September 1968 on Jurisdiction and the Enforcement of Judgments in Civil and Commercial Matters (OJ 1978 L304).

2

Historical Analysis on the Place of Performance as a Choice of Law Rule

I. Introduction

This chapter will critically analyse the history of the place of performance as a choice of law rule, and its significance pre-Rome Convention, Rome Convention and Rome I Regulation Proposal.[1]

Section II, first, will draw inspiration from the view of nineteenth century scholars, who had favoured the place of performance as a choice of law rule, where the parties do not make a choice of law. It will be observed that some courts which applied the place of performance as a choice of law rule exposed the weakness of the place of performance. This book then subscribes to some scholar's view in the middle of the twentieth century that the place of characteristic performance is a better choice of law rule in determining the country of closest connection.

Second, an analysis is made on the history of the place of business of the characteristic performer as the principal choice of law rule, where the parties do not make a choice of law. It is then opined that based on the Swiss experience, the doctrine of the place of business of the characteristic performer was contrived as a basis of solving the problem of classifying or identifying the place of performance. In effect, if the place of performance was easy to identify, it is possible that this doctrine may never have been invented or utilised. This book then subscribes to a French decision from the middle of the twentieth century which regarded the place of characteristic performance as the criteria for closest connection, especially where it coincides with the place of business of the characteristic performer.

In Section III, the significance of the place of performance will be considered under the Rome Convention, particularly in the context of the relationship between Article 4(2) and (5). It will be observed that there were divergent interpretations among scholars and Member State courts. The place of performance triumphed over Article 4(2) in English courts, but other courts in the Netherlands, Scotland and France gave the place of performance a subordinate or marginal role. Though the Court of Justice of the European Union (CJEU) ruled on the

[1] Proposal for a Regulation of the European Parliament and the Council on the Law applicable to Contractual Obligations (Rome I), December 15, 2005, COM (2005) 650 final.

criteria for interpreting the relationship between Article 4(2) and (5), its judgments inter alia did not specifically pronounce on the weight to be given to the place of performance.

In Section IV, the significance of the place of performance under Article 4 of Rome I Proposal will be considered. Fixed rules were used to replace the presumptions. It will be noted that there was no recorded consideration or suggestion that the place of characteristic performance should be the principal connecting factor under Article 4 of Rome I Proposal. However, the United Kingdom inter alia suggested that the place of performance should be given special significance in utilising the escape clause under Article 4(3) of Rome I Proposal.

Section V concludes.

II. Pre-Rome Convention

In this section, the early history of the significance of the place of performance as a choice of law rule is considered. This is important for three reasons. First, it will demonstrate that the idea that the place of performance is of considerable significance in international commercial contracts is not new. Second, it will demonstrate why the place of performance witnessed a decline, and why the invention of the doctrine of the habitual residence of the characteristic performer was aimed at curing the defect of the place of performance as a choice of law rule. Third, it would demonstrate that there eventually was a shift by some Swiss scholars, Swiss courts and legislators, from the place of performance to habitual residence of the characteristic performer.

Interestingly, there was an alternative connecting factor – the place of characteristic performance – suggested by a leading French scholar, which was later adopted by the Paris Court of Appeal. The historical shift to the habitual residence of the characteristic performer instead of place of characteristic performance is the underlying theme that motivates the historical account on the place of performance that is provided below.

A. Early Scholarly Opinion and Cases

Prior to entry into force of the Rome Convention, the place of performance was one of considerable significance, particularly from the nineteenth century.

Savigny, a German scholar of the nineteenth century, submitted that choice of law rules should be substance neutral – without a preference for the parties' laws, jurisdictions or nationality.[2] To conform to this principle, he suggested that every

[2] FC Von Savigny, *Private International Law – A Treatise on the Conflict of Laws* (William Guthrie trans, London, T & T, Law Publishers, 1869) 110–11, 114, 248. See also M Reimann, 'Savigny's Triumph? Choice of Law in Contracts Cases at the Close of the Twentieth Century' (1999) 39 *Virginia Journal of International Law* 571, 594–95.

legal relationship should be governed by the law of the State to which it has its 'seat'. Savigny's conception of 'seat' of a legal relationship mirrors what is now referred to as the principle of 'closest connection', 'centre of gravity' or 'proximity' in the classical conflict of law choice of law rules. The main purpose of a neutral choice of law rule was to enhance international uniformity and reduce forum shopping.

In determining the seat of a contractual obligation, Savigny proposed the place of performance as a choice of law rule for contractual obligations on the basis that the place of performance was the most important element of a contract, which constitutes the essence of the obligation and would likely meet the expectation of the parties.[3] In the words of Savigny:

> The forum of the obligation (which coincides with the true seat of obligation) depends on the voluntary submission of the parties, which, however, is generally indicated, not in an express, but in a tacit declaration of will, and thus always excluded by an express declaration to the contrary. We have therefore to inquire what place the expectation of the parties was directed – what place they had in their mind as the seat of obligation.[4]

Savigny argued that in determining the applicable law for a contractual relationship, the seat of the legal relationship is to be identified separately, which coincides with the place of performance. Thus, it is the localisation of each obligation's place of performance which determines its applicable law. In the eyes of Savigny, the place of performance was of great significance in determining the seat of obligation when compared to other connecting factors such as the place of contracting.

Savigny was not the first scholar to give considerable significance to the place of performance as a choice of law rule. Story, a United States' scholar and jurist, regarded the law of the place of performance as yielding to the intention of the parties. In the words of Story:

> The performance of the contract is to be in the place where it is made, either expressly or by tacit implication. But where the contract is either expressly or tacitly to be performed in any other place, there the general rule is, in conformity to the presumed intention of the parties, that the contract, as to its validity, nature, obligation, and interpretation, is to be governed by the law of the place of performance.[5]

It does not appear that Savigny's idea on the place of performance as a choice of law rule was influenced by Story. Indeed, though Savigny's first book on conflict of laws was published 15 years after Story's first book on conflict of laws (Story 1834; Savigny 1849), Savigny did not cite Story's work.[6] The difference between Savigny's approach and Story's is that Savigny regarded the place of performance as a choice of law rule, where the parties did not exercise party autonomy. The place of performance was justified as meeting the parties' expectations, rather than intention. On the other hand, Story regarded the place of contracting as the principal choice

[3] Savigny, ibid 269.
[4] ibid 198.
[5] J Story, *Commentaries On The Conflict Of Laws, Foreign And Domestic* (1834) s 283.
[6] G Kegel, 'Savigny and Story' (1989) 37 *American Journal of Comparative Law* 39, 47 (citing others).

of law rule for contractual obligations. It is only where the place of contracting differed from the place of performance that the place of performance was to be used in determining the parties' presumed intention to make a choice of law.

Savigny's idea on a substance-neutral conflicts justice system dominated the thinking in Europe, such that he could be regarded as the intellectual godfather of the European conflict justice system that generally uses territorial and geographical connections in determining the applicable law in the absence of choice.

Savigny's ideas also attracted some other European scholars, including English common law scholars in the early twentieth century. Westlake formulated the test of 'closest and most real connection',[7] and it was apparent that Westlake's test of 'closest and most real connection' was influenced by Savigny's theory of 'the seat of the relationship'.[8] Westlake's theory of 'closest and most real connection' was in turn refined by Dicey who coined the term 'proper law of contract',[9] which gave supremacy to the law intended by the parties, and then principal significance to the place of performance in determining the applicable law in the absence of choice. It was also apparent that Dicey's formulation on giving principal significance to the place of performance in the theory of proper law of contract was also influenced by Savigny.[10]

Following Savigny and Story's teachings, where the parties did not make an express or implied choice of law, some Member State courts prior to their entry into the EU choice of law rules, applied neutral conflict of law rules and gave considerable significance to the place of performance as a connecting factor.[11] It must however be opined that Savigny's methodology and proposal on the law of the place of performance appeared to be more dominant among some Member State courts of the EU.

In the late nineteenth century, in England, the approach at one time was to apply Story's approach. Thus, Lord Esher once held that:

> if a contract is made in one country to be carried out between the parties in another country, either in whole or in part, unless there appears something to the contrary, it is to be concluded that the parties must have intended that it should be carried out according to the law of that other country.[12]

In later English cases, the significance given to the place of performance in determining the presumed intention of the parties, as advanced by Story, witnessed a

[7] J Westlake, *A Treatise on Private International Law* 6th edn (London, Sweet and Maxwell, 1922) 227–31 (quoting from Savigny). See also Reimann (n 2) 598.

[8] See also Reimann (n 2) 598, fn 109.

[9] AV Dicey, *Conflict of Laws* 2nd edn (London, Sweet and Maxwell, 1908) Rule 146, at 529, 556 (citing Savigny).

[10] See also Reimann (n 2) 598, fn 110.

[11] Reimann (n 2) 571. See also OA Borum, 'Principles of the Private International Law on Contracts' (1940) 11 *Nordisk Tidsskrift for International Ret* 121, 123.

[12] *Chatenay v Brazilia SubmarineTelegraph Co* [1891] 1 QB 79 (CA), 82–83. Story's rule was initially applied by the US Supreme Court in the nineteenth century. See *Andrews v Pond*, 13 Pet 65 (US 1839).

steady decline.[13] The English practice applied party autonomy as the main rule, and gave considerable significance to the place of performance in determining the applicable law in the absence of choice, though the place of performance was not given absolute significance.[14] In other words, the English practice applied the principle of closest connection where it was established that the parties did not make a choice of law, which involved weighing the significance of connecting factors, with great weight being given to the place of performance.[15]

In the middle of the twentieth century, Dicey's formulation on the proper law of contract and significance to be given to the place of performance became firmly entrenched in the English common law jurisprudence, when Lord Simonds held that:

> the substance of the obligation must be determined by the proper law of the contract, i.e., the system of law by reference to which the contract was made or that with which the transaction has its closest and most real connexion. In the consideration of the latter question, what is the proper law of the contract, and therefore what is the substance of the obligation created by it, it is a factor, and sometimes a decisive one, that a particular place is chosen for performance.[16]

The German practice was more in line with Savigny's teachings. In German domestic law the solution adopted by the courts in determining the law of the contract in the absence of choice by the parties:

> was based largely upon the search for 'pointers' capable of showing the 'hypothetischer Parteiwille', the presumed will of the parties, having regard to the general interests at stake in each particular case. If this gives no result, the law applicable to the contract according to German case law was determined by the place of performance: more precisely, by the place of performance of each of the obligations arising from the contract, because the German courts take the view that if the various contractual obligations are to be performed in different countries, each shall be governed by the law of the country in which it was performed.[17]

Thus, 'if one party performs services in country A and the other pays him in country B, the obligation to perform is governed by the law of A but the obligation to pay by the law of B'.[18]

[13] *Hamlyn & Co v Talisker Distillery* [1894] AC 202, 207–08; *NV Kwik Hoo Tong Handel Maatschappij v James Finlay* [1927] AC 604, 609.

[14] *Jacobs, Marcus and Co.v Crèdit Lyonnais* (1884) 12 QB 589 (CA) 601; *Tzotzis v Monark Line A/B* [1968] 1 WLR 406; *Miller v Whitworth Street Estates* [1970] 1 All ER 769, 809; *Compagnie Tunisienne de Navigation SA v Compagnie d'Armement Maritime SA* [1971] AC 572.

[15] *Bonython v Australia* [1951] AC 201, 221–23; *Amin Rasheed Shipping Corp v Kuwait Insurance Co* [1984] AC 50 (HL); *Coupland v Arabian Gulf Oil Co* [1983] I WLR 1136, 1150; *Definitely Maybe v Marek Lieberberg* [2001] 1 WLR 1745 [7].

[16] *Bonython*, ibid 219–20.

[17] Giuliano-Lagarde Report [1980] OJ C282/1, 19. See also O Lando, 'Scandinavian Conflict of Law Rules Respecting Contracts: Party Autonomy and Center of Gravity' (1957) 6 *American Journal of Comparative Law* 1, 2; O Lando, 'The Proper Law of the Contract' (1964) 8 *Scandinavian Studies in Law* 105, 153–54; J Blom, 'Choice of Law Methods in the Private International Law of Contract' (1978) 16 *Canadian Yearbook of International Law* 230, 253–54; O Lando, 'EEC Convention on the Law Applicable to Contractual Obligations' (1987) 24 *Common Market Law Review* 159, 196.

[18] Blom (n 17) 270–71.

In the words of the German Supreme Court for Civil Matters:

> According to German private international law, in the area of contract the parties to the transaction are fundamentally free to determine by agreement what system of law shall govern their contractual relationship. In this case the appeal court has not found, and the parties have not argued before us, that the parties made such a choice of law by agreeing on it either expressly or impliedly in the appropriate terms. In this situation, according to the firm line of precedent laid down by Bundesgerichtshof, the matter is to be decided by the so-called hypothetical intention of the parties in relation to the law governing the contract, and in cases where such hypothetical intention cannot be established the law of the place of performance determines the rule applicable to the particular obligation in issue.[19]

Indeed, the German practice gave absolute significance to the place of performance where the intention of the parties to make a choice of law could not be established. In other words, the German practice did not give significance to other factors such as the place of contracting, language of the contract and currency of payment.

The major problem with applying the law of the place of performance as evidenced by the German practice was that it led to a split in the applicable law so that different laws governed the parties' obligations. The obligation in issue was also difficult to classify. Thus, some scholars were very critical of Savigny's proposal on the law of the place of performance as evidenced by the German practice.[20] Rabel was one of such scholars. While he conceded 'that performance has in many cases more significance in the eyes of parties to a contract than the locality where they declare their consent, if such a common locality exists',[21] he submitted that:

> Such fruits of the theory of place of fulfillment resulting in bisection of bilateral contracts are particularly objectionable. They cannot be removed by a fictional pretension that a contract producing two main obligations of different location has only one place of performance. The relations between creditor and debtor are often necessarily localized at more than two places. Conflicts law cannot schematically rely on such a device.[22]

Some scholars suggested that the solution to this problem of identifying or classifying the place of performance, was to apply the personal law of one of the parties to the contractual relationship, so that a single law would apply to the parties' contract.[23] If a single law was applied, there would be certainty and simplicity

[19] Eight Civil Senate of the Bundesgerichtshof in a decision of September 22, 1971, cited in Blom (n 17) 253–54.

[20] See generally, E Rabel, *The Conflict of Laws: A Comparative Study* Vol 2, 2nd edn (Michigan, The University of Michigan Press, 1960) 474; Lando (1964) (n 17) 124–25; Blom (n 17) 265–68. See also F Jamal, 'The Law Governing the Validity of a Contract – A Reconsideration' (1983) 4 *Singapore Law Review* 111; Lando (1987) (n 17) 167.

[21] Rabel, ibid 474.

[22] ibid.

[23] See Lando (1964) (n 17) 123–24; G Kegel, *Internationales Privatrecht: Ein Studienbuch* 4th edn (Munich, Schwerpunktbereich, 1977) 293 for a historical discussion of this point.

in the determination of the applicable law in the absence of choice. It was this kind of thinking that later sowed the seeds for the germination of the doctrine of habitual residence of the characteristic performer in Switzerland. This approach however did not best reflect the idea of the principle of closest connection, since the residence of one of the parties, without more, would likely not have sufficient connection to an international commercial transaction.

Thus, Batiffol, the leading French scholar in the middle of the twenteith century, better reformulated Savigny's idea when he submitted that:

> the parties should be presumed to have localized their contract at the place of performance … performance is the object of the agreement. At the time of performance the contract will 'manifest' itself to the outer world. The expectations of the parties are directed towards the fulfillment of the obligations and that fulfillment will occur at the place of performance. In carrying out many of his acts, the performing party is bound to obey the law in force at the place of performance. When each of the parties to a bilateral contract has to perform in the country of his residence, two legal systems might apply, but such a 'scission' of the contract must be avoided. One of the possible places of performance of the bilateral contract must prevail … this must be the place where the characteristic obligation is to be performed.[24]

Based on the above historical analysis, this book subscribes to Batiffol's idea on the significance of the place of performance and using the concept of characteristic performance to better identify and locate the obligation. In other words, this book argues that the place of characteristic performance should normally triumph over the residence of the parties. Batiffol's approach to utilising the place of characteristic performance as a connecting factor could also be defended as a pragmatic one. Since the problem of identifying the place of performance and splitting the applicable law based on the obligation of the parties was an approach that historically complicated the determination of the applicable law in the absence of choice, Batiffol's theory of selecting the place of characteristic performance is one that yielded to certainty and commercial common sense, and at the same time satisfying the requirement of proximity.

B. Switzerland: History of the Place of Business of the Characteristic Performer as a Connecting Factor

The concept of habitual residence of the characteristic performer which is the principal connecting factor for most commercial contracts in the EU choice of

[24] H Batiffol, *Les Conflits de Lois en Matière de Contrats* (Paris, Rec Srirey, 1938) 78–85 – quotation translated in P Hay et al in M Cappelletti, 'Conflict of Laws as a Technique for Legal Integration' in M Seccombe and J Weiler. *Integration through Law: Europe and the American Federal Experience Methods, Tools and Institutions* Vol 1 (New York, Walter de Gruyter and Co, 1986) 242.

law rules owes its roots to Switzerland.[25] Swiss law traditionally distinguished between (a) issues relating to the validity and conclusion of a contract which was governed by the law of the place of contracting ('*lex loci contractus*'); and (b) issues relating to either party's performance under the contract which was governed by the law of the place of performance. The result of this was that there was a split in the applicable law. In trying to reduce this split, the Swiss courts adopted a preference for the law of the place of performance to govern these issues. The Swiss courts thereby applied Savigny's approach which regarded the place of the performance as the most relevant element of a contractual relationship.

The adoption of the place of performance was not a perfect solution particularly in bilateral and complex contracts involving multiple obligations which gave rise to different laws applying. Also where the contract was to be performed in different places different laws applied to the contract. Thus, the application of the law of the place of performance also resulted in splitting the applicable law, as was the case in the German practice. In later cases, the Swiss Federal Court resolved contractual obligations by trying to ascertain the objective hypothetical intention of the parties, and also the principle of closest connection started gaining ground in determining the applicable law where the parties did not make a choice of law.

In a bid to reduce the split arising from the law of the place of performance, close to the middle of the twentieth century, Schnitzer suggested that in the absence of a choice of law, express or implied, Swiss law should focus on the law of the domicile or place of business of the party who was to perform the 'characteristic obligation of the contract'.[26] He argued that the domicile or place of business of the characteristic performer could give guidance as to the law most closely connected with the contract. The characteristic performer was generally the professional in the contractual relationship, such as a lawyer, doctor, seller, architect etc. He argued that the law of the place of business of the characteristic performer should be uniformly applied to all his clients. This was likely to make the law certain and the principle of closest connection easier to apply. Schnitzer's ideas attracted the attention of other academics such as Vischer who explained the doctrine of characteristic performance in terms of localising a legal relationship in accordance with its purpose and function. 'Later the doctrine moved from Switzerland into

[25] See generally Lando (1964) (n 17) 121–22; HUJ d'Oliviera, '"Characteristic Obligation" in the Draft EEC Obligation Convention' (1977) 25 *American Journal of Comparative Law* 303; K Lipstein, 'Characteristic Performance – A New Concept in the Conflict of Laws in Matters of Contract for the EEC' (1981) 3 *Northwestern Journal of International and Business* 402; F Vischer, 'The Principle of the Typical Performance in International Contracts and the Draft Convention' in P North (ed), *Contract Conflicts, The EEC Convention on the Law Applicable to Contractual Obligations: A Comparative Study* (Amsterdam, North-Holland Publishing Company, 1982) 25, 25–27; PR Beaumont and PE McEleavy, *Private International Law A.E ANTON* 3rd edn (Edinburgh, W Green, 2011) 464, [10.134].

[26] AF Schnitzer, *Handbuch des Internationalen Privatrechts* vol II, 2nd edn (Zurich/Leipzig, 1944) 514–17.

the case law of France and of the Netherlands. This as de Winter explained, was the historical background to Article 4(2) of the Rome Convention.'[27]

While Schnitzer was not the first to advocate the search for the law applicable to the contract by means of the notion of characteristic performance,[28] he was however the first scholar to have proposed a theoretical basis for this method of resolving choice of law issues in contractual obligations. Some scholars submit that the gestation period of Schnitzer's ideas was in Germany where he studied, and observed the German practice that had difficulties in applying the connecting factor of the place of performance.[29] This might explain why, unlike Batiffol's reliance on the place of characteristic performance, Schnitzer argued for a shift to the habitual residence of the characteristic performer.

Thus, the true historical reason for formulating the concept of habitual residence of the characteristic performer was to avoid the split in the applicable law caused by applying the law of the place of performance. Schnitzer and his disciples also regarded the habitual residence of the characteristic performer as the 'true' place of performance on the basis that it is where the professional makes the real arrangements in respect of fulfilling his obligations under the contract. The doctrine of habitual residence of characteristic performance was thus a way of 'properly' locating the place of performance.[30]

Schnitzer's ideas influenced the Swiss Federal Tribunal in *Arret Schevalley*[31] to hold that:

> By virtue of the rules of Swiss Private International Law and in the absence of a choice of law by the parties, the law applicable to an obligation of an international character is that of the country with which the contract presents the closest territorial relationship, normally that of the domicile of the party whose presentation (i.e performance) is characteristic of the contract in issue.

The Swiss court was very critical about the split in the applicable law caused by applying the law of the place of performance and emphasised that this split led to uncertainty. Thus, it advocated a single law to govern the formation, validity, conclusion and performance of a contract.

The Swiss legislator later in codifying their choice of law rules also adopted the habitual residence of the characteristic performer as a general rule in determining

[27] Beaumont and McEleavy (n 25) 465, [10.137].

[28] A Homberger, *Die obligatorischen Vertrage im internationalen Privatrecht nach der Praxis des schweizerischen Bundesgerichts* (Berne, 1925) 10 and 48; HL Oser and W Schönenberger, *Kommentar zum schweizerischen Zivilgesetzbuch, Das Obligationenrecht, Allgemeine Einleitung* (Zurich, 1929) cited in C Robitaille, 'La doctrine de la prestation caractéristique en droit international privé des contrats' – www.memoireonline.com/a/fr/cart/download/t1TQK3lCZSqh. See also P Mankowski, 'The Principle of Characteristic Performance Visited Yet Again' in K Boele-Woelki et al (eds), *Convergence and Divergence in Private International Law:Liber Amicorum Kurt Siehr* (The Hague, Schultess and Eleven International Publishing, 2010) 433, 434; Beaumont and McEleavy (n 25) 464.

[29] Robitaille, ibid.

[30] For a detailed analysis of this point see d'Oliviera (n 25) 307–08.

[31] *Arret Schevalley* BGE 78 II 74, 80 (12 February 1952).

the applicable law in the absence of choice for contractual obligations. Article 117 of the Swiss Private International Law Act[32] provided thus:

> 1 Failing a choice of law, contracts are governed by the law of the state with which they have the closest connection.
> 2 Such a connection is deemed to exist with the state of the habitual residence of the party having to perform the characteristic obligation or, if the contract is entered into in the course of a professional or business activity, with the state of such party's place of business.
> 3 Characteristic obligation means in particular:
>
> a. in contracts for the transfer of property: the transferor's obligation;
> b. in contracts pertaining to the use of property or of a right: the obligation of the party conferring such use;
> c. in contracts of mandate, contracts for work and other contracts to perform services: the service obligation;
> d. in contracts of deposit: the obligation of the depositary;
> e. in guarantee or suretyship agreements: the obligation of the guarantor or surety.

It is important to stress that historically, the true reason for applying the law of the place of business of the characteristic performer was because the application of the law of the place of performance as advocated by Savigny led to a split in the applicable law, and the place of performance was not so easy to identify. If there was no split in the applicable law, or the place of performance was easy to apply, it does not appear that there would have been a need for Schnitzer and his disciples to formulate the application of the law of the place of business of the characteristic performer, and for the Swiss Court to apply this formulation. Thus, the true historical reason for applying the law of the place of business of the characteristic performer was to isolate a particular performance – the 'characteristic performance' – and preferentially apply the law of the place of business of the characteristic performer. There are other scholars who correctly appreciate this view point, and they are worthy of quotation.

Vischer, who is an academic disciple of Schnitzer submits that:

> The principle's main purpose, as the development in the practice of the Swiss Federal Tribunal shows, is the avoidance of a split in the applicable law. It is justified by the fact that mutual obligations of the parties are interrelated and inter-dependent and that therefore one single law should govern the main issues of the contract.[33]

This book is indebted to Lipstein who captures the point lucidly when he submits that:

> In referring to the 'place of performance which is characteristic of the contract', the emphasis is placed only in part on the particular place of performance. Characteristic

[32] Federal Act on Private International Law of 18 December 1987.
[33] Vischer (n 25) 27.

performance is also made to depend upon the type of contract to be performed; the characteristic performance is identical with the characteristic obligation owed in a contract which gives this type of contract its individual features. Thus, what appears in the guise of a connecting factor (place of performance) is in reality a category of legal relationships (commonly called 'operative facts' for want of a better term) which are joined to the connecting factors: place of habitual residence, central administration or principal place of business of the contracting party owing the obligation which is characteristic of the particular type of contract.[34]

Lipstein then rightly submits that:

it must be admitted that the description of the criteria for determining the characteristic performance, i.e. of the essence and function of the obligation involved, is turgid. It *conceals the real purpose of the exercise* which is *the search for one place of performance in order to concentrate the legal relationship there.*[35]

Juenger rightly submits that:

the notion of characteristic performance was developed against a different background. In essence, *it amounts to an attempt to escape from the lex loci solutionis* rule which, under the spell of Savigny's teachings, some European courts and writers once espoused. *This rule implies that the obligation of each party is governed by the law of the place where that party is required to perform, with the result that different laws may control the different obligations arising from the same agreement. This consequence might be mitigated by focusing on the personal laws of the parties rather than on the places where they were required to carry out their obligations …*[36]

Collins submits that:

The use of the concept is limited to cases where each of the parties is to perform in a different country. In such a case there is more than one place of performance. The concept seeks to isolate the place of performance of one of the parties, by identifying the performance of that party as more 'characteristic' of the contract as a whole.[37]

Lando submits that:

A party to an international contract generally have their places of business in different states or countries. As a contract should not be governed by two laws, the law of one of the parties must be preferred, and here too, the place of business of the party should be chosen …[38]

[34] Lipstein (n 25) 404.

[35] ibid (emphasis added).

[36] FK Juenger, 'The EEC Convention on the Law Applicable to Contractual Obligations: An American Assessment' in P North (ed), *Contract Conflicts, The EEC Convention on the Law Applicable to Contractual Obligations: A Comparative Study* (Amsterdam, North-Holland Publishing Company, 1982) 301 (emphasis added). See also FK Juenger, 'The European Convention on the Law Applicable to Contractual Obligations: Some Critical Observations' (1981–82) 22 *Virginia Journal of International Law* 123, 132–34.

[37] L Collins, 'Contractual Obligations – The EEC Preliminary Draft Convention on Private International Law' (1976) 25 *International and Comparative Law Quarterly* 35, 47.

[38] Lando (1987) (n 17) 202.

The editors of Cheshire, North and Fawcett submit that:

> As far as English law is concerned, the place of performance is well known as a connecting factor, but it suffers from the obvious defect that in a typical contract both parties have to perform and may have to do so in different states. The concept of characteristic performance seeks to avoid this difficulty by concentrating on just one performance, the one which is characteristic of the contract as a whole – ie the one which constitutes the essence of the contract. It is this feature of characteristic performance which was used … to justify its elevation.[39]

Plender and Wilderspin submit that the doctrine of characteristic performance

> was likely to serve a useful purpose where mutual obligations created by a contract were to be performed in different jurisdictions; for in such an event there are two *leges solutionis*, each of which might be taken as a pointer to the applicable law.[40]

Lord Collins et al also submit that 'In Switzerland, it was a method of subjecting most of the incidents of a contract to one system of law, when previously the obligations of the respective parties had been governed by different laws.'[41]

Though the Swiss courts and legislator following Schnitzer applied the habitual residence of the characteristic performer as a choice of law rule, some other Member State courts at a contemporary time opted for the place of characteristic performance as a choice of law rule.

Thus, the Paris Court of Appeal in the middle of the twentieth century held that:

> The place with which the contractual transaction has its closest connection is the place where the specific acts of performance of the contract, in the execution of the obligation that is characteristic of that type of contract, must be performed … [T]he law of the country where this obligation is executed still has a stronger claim to govern the contract where the party on whom his obligation rests has his domicile in the same country.[42]

The Paris Court of Appeal's approach is quite similar to Batiffol's proposal, and is one which this book subscribes to rather than the habitual residence of the characteristic performer as the principal connecting factor. The divergence of approach between the Paris Court of Appeal and the Swiss courts is a critical element of this book, because as would be seen later in this study, the EU legislator preferred the habitual residence of the characteristic performer over the place of characteristic performance in determining the applicable law in the absence of choice for commercial contracts.

[39] P Torremans et al, *Cheshire, North and Fawcett, Private International Law* 15th edn (Oxford, Oxford University Press, 2017) 732.

[40] R Plender and M Wilderspin, *European Private International Law of Obligations* 4th edn (London, Sweet and Maxwell, 2014) 177, para 7-005.

[41] L Collins et al, *Dicey, Morris & Collins, The Conflict of Laws* 15th edn (London, Sweet and Maxwell, 2012) 1822, para 32-076.

[42] *Sociètè Jansen v Société Heurty*, [January 27, 1955], cited in Blom (n 17) 243.

III. Rome Convention

During the negotiation process for a Rome Convention, the provisions on the determination of the applicable law in the absence of choice for commercial contracts stirred controversy among Member State representatives involved in drafting the Rome Convention, scholars and other interest groups. Article 4 of both the 1972 Draft Convention[43] and the Rome Convention were substantially drafted in the same way.

Article 4(1) of the Rome Convention provided that, where the applicable law was not chosen, the contract shall be governed by the law of the country with which it is most closely connected. Article 4(1) in particular did not initially generate controversy because some Member State jurisdictions had already started applying the principle of closest connection, prior to entering into the Rome Convention.[44]

Article 4(2) of the Rome Convention provided that subject to the provisions of Article 4(5) of the Rome Convention:

> it shall be presumed that the contract is most closely connected with the country where the party who is to effect the performance which is characteristic of the contract has, at the time of conclusion of the contract, his habitual residence, or, in the case of a body corporate or unincorporate, its central administration. However, if the contract is entered into in the course of that party's trade or profession, that country shall be the country in which the principal place of business is situated or, where under the terms of the contract the performance is to be effected through a place of business other than the principal place of business, the country in which that other place of business is situated.

It is opined that the logic of Article 4(2) of the Rome Convention was to utilise the habitual residence of the characteristic performer as a way of locating the 'true' place of performance. This was the way in which Schnitzer and his disciples had historically conceived the concept of habitual residence of the characteristic performer.[45]

Article 4(2) generated controversy during the negotiation stage. During the negotiation stage, the working group made it clear that 'Article 4 abolishes the *lex loci contractus* and the *lex loci solutionis* as general points of connection'.[46]

In addition, the Giuliano-Lagarde Report (Report) stressed the fact that significance was to be placed on the place of business of the characteristic performer

[43] The EEC Draft of a Convention on the Law Applicable to Contractual and Non-Contractual Obligations, 1972.

[44] See Giuliano-Lagarde Report (n 17) 19.

[45] See generally d'Oliveria (n 25) 307–08 for this view point.

[46] BV Hoffmann, 'General Report on Contractual Obligations' in O Lando et al (eds), *European Private International Law of Obligations: Acts and Documents of an International Colloquium on the European Preliminary Draft Convention on the Law Applicable to Contractual and Non-Contractual Obligations* 1st edn (Berlin, Mohr, 1975) 1, 7.

when compared to the place where the characteristic performance was effected, or other connecting factors. In the words of the Report:

> As for the geographical location of the characteristic performance, it is quite natural that the country in which the party liable for the performance is habitually resident or has his central administration (if a body corporate or unincorporate) or his place of business, according to whether the performance in question is in the course of his trade or profession or not, should prevail over the country of performance where, of course, the latter is a country other than that of habitual residence, central administration or the place of business. In the solution adopted by the Group the position is that only the place of habitual residence or of the central administration or of the place of business of the party providing the essential performance is decisive in locating the contract.[47]

The Report then concluded that:

> Article 4 (2) gives specific form and objectivity to the, in itself, too vague concept of 'closest connection'. At the same time it greatly simplifies the problem of determining the law applicable to the contract in default of choice by the parties. The place where the act was done becomes unimportant. There is no longer any need to determine where the contract was concluded, with all the difficulties and the problems of classification that arise in practice. Seeking the place of performance or the different places of performance and classifying them becomes superfluous.[48]

In this connection, the Report appeared to pay too much attention to the weakness of the place of performance without considering its strengths. In effect, like Schnitzer, the Report favoured a complete shift to the habitual residence of the characteristic performer, without comparing the criteria of place of characteristic performance, in order to ascertain what connecting factor works better.

Interestingly, it was evident that the Report was aware of the criteria of 'place of characteristic performance' and 'main place of performance', which was utilised by the Paris Court of Appeal as a way of better identifying and classifying the place of performance. It is important to provide the relevant quotation:

> [T]he Paris Court stated in its judgment of 27 January 1955 (Soc. Jansen v. Soc. Heurtey) that, in default of an indication of the will of the parties, the applicable law 'is determined objectively by the fact that the contract is located by its context and economic aspects in a particular country, the place with which the transaction is most closely connected being that in which the contract is to be performed in fulfillment of the obligation characteristic of its nature'.

It is this concept of the location of the contracts that is referred to, in terms clearly modelled on the above judgment, in the second paragraph of Article 2313 of the French draft, which states that in default of the expressed will of the parties 'the contract is governed by the law with which it is most closely connected by its economic aspects, and notably by the main place of performance'.[49]

[47] Giuliano-Lagarde Report (n 17) 20–21.
[48] ibid 21.
[49] ibid 19 (footnotes omitted in quotation).

In effect, the Report did not explicitly consider whether the criteria of main place of characteristic performance (when compared to the habitual residence of the characteristic performer), would be a better choice of law rule in reconciling certainty on the one hand, and flexibility and proximity on the other hand. In this connection, this divergence of approach is an important theme that is critically analysed in Chapter 3 of this book.

Though Article 4 of the Draft Convention and 4(2) of the Rome Convention was hailed by some scholars as favouring the triumph of the law of the professional,[50] some scholars and interest groups in the common law jurisdictions were very critical of using the connecting factor of the place of business of the characteristic performer as a presumption to determine the country that is most closely connected to the contract. The common law approach at the time was two-fold. It either preferred that the applicable law should be determined without presumptions (including the presumption of law of the place of performance or characteristic performance) in determining the country or legal system that is most closely connected with a commercial transaction, or in the alternative, the presumption of the place of performance or characteristic performance (rather than the place of business of the characteristic performer) should be utilised in determining the country or legal system that is most closely connected with a commercial transaction.

The first approach was favoured by Collins when he submitted thus:

> In the first place there must be some doubt as to whether residence or place of business is the proper connecting factor in the case of commercial contracts, which represent the vast bulk of contracts containing a foreign element; in the second place, the concept of 'characteristic performance' as a test does not, rightly, find much favour among the EEC countries. The combination of these tests does not, it is submitted, lead to an appropriate law. To put it in terms of English law, it amounts to the very least to a resurrection in favour of the law of the place of performance ...[51]

He also submitted thus:

> What, then of the place of 'characteristic performance'? If this were the governing presumption (entirely without reference to the residence or place of business establishment) it would not do very much than represent a revival of the presumption that the law of the place of performance is to govern the contracts, merely refining the presumption by making it the performance not of both parties but of one party only.[52]

[50] Hoffmann (n 46) 7–8; Lando (1987) (n 17) 202; Vischer (n 25) 27; AJE Jaffey, 'Choice of Law in Relation to Ius Dispositivum with particular reference to the E.E.C Convention on the Law Applicable to Contractual Obligations' in P North (ed), *Contract Conflicts, The EEC Convention on the Law Applicable to Contractual Obligations: A Comparative Study* (Amsterdam, North-Holland Company, 1982) 33, 37–40; AJE Jaffey, 'The English Proper Law Doctrine and the EEC Convention' (1984) 22 *International and Comparative Law Quarterly* 531, 541–47; Mankowski (n 28) 433.

[51] Collins (n 37) 45–46.

[52] ibid 35, 47.

The alternative approach was considered by the English and Scottish Law Commissions, when they submitted at the time that:

> Even if the theory of characteristic performance is accepted, it does not follow that it would be satisfactory to select the law applicable by reference to the residence or place of the principal establishment of the party who has to make the characteristic performance. If the characteristic performance is so important it might be thought that it would be more consistent to apply the law of the place where the characteristic performance is to take place ...[53]

In addition, Williams submitted that 'Perhaps the adoption of the law of the place of performance would have been preferable and recourse to the country of habitual residence etc. as a final resort in those cases where performance is not predominantly centred in one particular country.'[54] He also submitted that 'Admittedly, laws often differ as to where is the place of performance, but it is submitted that in general that country would have a more significant bearing on the contract than the country of residence.'[55]

Article 4(2) of the Rome Convention was further complicated by Article 4(5) of the Rome Convention, which provided, inter alia, that Article 4(2) shall be disregarded if it appears from the circumstances as a whole that the contract is more closely connected with another country.

The relationship between Article 4(2) and Article 4(5) was controversial. Was Article 4(2) a true presumption for determining the country or legal system that is most closely connected to a commercial contract? Was the place of performance better suited to determining the country or legal system that is most closely connected to a commercial contract? Was Article 4(2) a strong rule or a weak rule? What factors were to be considered significant, singly or cumulatively, in disregarding Article 4(2)?

Prior to the entry into force of the Rome Convention, and before the relationship between Article 4(2) and Article 4(5) was tested in practice, some scholars in their early and timely publications had already warned that the relationship between Article 4(2) and Article 4(5) of the Rome Convention was likely to generate uncertainty. At the time, Collins submitted that:

> The search initially is for the law of the country with which the contract is most closely connected. Article 4 contains a rule of habitual residence/principal establishment/characteristic performance indicating which country 'shall be' the country with which the contract is most closely connected. And yet there is an overriding rule that the

[53] www.scotlawcom.gov.uk/files/4413/1739/0072/Private_International_Law__Consultative_Document_on_EEC_Preliminary_Draft_Convention_on_the_Law_applicable_to_Contractual_and_Non Contractual_Obligations.pdf.

[54] PR Williams, 'The EEC Convention on the Law Applicable to Contractual Obligations' (1986) 35 *International and Comparative Law Quarterly* 1, 16.

[55] ibid 16, fn 38.

> characteristic performance rule does not apply if from the circumstances as a whole it is clear that the contract is more closely connected with another country. Why then have a complicated rule which is deprived of meaning by the overriding provision that in any event the search is for the country with which the contract is most closely connected? It would be surely better, if a close connection rule is to be elaborated, to indicate what are the factors (place of performance/residence/place of contracting/form of contract/ language of contract, etc.) by way of example rather than have a dubious rule subject to an exception which may deprive it of all meaning.[56]

Having regard to the complicated relationship between Article 4(2) and 4(5) in determining the law of the country, which is most closely connected to the commercial contract in the absence of a choice of law, some courts of Member States and academic commentators were in disagreement on the proper relationship between these Articles.

Four major approaches feature in judicial opinions and academic writings on the appropriate relationship between Article 4(2) and 4(5) in determining the law of the country, which is most closely connected to the commercial contract in the absence of a choice of law.[57] These approaches are (a) the weak presumption approach, (b) the strong presumption, (c) the intermediary approach and (d) the doctrine of commercial expectations. These approaches exposed the tension between flexibility[58] and justice in individual cases on the one hand, and legal certainty, predictability and uniformity on the other hand, in addressing choice of law problems in commercial transactions under the Rome Convention. Of particular importance to this book, these approaches also aroused the question as to the weight to be given to, inter alia, the place of performance, in displacing Article 4(2) of the Rome Convention. These approaches are critically considered and reviewed below.

[56] Collins (n 37) 48–49. See also Jeunger (n 36) 302.

[57] The literature on this subject is vast. For the scholarly literature in English see A Arzandeh, 'The Law Governing International Contractual Disputes in the Absence of Express Choice by the Parties' (2015) *Lloyd's Maritime and Commercial Law Quarterly* 525; MP Fons, 'Commercial Choice of Law in Context: Looking Beyond Rome' (2015) 78 *Modern Law Review* 241; CSA Okoli and GO Arishe, 'The Operation of the Escape Clauses in the Rome Convention, Rome I Regulation and Rome II Regulation' (2012) 8 *Journal of Private International Law* 513; A Dickinson, 'Rebuttable Assumptions (*ICF* v *Balkenende*)' (2010) *Lloyd's Maritime and Commercial Law Quarterly* 27; U Magnus, 'Article 4 Rome I Regulation: the Applicable Law in the Absence of Choice' in F Ferrari and S Leible (eds), *Rome I Regulation: the Law Applicable to Contractual Obligations in Europe* (Sellier, Munich, 2009); Z Tang, 'Law Applicable in the Absence of Choice – The New Article 4 of the Rome I Regulation' (2008) 71 *Modern Law Review* 785; S Atrill, 'Choice of Law in Contract: the Missing Pieces of the Article 4 Jigsaw' (2004) 53 *International and Comparative Law Quarterly* 549–577; W O' Brian, 'Choice of Law under the Rome Convention: the Dancer or the Dance' (2004) *Lloyd's Maritime and Commercial Law Quarterly* 375; J Hill, 'Choice of law in Contract under the Rome Convention: The Approach of the UK Courts' (2004) 53 *International and Comparative Law Quarterly* 325.

[58] On the concept of flexibility in private international law, see generally LC Wolff, 'Flexible Choice-of-Law Rules: Panacea or Oxymoron?' (2014) 10 *Journal of Private International Law* 431.

A. The Strong Presumption Approach

In some early publications (prior to judicial practice), some scholars argued that Article 4(2) should be applied as a strong rule and rarely displaced. In applying Article 4(2) significant connecting factors such as the place of performance cannot be used to displace Article 4(2) even if the place of performance is cumulatively corroborated qualitatively and quantitatively by other significant connecting factors. The logic behind the strong presumption approach was to enhance certainty, uniformity and predictability and favour the triumph of the law of the professional in international commercial contracts.

Lagarde in his early and timely publication argued in favour of the strong presumption approach thus:

> The judge's discretion with respect to disregarding the presumption is comparable to the judge's power in exceptional cases to sever a part of the contract and then to submit this part to the law of the country with which it has its closest connection, even if this law is not the proper law of the contract.[59]

Jaffey also submitted that:

> The rule in favour of the law of the party rendering the characteristic performance does go a long way to produce certainty and convenience – but only so long as the parties can be confident that it will be departed from only in exceptional circumstances. If the presumption is readily departed from, the whole advantage intended by the provision will be lost, and the desirable uniformity which the Convention was designed to produce will not be obtained.
>
> Thus the correct approach is for paragraph 5 to be invoked to override the presumption of paragraph 2 only in exceptional circumstances.[60]

In judicial practice, the strong presumption approach has also been labelled as the Dutch and Scottish approach.[61] The approach was primarily given judicial endorsement by the Supreme Court of the Netherlands in *Société Nouvelle des Papeteries de l'AA SA v BV Machinefabriek BOA*.[62] In that case, a Dutch producer of paper presses (the Seller) sold a paper press to a company in France (the Buyer). After the delivery had taken place and part of the price had been paid, a dispute arose between the parties in respect of the payment of the balance of the price: the Seller claimed payment of the balance, whereas the Buyer contested this claim on

[59] P Lagarde, 'The European Convention on the Law Applicable to Contractual Obligations: An Apologia' (1981) 22 *Virginia Journal of International Law* 91, 96–97, fn 35.

[60] Jaffey (1984) (n 50) 554.

[61] See also AG Bot in C-133/08 *Intercontainer Interfrigo SC (ICF) v Balkenende Oosthuizen*, EU:C:2009:319 [71]–[72].

[62] *Société Nouvelle des Papeteries de l'AA SA v BV Machinefabriek BOA* [1992] Nederlandse jurisprudentie 750. re-affirmed in *Baros AG (Switzerland) v Embrica Martim Hotelschiffe GmBH* [Hoge Road, 17 October 2008, No C07/037HR; LJN: BE7201].

the basis of alleged faults of the paper press. The negotiations of the sale agreement, as well as the negotiations connected with the claim for payment of balance, were carried out through an agent of the Seller, based in France, the negotiations and documentation (including also the contract) was in French language, and the currency of payment was in Francs. More importantly, according to the terms and conditions of the contract, the paper press was to be (and actually was) delivered and installed, by the Seller, at the Buyer's premises in France.

The Dutch Supreme Court applied the strong presumption approach, as follows:

> The Court of Appeal apparently and rightly proceeded from the view that it follows from the wording and the structure of art 4, as well as from the uniformity in the application of the law which has been intended with the Convention, that this exception to the main rule of [paragraph] 2 has to be applied restrictively, to the effect that the main rule should be disregarded only if, in the special circumstances of the case, the place of business of the party who is to effect the characteristic performance has no real significance as a connecting factor.[63]

The Supreme Court referred to Article 4(2) as containing 'the main rule'; regarded Article 4(5) as an exception and not merely another expression of the principle of closest connection under Article 4(1). It stated that special circumstances were needed in order to justify the application of Article 4(5) on the ground that the desire to create uniform law required a restrictive application to be given to Article 4(5,) and stressed that the place of business of the characteristic performer was the predominant connecting factor.

The Dutch Supreme Court may however be criticised for applying Article 4(2) as an inflexible rule. It paid little or no regard to the fact that the connecting factors, other than the place of business of the characteristic performer, all pointed to France. More importantly, the place of performance was exclusively located in France, and was corroborated by other connecting factors such as the place of negotiation and conclusion of the contract, language and form of the contract, and currency of payment. In essence, the Dutch Supreme Court robbed Article 4(1) of its prevailing significance.

This trend of judicial thinking was followed by a majority of the Members of the Court of Session in the Scottish case of *Caledonia Subsea Ltd v Microperi Srl*.[64] In that case, the claimant, a diving contractor based in Scotland, entered into a contract with the defendant, an Italian company, to carry out work in Egyptian waters. The defendant was working under a contract with an Egyptian company that included an express choice of law clause naming the Arab Republic of Egypt. The claimant brought an action in the Court of Session against the defendant for sums allegedly due under the contract. A preliminary proof was heard on the

[63] THD Struycken, 'Some Dutch Reflections on the Rome Convention, Art 4(5)' (1996) *Lloyd's Maritime and Commercial Quarterly* 18, 20.

[64] *Caledonia Subsea Ltd v Microperi Srl* 2001 SLT 1186.

issue of the law applicable to the contract. The claimant conceded that if the Rome Convention presumption of the habitual residence of the characteristic performer applied then Scots law would be the law applicable, but argued that the presumption did not apply because the contract was more closely connected to Egypt where it was to be performed.

Lord Hamilton, at the Court of First Instance, favoured a strong presumption approach and rejected the idea that the place of performance would ordinarily triumph over the place of business of the characteristic performer. He held that:

> Having regard to the terms and structure of art 4 and to the explanations given in the report, I am of opinion that the presumption laid down by para (2) was designed (in the interests of certainty and of the taking into account of social and economic considerations) prima facie to localise the contract in the country where the party to effect the characteristic performance is established. The place (or places) where the characteristic performance is to take place or in fact takes place is subordinated to the place of the performer's establishment. I am unable to accept counsel for the defender's submission that this is because performance will ordinarily take place in the country of such establishment. The true reason, it seems, is that the social and economic source from which the performance comes (and to which in ordinary course the economic benefit of payment may be expected to return) is in the country of establishment. If the place of performance had been the dominant factor, it would have been easy so to provide.[65]

In addition, he observed that the place of business of the characteristic performer in this case was of real significance as a connecting factor in determining the applicable law, so that it should not be displaced. In this connection, Lord Hamilton held that:

> I accept that the place where the characteristic performance is effected is a material consideration for the purposes of para (5). I also accept that in the circumstances of this case such performance was substantially, albeit not exclusively, in Egypt. It was there and there alone that actual diving operations took place. However, other activities connected with such operations took place outside Egypt. Necessary preparatory work took place at Siracusa and elsewhere en route from Dundee to Port Said. More importantly, activities critically linked to the diving operations were localised in Aberdeen. It was there that the pursuer's project management and administrative staff were based throughout the performance of the contract and it was to there that the superintendent reported daily. It was there that, as illustrated by the issue over diving without through-water communication, matters of major consequence to the continuation of the diving operations were referred and decided – notwithstanding that day to day decisions were taken by the superintendent in Egypt. Accordingly, this is not a case in which the effecting of the characteristic performance was unrelated or insignificantly related to the country where the performer had its principal place of business at the time of the conclusion of the contract. There was a continuing and important connection between the latter place and the place of performance. Additionally it was to Aberdeen alone that payments under the contract were remitted.[66]

[65] ibid [26].
[66] ibid [29].

The majority of the Inner House of the Court of Session favoured a stringent test in determining whether or not to displace Article 4(2) and reasoned that the presumption must be strong and only in exceptional circumstances or very special circumstances can it be disregarded under Article 4(5). The court also unanimously held that though the place of performance was a significant factor under Article 4(5), it was to be subordinated to the place of business of the characteristic performer in determining the law that is most closely connected to a commercial contract.

The majority defended the strong presumption approach as advocated by the Dutch Supreme Court on three main grounds. First, it supported the underlying objective of Article 4 in promoting certainty and uniformity in determining the applicable law in the absence of choice.[67] In other words, it was also honouring the claim in Article 18 of the Rome Convention that the Rome Convention should be interpreted with an objective international flavour and not with a domestic bias. Second, 'looking for the law of the country in which the performance takes place is not the primary aim in any determination of what is to be the applicable law'.[68] Third, it is only by giving considerable weight to the presumption of the place of business of the characteristic performer in Article 4(2) 'that the real and practical effect can be given to the objective of Article 4 … namely that of clarifying and simplifying the law'.[69] In other words, the constant use of the escape clause complicated the determination of what the applicable law in a contract should be in the absence of choice.

Advocate General Bot also favoured the strong presumption approach when he opined that:

> [F]or reasons related to compliance with the principle of legal certainty and in order to ensure the objective of predictability which the Rome Convention seeks to achieve, it is appropriate to apply Article 4(5) of that Convention in so far as it has been shown that the presumptions laid down in Article 4(2) to (4) of the Convention do not reflect the true connection of the contract with the locality thus designated.[70]

The main advantage of the strong presumption approach is that parties can easily determine what law applies to their transaction if they fail to make a choice. It was a strong attraction for the parties to make an express choice of law under Article 3 of the Rome Convention so as to avoid the inflexible rules of the strong presumption approach.[71]

The major criticism of the strong presumption approach is that it construed Article 4(2) as an inflexible rule, and failed to give due consideration to the relevant phrase in Article 4(5) that 'if it appears from the circumstances as a whole that the contract is more closely connected with another country', the presumption

[67] ibid [2] (Lord Marnoch).
[68] ibid [3] (Lord Cameron).
[69] ibid [4] (Lord Marnoch).
[70] *Intercontainer* (61) [74] (footnote omitted in the quotation).
[71] JV Hein, 'The Contribution of the Rome II Regulation to the Communitarisation of Private International Law' (2009) 73 *RabelsZ* 461, 484.

in paragraph 2 'shall be disregarded'. Second, the primary aim of Article 4 of the Rome Convention is to determine the law of the country which is most closely connected to the contract in the absence of choice.[72] Thus, the excessive concern with the presumption in Article 4(2), where there are other justifiable connecting factors, such as the place of performance, that require displacing Article 4(2), make the strong presumption approach open to objection. Third, the strong presumption approach made the escape clause in Article 4(5) of the Rome Convention of little utility in locating the law of the country that was most closely connected to the contract where the parties for good reasons failed to agree on a choice of law.

B. The Weak Presumption Approach

In some early publications (prior to judicial practice), some scholars, particularly from England, argued that the presumption in Article 4(2) was weak because it was likely to be displaced by other significant connecting factors such as the place of performance. In essence, there was hostility to the idea that the place of business of the characteristic performer best embodied the principle of closest connection, when compared to other significant connecting factors such as the place of performance.

North, a leading English private international law scholar at the time, who was part of the UK team that negotiated the Rome Convention, submitted that:

> The law applicable in the absence of choice is that of the country with which the contract is most closely connected – the proper law approach. It is true that presumptions, recently ousted from the English choice of law rules, will re-appear but they are not likely significantly to affect the determination of the law applicable in any particular case – not even the presumption relating to 'characteristic performance'.[73]

Some other English scholars at the time denigrated the presumption in favour of the law of the party rendering the characteristic performance as applying only after the contract's connections with two or more countries have been shown to be equally close.[74] Indeed, some English scholars even went as far as submitting that 'the presumption in Article 4(2) is to be used as a matter of last resort is evident from the fact that the place of habitual residence etc. of the party in question may have no relevance to the transaction whatsoever'.[75]

In judicial practice, the weak presumption approach has also been labelled as the English, French and Danish approach.[76] The English practice was the most

[72] C-133/08 *Intercontainer*, EU:C:2009:617 [26], [54].

[73] P North (ed), *Contract Conflicts, The EEC Convention on the Law Applicable to Contractual Obligations: A Comparative Study* (Amsterdam, North-Holland Publishing Company, 1982) 1, 22.

[74] See the discusiion in Jaffey (1984) (n 50) 553.

[75] Williams (n 54) 15–16.

[76] AG Bot in *Intercontainer* (n 61) [73]; R Plender and M Wilderspin, *European Private International Law of Obligations* 3rd edn (London, Sweet & Maxwell, 2009) 174–75.

prominent in displacing the presumption under Article 4(2), and is thus deserving of attention. Indeed, in one case, Hobhouse LJ expressly labelled the presumption in Article 4(2) as 'very weak'.[77]

Historically, English common law was hostile to the idea of using presumptions to determine the applicable law in the absence of choice for international commercial contracts.[78] It was also not used to utilising the technique of using the presumption of the place of business of the characteristic performer. But the principle of closest connection, under which the place of performance was of considerable significance in determining the law that applies to a contract, was part of the common law, and probably influenced its approach in the determination of the applicable law in the absence of choice.[79]

The relationship between Articles 4(2) and 4(5) was described as 'a tie-breaker' that could tilt in favour of the law of the country that is most closely connected to the contract based on the centre of gravity of the commercial transaction.[80] Thus, English courts were quick to disregard the presumption of characteristic performance in favour of other connecting factors in determining the law that applies to a contract based on deploying the escape clause under Article 4(5).

There were three material factors that played a pivotal role in utilising the escape clause to displace Article 4(2). The first was the use of the place of performance, or the place where the characteristic performance was effected. The second was the use of factors in determining the existence of an implied choice of law under Article 3(1) of the Rome Convention[81] to also determine the existence of a close connection under Article 4(5).[82] The third factor was the use of the law of the country which is closely connected to a contractual transaction to govern another closely connected contract. This factor played a prominent role in letter of credit transactions, reinsurance contracts and guarantee agreements which had independent contractual obligations subsumed under a similar contract.[83]

However, it must be noted that some English courts claimed that they payed due respect to the presumption in Article 4(2).[84] Some English courts discussed the various approaches to the interpretation of the escape clause, such as the judicial approach in Netherlands and France, and claimed to steer a middle course. In this connection, Morrison J held that 'if a wide effect were given to article 4(5),

[77] *Credit Lyonnais v New Hampshire Insurance Company* [1997] CLC 909, 914.

[78] See generally *Coast Lines Limited v Hudig and Veder Chartering NV* [1972] 2 QB 34, 44, 47.

[79] *Bonython* (n 15) 221–23; *Definitely Maybe* (n 15) [7].

[80] *Caledonia* (n 64) (Lord President Cullen).

[81] Such as 'dispute-resolution clauses', 'standard forms', 'previous course of dealing', 'express choice of law in related transactions' and 'reference to particular rules' etc. See generally Giuliano-Lagarde Report (n 17) 1, 17 for an exhaustive discussion of these factors.

[82] For an analysis of this issue Okoli and Arishe (n 57) 524–29.

[83] For a detailed treatment see CSA Okoli, 'The Significance of the Doctrine of Accessory Allocation as a Connecting Factor under Article 4 of Rome I Regulation' (2013) 9 *Journal of Private International Law* 449–97.

[84] On this basis, one might argue that the English approach is an intermediary one that reconciles the requirement of legal certainty and flexibility. However, the frequency with which English courts applied the escape clause demonstrated that they were at best paying lip service to the presumptions.

it would render the presumption in article 4(2) of no value'.[85] Potter LJ held that the presumption should 'only be disregarded in circumstances which clearly demonstrate the existence of connecting factors justifying the disregarding of the presumption in article 4(2)'.[86] Keene LJ also held that 'If the presumption is to be of any real effect, it must be taken to apply except where the evidence clearly shows that the contract is more closely connected with another country.'[87]

For the purpose of this book, suffice it to say that the reason why the English practice is regarded as favouring the weak presumption approach is that it treated the place of performance as almost decisive in displacing Article 4(2). This approach was influenced by the academic disciples of Dicey, who submitted that:

> Inevitably the solution of individual cases will depend on the facts, but in principle it is submitted that the presumption may be most easily rebutted in those cases where the place of performance differs from the place of business of the party whose performance is characteristic of the contract. It has already been seen that the presumption is designed to lead to the country of the residence or place of business of the party whose performance is characteristic, and that usually that country will coincide with the place of performance, because normally contracts are performed in the country of that party's place of business. The situations in which they are performed elsewhere may (but by no means inevitably) provide material to rebut the presumption.[88]

The view advanced by the academic disciples of Dicey has been followed by a significant number of English judges in decided cases.[89] In many cases, English courts were quick to disregard the presumption in Article 4(2) where the place of performance (or characteristic performance) differed from the place of business of the party who is required to effect the characteristic performance. Such was the undue elevation of the place of performance that in one case, the Court of Appeal had to correct an expression used by a lower court judge, who had held that the relationship between Article 4(2) and Article 4(5) was simply concerned with locating the place of characteristic performance.[90] It is important to discuss here some of these cases, so that one can better appreciate how the significance of

[85] Keene LJ in *Ennstone Building Products Ltd v Stranger Ltd* [2002] 1 WLR 3059 [41] summarising *Definitely Maybe* (n 15) [14]–[15].

[86] *Samcrete Egypt Engineers v Land Rover Exports Limited* [2001] ECWA 2019 [45].

[87] *Ennstone* (n 85) [41].

[88] L Collins (ed), *Dicey and Morris on the Conflict of Laws* 12th edn (London, Sweet and Maxwell, 1993) 1237–38.

[89] *Bank of Baroda v Vysya Bank Limited* [1994] CLC 41, 49; *Definitely Maybe* (n 15) [15]; *Samcrete* (n 86) [47]; *Kenburn Waste Management Ltd v Bergmann* [2002] EWCA 99 [20]–[23]; *Marconi Communications International v PT Pan Indonesia Bank Ltd* [2005] ECWA 422 [66]; *Habib Bank Limited v Central Bank of Sudan* [2006] EWHC 1767 [43]–[44]; *Albon (t/a NA Carriage Co) v Naza Motor Trading Sdn Bhd* [2007] 1 WLR 2489; *Mrs Daad Sharab v His Royal Highness Prince Al-Waleed Bin Talal Bin Abdal Aziz Al Saud* [2008] EWHC 1893 [74]–[75]; *Commercial Marine Piling Limited v Pierse Contracting Limited* [2009] EWHC 2241 [33]–[37]; *Cecil v Byatt* [2010] EWHC 641 (Comm) [82]–[94] (this aspect of the High Court's decision was not overturned by the Court of Appeal in [2011] EWCA Civ 135); *Donkers v Storm Aviation Ltd* [2014] EWHC 241 (QB) [50–52].

[90] *Kenburn*, ibid [20]–[23].

the place of performance under Article 4(5) of the Rome Convention worked in the English practice.

In letter of credit contracts, English courts applied the place of performance in the sense that the law that governs a letter of credit transaction is 'the place where the documents necessary to procure payment to the seller/beneficiary are to be presented and checked, and the place where payment to the seller/beneficiary is to be made against those documents'.[91] In fact, prior to the Rome Convention, the English position of applying the law of the place of performance in relation to letter of credit appears to have been influenced by Gutteridge and Megrah, who submitted that:

> Men of business do not, perhaps, often express their choice of law either openly or by inference, and very frequently it becomes the duty of the court to ascertain, not what the parties intended to be the proper law of the contract, but what law would be selected by reasonable men of business in all the circumstances of any particular transaction. In this event it is submitted that the presumption must be that matters connected with the performance by the banker of his contract under a commercial credit are to be regulated by the law prevailing at the place of performance, i.e. the law of the territory in which the seller's draft is presented to the banker for acceptance or payment.[92]

In the *Bank of Baroda* the case was concerned with whether the court had jurisdiction based on a good arguable case relating to application of the *forum conveniens* principle to grant leave to order service of a writ out of jurisdiction on the foreign defendants. An issuing bank (from India) had issued a letter of credit in favour of an Irish seller. Mance J (as he then was) determined the characteristic performer between the issuing bank and the confirming bank (from India) under Article 4(2). He was of the view that the party (confirming/advising bank) charged with the responsibility of adding its confirmation to make payment against the presentation of compliant documents by the seller is the characteristic performer, and the duty of reimbursement by the issuing bank was merely a consequential obligation. In this connection, Article 4(2) led to the application of English law because the confirming/advising bank effected performance through an office in London. He further considered the relationship between the confirming bank and seller, and held that it was governed by English law, and applied these contracts that were governed by English law to govern the contract between the issuing bank and the seller that will ordinarily have been governed by Indian law if Article 4(2) was applied as well. In reaching this conclusion, considerable weight was given to the fact that the performance of the obligation of the letter of credit was to take place in England.

[91] *Marconi* (n 89) [63] (Potter LJ). See also *Bank of Baroda* (n 89). cf *Credit Agricole Indosuez v Chailease Finance Corp* [2000] CLC 754.

[92] HC Gutteridge and M Megrah, *The Law of Bankers' Commercial Credits* 5th edn (Abingdon, Taylor & Francis, 1976) 198. Approved in *Offshore International SA v Banco Central SA and Another* (1977) 1 WLR 399, 402.

The approach in *Bank of Baroda* might be supported on the basis that though the place of performance was given considerable significance, the court was seeking to apply a single law to the sub-contracts arising out of the letter of credit transaction, so as to enhance legal and commercial certainty, and convenience for the parties. This approach has now been legitimised by Recital 20 to Rome I, and is also regarded as a legitimate approach under the Rome Convention.[93]

Similarly in *Marconi*, the case was concerned with whether the court had jurisdiction based on a good arguable case relating to the application of the *forum conveniens* principle to grant leave to order service of a writ out of jurisdiction on the foreign defendants. The seller/beneficiary claimed against the confirming bank for refusing to pay against apparently compliant documents despite the advice of the negotiating bank. The application of the presumption under Article 4(2) with regard to the contracts between the seller/beneficiary and issuing bank, issuing bank and confirming bank, and confirming bank and seller led to the application of Indonesian law. The Court of Appeal gave considerable weight to the place of performance and payment, instead of the place of contracting and residence of the parties, and held that since the place of performance and payment was in England, where the presentation and checking of the documents was carried out through the bank negotiating on behalf of the seller, Article 4(5) should displace Article 4(2) and govern the relationship between the parties under the letter of credit.

The Court of Appeal in *Marconi* may be criticised on the basis that it should have applied Indonesian law through the application of Article 4(2) to the three component contracts that formed the core of the letter of credit transaction where no inconvenience or legal and commercial uncertainty would have arisen as was the case in *Bank of Baroda*. The Court of Appeal's undue reliance on the contract between the seller and negotiating bank based on the place of performance appears to give too much weight to Article 4(5), and undermine the goal of certainty.

In *Definitely Maybe*,[94] the defendant applied to set aside the service of claim for breach of contract on the ground that under the Brussels Convention the court had no jurisdiction to hear the case. The plaintiff, an English company, had commenced the claim against the defendant, a German company, for the unpaid balance of two performances by the plaintiff's music band, which had taken place in Germany. The Court of First Instance held that the subject matter of the contract had been exclusively performed in Germany and, in accordance with Article 4 of the Rome Convention, the applicable law was German law. The Court noted that:

> The characteristic performance of the contract, although made by the claimant in England, was to provide performances in Germany. The defendant, leaving aside his obligation to make payment, had to provide certain facilities in Germany. The marketing

[93] C-305/13 *Haeger & Schmidt GmBH v Mutuelles du Mans assurances IARD (MMA IARD) and others* EU:C:2014:2320. See also Okoli (n 83); N Enonchong, 'The Law Applicable to Demand Guarantees and Counter-Guarantees' (2015) *Lloyd's Maritime and Commercial Law Quarterly* 194–215.

[94] *Definitely Maybe* (n 15).

> and promotion of the concerts took place in Germany. There were certain territorial exclusions which related to Germany and the defendant was clearly entering into a series of contracts, each one of which was to result in performance by artists in Germany.[95]

On appeal, the High Court (per Morison J) was in a dilemma as to whether to give principal effect to the presumption in Article 4(2) of the Rome Convention or the place of performance by applying Article 4(5) of the Rome Convention which arguably was a better representation of the closest connection test. Morison J expressed his frustration in the following words:

> The real issue between the parties centres on the relationship between these two paragraphs of art 4. Whilst para 2 looks to the location of the principal performer, para 5 looks more widely to a connection between the contract and a country. If there is a divergence between the location of the principal performer and the place of substantial or characteristic performance, what then? On the one hand, were the presumption to be displaced whenever such divergence existed, the presumption would be of little weight or value. Paragraph 2 must have been inserted to provide a 'normal' rule which is simple to apply. Giving wide effect to para 5 will render the presumption of no value and represent a return to the English common law test of ascertaining the proper law, which places much less weight on the location of the performer and much more on the place of performance, and the presumed intention of the parties.[96]

In his final analysis he endorsed the views of the academic disciples of Dicey which gives considerable significance to the place of performance in utilising the escape clause.[97] Morison J's decision in *Definitely Maybe* exposes the difficulty in determining what weight should be given to the place of performance in applying Article 4(5). The contract inter alia was exclusively performed in Germany, so that Germany was the country where the 'main action' of the contract took place. This might explain why despite the difficulties in interpreting Article 4(2) and 4(5), the English court gave considerable weight to the place of performance.

Similarly, in the case of *Samcrete*[98] the defendant appealed against the dismissal of its application for a stay of proceedings on the ground of *forum non conveniens*. The defendant, an Egyptian company, had entered into a contract of guarantee with the claimant in respect of credit offered by the claimant to a company called Technotrade, another Egyptian company of whom the defendant was 20 per cent shareholder. Technotrade was the claimant's distributor in Egypt and the contract between the claimant and Technotrade contained a choice of law clause granting jurisdiction to the English court. The contract of guarantee contained no such clause. The judge in the court below held that under Article 4 of the Rome Convention the contract was most closely connected with England because of the choice of law clause in the contract between Technotrade and the claimant. On appeal,

[95] ibid [8].
[96] *Definitely Maybe* (n 15) [15].
[97] ibid [15]. See also *Surrey (UK) Ltd v Mazandaran Wood & Paper Industries* [2014] EWHC 3165 (Comm) [23]–[27].
[98] (n 86).

the defendant argued that the judge had taken the wrong approach to Article 4 of the Rome Convention. In this connection Potter LJ observed that:

> The facts … which appear to me to be of greater significance in connecting the contract with England are that the obligation of payment under the guarantee was to be performed in England so that any breach of the guarantee by failure to pay in accordance with a valid demand would similarly take place in England and there give rise to the cause of action under the guarantee. It has been argued by Mr Tolley that, in an international trading contract of this kind, the place of payment is a technical accounting matter rather than one of commercial significance. Nonetheless, from the point of view of the enforcement of the guarantee, it is a matter of considerable importance to the creditor.[99]

Some scholars have been critical of the considerable significance given to the place of performance in *Samcrete*. Hill observes that:

> It is far from clear why the place of performance of the claimant's obligations under the distribution contract was relevant at all.
>
> Furthermore, the Court of Appeal's conclusion basically has the effect of replacing the connecting factor identified in paragraph 2 (the characteristic performer's principal place of business) with the place of performance of the characteristic obligation; nothing else of substance linked the guarantee with England. The *Samcrete* case is the sort of situation for which the presumption was intended to provide the degree of certainty which a general 'closest connection' test is unable to achieve. The Court of Appeal's decision to attach little, if any, weight to the presumption is difficult to support and undermines the operation of the Rome Convention.[100]

Samcrete is another case that exposes the problem of what significance should be given to the place of performance in applying Article 4(5) of the Rome Convention, given that the habitual residence of the characteristic performer, without a corroboration of other connecting factors is not suitable for determining the principle of closest connection.

The advantage of the weak presumption approach is that it shows that in determining the closest connection with the country and contract, the place of business of the characteristic performer may in many cases have little or no connection with the contract in question, when compared with the place where the performance was effected.[101] Second, it made the escape clause in the Rome Convention a strong tool in addressing choice of law problems in commercial transactions by flexibly locating the law that is most closely connected to the contract in question.

The disadvantage of the weak presumption approach is that it functionally made the presumption in Article 4(2) of no material significance by displacing it quite often through the deployment of the escape clause thereby undermining legal certainty.[102] Second, the undue elevation of the place of performance as a special

[99] ibid [47].
[100] Hill (n 57) 341–42.
[101] See also *Definitely Maybe* (n 15) [12].
[102] See also PA De Miguel Asensio, 'Applicable Law in the Absence of Choice to Contracts Relating to Intellectual or Industrial Property Rights' (2008) 10 *Yearbook of Private International Law* 199, 203.

connecting factor in disregarding the presumption in Article 4(2) has no textual legitimacy under Article 4 of the Rome Convention.[103] The place of performance ought to be considered alongside other material connecting factors in determining whether it is justifiable to disregard the presumption of characteristic performance in Article 4(2). Third, the escape clause was abused in such a way that the law of the forum was often interpreted by some courts of Member States to be the most closely connected law in the absence of choice.[104]

C. Commercial Expectations

The doctrine of commercial expectations assesses the significance of connecting factors under Article 4 of the Rome Convention in commercial terms. Some advocates in favour of the triumph of the law of the professional argue, inter alia, that the rationale for applying Article 4(2) as the principal connecting factor was for the commercial convenience of the professional, which would result in the reduction of transaction costs.[105] However, in the eyes of some common law scholars and judges, the commercial expectation of the parties is that the 'The presumption is especially vulnerable because it will so seldom be appropriate to apply the supplier's law, the law of the place of performance frequently, having a stronger claim to govern.'[106]

In the context of the relationship between Article 4(2) and Article 4(5) of the Rome Convention, Fentiman is credited with expressly propounding the above theory in academic writings.[107] The theory was further reformulated by Atrill.[108] The theory asserts that the true purpose for the justification of the deployment of the escape clause in disregarding the presumption of characteristic performance is not explicitly stated in the Rome Convention. In other words, the Rome Convention neither makes an exhaustive list of connecting factors that justify using the escape clause nor the measure of significance or weight to be attached to these factors in disregarding the presumption of characteristic performance. The rationale for this is that the European drafters of the Rome Convention did not intend to fetter the discretion of the courts of Member States in ascertaining what material connecting factors justify the utilisation of the escape clause in disregarding Article 4(2).

[103] See also *Caledonia* (n 64) [41].

[104] Struycken (n 63) 18; *Samcrete* (n 86) [42]; E Lein, 'The New Rome I/Rome II/Brussels I Synergy' (2008) 10 *Yearbook of Private International Law* 177, 185.

[105] Lando (1987) (n 17) 202; Jaffey (1982) (n 50) 37–40; Jaffey (1984) (n 50) 541–47; Mankowski (n 28) 433.

[106] R Fentiman, 'Commercial Expectations and the Rome Convention' (Case Comment) (2002) 61 *Cambridge Law Journal* 50.

[107] ibid; R Fentiman, 'The Significance of Close Connection' in J Ahern and W Binchy (eds), *The Rome II Regulation on the Law Applicable to Non-Contractual-Obligations: A New International Litigation Regime* (The Hague, Martinus Nijhoff, 2009) 94–98; R Fentiman, *International Commercial Litigation* (Oxford, Oxford University Press, 2015) 208–15.

[108] Atrill (n 57).

Fentiman states the main purpose of Article 4 of the Rome Convention is to identify the commercial gravity of a contract. Thus, a purposive approach which looks into the socio-economic function of the contract is required in determining whether Article 4(5) should be utilised in displacing Article 4(2); and not a 'mere accumulation of connecting factors',[109] 'an arithmetical preponderance of elements'[110] or 'simply a matter of judicial intuition'.[111] The theory posits that close connection is equivalent to significant connection and 'requires a court to give such weight to connecting factors as reflects their practical importance'.[112] It is also stated that the strong and weak presumption approaches are not useful in this task because they offer a deceptive choice between the requirements of legal certainty and flexibility in commercial transactions.[113]

Fentiman submits that the purpose of the escape clause in Article 4(5) of the Rome Convention is:

> intended to capture a contract's commercial context and presumably thereby to ensure its commercial effectiveness, and indirectly the parties' expectation that their contract shall be commercially viable. The animating principle is that the significance of the relevant connecting factors should be assessed in commercial terms.[114]

Thus, it is advocated that in justifying the deployment of the escape clause in displacing the presumption of characteristic performance, material connecting factors such as the place of performance or payment, object of the contract, and the closeness of one contract to another are of commercial significance to the parties involved in a contract and should be given due attention by the court. However, connecting factors such as the place where the contract was negotiated or concluded, the language in which the contract was expressed, reference to a foreign law and the country's currency of payment are not of any commercial significance to the parties involved in a contract.

The commercial expectations doctrine appears to have been supported by some judges. In this connection, let us consider for example the significance of the place of contracting and language of the contract in determining the principle of closest connection.

Though some judges hold that the place of contracting might have the advantage of certainty, predictability and simplicity;[115] in the context of modern

[109] Fentiman (2015) (n 107) 209.
[110] ibid.
[111] ibid 210.
[112] ibid 211.
[113] Atrill (n 57) 556.
[114] Fentiman (2015) (n 107) 211. Commercial expectations' proponents draw support from the cases of *Apple Corps Limited v Apple Computers Incorporated* [2004] 2 CLC 720 [49], [56]–[64]; *Bank of Baroda* (n 89) 48–49; *Marconi* (n 89) [62]–[66]; *Iran Continental Shelf Oil Co Ltd v IRI International Corp* [2004] CLC 696 [73]; *Ennstone* (n 85) 3067–70; *Samcrete Egypt Engineers v Land Rover Exports Limited* [2001] ECWA 2019 [22], [24], [47]–[51]; *Caledonia* (n 64) [44]; *British Arab Commercial Bank Plc v Bank of Communications and Commercial Bank of Syria* [2011] EWHC 281 (Comm) [25]; and *Gard Marine and Energy Limited v Glacier Reinsurance AG* [2010] EWCA Civ 1052 [41], [45].
[115] *Sturiano v Brooks*, 523 So 2d 1126, 1129 (Fla 1988).

international commercial transactions, it has been submitted by some jurists[116] and judges,[117] on the contrary, that less weight should be accorded to the place of contracting. This is because in modern commercial transactions, the place of contracting has limited practical significance. For technological and commercial reasons, it has also been held that the place of contracting has less significance because it is 'essentially a matter of business convenience, and not a contractual connection'.[118] In other words, the place of contracting could simply be a matter of chance or fortuitous, and not one that has significance to the commercial transaction in question.[119] The place of contracting could also be difficult to identify where it takes place in different countries, or impossible to identify where it takes place in more than one country at the same time,[120] thereby leading to uncertainty.

Though the language of the contract might be easy to determine and could be significant where it was used as a neutral means of negotiating a contract between the parties,[121] for practical commercial reasons it has been held that the language of the contract is not a significant connecting factor, and little weight should be given to it.[122] Thus, Potter LJ held that the significance of English language as a connecting factor is of 'little consequence, given the general use of English as a language of international commerce'.[123] Popplewell J also held that English language as a connecting factor 'provides no relevant connection. English is the first language of many countries and a primary language employed in international trade, whose use betrays no significant connection between the transaction itself and England.'[124]

The advantage of the commercial expectations theory is that it offers a pragmatic solution in justifying which factors, such as the place of performance, are significant or material in displacing the presumption of the habitual residence of the characteristic performer in a contract where the parties fail to make a choice. In other words, the true value of the commercial expectations theory is that it provides a normative approach on how connecting factors should be assessed according to their significance.

However, it is open to three main objections. First, the doctrine of commercial expectations has no explicit textual legitimacy in the Rome Convention. The major quarrel with the doctrine is not that Article 4 of the Rome Convention is not in any way connected with the goal of commercial certainty or proximity. The major

[116] AG Wahl in C-64/12, *Schlecker v Boedeker* EU:C:2013:241 [70].

[117] *Amin* (n 15) 63; *Transworld Ltd v Bombardier Inc* [2012] 1 CLC 145.

[118] *Marconi* (n 89) [62].

[119] 'The fact that seven of the contracts were made in London is accounted for by the fact that it was in London that Mr Mirchandani usually met Mr Somaia but that does not make the resulting contracts more closely connected with England. The meeting might just as well have taken place in Dubai, the US or Mauritius' – *Mirchandani and Others v Ketan Somaia and Others* 2001 WL 239782 Chancery Division [25].

[120] *Apple* (n 114).

[121] *Latchin (t/a Dinkha Latchin Associates) v General Mediterranean Holdings SA* [2003] EWCA Civ 1786.

[122] *Sapporo Breweries Ltd v Lupofresh Ltd* [2013] EWCA Civ 948.

[123] *Samcrete* (n 86) [46].

[124] *Martrade Shipping & Transport GmbH v United Enterprises Corp* [2014] EWHC 1884 (Comm) [22].

objection to the doctrine is that the overriding goal of Article 4 of the Rome Convention is based on the principle of closest connection, and not commercial expectations.

Second, the theory is likely to produce almost as much uncertainty as the weak presumption approach. The determination of whether a connecting factor meets the commercial expectations of a contract, or the determination of the measurement or assessment of a contract's commercial significance will in a variety of cases amount to embarking on a voyage of discovery beyond the scope envisaged by the Rome Convention. For example, in a service contract, where the service provider's ('A') place of business is in New York, for services to be provided to B in London, and a very closely related contract to the service contract provides for Swiss law to apply, the doctrine of commercial expectation could produce different results. First, it could be argued that since the service provider's place of business is in New York, his law should apply because of the commercial expectation that his law should be uniformly applied to all clients he deals with, so at to reduce transaction costs. Second, it could be argued that the commercial expectation of the parties is that English law should apply because the essence of the contract takes place in London. Third, it could be argued that Swiss law should apply because it already governs a very closely related contract to the service contract, so that transaction costs would be reduced by applying a single law to the parties' contract, and the parties can consistently allocate their risk by applying a single law. Which of these commercial expectations should the court give effect to? Furthermore, it does not allay the fears of uncertainty by suggesting that in such a situation the court should look for a commercially effective solution.

Third, Article 4(5) is concerned with the circumstances as a whole in determining whether the presumption should be displaced, and not just the commercial expectation, consequence or effectiveness of the contract. In embarking on this exercise the judge ought not to be fettered by precedent in determining what type of factors are significant. For example, a factor such as the place of payment may be a significant factor for the creditor in respect of a contract of guarantee,[125] but may turn out to be insignificant in another case where no term of the instrument gave the place of payment contractual effect.[126]

D. Intermediary Approach

The intermediary approach recognises that there is an underlying dilemma and tension between achieving the goals of legal certainty and predictability in

[125] *Samcrete* (n 86) [47].

[126] *British Arab* (n 114) [35]. Furthermore, 'currency of payment' and the 'place of negotiation and conclusion of the contract', which is regarded as an insignificant connecting factor by commercial expectations' proponents was utilised as a significant factor in *Definitely Maybe* (n 15) [8] and *Opthalmic Innovations Limited (UK) v Opthalmic Innovations International Incorporated (USA)* [2004] EWHC 2948 [32], [49].

commercial transactions on the one hand, and flexibility and justice on the other hand. The intermediary approach argues that principal weight should be given to Article 4(2) but it could be displaced where it is sufficiently outweighed inter alia by other connecting factors such as the place of performance. The use of the intermediary approach has been favoured by some judges in Scotland, France and the jurisprudence of the CJEU.

In Scotland, initially it appeared that the place of performance was given considerable significance in displacing Article 4(2). Thus, in *Ferguson Shipbuilders Ltd v Voith Hydro GmbH & Co KG*[127] a Scottish shipbuilding company entered into a contract with a marine engineering company domiciled in Germany. The German company agreed to deliver to the Scottish company in Scotland propeller systems which were to be incorporated into ships there being built for Scottish buyers. Lord Penrose held that Article 4 of the Rome Convention led to the application of Scots law, because the contract had a real connection with Scotland. The crucial factors in reaching this conclusion were that the place of performance of the German company's obligation was Scotland, where the machinery was to be delivered, and the contract for the construction and delivery of the propellers was proximate construction of the ships in Scotland.

In a later Scottish case, the significance of the place of performance was attributed with a subordinate role. The use of the intermediary approach in deploying the escape clause under the Rome Convention featured in the dissenting opinion of Lord President Cullen in *Caledonia Subsea Ltd v Microperi Srl* ('*Caledonia*').[128] Though the majority in the Inner House argued for Article 4(2) to be applied almost strictly, Lord President Cullen rejected a strong or weak presumption approach, and alternatively held that the place of performance, though very significant, should not ordinarily triumph over the place of business of the characteristic performer, unless there was good justification.[129] He held that both the weak and strong presumption approaches are open to objection as they are extreme versions of what is intended in the Rome Convention.[130]

He held that:

> art 4 intended to accord a special significance to the place of business of the principal performer as the indicator of the country with which the contract had the closest connection. I am not disposed to agree with the view that this was because in most cases the contract was likely to be performed in that country; or with the view suggested by Dicey and Morris … that the presumption may most easily be rebutted in those cases where the place of performance differs from the place of business of the party whose performance is characteristic of the contract, a statement approved by Mance J … in *Bank of Baroda v Vysya Bank Ltd*. If the framers of art 4 had intended to attach such significance to the place of performance they could have readily indicated that, but they

[127] [2000] SLT 229.
[128] *Caledonia* (n 64) [35]–[41].
[129] ibid.
[130] ibid [35].

> did not do so. Indeed when the place of performance is such an obvious candidate as the test, the fact that it is not mentioned suggests a movement away from it .... No doubt the place where the contract is performed is of relevance, either directly or indirectly, but it may be only one of a number of factors to be assessed in the exercise under para 5. In the result I consider that the presumption under para 2 should not be 'disregarded' unless the outcome of the comparative exercise referred to in para 5 – which, unlike para 2, may involve difficulty and uncertainty – demonstrates a clear preponderance of factors in favour of another country.[131]

The CJEU in *Intercontainer*[132] also gave legitimacy to the intermediary approach. In that case one of the issues before the CJEU was the interpretation of the relationship between Article 4(2) and (5) of the Rome Convention.

The CJEU held that the primary consideration in Article 4 of the Rome Convention is the determination of the law that is most closely connected with a contract in the absence of choice.[133] The presumption in Article 4(2) is aimed at achieving the goals of legal certainty and foreseeability in the contract between the parties with regard to determining the law that is most closely connected to the contract in the absence of choice.[134] The escape clause in Article 4(5) is aimed at achieving the goal of flexibility and justice in individual cases by leaving a margin of discretion for a judge to disregard the presumption in Article 4(2) if there are other connecting factors that justify such an exercise.[135]

The relationship between Article 4(2) and Article 4(5) involves a counterbalance between the requirements of legal certainty and predictability in commercial transactions on the one hand, and the requirements of flexibility and justice in individual cases on the other hand.[136] Thus, where it is clear from the circumstances as a whole that the contract is more closely connected with a country other than that identified on the basis of the presumptions set out in Article 4(2), it is for the court to refrain from applying Article 4(2).[137]

The intermediary approach as advocated by Lord President Cullen in *Caledonia* and the CJEU in *Intercontainer* is the appropriate, 'literal'[138] or natural meaning of the deployment of the escape clause in the Rome Convention. The approach is sound and has textual legitimacy in the Rome Convention.

The main advantage of the intermediary approach is that it steers a middle course between meeting the requirements of legal certainty and predictability in commercial transactions on the one hand, and the requirements of flexibility and justice in individual cases on the other hand.[139]

[131] ibid [41].
[132] (n 72).
[133] ibid [55], [60].
[134] ibid [55], [60], [61].
[135] ibid [58].
[136] ibid [59].
[137] ibid [63].
[138] Beaumont and McEleavy (n 25) 477–78.
[139] For a critique, see Wolff (n 58).

However, its major shortcoming is that it does not sufficiently describe the threshold of displacement under Article 4(5). The CJEU's ruling also appears to rewrite the words of Article 4 of the Rome Convention simpliciter. Thus, the intermediary approach is susceptible to manipulation and infiltration by both the weak and strong presumption approaches. In other words, both the weak or strong presumption judicial disciples can claim that they are honouring the intermediary approach as decided by the CJEU in *Intercontainer*, but they can still functionally deploy their extreme versions of the escape clause under the Rome Convention.[140]

Another shortcoming of the CJEU's decision is that it did not provide any guidance on the weight to be given to other connecting factors such as the place of performance in displacing Article 4(2). A counter-argument might be that creating an exhaustive list of significant factors that determines the threshold of displacement ultimately fetters the discretion of the judge or decision maker, and may lead to injustice in individual cases. In other words, a significant factor in one case may turn out to be insignificant when dealing with the same or another type of contract in the circumstances of the case.

Though it is conceded that the issue of what significance should be given to the place of performance under the Rome Convention was not expressly an issue before the CJEU, the CJEU may have provided some guidance on this issue, given the controversy generated on the significance of the place of performance in scholarly writings and judicial decisions.

Interestingly, one did not have to wait too long for a court of a Member State to pronounce again on the significance of the place of performance under Article 4 of the Rome Convention. In the French case of *La Société JFA Chantier Naval v La Société Kerstholt Teakdecksystems BV*[141] the principal issue was whether the place of business of the characteristic performer should be attributed with special significance where Article 4(2) is not corroborated by other significant factors. In such a case should the law of the place of performance not automatically be a stronger candidate for determining the applicable law? This was an important issue raised, at least from the perspective of this book.

Interestingly Cuniberti in an earlier publication, had argued that it would be a good thing for the French Cour de Cassation to make a pronouncement on the relationship between Article 4(2) and (5).[142] Like some common law scholars and judges, he was very critical of using the place of business of the characteristic performer as a presumptive criterion for closest connection when compared

[140] See also P Rogerson, 'Conflict of Laws' (2009) *All England Annual Review* 5 [5.38].

[141] Arrêt n° 1017 du 19 octobre 2010 (09-69.246) www.courdecassation.fr/publications_26/arrets_publies_2986/chambre_commerciale_financiere_economique_3172/2010_3324/octobre_3694/1017_19_17959.html.

[142] G Cuniberti, 'L'incertitude du lieu d'exécution sur la loi applicable au contrat. La difficile cohabitation des articles 4-2 et 4-5 de la Convention de Rome du 19 juin 1980' (2003) *Juris-Classeur Pèriodique* (general edition) 153.

to the place where the performance takes place. He drew inspiration from old continental scholars such as Savigny and Batiffol to argue that the place of performance was arguably a better criterion for determining the principle of proximity. He was puzzled as to what significance would be given to the place of performance in the context of Article 4 of the Rome Convention. His wishes came to pass.

The French Cour de Cassation held that it does not result from the combination of paragraphs 1, 2 and 5 of Article 4 of the Rome Convention on the law applicable to contractual obligations, that when the principal connecting factor of the habitual residence of the characteristic performer is not corroborated by any other connecting factor, the law of the place of performance should necessarily apply. The Court favoured an intermediary approach that does not give decisive weight to the place of performance. Its decision may have been stronger if it provided further guidance on what weight should be attributed to the place of performance in disregarding Article 4(2).

The CJEU, in the later case of *Haeger*,[143] implicitly gave significance to the place of performance as a connecting factor for a commercial contract of carriage of goods. The CJEU in this case was also concerned with the relationship between Article 4(2) and (5) of the Rome Convention. It held inter alia that the court of a Member State 'must conduct an overall assessment of all objective factors characterising the contractual relationship and determine which of those factors are, in its view most significant';[144] and, further held that the place of delivery of the goods should be taken into account in interpreting the escape clause under Article 4(5) of the Rome Convention.

It could be argued that the CJEU's explicit reference to the place of delivery of the goods which is the performance of the obligation for a contract of carriage of goods, by way of analogy, could be regarded as the CJEU giving implicit endorsement to the place of performance as a factor that should be taken into account in interpreting the escape clause for commercial contracts under Article 4(5) of the Rome Convention. A contrasting view is that the CJEU's judgment was simply restricted to giving significance to the place of delivery as a significant connecting factor in displacing the main connecting factors for a contract of carriage of goods under Article 4(4) of the Rome Convention (and by extension Article 5(1) of Rome I). A contract of carriage of goods is a special commercial contract and is not to be equated or compared with other commercial contracts.

In summation, though the intermediary approach is the proper approach to interpreting Article 4(5) of the Rome Convention, it does not clearly articulate the significance to be given to other significant connecting factors such as the place of performance, so that the intermediary approach can be applied in a weak or strong presumption form.

[143] *Haeger* (n 93).
[144] *Schlecker*, EU:C:2013:551 [40]; C-305/13, *Haeger* (n 143) [49].

IV. Rome I Regulation Proposal

There was a Rome Convention Green paper which highlighted the problems of Article 4 of the Rome Convention, and in particular, the complicated relationship between Article 4(2) and (5).[145]

Subsequently, there was a European Commission Proposal relating to Article 4 of Rome I, dealing with the law applicable in the absence of choice.[146] The European Commission's proposal on Article 4 of Rome I initially proved controversial.[147] In this connection, there are two issues that are worth noting. The first issue was that fixed rules rather than presumptions were to be used in determining the applicable law. The second was that there was a controversy as to whether the escape clause should be abolished.

A. Fixed Rules: Exclusion of the Place of Characteristic Performance

The European Commission proposed fixed rules for eight categories of commercial contracts under Article 4 of Rome I.[148] The use of fixed rules differed from the structure of Article 4 of the Rome Convention which used presumptions. In the final draft, Article 4 of Rome I retained the solution of fixed rules for commercial contracts with slight amendments.[149] Thus, Article 4 of Rome I is built on fixed rules in determining the applicable law in the absence of choice, and does away with the style of presumptions, as was the case under the Rome Convention. It also does away with expressly regarding the principle of closest connection as its driving force, as was the case under the Rome Convention. There is no clear indication as to what is the driving force of these fixed rules under Article 4(1) and (2) of Rome I other than they are aimed at legal certainty, predictability and foreseeability in judicial proceedings for the purpose of determining the applicable law in the absence of choice.

[145] The Green Paper on the Conversion of Rome Convention of 1980 on the law Applicable to Contractual Obligations into a Community Instrument and its Mordernisation, COM (2002) 654 final, 14 January 2003, para 3.2.5.

[146] Rome I Proposal (n 1) 16.

[147] See generally M McParland, *The Rome I Regulation on the Law Applicable to Contractual Obligations* (Oxford, Oxford University Press, 2015) 357–432, paras 10.76–10.379.

[148] Rome I Proposal (n 1) 16.

[149] Article 4(1)(c) of the Commission's proposal provided that the law applicable to a contract of carriage of goods should be the habitual residence of the carrier. Article 4(1) (f) of the Commission's proposal provided that a contract relating to intellectual or industrial property rights shall be governed by the law of the country in which the person who transfers or assigns the rights has his habitual residence. Both paragraphs were deleted in the final provision of Article 4 of Rome I. Article 5 of Rome I governed the law applicable to contract of carriage of goods, and contracts of intellectual and industrial property rights were not specifically accounted for under the Rome I.

During the period of negotiation among Member States, for the Rome Convention to be converted into Rome I, there was no recorded suggestion that the place of characteristic performance should triumph over habitual residence of the characteristic performer.[150] In this connection, the European legislator may have justified this approach on the basis that the principal concern was with certainty, predictability and uniformity in determining the applicable law, when compared to proximity and justice in individual cases. On this basis, the European legislator may have taken the view that the habitual residence of the characteristic performer is easier to ascertain and apply, and should thus triumph over the place of characteristic performance.

A counter-argument would be that the place of characteristic performance would have a better claim to determining the principle of closest connection when compared to the habitual residence of the characteristic performer. In effect, there should have been a consideration on whether to utilise the place of characteristic performance as the principal connecting factor for commercial contracts.

Considering the theoretical and practical controversy on the significance given to the place of performance, especially the place where the characteristic performance was effected, it is opined that this argument should have been expressly considered and advanced. In other words, if the place of characteristic performance was regarded as almost decisive by most English courts, on the basis that it best satisfied the requirement of the proximity, the UK or any other Member State may have advanced the view that the place of characteristic performance should be made to triumph over the habitual residence of the characteristic performer, so that the habitual residence of the characteristic performer is used as a last resort, where the place of characteristic performance cannot be determined. In effect, there is no record to show that the UK,[151] or its lobby group[152] or indeed any other Member State during the negotiation period for Rome I Proposal made this suggestion.[153]

B. Escape Clause: Exclusion of the Place of Performance

The European Commission initially proposed that only fixed rules should apply and the escape clause should be abolished. The proposed abolition of the escape clause was probably due to strong criticisms regarding the abuse of the escape clause in the Rome Convention to mostly favour the law of the forum of Member

[150] For a detailed history on the negotiation of Article 4 see generally McParland (n 147) 357–432, [10.76]–[10.379].

[151] ibid.

[152] Financial Markets Law Committee, 'Legal Assessment of the Conversion of the Rome Convention to a Community Instrument and the Provisions of the Proposed Rome I Regulations' – European Commission Final Proposal for a Regulation on the Law Applicable to Contractual Obligations ('Rome I') (2006) 121(3) 12–14. www.fmlc.org/Documents/April06Issue121.

[153] See generally McParland (n 147) 357–432, [10.76]–[10.379].

States and its leading to so much uncertainty. The Commission rationalised its position on the basis that:

> The rule in the Convention, whereby the applicable law is the law of the place where the party performing the service characterising the contract has his habitual residence, is preserved, but the proposed changes seek to enhance certainty as to the law by converting mere presumptions into fixed rules and abolishing the exception clause. Since the cornerstone of the instrument is freedom of choice, the rules applicable in the absence of a choice should be as precise and foreseeable as possible so that the parties can decide whether or not to exercise their choice.[154]

If the Commission's proposal had been accepted, the escape clause and inter alia the significance attributed to the place of performance as a significant connecting factor would have been extinct. However, Member States in the Council were not keen on the Commission's proposal to abolish the escape clause.[155] Some scholars also criticised the proposal for only concerning itself with certainty, predictability and uniformity, while ignoring the concerns of flexibility, justice in individual cases, commercial solutions and the expectation of the parties.[156]

In the final draft of Rome I, the escape clause was eventually retained. It is important to note that during the negotiations for the Rome Convention to be converted into Rome I, the Financial Markets Law Committee (FMLC), a lobby group of the UK, had proposed that in interpreting the escape clause for commercial contracts, the connecting factors of the doctrine of infection (or accessory allocation), and place of performance should be expressly provided for as connecting factors that should be utilised in interpreting the escape clause.[157] The argument was made so as to take into account the commercial expectations of the parties in the legal market.

The UK in proposing an escape clause (draft Article 4(3)) suggested that a new draft Article 4(3) should read as follows:

> Notwithstanding paragraphs 1 and 2 of this Article, where it is clear from all the circumstances of the case that the contract is manifestly more closely connected with a country other than that indicated by those paragraphs, the law of that other country shall apply. In particular, a manifestly closer connection with another country might exist where:
>
> the characteristic performance is to be effected in that other country; or
>
> the contract is closely linked to another contract which constitutes part of the same transaction and the transaction as a whole is most closely connected with that other country.[158]

[154] Rome I Proposal (n 1) 6.

[155] See generally McParland (n 147) 427–28, [10.354]–[10.386].

[156] P Lagarde, 'Remarques sur la proposition de règlement de la Commission européene sur la loi applicable aux obligations contractulles' (2006) *Revue Critique de Droit International Privè* 331, 338; S Dutson, 'A Dangerous Proposal: the European Commission's Attempt to Amend the law Applicable to Contractual Obligations' (2006) *Journal of Business Law* 608, 610–14; Hein (n 71) 483–84.

[157] (n 152).

[158] Council Document 13035/06 ADD 4 (22 September 2006), Annex A.

In the final draft of Article 4 of Rome I, Recital 20 to Rome I only accounted for the doctrine of infection (or accessory allocation) in providing that in interpreting the escape clause, account should be taken inter alia of whether the contract has a very close relationship with another contract or contracts. None of the recitals or Article 4 of Rome I explicitly accounted for the place of performance as a connecting factor in interpreting the escape clause. Moreover, there is no official explanation contained in Rome I, or the discussions of the expert group that negotiated a new Rome I, as to why the place of performance was not explicitly given special significance in interpreting Article 4(3) of Rome I.[159]

The lesson is that the European legislator's approach in not explicitly giving special significance to the place of performance under Article 4 of Rome I Proposal was devoid of a proper appreciation of the history that led to the concept of habitual residence of the characteristic performer to be used as a connecting factor rather than the place of performance. It appears the European legislator failed to appreciate that the logic behind the connecting factor of the habitual residence of the characteristic performer was also a way of locating the 'true' place of performance, and that place of characteristic performance was also a candidate for locating the place of performance, while satisfying the requirement of proximity (when compared to the habitual residence of the characteristic performer).

V. Conclusion

The idea that the place of performance is of considerable significance in international commercial contracts is not new. If the EU choice of law rules claim to honour Savigny's methodology, and the principle of proximity is in the foundation of its rules in determining the applicable law in the absence of choice, it is questionable why the EU legislators favoured the shift from the place of performance to habitual residence of the characteristic performer as proposed by Schnitzer and his disciples.

Apparently, the expert group that drafted the Rome Convention only paid attention to the weaknesses of the place of performance, and not its strengths. The significance of the place of performance was thereby denigrated and underestimated. If the problem was that there would be a split in the applicable law if the place of performance was applied, the leading French scholar of the twentieth Century, Batiffol, had already suggested the place of characteristic performance as a remedy to the defect of the place of performance. So why then was there a complete shift from the place of performance to habitual residence? Why was the place of performance not explicitly given any special role in determining the applicable law in the absence of choice for commercial contracts?

[159] McParland (n 147) 427–28, [10.354]–[10.386].

Given that proximity is in the foundation of Article 4 of the Rome Convention, Batiffol's approach as applied by the Paris Court of Appeal should have found its way to the Rome Convention as the principal connecting factor. Accepting the shift made by Schnitzer and his disciples to the habitual residence of the characteristic performer was what resulted in the divergent approaches taken by Member State courts in interpreting Article 4(2) and (5) of the Rome Convention. This is because the idea that the habitual residence of the characteristic performer without a corroboration of other connecting factors would satisfy the requirement of proximity, could not withstand the practice of English courts. If the place of characteristic performance was the principal connecting factor, it is likely that the presumption of closest connection would have been strongly tamed, so that the escape clause would have been applied rarely in practice. In this connection, the goal of uniformity sought by the EU legislator would likely have been better achieved.

Despite the experience of the divergent approaches between Member State courts in interpreting Article 4(2) and (5) of the Rome Convention, the EU legislator did not accept the alternative view advanced by the FMLC and UK government, that the place of performance should be expressly given special significance as a connecting factor in utilising the escape clause that is based on proximity.

In summation, the EU legislator's approach failed to fully appreciate the historical significance of the place of performance in determining the applicable law in the absence of choice for international commercial contracts.

3

Should the Place of Performance be Given Special Significance under a Revised Article 4 of Rome I Regulation?

I. Introduction

This chapter is concerned with the central proposal in this book as to whether the place of performance should be given special significance under a revised Article 4 of Rome I.

In chapter two, it was observed that the principal weakness of Article 4 of the Rome Convention is that the presumption of the habitual residence or place of business of the characteristic performer, under Article 4(2) of the Rome Convention, was arguably not a connecting factor that best honoured the aims of the principle of proximity or closest connection. This is what gave rise to divergent interpretations among Member State courts.

Article 4 of Rome I inherits this weakness by designating the habitual residence (or place of business)[1] of the characteristic performer for most categories of commercial contracts. Article 4(1)(a) provides that a contract for the sale of goods shall be governed by the law of the country where the seller has his habitual residence; Article 4(1)(b) provides that a contract for the provision of services shall be governed by the law of the country where the service provider has his habitual residence; Article 4(1)(e) provides that a franchise contract shall be governed by the law of the country where the franchisee has his habitual residence; Article 4(1)(f) provides that a distribution contract shall be governed by the law of the country

[1] Article 19 provides that:

1. For the purposes of this Regulation, the habitual residence of companies and other bodies, corporate or unincorporated, shall be the place of central administration.
   The habitual residence of a natural person acting in the course of his business activity shall be his principal place of business.
2. Where the contract is concluded in the course of the operations of a branch, agency or any other establishment, or if, under the contract, performance is the responsibility of such a branch, agency or establishment, the place where the branch, agency or any other establishment is located shall be treated as the place of habitual residence.
3. For the purposes of determining the habitual residence, the relevant point in time shall be the time of the conclusion of the contract.

where the distributor has his habitual residence; and Article 4(2) provides that where the contract is not covered by Article 4(1) or where the elements of the contract would be covered by more than one of points under Article 4(1)(a)–(h), the contract shall be governed by the law of the country where the party required to effect the characteristic performance of the contract has his habitual residence. Contracts of sale, provision of services, distribution contracts, franchise contracts and other types of commercial contracts, falling under Article 4(2) (such as contracts of guarantee), are the type of commercial transactions that usually arise in practice, and would attract the application of the law of the habitual residence of the characteristic performer.

Given the considerable significance of the place of performance as a connecting factor, it is proposed that it should be given principal significance as the connecting factor for commercial contracts under a revised Article 4 of Rome I.

In this connection, it is also proposed that the habitual residence of the characteristic performer which is currently the principal connecting factor for commercial contracts under a revised Article 4 of Rome I should be made a subsidiary connecting factor. In other words, a proposal is made for the place of characteristic performance to be the principal connecting factor for commercial contracts, and the habitual residence of the characteristic performer resorted to where the place of performance of the characteristic obligation cannot be easily identified.

In the alternative, it is proposed that the place of performance should be explicitly given special significance as a connecting factor that can displace the principal connecting factor (usually habitual residence of the characteristic performer) under a revised Article 4(3) of Rome I.

Section II contains a critical analysis of the rationale in favour of the rule of the habitual residence of the characteristic performer under the EU choice of law rules. It also exposes reasons why the place of performance was downplayed as a connecting factor under the EU choice of law rules.

Section III contains an argument in favour of retaining the escape clause, while utilising the concept of place of characteristic performance as the principal connecting factor for commercial contracts. In the alternative, it is proposed that the current rule could be retained, while special significance is explicitly given to the place of performance under a revised Article 4(3) of Rome I.

Given that it is proposed that the concept of the place of characteristic performance should be the principal connecting factor, Section IV addresses some issues that might arise in relation to the application of the concept. Section V concludes.

II. A Critical Analysis of the Rationale for the Doctrine of the Habitual Residence of the Characteristic Performer

It is important to critically analyse the arguments in favour of the doctrine of habitual residence of the characteristic performer as the principal connecting factor under the EU choice of law rules in determining the applicable law in the absence of choice. This is important because it would put one in a better position to propose whether the place of performance is a better candidate as the principal connecting factor under Article 4 of Rome I.

Section A discusses the issues of classification or identification of the place of performance. Section B discusses the issue of triumph of the law of the professional. Section C discusses the country-of-origin principle.

The underlying theme running through section II is that the attack levelled against the place of performance as a connecting factor, or the arguments in favour of the doctrine of habitual residence of the characteristic performer, do not sufficiently justify stripping the place of performance of its special significance under a revised Article 4 of Rome I.

A. Classifying or Identifying the Place of Performance

The issue of classifying or identifying the place of performance is important. If the place of performance was always easy to define or classify, it appears that the EU legislator would probably have selected the place of performance as the principal connecting factor for commercial contracts. As stated in chapter two, the doctrine of the habitual residence of the characteristic performer was contrived by Schnitzer and his disciples as a solution to the problem of identifying or classifying the place of performance for commercial contracts.[2]

Schnitzer's proposal on the habitual residence of the characteristic performer raises four questions. First, is the habitual residence of the characteristic performer the 'true' place of performance? Second, does the habitual residence of the characteristic performer always lead to certainty and predictability? Third, does the place of performance always lead to judge made *dépeçage*? Fourth, what is the solution to the problem that the place of performance might occur in more than one country? These issues are addressed below.

i. From Place of Performance to Habitual Residence

Schnitzer made a shift from the place of performance to the habitual residence of one party when he proposed to rely on the characteristic obligation.[3] In reality, utilising the connecting factor of the habitual residence of the characteristic performer aims at locating the place of performance in a mysterious way because the habitual residence of the characteristic performer is regarded by Schnitzer and some of his disciples as the 'true' place of performance.[4]

[2] See ch 2, s II.B.

[3] ibid.

[4] 'Moreover, the principal place of business is the real place of performance of most contracts made by an enterprise. At this place most of its contracts are prepared, calculated, decided upon and performed. In some contracts, as for instance contracts of sale, clauses such as f.o.b and "free delivered" may locate the technical place of performance at another place, but the centre of the real obligation of

In situations where the professional's habitual residence and the place where his obligations are carried out coincide, the professional's habitual residence would obviously be the place of characteristic performance, and the law of the professional in such cases is very suitable to govern an international commercial contract, in the absence of a choice of law by the parties.

However, this is not always the case. In reality, multinational companies do not carry out their obligations only in their place of habitual residence. Multinational companies have clients from various countries. In situations where the obligation of the characteristic performer is carried out in a country, other than its habitual residence, the focus should be on the place where such obligation is executed.

It is opined that the logic would have been that, after singling out one obligation, the connecting factor would have been the place of performance of such characteristic obligation, instead of the habitual residence of the characteristic performer. The habitual residence of the characteristic performer appears to deviate too much from the place of performance when compared to the place of characteristic performance.

The performance of the professional is not really in its habitual residence especially in cases where the client is located in another country, or cases where the professional carries out its obligation in another country. The performance of the professional is in the place where its obligation is provided to the client. The habitual residence of the professional and the place where the professional carries out his obligation to the client are different.

The habitual residence of the professional is mainly significant to the extent that it is the place where preparation is usually carried out on how to execute the contract. However, the habitual residence of the professional does not have more significance over the place where the contract is executed, and its significance should not be confused with the place of characteristic performance.

Where for example, a professional is habitually resident in country A and services are provided to the client in country B, it is not correct to say that the professional's obligation is carried out in country A. The professional's obligation is actually carried out in country B because that is where services are actually provided to the client.

Thus, locating the place of performance through the habitual residence of the characteristic performer is fallacious and amounts to a legal fiction. It is an approach that avoids the issue or problem of the place of performance instead of remedying it. Whereas the place of characteristic performance addresses and to a large extent remedies the problem of classifying and identifying the obligation in question.

the seller remains at his principal place of business.' – O Lando, 'The EC Draft Convention on the Law Applicable to Contractual and Non-Contractual Obligations: Introduction and Contractual Obligations' (1974) 38 *Rabel Journal of Comparative and International Private Law* 6, 30–31; O Lando, 'EEC Convention on the Law Applicable to Contractual Obligations' (1987) 24 *Common Market Law Review* 159, 202. See also HUJ d'Oliveria, 'Characteristic Obligation' in the Draft EEC Obligation Convention' (1977) *American Society of Comparative Law* 303, 307–08 for a detailed analysis.

ii. Certainty and Predictability

One of the counter-arguments to the proposal in this book is that the place of performance is too flexible, and not easy to identify or determine. One of the principal goals of the EU legislator is legal certainty in judicial proceedings in determining the applicable law.[5] Legal certainty is given principal significance because it also leads to predictability, foreseeability and uniformity in the determination of the applicable law. Rome I being a community instrument, honouring the goals of legal certainty is generally regarded as its driving force so that there are both uniform approaches and outcomes among Member State courts on the law that applies in the absence of choice. Arguably, honouring the goals of legal certainty reduces forum shopping and excessive litigation in determining the applicable law in the absence of choice. If these goals of the EU legislator are regarded as sacrosanct, it requires that the connecting factor that is designated or utilised in determining the applicable law should not be one that results in uncertainty in determining the applicable law in judicial proceedings. It is thus argued that Article 4(1) and (2) of Rome I principally utilises the habitual residence of the characteristic performer as a basis for determining the applicable law in judicial proceedings because it generally leads to legal certainty and predictability in determining the applicable law in judicial proceedings.

The proponents of the habitual residence of the characteristic performer envisage that it is much easier to identify and apply when compared to the place of performance. Thus, the simplicity in identifying the habitual residence of the characteristic performer is what leads to certainty and predictability in determining the applicable law in the absence of choice. This explains why the Giuliano-Lagarde report[6] submits that the rule of the habitual residence of the characteristic performer:

> gives specific form and objectivity to the, in itself, too vague concept of 'closest connection'. At the same time it greatly simplifies the problem of determining the law applicable to the contract in default of choice by the parties. The place where the act was done becomes unimportant. There is no longer any need to determine where the contract was concluded, with all the difficulties and the problems of classification that arise in practice. Seeking the place of performance or the different places of performance and classifying them becomes superfluous.[7]

Some other scholars similarly submit that 'the place of business is intended to introduce certainty and to avoid the difficulties in seeking the place of performance'.[8]

The idea that the habitual residence of the characteristic performer leads to certainty, predictability and simplicity when compared to the place of performance

[5] See Recital 6 and 16 to Rome I.
[6] [1980] OJ C282/1.
[7] ibid 21.
[8] R Schu, 'The Applicable Law to Consumer Contracts made over the Internet: Consumer Protection through Private International Law' (1997) 5 *International Journal of Law and Information Technology* 192, 221–22.

is open to question.[9] In reality, the concept of habitual residence is not so straightforward. Some scholars even regard it as an 'amorphous connecting factor'[10] that 'can trigger uncertainty'.[11] Habitual residence has varied interpretations in EU private international law.[12] There is no consensus on what habitual residence means in European private international law.[13] This might explain why there is no precise definition of habitual residence in private international law. Indeed, habitual residence is a question of fact[14] and could vary depending on the case before a court. If the major flaw of the place of performance is that it is too flexible, the concept of habitual residence is also susceptible to the problems of flexibility.[15]

Even in matters of choice of law for contractual obligations, Rome I has no consistent or coherent definition of habitual residence in determining the applicable law for commercial contracts,[16] consumer contracts,[17] insurance contracts[18] and matters of consent and material validity for contractual obligations.[19] This is

[9] 'On further inspection it becomes apparent that habitual residence is not so uncomplicated. The courts and the commentators are being rather disingenuous to suggest otherwise … the concept of habitual residence contains within itself a considerable subjective element which necessitates an investigation "into the minds of men"' – P Rogerson, 'Habitual Residence: The New Domicile' (2000) 49 *International and Comparative Law Quarterly* 86, 89.

[10] J Carruthers, 'Party Autonomy in the Legal Regulation of Adult Relationships: What Place for Party Choice in Private International Law?' (2012) 61 *International and Comparative Law Quarterly* 861, 889.

[11] ibid.

[12] See generally Articles 3(1)(a), Article 6(a), Article 8(1), Article 7(2), Article 9(1) and (2), Article 12(3)(a), Article 13(1), Article 15(3)(b) and (d) of Brussels II-Ibis (Council Regulation (EC) No 2201/2003 of 27 November 2003 concerning jurisdiction and the recognition and enforcement of judgments in matrimonial matters and the matters of parental responsibility); Article 3(a) and (b), Article 4(1)(a) and (c)(ii), Article 8(1), Article 11(1) of Maintenance Regulation (Council Regulation (EC) No 4/2009 of 18 December 2008 on jurisdiction, applicable law, recognition and enforcement of decisions and cooperation in matters relating to maintenance obligations); Article 5(1)(a) and (b), Article 6(2), Article 7(2)–(4), Article 8(a)–(b), Article 14(b) of Rome III Regulation (Council Regulation (EU) No 1259/2010 of 20 December 2010 implementing enhanced cooperation in the area of the law applicable to divorce and legal separation); Article 3(1) of European Payment Order Regulation (Regulation (EC) No 1896/2006 of the European Parliament and of The Council of 12 December 2006 creating a European order for payment procedure); Article 3(1) of European Small Claims Procedure Regulation (Regulation (EC) No 861/2007 of The European Parliament and of The Council of 11 July 2007 establishing a European Small Claims Procedure); Article 6(a), Article 21(1), Article 27(d) of the Succession Regulation (Regulation (EU) No 650/2012 of The European Parliament and of The Council of 4 July 2012 on jurisdiction, applicable law, recognition and enforcement of decisions and acceptance and enforcement of authentic instruments in matters of succession and on the creation of a European Certificate of Succession). However, there is coherence between Rome I and Rome II on the concept of habitual residence for persons and companies. See Article 19 of Rome I and Article 23 of Rome II.

[13] J Harris, 'The Proposed EU Regulation on Succession and Wills: Prospects and Challenges' (2008) 22 *Trust Law International* 181, 210–13.

[14] *Winrow v Hemphill* [2014] EWHC 3164 (QB) [45] – reliance placed on *IN Re Children* [2014] 2 WLR 124; *A v A* (Habitual Residence) [2014] AC 1; C-497/10 PPU, *Mecredi v Chaffe* EU:C:2010:829 [47].

[15] See also A Fiorini, 'The Codification of Private International Law: the Belgian Experience' (2005) 54 *International and Comparative Law Quarterly* 499, 509.

[16] Article 4(1)(a),(b),(e) and (f) and (2), Article 5(1) and 19 of Rome I.

[17] Article 6(1)(a) and (4)(a) of Rome I.

[18] Article 7(3)(b) of Rome I.

[19] Article 10 of Rome I.

because Article 19 of Rome I, which defines habitual residence, is more focused on the habitual residence for commercial persons (natural persons or companies), so that its interpretation might diverge in the case of consumers and insured persons.[20] In other words, Article 19 is concerned with persons acting in the course of their business activity, so that a non-commercial person or entity (such as a passive consumer or insured person) does not fall within that category.

On the other hand, for commercial contracts the place of characteristic performance is not difficult to identify in private international law, especially in simple contracts.[21] The place of characteristic obligation for a contract of sale is the place of delivery and the place of characteristic obligation for a contract of provision of services is the place where the services are provided. The place of characteristic performance thus works well in most cases as a connecting factor in private international law.

It might be counter-argued that the place of performance might take place in different countries even in simple contracts, and that the characteristic obligation may be difficult to identify in complex contracts involving mutual obligations. The response to such counter-arguments is that this chapter addresses these issues, and provides a proposal on what criteria to use in identifying the place of performance, where it takes place in different countries;[22] and suggests a reformulation of the doctrine of characteristic obligation in the case of complex contracts involving mutual obligations.[23]

It is important to specifically consider the provisions of Article 19, in order to ascertain if the concept of habitual residence is so easy to determine and leads to certainty and predictability. It may be argued that Article 19 provides sufficient clarity on the concept of habitual residence in the case of commercial contracts. In addition, it leads to certainty and predictability by restricting the concept of habitual residence to the time of conclusion of the contract.[24] It is opined on the contrary that Article 19 does not always lead to certainty and predictability in commercial contracts.[25]

a. Habitual Residence of a Company

Article 19(1) provides that the habitual residence of companies and other bodies, corporate or unincorporated, shall be the place of central administration. The question is then: where is the place of central administration of a company and how is it located? Article 19(1) does not provide an answer to this question. Surely, the

[20] Although Article 19 of Rome I does not explicitly state that it applies only to commercial contracts, the manner in which it is drafted suggests so. For example, how is the habitual residence of a natural person who is a consumer or insured person, and has no principal place of business determined?

[21] See Article 7(1)(b) of Brussels Ia and Article 4 of Rome I.

[22] See s II.A.iv of this chapter.

[23] See s IV.A of this chapter.

[24] Article 19(3) of Rome I.

[25] See s II.A.ii.a–c of this chapter.

concept of place of central administration in determining the habitual residence of a company under Rome I would have to be given an autonomous meaning, but at the moment, no autonomous meaning has been given to the concept of place of central administration under Rome I.

It is not so clear if the concept of place of central administration under Brussels Ia[26] should be given the same meaning as that of Article 19 of Rome I.[27] The concept of place of central administration is one of the ways of determining the domicile of a company under Brussels Ia. On the one hand, it might be argued that since domicile and habitual residence are not exactly the same concepts, the concept of place of central administration should not have a consistent interpretation under Brussels Ia and Rome I. In addition, since the concept of jurisdiction and choice of law are conceptually different subject areas, it could be argued that the place of central administration of a company should not have a consistent meaning under Article 19 of Rome I and Article 63(1)(b) of Brussels Ia. On the other hand, it might be argued that for the purpose of coherence in EU private international law, the concept of place of central administration should have a consistent meaning in both Brussels Ia and Rome I.[28]

There has been no judicial definition of place of central administration of a company in the context of Article 19 of Rome I, but there has been judicial controversy as to how such a concept is defined under Article 60(1)(b) of Brussels I (now Article 63(1)(b) of Brussels Ia). Varied interpretations have been given to the definition of the place of central administration of a company under Article 60(1)(b) of Brussels I. These varied definitions lead one to the conclusion that the concept of place of central administration in locating the habitual residence of a company is not one that is so straightforward or leads to certainty, predictability and simplicity as suggested by some scholars.

In *King v Crown Energy Trading AG*[29] HH Judge Chambers QC defined the concept of place of central administration under Article 60(1)(b) of Brussels I in the following way:

> Administration is clearly an aspect of the conduct of business. That aspect has something of the 'back office' about it. Boards decide upon policy and important aspects of its implementation. Employees sell, supply and produce. Administration ensures that all runs smoothly: money is got in, debts are paid, leases and transport are arranged, personnel are looked after. But what of central administration?
>
> In a small organisation there may be a considerable blurring of functions because the same person will often discharge a variety of roles. The larger the organisation the easier it should be to discern a division of responsibilities. The location of the company secretary's office in a major organisation might provide a good clue. However, without attempting to be exhaustively precise, I think that in this case a simple listing of those

[26] See Article 63(1)(b) of Brussels Ia.
[27] See Recitals 7 and 39 to Rome I.
[28] It is not the focus of this book to give a verdict on these counter-arguments.
[29] *King v Crown Energy Trading AG* [2003] EWHC 163 (Comm) 540.

> with important responsibilities ... will be enough to show where the central administration is to be found ...[30]

More recently, the English judges defined the place of central administration under Article 60(1)(b) of Brussels I in a 'European autonomous way'[31] to the effect that it is the place where the company concerned through its constitutional organs, takes decisions that are essential for the company, which is the place where the company takes its entrepreneurial decisions.[32]

Despite this 'European autonomous' definition offered by English judges on the concept of place of central administration, there is no consensus on the precise criteria used in identifying the place of central administration.[33] Silber J gave little or no significance to the place where the Board of Directors (BOD) and Annual General Meetings (AGM) meet for the purpose of determining where the place of central administration of a company is.[34]

Andrew Smith J did not adopt the same approach. He held that the place where the BOD meets is a significant part of the administration of a company, and could be a critical determinant of the place where a company has its central administration.[35]

In addition, another area where previous English decisions on the subject of Article 60(1)(b) of Brussels I were questioned and doubted was the position taken by HH Judge Chambers QC in *King*[36] that administration implies 'back office' functions;[37] and second, the acceptance by English judges of the position advanced by Briggs in an academic commentary,[38] that in determining what constitutes central administration, a helpful approach is to examine the place where those who have serious responsibilities have their place of work.[39] Andrew Smith J qualified his acceptance of the concept of 'back office' functions to mean that central administration under Article 60(1)(b) means important administration and not the bulk of administration – which possibly indicates the difference

[30] ibid 545. See also *Ministry of Defence and Support of the Armed Forces for Iran v Faz Aviation and another* [2007] ILpr 42 (Langley J); *Alberta Inc v Katanga Mining Limited* [2008] EWHC 2679 (Comm.) [23] (Tomlinson J); A Briggs and P Rees (P Rees as editor with no authorial role), *Civil Jurisdiction and Judgments* 4th edn (London, Informa/Lloyds of London Press, 2005) [2.115]; A Briggs and P Rees, *Civil Jurisdiction and Judgments* 5th edn (London, Informa, 2009) [2.138].

[31] It is open to question whether providing such 'European autonomous interpretation' should be done by the CJEU rather than a national court.

[32] *Vava & Ors v Anglo American South Africa Limited* [2012] EWHC 1969 (QB). *Vava & Ors v Anglo American South Africa Limited; Young v Anglo American South Africa Limited* [2013] EWHC 2131(QB) [23], [71]; *Young v Anglo American South Africa Limited* [2014] EWCA Civ 1130.

[33] One agrees with the decision of English judges in this case on the principle stated. However, one thinks the case should have been referred to the CJEU. See generally CSA Okoli, 'AASA: Locating the Central Administration of a Subsidiary Company which is part of a Group of Companies under Article 60 of Brussels I Regulation' (2015) *European Company Law* 13–18.

[34] *Vava* [2012] (n 32) [43].

[35] *Vava* [2013] (n 32) [22], [24].

[36] (n 29) [12]–[13].

[37] ibid. See also *Ministry of Defence* (n 30) (Langley J); *Alberta Inc* (n 30) [23] (Tomlinson J).

[38] Briggs and Rees (2005) (n 30) [2.115]; Briggs and Rees (2009) (n 30) [2.138].

[39] *King* (n 29) (HH Judge Chambers QC) [13]; *Alberta* (n 30) [23] (Tomlinson J).

between principal place of business and central administration.[40] Second, Andrew Smith J expressed the view that although a listing of those with important responsibilities in a company can be helpful in indicating the central administration of company under Article 60(1)(b), it was not a decisive factor.[41]

Aikens LJ (with whom other Justices of the Court of Appeal agreed with) on the contrary held that the utilisation of the suggestion of 'back office' and 'a simple listing of those with important responsibilities in a company' by previous English authorities to interpreting Article 60(1)(b) was unhelpful and should be disregarded.[42]

Thus, since there is no precise way in which the place of central administration of a company can be identified, the concept of place of central administration in determining the concept of domicile or habitual residence is just as flexible and fact dependent as the place of performance as a connecting factor.

Identifying the place of central administration of a company would even be more problematic in the case of corporate groups. Neither Brussels Ia nor Rome I explicitly offers a solution on how to identify the central administration of a company in the case of corporate groups. Although the English Court of Appeal[43] claimed to provide an autonomous 'European' interpretation of Article 60(1)(b) of Brussels I in the case of individual companies and corporate groups,[44] it is open to question whether the English Court of Appeal had the authority to provide an autonomous interpretation in the case of corporate groups.[45]

The principal reason for the above stated is that, at the moment, it is doubted if there can be a uniform application of the concept of central administration to corporate groups under Article 63(1)(b) of Brussels Ia. English judges overlooked the recent Court of Justice of the European Union (CJEU) decision in *Impacto*[46] which was not brought to their attention. In *Impacto*, the question referred to the CJEU was whether Portuguese law which provides for joint and several liability of parent companies vis-à-vis the creditors of their subsidiaries only in respect of parent companies having their seat in Portugal was a violation of Article 49 TFEU (Treaty of the Functioning of the European Union) that requires the abolition of restrictions of the freedom of establishment (such as discrimination on grounds of nationality) in the European Community. The CJEU in holding in the negative pointed out that '*the rules concerning corporate groups are not harmonised at the*

[40] *Vava* [2013] (n 32) [23].
[41] ibid [20].
[42] *Young* [2014] (n 32) [43]–[44].
[43] ibid.
[44] The English judges were persuaded by U Everling's submission in *The Right of Establishment in the Common Market* (New York, Commerce Clearing House, 1964) 75, [214] to the effect that '[T]he central administration is located where the company organs take the decisions that are essential for the company's operations. In this connection only the organs of the company itself count; *it is irrelevant whether the company depends on the decision of a parent company which has its domicile outside the community*' (emphasis added).
[45] For a critique see Okoli (n 33).
[46] C-186/12, *Impacto Azul Lda v BPS*, EU:C:2013:412.

European Union level, the Member States remain, in principle, competent to determine the law applicable to a debt of a related company'.[47]

It is opined that if there is indeed a uniform application of the concept of central administration to corporate groups in determining the domicile of a company under Article 63(1)(b) of Brussels Ia, it is the CJEU that would have been in the best position to fill the gap and provide authoritative guidance to other Member State courts.

In summation, the concept of place of central administration in determining the habitual residence of a company under Article 19(1) of Rome I is not so certain. There has been no recorded autonomous definition of the place of central administration of a company under the EU choice of law rules. The concept of place of central administration of a company may also be difficult, impossible to identify and lead to uncertainty in the case of corporate groups.

b. Habitual Residence of Natural Persons

Article 19(1) also provides that the habitual residence of a natural person acting in the course of his business activity shall be his principal place of business. There is however no autonomous definition of what principal place of business of a natural person means under Rome I.[48] Identifying the principal place of business of a natural person is not always easy.

Assume A, an agent and natural person, enters into a contract with B, a manufacturing company, to promote and market the goods of B in several countries. A promotes and markets the goods of B in over a dozen countries. A dispute subsequently arises between A and B, and the applicable law is in issue, having regard to the fact that the parties made no choice of law. How is the principal place of business of A established?[49] Would it be the place where A principally resides and works when he does not travel to promote and market goods? Would it be the place where A principally promotes and markets the goods of B? Should the place where A principally promotes goods be determined by the time spent in the relevant country, or by the amount of business made there? Could it be that no principal place of business can be established in this case? Identifying the principal place of business of A in this scenario is not so straightforward.

The lesson from the above scenario is that there is likely to be confusion and uncertainty in determining the principal place of business of a natural person who carries out business in many countries. It is indeed possible that there might be cases where it would be impossible to determine the principal place of business of a natural person. Any criteria for generally determining the principal place of

[47] ibid [35] (emphasis added).

[48] The 'principal place of business' would be given an autonomous definition as well under Article 19(1) of Rome I.

[49] See also *Lawlor v Sandvik Mining and Construction Mobile Crushers and Screens Ltd* [2012] EWHC 1188.

business of a natural person who carries out business in many countries would certainly not be a precise one. It is a criteria that would have to be applied flexibly to the facts of individual cases.

Thus, the argument that the principal place of business of a natural person is easier to determine and apply when compared to the place of performance is not always true. Thus, the determination of habitual residence of a person through the principal place of business (of a natural person) could just be as flexible and fact dependent as the place of performance.

c. Habitual Residence through Branch, Agency or Other Establishment

Article 19(2) of Rome I provides that where

> the contract is concluded in the course of the operations of a branch, agency or any other establishment, or if, under the contract, performance is the responsibility of such a branch, agency or establishment, the place where the branch, agency or any other establishment is located shall be treated as the place of habitual residence.

Article 19 (2) takes into account situations where an international commercial contract is concluded, or under the contract, performed by a branch, agency or any other establishment. In such a situation, the central administration of a company, or principal place of business of a natural person, might be fortuitous and entirely unconnected to the international commercial contract, and thus the branch, agency or establishment that concludes or under the contract performs the contract stands in a better position as the governing law.

In reality, the determination of what 'under the contract' means in the context of the branch, agency or other establishment that assumes responsibility to perform the contract, for the purpose of determining habitual residence is not so clear. This is particularly evident from two English cases that interpreted an equivalent concept ('under the terms of the contract')[50] under Article 4(2) of the Rome Convention. The relevant text of Article 4(2) of the Rome Convention reads:

> However, if the contract is entered into in the course of that party's trade or profession, that country shall be the country in which the principal place of business is situated or, where under the terms of the contract the performance is to be effected through a place of business other than the principal place of business, the country in which that other place of business is situated.

In *Iran Continental Shelf Oil Co v IRI International Corp*,[51] the question before the court was whether, once it had been decided that the parties had not made a choice of law, the contract was governed by the law of Texas (where the defendant's principal place of business was located) or the law of England (where the defendant

[50] In the spirit of continuity, equivalent concepts in the Rome Convention would be interpreted in the same light as Rome I.

[51] *Iran Continental Shelf Oil Co v IRI International Corp* [2002] CLC 372 (McCombe J); [2002] EWCA Civ 1024 (CA).

had an office through which, so the claimant argued, the defendant's performance was to be effected).

In this case, the claimants were three Iranian companies, while the defendant was a Delaware corporation with its principal place of business in Texas and a branch in England. In 1990 the parties entered into a contract for the supply by the defendant of rigs to the claimants, the contract providing that contract disputes were to be resolved in Iranian courts applying Iranian law. The parties subsequently entered into negotiations for a further contract. The new contract of the parties contained no choice of law. After providing further quotations the defendant accepted the claimant's purchase order, which was sent to the defendant's English offices but which contained no provision as to choice of law. After the contract was agreed, the defendant was prohibited by executive order in the United States from performing the contract. The claimants sued the defendant in England and Article 4(2) of the Rome Convention (inter alia) was in issue.

At the High Court, McCombe J decided that the presumption in Article 4(2) pointed to Texas, since the defendant (as seller of the parts and provider of the services) was the characteristic performer and its principal place of business was in Texas.[52] He rejected the claimant's argument that the characteristic performance was, under the contract, to be effected through the defendant's English branch office, which was, in his view, no more than a 'conduit of communication' between the claimants in Iran and the defendant in Texas.[53]

However, the Court of Appeal in a unanimous decision allowed the claimants' appeal against the defendant.[54] The Court of Appeal did not agree with McCombe J that the English branch office was only a conduit of communication. It held that the arrangements made between the parties involved the defendant's English office in order to comply with the Iranian government's policy which prohibited the purchase by Iranian entities of goods from the US. The contract was in part a CFR contract (which included making out an invoice; shipping the goods at the port of shipment; procuring a contract of affreightment; and tendering the shipping documents to the buyer under the terms of the contract) for the sale of goods and in part a contract for services. On the assumption that the characteristic performance to be carried out by the defendant was the supply and delivery of goods in the US under the CFR contract, that performance was to be effected through the English branch office. The defendant's obligation to deliver the goods to the vessel in Houston, Texas was to be arranged or effected by the English branch office. The contractual documents were carefully prepared, structured and agreed in order to show the English place of business as the supplier and shipper without any express reference to the defendant in the US. That was not by chance but by agreement. Therefore the effect of Article 4(2) of the Rome Convention was that English law applied.

[52] ibid [41].
[53] Ibid at 384, [45].
[54] (n 51).

It is important to note that Clarke LJ who delivered the leading judgment of the Court of Appeal, expressed some uncertainty as to the proper way to interpret the phrase 'where under the terms of the contract the performance is to be effected'. Counsel for the defendant had argued that, to bring the last part of the presumption in Article 4(2) into play, the relevant performance must, as a matter of *contractual obligation*, be effected through the other place of business. However, Clarke LJ 'doubted whether the expression "to be effected" should be so narrowly construed'.[55]

A similar argument was considered in *Ennstone Building Products Ltd v Stanger Ltd.*[56] In this case, the claimant was a supplier of stone for building work and the defendant provided testing and consultancy services. The principal place of business of both parties was located in England, but the defendant had a number of regional offices including one in Scotland. The defendant contracted to undertake some tests and give advice in relation to some stone that the claimant had provided for a building in Scotland. The contract did not include a choice of law. A dispute arose between the parties when the claimant alleged that the defendant's advice had been given in breach of contract and negligently. It was common ground that the characteristic performance was the defendant's provision of testing and consulting services to the claimant. What was in issue was the identification of the habitual residence of the defendant for the purpose of Article 4(2) of the Rome Convention.

The claimant argued that, as the defendant was the characteristic performer whose principal place of business was England, the effect of Article 4(2) was that the contract was governed by English law. According to the defendant, Scots law was the governing law on the basis that, as both parties had envisaged that the characteristic performance was to be effected through the regional office, the relevant connecting factor was the defendant's regional office in Scotland. At the High Court, Kirkham J agreed with the argument of the claimant and held that Scots law was the applicable law. However, the Court of Appeal allowed the claimant's appeal. Keene LJ (with whom Potter LJ agreed) considered that, even though both parties had clearly envisaged that the defendant would undertake the characteristic performance through its Scottish office, this was not enough to bring the 'other place of business' into play as the connecting factor for the purposes of Article 4(2). He held that, for the relevant connecting factor not to be the characteristic performer's principal place of business, it must be a term of the contract, whether express or implied,[57] that the defendant is bound to perform the contract through some place of business other than the principal place of business, such that failure by the defendant to do so would found a claim for breach of contract.[58]

[55] ibid [65].
[56] *Ennstone Building Products Ltd v Stanger Ltd* [2002] 1 WLR 3059, 3067.
[57] On the concept of an 'implied' term of the contract see also Mance LJ in *American Motorists Insurance Co v Cellstar Corporation* [2003] ILPr 370, 394 [47].
[58] *Ennstone* (n 56) [[29].

Such a strict interpretation was justified on the basis that it would contribute to the aims of legal certainty and predictability.[59]

It is conceded that a strict interpretation might better enhance the aims of certainty and predictability, given that the central administration of a company or principal place of business of a natural person, would always be applicable unless the contract of the parties expressly or implicitly requires that another place of business effects the contract, so that if such other place of business did not effect the contract, it would amount to a breach of contract.[60] However, the rule might be too rigid and lead to fortuitous situations where the central administration of a company, or principal place of business of a natural person, which does not in reality perform or conclude the contract, is generally the connecting factor that designates the applicable law for the parties in the absence of choice.

On the other hand, a liberal interpretation might better enhance the aims of proximity and flexibility, where another place of business actually performs or concludes the contract, rather than the central administration of a company, or principal place of business of a natural person, which might be fortuitous in such a case. However, it might lead to uncertainty and increase in transaction costs if the parties are unable to predict in advance before litigation whether the central administration of a company (or principal place of business of a natural person) or other place of business would be used in determining the concept of habitual residence, for the purpose of determining the applicable law in the absence of choice.

The truth is that the interpretation of habitual residence under Article 19(2) of Rome I is not so clear. The English Court of Appeal decisions in *Iran Continental Shelf Oil* and *Ennstone* expose the problem of uncertainty in interpreting the concept of habitual residence. While the Court of Appeal in *Iran Continental Shelf Oil* favoured a liberal interpretation, it later favoured a strict interpretation in *Ennstone*. In addition, since divergent interpretations were given by English judges at both the High Court, and the Court of Appeal in interpreting the concept of habitual residence under Article 19(2) of Rome I (then Article 4(2) of the Rome Convention), it demonstrates that the concept of habitual residence in this context is not so clear.

iii. *Avoidance of Judge Made* Dépeçage

The issue of judge made *dépeçage* is relevant in this section on the basis that it seeks to respond to the counter-argument that a commercial contract would usually have more than one obligation to be performed by the parties. This is however a minor issue, given that this book argues for the place of characteristic obligation

[59] See also J Hill, 'Choice of Law in Contract under the Rome Convention: The Approach of the UK Courts' (2004) 53 *International and Comparative Law Quarterly* 325, 338–39 supporting this view point.

[60] It is likely that a strict interpretation might be favoured by the CJEU in light of recital 6 and 16 to Rome I, which underscores the importance of certainty in legal proceedings.

to be the principal connecting factor for commercial contracts in determining the applicable law in the absence of choice.

The issue of judge made *dépeçage* is a more important issue in the context of the counter-argument that the place of characteristic performance might take place in several countries. This issue is addressed separately in the next section.[61]

Dépeçage is the process of applying different laws to issues arising out of a contract.[62] Where the parties do not make a choice of law, allowing a judge to apply different laws arising from the obligation in question of the parties is particularly controversial. Historically, it was demonstrated that it is an unattractive and undesirable situation.[63]

The purpose of utilising the habitual residence of the characteristic performer avoids the problem of judge made *dépeçage*. The place of performance usually leads to different laws applying. If you apply the laws of the service provider, who provides services, and the client who pays, you would be applying at least two laws, if the place of payment and place of provision of services are in different countries. This is the kind of problem, the doctrine of habitual residence of characteristic performer avoids. The issue of judge made *dépeçage* in the context of applying the place of performance is therefore a significant issue.

In this connection, Vischer, who is an academic disciple of Schnitzer submits that:

> The principle's main purpose, as the development in the practice of the Swiss Federal Tribunal shows, is the avoidance of a split in the applicable law. It is justified by the fact that mutual obligations of the parties are interrelated and inter-dependent and that therefore one single law should govern the main issues of the contract.[64]

Lando submits that:

> A party to an international contract generally have their places of business in different states or countries. As a contract should not be governed by two laws, the law of one of the parties must be preferred, and here too, the place of business of the party should be chosen ...[65]

Lord Collins et al also submit that 'In Switzerland, it was a method of subjecting most of the incidents of a contract to one system of law, when previously the obligations of the respective parties had been governed by different laws.'[66]

[61] s II.A.iv.

[62] See generally WLM Reese, '*Dépeçage*: A Common Phenomenon in Choice of Law' (1973) 73 *Columbia Law Review* 58–75.

[63] See ch 2, s II.A.

[64] F Vischer, 'The Principle of the Typical Performance in International Contracts and the Draft Convention' in P North (ed), *Contract Conflicts, The EEC Convention on the Law Applicable to Contractual Obligations: A Comparative Study* (Amsterdam, North-Holland Publishing Company, 1982) 25, 27. See also F Vischer, 'The Concept of Characteristic Performance Reviewed' in G Droz et al (eds), *E Pluribus Unum on the Progressive Unification of Private International Law, Liber Amicorum* (The Hague/Boston/London, Martinus Nijhoff, 1996) 499–515.

[65] Lando (1987) (n 4) 202.

[66] L Collins et al, *Dicey, Morris & Collins, The Conflict of Laws* 15th edn (London, Sweet and Maxwell, 2012) 1822, [32-076].

The issue of judge made *dépeçage* is an approach that is not generally favoured in the EU choice of law rules. Despite its existence under Article 4 of the Rome Convention, the CJEU held that it was to be applied in truly exceptionally circumstances where the contracts in question are independent of each other and could be severed.[67] Under the current Article 4 of Rome I, there is no express provision for judge made *dépeçage* as the Rome Convention had, but there remains an argument as to whether its existence is still preserved and to be left at the discretion of courts of Member States.[68] The view held here is that judge made *dépeçage* has no place in Rome I based on two main reasons. First, it is not explicitly mentioned in Article 4.[69] Second, the high bar set by the CJEU in stating that splitting the applicable law (which is expressly provided for in Article 4 of the Rome Convention) should only be deployed on exceptional grounds is good reason to hold that the absence of the mention of its use in Article 4 of Rome I means that it is not to be resorted to.

It may be argued that in the context of the place of performance, applying judge made *dépeçage* is appropriate in this situation, because it

> (a) would result in the application to each issue of the rule of the State with greatest concern in the determination of that issue, (b) would serve to effectuate the purpose of each of the rules applies, and (c) would not disappoint the expectation of the parties.[70]

In other words, applying judge made *dépeçage* is to subject a contract to those rules, which best advances the expectation of the parties which is the law of the countries where each of the obligations is executed.

In addition, it might be argued that it would be flexible to apply different laws to obligations arising out of the contract, such that for example, in a contract of sale, the law of the place of delivery governs the seller's obligations, while the law of the place of payment governs the buyer's obligations.

[67] C-133/08, *Intercontainer Interfrigo SC (ICF) v Balkenende Oosthuizen*, EU:C:2009:617 [42–9]; Giuliano-Lagarde Report (n 6) 23.

[68] C Nourrissat, 'Le Dépeçage' in S Corneloup and N Joubert (eds), *Le règlement communautaire 'Rome I' et le choix de loi dans les contrats internationaux* (Paris, LexisNexis Litec, 2011) 205; BA Marshall, 'Reconsidering the Proper Law of Contract' (2012) 13 *Melbourne Journal of International Law*' 505, 532. See also PA De Miguel Asensio, 'Applicable Law in the Absence of Choice to Contracts Relating to Intellectual or Industrial Property Rights' (2008) 10 *Yearbook of Private International Law* 199, 201; U Magnus, 'Article 4 Rome I Regulation: The Applicable Law in the Absence of Choice' in F Ferrari and S Leible (eds), *The Law Applicable to Contractual Obligations in Europe* (Munich, Sellier European Law Publishers, 2009) 27, 31; A Mills, 'The Application of Multiple Laws under the Rome II Regulation' in J Ahern and W Binchy (eds), *The Rome II Regulation on the Law Applicable to Non-Contractual-Obligations: A New International Litigation Regime* (The Hague, Martinus Nijhoff Publishers, 2009) 133.

[69] By way of analogy, in the Irish case of *ICDL GCC Foundation FZ-LLC and others v European Computer Driving Licence Foundation Ltd* [2011] IEHC 343 [9.7]–[9.8] the High Court per Clarke J held that Article 4 of Rome II does not provide for judge made *dépeçage* (as regards deploying the escape clause) since there is no express mention of its use.

[70] Reese (n 62) 60. See also PL Stein, 'Choice of Law: Defining the Place of Performance for General Contract Disputes in Oklahoma' (2011) 64 *Oklahoma Law Review* 17, 53.

This book does not agree with these views. The potential multiplicity of applicable laws could threaten the stability of contractual relationships if parties cannot reasonably predict a single law that governs their contract. Applying different laws based on the obligation in question carried out in different countries could also lead to an incoherent solution in the determination of rights and liabilities of the parties. For example, the law of the place of delivery may regard the buyer as liable to pay for certain goods, while the law of the place of payment may excuse the buyer from liability. Reconciling these inconsistent laws could be problematic for the parties and the courts. In addition, the parties would incur more costs in investigating more than one law relating to their obligations instead of a single law.

Admittedly, it is true that the rule of the habitual residence of the characteristic performer would usually result in a single law. Again, the response to this is that instead of the shift to the habitual residence of the characteristic performer, the place of characteristic performance would be a better connecting factor, since it would also lead to a single law applying.

Where the characteristic obligation has been identified, it leads to a single law applying and at the same time remedies the defect of the place of performance as a connecting factor. Thus, the problems of judge made *dépeçage* no longer arises. Applying the concept of place of characteristic performance would be consistent with the scheme of Article 4 of Rome I that does not provide for judge made *dépeçage*.

iv. Characteristic Obligation Performed in Different Countries

Schnitzer probably envisaged that the place of performance (including the characteristic obligation) usually takes place in more than one country, and thus he sought to concentrate the legal relationship in the habitual residence of the characteristic performer. Admittedly, it is true that it may be difficult to determine the place of performance in cases where the characteristic obligation takes place in more than one country.[71]

However, the problem with Schnitzer's idea is that it is not in all situations that the characteristic obligation is executed in different countries, and thus there often is no problem to resolve. Utilising the concept of habitual residence of the characteristic performer as the principal connecting factor creates the wrong impression that a vast majority of international commercial contracts are 'characteristically performed' in different countries. In reality, except in unusual cases, the characteristic obligation is rendered to a client in a single country.

[71] PR Williams, 'The EEC Convention on the Law Applicable to Contractual Obligations' (1986) 35 *International and Comparative Law Quarterly* 1, 30, fn 63. See also L Collins, 'Contractual Obligations – The EEC Preliminary Draft Convention on Private International Law' (1976) 25 *International and Comparative Law Quarterly* 35, 47; R Plender and M Wilderspin, *European Private International Law of Obligations* 4th edn (London, Sweet and Maxwell, 2014) 177, [7-005]; P Torremans et al, *Cheshire, North and Fawcett, Private International Law* 15th edn (Oxford, Oxford University Press, 2017) 732.

Notwithstanding the above, it is important to consider situations where the characteristic obligation is carried out in different countries and offer a solution to such problems. In other words, this book would not avoid or gloss over the possibility that problems might arise where the characteristic obligation is effected in different countries.

In situations where the party who effects the characteristic performance carries out its obligations in more than one country, identifying the *place* where the performance is effected could also lead to uncertainty and result in a multiplicity of potentially applicable laws to a commercial transaction if the law of each country where the characteristic performance is effected is applied. This approach is equivalent to judge made *dépeçage*. In this chapter, the pros and cons of judge made *dépeçage* were considered in the context of the EU choice of law rules, and it was opined that it is better to avoid or do away with judge made *dépeçage*.[72]

In this connection, it is suggested that a better alternative or solution to this problem is to identify the principal, main or essential place where the professional carries out (or agreed to carry out) the characteristic obligation. The idea behind this approach is to identify a single law to govern the parties' relationship rather than a multiplicity of potentially applicable laws. Applying a single law in this context promotes efficiency and simplicity for the court and the parties: less time is expended in determining the applicable law in the absence of choice. Applying a single law also reduces transaction and litigation costs that would be expended in investigating the content of potential applicable laws by legal experts versed in these laws.

By way of analogy, this solution has consistently been adopted by the CJEU under the Brussels I regime for commercial contracts as a way of avoiding fragmentation of jurisdiction or multiplicity of judicial proceedings where different courts of Member States, where the place of characteristic performance is carried out assume jurisdiction. Thus, it was initially uncertain if Article 5(1)(b) of Brussels I (now Article 7(1)(b) of Brussels Ia) applied where there are several places of delivery within one Member State and, second (if Article 5(1)(b) applied) which courts the plaintiff could sue within one Member State. In *Color Drack*,[73] the CJEU held that Article 5(1)(b) applied where delivery occurred in several places within one Member State.[74] The CJEU reasoned that this approach met the requirement of legal certainty, since the parties can predict or reasonably foresee the courts in which the dispute will be brought within one Member State; and flexibility, since 'it will in any event be the courts of that member state which will have jurisdiction to hear the case'.[75] In answering the second question, the CJEU held that in identifying the court, which has jurisdiction within that Member State, 'the place of performance' must be understood as 'the place

[72] See s II.A.iii of this chapter.
[73] C-386/05, *Color Drack Gmbh v Lexx International Vetriebs GMBH*, EU:C:2007:262.
[74] ibid [36]–[38].
[75] ibid.

with the closest linking factor between the contract and the court having jurisdiction' which will as 'a general rule be at the place of principal delivery, which must be determined on the basis of economic criteria'.[76] The CJEU justified its reasoning on the ground that legal certainty and avoidance of fragmentation are achieved where one central court is identified by the parties within one Member State to resolve all contractual disputes, and flexibility is achieved since the court called upon to hear the case is within the same Member State, with a view to efficient organisation of proceedings.[77]

In *Wood Floor*,[78] the claimant, an Austrian company, brought proceedings in Austria against the defendant, a Luxembourgish company, seeking compensation for the termination of a commercial agency contract. In order to found the jurisdiction of the Austrian court, the claimant relied on Article 5(1)(b) of Brussels I, claiming that the place where the services under the contract were provided was Austria as that was where it carried on business and, therefore, where the work of signing up and acquiring of clients took place. The defendant challenged the jurisdiction of the Austrian court by arguing that more than three quarters of the claimant's turnover was generated in countries other than Austria and that Article 5(1), which did not expressly provide for such a case, was inapplicable. A reference was made by the Austrian Court to the CJEU for a preliminary ruling as to whether Article 5(1)(b) was applicable where services were provided in several Member States and, if so, on the basis of what criteria was the place of performance of the contract to be determined in the case of a commercial agency contract. The CJEU in its decision applied the rule in *Color Drack* and held that a single court should be identified by the centralisation of jurisdiction for all claims arising out of the contract in a court of a Member State, where there are multiple places of performance of services in different Member States in order to enhance the objectives of predictability, unification and proximity, and the avoidance of fragmentation.[79] The CJEU adapted the rule in *Color Drack* to the case of a commercial agency contract performed in different countries and held inter alia that, the place of performance as a general rule is the place where under the contract, the commercial agent is to perform the main services on behalf of his principal.[80]

In this regard, by way of analogy, the CJEU has also applied this approach of centralisation of jurisdiction in one court and avoidance of multiplication of proceedings consistently in relation to determining the (habitual) place of performance of the characteristic obligation for employment contracts in the choice

[76] ibid [40]–[42].

[77] ibid [36]–[38].

[78] C –19/09, *Wood Floor Solutions Andreas Domberger Gmbh v Silva Trade Sa*, EU:C:2010:137.

[79] ibid [27]–[29].

[80] This decision probably influenced the withdrawal of C-147/09: Order of the President of the Court of 29 April 2010 (reference for a preliminary ruling from the Oberlandesgericht Wien (Austria)) – *Ronald Seunig v Maria Holzel* (OJ C 153, 4.7.2009) p. 30 since the reference in *Wood Floor* was similar. See also *Saey Home & Garden NV/SA v Lusavouga-Máquinas e Acessórios Industriais SA*, EU:C:2018:173 [41–44]; C-47/14, *Holterman Ferho Exploitatie BV v Spies von Bullesheim*, EU:C:2015:574; *EPN (Société) v Simax Trading (Société)* (2013) ILPr 9.

of jurisdiction rule for employment contracts under Article 5(1) of the Brussels Convention.[81] In *Mulox*[82] the defendant was a company incorporated under English law with its registered office in London. The claimant worked for the defendant in a number of countries including France but was resident in France. Following the termination of his employment contract, the claimant brought an action against the defendant before the French court for compensation in lieu of notice plus damages. The defendant argued that the French courts had no jurisdiction because the place of performance of the employment contract in question was not restricted to France and that the defendant was established in the UK. The CJEU held inter alia that Article 5(1) of the Brussels Convention cannot be interpreted as meaning that it confers concurrent jurisdiction on the courts of each Contracting State in which the employee carries out part of his work. Where the employee's work covers several Contracting States, Article 5(1) of the Brussels Convention, must be interpreted to mean the place where or from which the employee mainly discharges his obligations to his employer.[83]

In *Rutten*,[84] the defendant was a subsidiary of a company incorporated under English law whose registered office was situated in London. The defendant was incorporated under Netherlands law and its registered office was situated in the Netherlands. The claimant in this case carried out his duties for the defendant and the principal company in the Netherlands and approximately one third of his working hours in the United Kingdom, Belgium, Germany and the United States of America. The Dutch Court inter alia asked the CJEU for a preliminary ruling thus:

> Where in the performance of an employment contract, an employee carries out his work in more than one country, what are the criteria according to which he should be regarded as habitually carrying out his work in one of those countries, within the meaning of Article 5(1) of the Brussels Convention?

The CJEU followed its approach in *Mulox* by holding inter alia that where a contract of employment is performed in several Contracting States, Article 5(1) of the Brussels Convention must be understood to refer to the place where the employee has established the effective centre of his working activities and where, or from which, he in fact performs the essential part of his duties towards his employer.[85]

Similarly, in *Weber*,[86] the claimant was employed as a cook over a period of six years by the defendant, a Scottish company, at first partly on board ships or drilling rigs operating on or over the Netherlands continental shelf and later

[81] See generally C-29/10, *Koelzch v Etat du Grand Duchy of Luxembourg*, EU:C:2011:151 citing with approval previous CJEU decisions on the subject.

[82] C-125/92, *Mulox IBC Ltd v Geels*, EU:C:1993:306.

[83] ibid [25]–[26].

[84] C-383/95 *Rutten v Cross Medical Ltd*, EU:C:1997:7.

[85] ibid [22].

[86] C-37/00, *Weber v Universal Ogden Services Ltd*, EU:C:2002:122.

on a floating crane in Danish territorial waters. A dispute arose in relation to the employment contract, and the claimant brought an action in Netherlands. The Dutch Court inter alia asked the CJEU whether the contract was 'habitually' carried out in Netherlands. The CJEU observed that though it is common ground that, during the period of employment of the claimant with the defendant, the claimant was engaged in at least two different Member States; unlike the employees in *Mulox* and *Rutten*, the claimant did not have an office in a Member State that constituted the effective centre of his working activities or from which he performed the essential part of his duties towards his employer. The CJEU thus held that in this present context, the relevant criterion for establishing an employee's habitual place of work, for the purposes of Article 5(1) of Brussels I, is, in principle, the place where he spends most of his working time engaged on his employer's business.[87]

Interestingly, the CJEU has by way of analogy applied this approach to choice of law for employment contract under the Rome Convention (and by extension Rome I). Thus, in *Koelzch*,[88] the problem with determining the place of performance where the employee habitually carries out his work arose as the main issue for consideration by the CJEU. In *Koelzch*, the claimant, a heavy goods vehicle driver domiciled in Germany, was engaged under a contract of employment as an international driver with a company established under Danish law which did not have offices in Germany. The claimant transported flowers and other plants from Denmark mostly to destinations in Germany but also in other European countries by means of lorries which, while stationed in Germany, were registered in Luxembourg. The claimant's contract contained a clause conferring exclusive jurisdiction on the courts of Luxembourg. When the employer terminated his employment, the claimant challenged the dismissal in the German courts, which declined jurisdiction. The claimant then brought an action against its employer at the Luxembourg courts. The Luxembourg Court of Appeal referred a question to the CJEU as to whether the conflict rule in Article 6(2)(a) of the Rome Convention was to be interpreted as meaning that, where the employee worked in more than one country but returned systematically to one of them, that country had to be regarded as the country in which the employee habitually carried out his work. The CJEU by way of analogy drew support from its jurisprudence (and applied it) in relation to the allocation of jurisdiction in employment contracts, which is aimed at protecting weaker parties. The CJEU in this regard held that Article 6(2)(a) should be given a broad interpretation. The CJEU in its final analysis concluded that:

> the answer to the question referred is that Article 6(2)(a) of the Rome Convention must be interpreted as meaning that, in a situation in which an employee carries out his activities in more than one Contracting State, the country in which the employee habitually carries out his work in performance of the contract, within the meaning

[87] ibid [50].
[88] (n 81).

of that provision, is that in which or from which, in the light of all the factors which characterise that activity, the employee performs the greater part of his obligations towards his employer.[89]

The solution of the CJEU in *Koelzch* is especially significant given that Article 8(3) of Rome I offered a default rule where the applicable law cannot be determined on the basis of the place of habitual work.[90] This means that the CJEU preferred to identify the main place of performance rather than resorting to another less significant factor which was clearly insignificant from a proximity perspective. The less significant factor for employment contracts under Rome I is the place from which the employee is engaged. The place is less significant because it has little connection with the employment contract.

I have also proposed this solution in respect of choice of law for contract of carriage of goods (under the proviso to Article 5 of Rome I where there is no required convergence of connecting factors), where the delivery obligation is carried out in different countries, so that the principal place of delivery should be utilised as a general rule.[91] Thus assume Party A, a carrier habitually resident in country B, is to deliver goods to Party Y, the recipient of the goods, habitually resident in country D. The places of delivery of the goods are in countries E, F and G. The consignor is habitually resident in country H. In this case, the main provision of Article 5 does not apply because there is no convergence between the habitual residence of the carrier, place of delivery and receipt of the goods, and the habitual residence of the consignor so that the law applicable is the place of delivery under the proviso to Article 5 of Rome I Regulation. The court of the Member State would have to identify the principal place of delivery of the goods amongst countries E, F and G.

The concept of 'economic criteria' which was proposed by the CJEU for determining the principal place of obligation under Article 5(1)(b) of Brussels I is usually the place where the professional spends most of the time and carries out the most important obligation to the client.

In summation, the principal, essential, greater or main characteristic obligation should be resorted to where the characteristic obligation is effected in several countries. This criteria is also likely to meet the requirements of legal certainty and proximity in commercial transactions. There is also some room for flexibility by the decision maker in looking at the contract and circumstances of the case in identifying the principal place of characteristic performance.

[89] ibid [50].

[90] Article 8(3) of Rome I provides that 'Where the law applicable cannot be determined pursuant to paragraph 2, the contract shall be governed by the law of the country where the place of business through which the employee was engaged is situated.' For a vigorous critique of this connecting factor see U Grüsic, 'Should the Connecting Factor of the "Engaging Place of Business" be abolished In European Private International Law?' (2013) 62 *International and Comparative Law Quaterly* 173–92.

[91] CSA Okoli, 'Choice of Law for Contract of Carriage of Goods in the European Union' (2015) 4 *Lloyds Maritime and Commercial Law Quarterly* 512, 521.

B. Triumph of the Law of the Professional

In seeking to identify the most desirable connecting factor, preference was given to the law of the place of business of the professional. This has resulted in some scholars justifying and applauding the doctrine on the basis that the law of the place of business of the professional triumphs.[92]

At this juncture, it is important to critically analyse the view of these scholars who advocate the triumph of the law of the professional as the principal success of Schnitzer's ideas and inter alia its transmission into the EU choice of law rules for commercial contracts.

The following issues are critically analysed below as it relates to the doctrine of the triumph of the law of the professional: is it linked to welfare economics in the context of saving costs for clients and/or consumers? Is it arbitrary? Is it consistent with the philosophy of protecting weaker parties? Is it consistent with the principle of proximity?

i. Welfare Economics

Welfare economics evaluates the economic prosperity and the economic welfare of a country in order to provide general equilibrium in the economy between economic efficiency and benefit versus the allocation of costs and resources. In general, welfare economics studies how legal and economic policies influence the prosperity of the society.[93]

Some proponents of the doctrine of the habitual residence of the characteristic performer argue that the application of such law is advantageous to the interest of the society. This is because it leads to economic efficiency in mass production

[92] O Lando, 'The Proper Law of Contract' (1964) 8 *Scandinavian Studies in* Law 105, 177–78; BV Hoffmann, 'General Report on Contractual Obligations' in O Lando et al, (eds), *European Private International Law of Obligations: Acts and Documents of an International Colloquium on the European Preliminary Draft Convention on the Law Applicable to Contractual and Non-Contractual Obligations* 1st edn (Berlin, Mohr, 1975) 1, 7–8; Lando (1987) (n 4) 202; J Blom, 'Choice of Law Methods in the Private International Law of Contract' (1978) 16 *Canadian Yearbook of International Law* 230, 285; Vischer (n 64) 27; AJE Jaffey, 'Choice of Law in Relation to Ius Dispositivum with Particular Reference to the EEC Convention on the Law Applicable to Contractual Obligations' in P North (ed), *Contract Conflicts, The EEC Convention on the Law Applicable to Contractual Obligations: A Comparative Study* (North-Holland Company, Amsterdam, 1982) 33, 37–40; AJE Jaffey, 'The English Proper Law Doctrine and the EEC Convention' (1984) 22 *International and Comparative Law Quarterly* 531, 541–47; IFG Baxter, 'International Business and Choice of Law' (1987) *International and Comparative Law Quarterly* 92, 105; FA Gabor, 'Private International Law Aspects of East-West Trade: A Synopsis of Recent Developments' (1989) 17 *International Journal of Legal Information* 144, 151; P Mankowski, 'The Principle of Characterisitic Performance Visited Yet Again' in K Boele-Woelki et al (eds), *Convergence and Divergence in Private International Law:Liber Amicorum Kurt Siehr* (The Hague, Schultess and Eleven International Publishing, 2010) 433.

[93] See generally CA Zebot, 'Efficiency and Equity in Welfare Economics' (1965) 88 *Monthly Labour Review* 528–34; D David, 'The Perils of Welfare Economics' (2002–03) 97 *Northwestern University Law Review* 351–94.

of goods and services, and reduction of costs for professionals (and thus potentially prices for clients) in international commercial transactions. Thus, the triumph of the law of the professional is linked to the philosophy of welfare economics.

Lando who is a strong advocate of this view point in a very early publication submitted that:

> There is in many bilateral contracts a sound basis for the application of the law of the *place of business* of that party whose performance is one that characterizes the type of contract in question ... it is generally 'the seller' who calculates the price, and his advantage on being able to predict the applicable law in all his contracts is presumably advantageous to the society. The 'seller' is also in most of his activities subject to the measures of control and interferences of the country he has his place of business.[94]

He then justifies this view point on the basis that:

> The basis of applying the 'seller's' law would then be that mass bargaining, like mass production, brings down the cost and the prices. The enterprise must calculate expenditures and risks on the basis of a multitude of contracts, and this calculation can be made safely only if all his contracts are governed by the same law, i.e., the law of the 'seat' of the enterprise.[95]

In addition, the performance of the professional is regarded as having more socio-economic significance to a country when compared to the performance of the other contracting party: this justifies why the law of the professional should be preferred.

Thus, d'Oliviera is of the view that:

> One of the more or less explicit assumptions of the doctrine of characteristic performance is that a contract is rooted in the national economy of that State where the characteristic performance is on one way to be located. This is bound up with the functional viewpoint which permeates the doctrine of characteristic performance and in the last resort constitutes its point of departure, that the national economy of one of the parties is more strongly involved in a given type of contract than that of the other. Two observations are called for. In the first place, this notion seems to repose upon an implicit value judgment, namely that it is more blessed to produce than to consume, and that the degree to which a national economy is involved is above all determined by the offering of goods and services, while the consumer for his part involves his national economy to a lesser extent.[96]

The Giuliano-Lagarde report also submits that:

> it is possible to relate the concept of characteristic performance to an even more general idea, namely the idea that his performance refers to the function which the legal

[94] Lando (1964) (n 92) 177 (italics in the original quotation). See also Lando (1974) (n 4) 30; O Lando, 'Some Issues Relating to the Law Applicable to Contractual Obligations' (1996–97) 7 *Kings College Journal* 66, 67–68.

[95] Lando (1964) (n 92) 177–78.

[96] HUJ d'Oliviera, '"Characteristic Obligation" in the Draft EEC Obligation Convention' (1977) 25 *American Journal of Comparative Law* 303, 327–28.

> relationship involved fulfils in the economic and social life of any country. The concept of characteristic performance essentially links the contract to the social and economic environment of which it will form a part.[97]

An underlying reason for advocating the triumph of the law of the professional on the basis of welfare economics is that the professional's job is more difficult and complex in benefiting the society, and his activities are more likely to be regulated by law when compared to the other contracting party.

Thus, Vischer, an academic disciple of Schnitzer holds the view that:

> The concentration on the position of the performer of the characteristic rights and duties, i.e. normally of the party to the contract which has to perform the non-pecuniary obligation, pays special regard to the fact generally this party has to take more care than the co-contractor, who owes the monetary consideration, that its obligation is more complicated and often regulated to a greater extent by rules of law. The application of the law of the residence of the performer of the characteristic obligation therefore attempts to take into account the interests of the parties.[98]

Jaffey also takes the position that:

> As to the question – which party's convenience is to be preferred? – the inquiry must be prefaced by the reminder that the law of either one of the parties (in a sale, say the seller's or the buyer's) will be better than any third law. It may often be said that there is no strong argument for preferring one party to the other; then a criterion that selects one rather than the other could verge on the arbitrary while still being as serviceable an approach as can be found. The case for the law of the party who renders the characteristic performance is that a sensible ground of convenience for choosing between the parties' laws is to select the law of the party who is more likely, or is likely more often, to have to ascertain and act on rules of law in the course of his performance: the party whose role under the contract is more active and substantial, whose performance is the more active and substantial, whose performance and the obligations in relation to it are more complex. That will normally be the law of the party who is to render the characteristic performance.[99]

He then goes on to express the view that:

> In most of these cases, it is the party whose performance is the characteristic one who has the more active role to play and thus, it may reasonably be supposed, is the more likely to consult the law during performance. It would be reasonable to prefer his convenience in being able to rely on his own law. This might indeed be economically more efficient in reducing costs of the transaction.[100]

To put the above submission of these scholars in one's own words, it is a case of applying the law of the professional who does the job rather than the party who 'buys' the performance, and a case of favouring production over consumption.

[97] (n 6) 20.
[98] Vischer (1982) (n 64) 27.
[99] Jaffey (1984) (n 92) 547.
[100] ibid 548 (footnotes omitted in quotation).

The argument is that the professional is the person who carries out the complex work in the contract he has with the client and is more likely to have his obligations regulated by law. The professional thus deserves more protection in planning and executing his contractual obligations, and possibly hedging against any potential legal and commercial risk. If the professional was exposed to the application of different laws, it might be difficult to hedge against potential legal and commercial risks in dealing with several clients in cross-border transactions. It is thus convenient and pragmatic to select the law of the place of business of the professional where the parties do not make a choice of law. The professional is able to standardise his contracts uniformly in relation to several clients, despite their nationality, residence or language barrier arising from dealing with clients in a cross-border transaction. Applying the law of the professional enhances economic efficiency since the application of the law of the professional might promote rapid economic development. Selecting the professional's law is viewed as an incentive to enhance economic development. In other words, the legal and commercial convenience of only applying his law in his relationship with several clients might result in mass production of goods and services. It also enhances business efficacy because it reduces transaction costs and litigation costs. In litigation proceedings the parties would only pay legal advisers to investigate the application of the law of the professional instead of the potential the application of various laws that might apply to the legal relationship. The parties would also reasonably predict in judicial proceedings that it is the professional's law that would apply.

It is opined that the welfare economics theory in justifying the triumph of the law of the professional is questionable. On the contrary, the triumph of the law of the professional is linked more to capitalism. The professional does not operate to save costs for clients but for himself. The main goal of the professional is to make a profit for himself. Standardising the commercial operations of the professional through Article 4 of Rome I saves costs for the professional, makes his business more efficient, productive, certain, and reduces his risks.

The professional saves costs by relying only on the content of his law in situations such as a dispute with clients in judicial or arbitral proceedings, or other commercial transactions. He makes his business more efficient by having his own law centralised to govern transactions with various clients in cross-border transactions. He makes his business more productive by spending less time on disputing or negotiating the law that would govern the transaction he has with his clients, and thus channels those saved resources to other goals. His transactions with clients are more certain if the professional can reasonably predict that his own law would regulate his relationship with his clients. He reduces the risk of having a foreign law applied to his transaction with clients, which he might not be very familiar with, or the foreign law might be hostile to his interest.

In essence, the truth is that professionals are not in the business of saving costs for clients. Professionals are not that benevolent or altruistic. It is common knowledge that what really brings down the cost of prices of goods and services for customers in a free market economy is efficiency and competition. Where professionals are efficient in the production of goods and services, and in competition to increase their client base, the price of goods and services are likely to reduce as a result of this.

Another major objection to using the welfare economics theory to support the idea of the triumph of the law of the professional is that the link between the theory of welfare economics and the doctrine of habitual residence of the characteristic performer has not been sufficiently proven or established. In other words, no concrete evidence has been provided to demonstrate that the application of the law of the professional is generally in the interest of the society and reduces transaction costs for clients. It is true that mass production of goods and services might also lead to a reduction in prices and cost for clients (though not conclusively and decisively), but there has been no empirical study (socio-economic, legal or otherwise) to back up this claim, in the context of the application of the law of the professional.

In this connection Juenger rightly submits that 'Though it has been argued that the preference is justified by socio-economic considerations, no empirical evidence has been adduced to support such "extravagant claims" and they have been challenged for cogent reasons.'[101]

d' Oliveria also submits that:

> until the contrary is proved, that 'economics' and 'sociology' serve merely as ventriloquists' dummies for the preconceived ideas of the writers. The abdication of legal analysis in favor of economics and sociology is only apparent. In actual fact, the writers once again represent their own evaluations as having been an application of the immutable scientific criteria of associated disciplines, which are supposed to be totally free of value judgments. The introduction of these disciplines is indeed extremely functional – in the sense that it serves to conceal the writers' own subjectivity.[102]

For the purpose of argument, let us assume that the welfare economics theory in favour of the triumph of the law of the professional is correct. The logic would be that the standardisation of the operations of the professional through his own law applying leads to a reduction in his own costs, which would eventually translate to a reduction in the price of goods and services for clients. Clients 'buying' goods and services at cheaper prices is in the general welfare of the society, and in such situations the clients can dedicate their saved resources to other goals. If the professional had to consult the law of every country where he provides goods and services for clients in cross-border transactions, transaction costs would increase. The clients would thus have to bear the burden of this transaction costs when paying the professional.

[101] FK Juenger, 'The EEC Convention on the Law Applicable to Contractual Obligations: An American Assessment' in P North (ed), *Contract Conflicts, The EEC Convention on the Law Applicable to Contractual Obligations: A Comparative Study* (Amsterdam, North-Holland Publishing Company, 1982) 301.

[102] D'Oliviera (n 96) 313.

In reality, the above argument does not always hold true. Conversely other costs could be saved, or benefits gained, by applying the same law to all transactions performed in a given country. If the law of the place of performance applies, all transactions performed in one country are governed by the same law. Instead, with the current rule, they are governed by different laws. In economic terms, this might not be favourable for the client who is likely to increase his own costs as a commercial entity, and eventually that of the customers the client deals with. The country where the obligation of the professional is performed might be also deprived of the economic benefit of having its substantive laws applied to such international commercial transactions, which are substantially connected with it.[103] In addition, the client might not feel 'safe' or 'protected' with applying various foreign laws to transactions professionals perform in its own jurisdiction. The client is likely to feel 'safer' with the law of the place of performance applying, which is more neutral and proximate to the transaction.

For example, assume client A is in the business of manufacturing cars in country A, but it sometimes engages several professionals who travel from other countries to assist in the manufacture of its cars. A in the course of its business also buys materials for making cars from other professionals located in different countries. The current rule would lead to A's business operations not being standardised, if the law of the place of performance is not applied. A would have to investigate the laws of different professionals that assist it in the manufacture of its cars, and also investigate the laws of different professionals that it buys materials from to manufacture its cars. This would thereby increase transaction costs for the client, and customers who purchase such cars from the client would have to pay more.

Moreover, and perhaps more importantly, the proper route to standardise an international commercial contract is through party autonomy under Article 3 of Rome I. Party autonomy is now the norm and practice in international commercial transactions.[104] There are relatively very few cases where party autonomy in choice of law is not effectively utilised. If the professional wants to reduce his transaction costs and ultimately benefit the client, he should expressly provide for a standard choice of law and forum clause in agreements he enters into with various clients. Article 4 of Rome I is not the route through which the concept of welfare economics should be applied.

Given that parties to international commercial contracts use party autonomy in most cases (maybe 80 per cent of cases), Article 4 can hardly achieve any standardisation or harmonisation, as it only concerns 20 per cent of international

[103] For empirical findings see also G Cuniberti, 'The International Market for Contracts: The Most Attractive Contract Laws' (2014) 3 *Northwestern Journal of International Law & Business* 455–516; G Cuniberti, 'The Laws of Asian International Business Transactions' (2016) 25 *Pacific Rim Law & Policy Journal* 35–86; MP Fons, 'Commercial Choice of Law in Context: Looking beyond Rome' (2015) 78 *Modern Law Review* 241, 257–59, 265–72.

[104] See also Fons (ibid) 281.

commercial contracts. In this connection, it must be stressed that one is only discussing consumer cases marginally (Article 4 does apply to some consumer contracts),[105] so that there is therefore potential bargaining power on both sides, which would thus not necessarily lead to the choice of the law of the characteristic performer.

Furthermore, and contrary to the welfare economics theory, from the perspective of State interests, it is trite that States are usually interested in regulating or attaching consequences to commercial transactions that are executed or performed in their country.[106] When compared to the place of business of the characteristic performer, the place of performance serves as a regulatory function in international commercial transactions and thus has a legitimate interest in governing such transactions, even when it is not the chosen law. For example, the law of the place of performance is more interested in the health and general welfare of its consumers in relation to goods that are delivered (or services rendered) to its territory. This might explain why the EU legislator under Article 9(3) of Rome I gives absolute significance to the place of performance in matters of foreign mandatory rules.[107]

The place of performance as a matter of policy has the greatest interest in regulating an international commercial transaction. In this connection, the place of performance being of considerable significance when compared to the place of business of the characteristic performer has a better claim to regulating international commercial transactions.

ii. Arbitrary

Favouring the triumph of the law of the professional is arbitrary. The professional is gifted with the advantage of having his law applied, where the parties do not make a choice of law. The obvious advantage for the professional is that he would save costs during his negotiation with his clients, as he should normally be familiar with his own law in the course of his business operations. The professional can thus negotiate with the client in such a way that the arrangement suits the interest of the law of the professional. On the other hand, the client would have to expend legal and transaction costs to investigate the content of the law of the professional in order to ascertain how that law suits his interest in the commercial transaction.

In addition, in judicial proceedings the professional would be confident that his law would generally be the applicable law, and this would save the professional litigation and transaction costs, as it relates to the content of his law. The professional is also likely to be more confident in applying his law in judicial proceedings, when compared to the client.

[105] See Article 6 of Rome I.

[106] AJE Jaffey, 'Essential Validity of Contracts in the English Conflict of Laws' (1974) 23 *International and Comparative Law Quarterly* 1, 11.

[107] See ch 4.

Generally speaking, the EU choice of law rules are concerned with the determination of the applicable law based on designated connecting factors that determine the applicable law. It is generally concerned with the geographical localisation of the legal relevant relationship and the determination of the country or legal system which has the closest connection. It is opined that the principal connecting factor utilised should not be one that generally favours the interest of *one* of the parties to an international commercial transaction.

It cannot reasonably be argued that applying the law of the place of business of the characteristic performer is objective. Thus, Juenger submits that favouring the law of the place of business of the professional attempts to:

> localize contracts by means of a 'mysterious, almost a mystical, concept' like earlier proposals having a similar thrust, is but another 'unconvincing production of divination rather than inquiry.' Since it focuses on the home state law of one of the parties, rather than their common concerns, that test cannot be reconciled with the proper law approach it is meant to clarify.[108]

It is important to stress that when compared to other connecting factors such as the place of business of the characteristic performer, the place of performance is an objective connecting factor. The application of the law of the place of business of the characteristic performer usually downplays the application of the law of another party thereby providing legal and commercial advantage to one party over another; whereas the law of the place of performance could be situated in the commercial residence of any of the parties or some other country that is not the residence of any of the parties. For example in a contract between A, whose place of business is in Luxembourg, and B, who is habitually resident in Scotland for the provision of services by A to B in Scotland. Assuming A sues B in a Scot's court and the court presumably holds that Luxembourgish law is applicable because of the place of business of A, B is likely to incur more cost and time in investigating the content of Luxembourgish law, when compared to A. In this scenario Scots law is more neutral and fair to the parties because A is performing his services in Scotland rather than Luxembourg, and Scots law has an interest in regulating the quality or standard of performance of A's contract rather than Luxembourgish law which simply has a connection to the contract because of A's place of business.

iii. Weaker Party

Favouring the triumph of the law of the professional betrays the claim that EU choice of law rules aims to protect the weaker party.[109] A counter-argument might be that the EU choice of law rules takes care of this situation in the case of consumers, employees, and insured persons.[110] The appropriate response to this

[108] Juenger (n 101) 302.
[109] Recital 23 to Rome I.
[110] Article 6, 7 and 8 of Rome I.

counter-argument is that in reality, in an international commercial contract, it is the professional that is usually the relatively stronger party, who should be in a better position to seek legal advice on how to hedge against his legal and commercial risk.

It may also be counter-argued that the substance of the law of the professional would not necessarily or always provide him with an advantage. The appropriate response to this argument is that the familiarity the professional has with his own law provides him with a significant advantage where the parties dispute the applicable law in the absence of choice. An obvious advantage is that the professional would likely incur less costs given that the professional in the course of his business is familiar with his own law.

If the professional is of the view that he would be exposed to risk by applying an uncertain neutral law, then he should hedge against this risk by inserting an express choice of law, jurisdiction and arbitration clause. The professional as a relatively stronger party is usually in a better position to insert a choice of law and jurisdiction clause in his favour. If the party is in breach, it is the client who will look at the law. Moreover, in any case, there is no obligation to choose between the laws of each of the parties: you could simply look at the law of the place of performance.

In international commercial transactions, the law should not be seen to give double protection to the professional, at the expense of the client, by favouring his hedging against his legal and commercial risk, both in the case of party autonomy and the applicable law in the absence of choice. In essence, the principal weakness of favouring the triumph of the law of the professional is that it promotes a form of unbridled capitalism.

In this connection, Blom submits that the connecting factor of the habitual residence of the characteristic performer:

> does tend generally to favor the interests of the stronger party to the contract, the one who sells the goods, provides the services, lends the money, and so forth. He will enjoy the convenience of having his own law govern the agreement, and, if he makes contracts with persons resident in various foreign countries, he will also derive the benefit of having a single law apply to all these agreements.[111]

Jaffey observes that:

> While conceding that the law of one of the parties should govern, it might be argued, however, that it is often the interests and convenience of the party who is not rendering the characteristic performance which should be preferred. He will often be the economically weaker party and, though it may be that he is likely to have to consult the law, when he does have his resources and opportunities to obtain legal advice about, and ability to adapt his expectation to foreign laws are much less than those of the business party with whom he deals.[112]

[111] Blom (n 92) 162.
[112] Jaffey (1984) (n 92) 550.

Juenger holds the view that the rule of the habitual residence of the characteristic performer:

> confers a choice of law privilege upon those who engage in a consistent course of conduct to supply goods or services. These are often the very parties able to evaluate the risk of doing business and hedge against it by means of choice-of-law and forum-selection or arbitration clauses. It is difficult to see why the conflict of laws should favour lawyers over laymen, or 'Helvetian hotel keepers and cukoo-clock makers' over their clientele. Not only is such a choice of law bonus incompatible with general policy considerations; it also clashed with the provisions of Article 5 and 6 of the Convention, which favour economically disadvantaged parties.[113]

d'Oliviera expresses the view that:

> the doctrine of characteristic performance, if not deliberately then at any rate in its actual working, operates in favor of the stronger party: employers, banks, insurance companies, the closed professions. The theory reveals itself as a functional and loyal handmaiden of capitalist society, in which the weaker party – consumers, employees, those needing insurance, those seeking specialized help, etc. – gets the wrong end of the stick. The doctrine of characteristic performance calls into being in private international law a leonine contract in favour of the stronger party, whilst pretending to be a neutral and objective method for connecting the contracts with a given law.[114]

The editors of Cheshire, North and Fawcett submit that:

> in terms of economic strength, the large enterprise, the manufacturer of goods, the provider of services (such as banks and insurance companies) and the professional is favoured against the other party who may well be in a weaker position. It is curious to find a pro-manufacturer stance being taken in a Convention which is sufficiently concerned about protecting weaker parties to have special rules for consumers and employees.[115]

Beaumont and McEleavy conclude that:

> the doctrine of characteristic performance tends, on the whole, to favour big battalions, the company which supplied the goods or services. This will not necessarily be so, but it is clearly a feature of the scheme which conduced to the inclusion within it of special provisions made in arts 5 and 6 for consumer and individual employment contracts.[116]

Article 4 of Rome I would apply to small scale businesses (companies or natural persons) as 'active' consumers, who are conversant with the business, which are in reality weaker parties, but are not taken into account to be protected under Article 6 of Rome I. Such small scale businesses in transacting with big companies

[113] Juenger (n 101) 301–02. See also FK Juenger, 'Two European Conflicts Conventions' (1998) 28 *Victoria Wellington Law Review* 527, 540.
[114] d'Oliviera (n 96) 327.
[115] Torremans (n 71)735.
[116] PR Beaumont and PE Mc Eleavy, *Private International Law A.E ANTON* 3rd edition (Edinburgh, W Green, 2011) 469–70, [10.152].

usually do not have the upper hand in insisting on a standard choice of law clause that would protect their interests. It is rather unfortunate that where the parties do not make a choice of law to govern their transaction, such small scale companies when dealing with big companies are in a position where the applicable law is generally not in their favour. For choice of law purposes, small scale businesses that do not qualify as consumers under Article 6 of Rome I are thus doubly at a disadvantage under both Article 3 and Article 4 of Rome I.

In addition, qualifying as a consumer in order to apply the law of the consumer's habitual residence under Article 6 (1) of Rome I is not so easy. It has to be established that: (a) the professional pursues his commercial or professional activities in the country where the consumer has his habitual residence, or (b) the professional by any means, directs such activities to that country or to several countries including that country.[117] In addition, the law of the habitual residence of the person who wants to qualify as a consumer would not be applied inter alia where the services are exclusively performed in a country other than his habitual residence.[118]

For example, assume a 'consumer' habitually resident in country X buys exotic shoes from a professional habitually resident in country Y. The 'consumer' later disputes the quality of the shoes ordered and requests a refund from the professional in court. The applicable law in the absence of choice would generally be the habitual residence of the professional (under Article 4(1)(a) of Rome I) if it is established that the professional does not pursue his activities in country X, or directs any of its activities to country X.

In summation, the idea of the triumph of the law of the professional in justifying the habitual residence of the professional as the applicable law in reality works against weaker parties in international commercial transactions.

iv. Proximity

Favouring the triumph of the law of the professional appears to be inconsistent with the principle of proximity,[119] which is in the foundation of the EU choice of law rules for commercial contracts. It has been observed that prior to the entry into the EU choice of law rules, under the influence of Savigny's teachings, some Member States courts applied the principle of closest connection in determining the applicable law in the absence of choice.[120] For example in *Bonython v Commonwealth of Australia*,[121] Lord Simonds held that '[T]he substance of the obligation must be determined by the proper law of the contract, ie the system of law by

[117] Article 6(1)(a) and (b) of Rome I.

[118] Article 6(4)(a) of Rome I. See also Article 6(4)(b)–(e) of Rome I.

[119] Proximity in this connection means that the country or law that has its closest or greatest connection to a particular situation should govern the dispute. In other words, the principle of proximity applies the nearest law to the parties' transaction.

[120] See ch 2, s II.

[121] *Bonython v Commonwealth of Australia* [1951] AC 201.

reference to which the contract was made or that with which the transaction has its closest and most real connexion.'[122]

Some authors have argued that Article 4(1) and (2) of Rome I are based on principled proximity.[123] In other words, the driving force of Article 4 of Rome I is the principle of closest connection. The idea that Article 4(1) and (2) are based on principled proximity is open to question. For example where the habitual residence of the seller is not corroborated by other significant connecting factors such as the place of performance, it is arguable that the habitual residence of the seller does not meet the criteria of proximity. It is opined that the better argument is that the rules in Article 4(1) and (2) are primarily based on the principle of legal certainty, predictability and uniformity rather than the principle of proximity. This is not to say the goals of proximity would not be met by applying Article 4(1) and (2). What is being said is that Article 4(1) and (2) standing on their own do not meet the requirement of proximity.

It is open to question whether the proponents of the habitual residence of the characteristic performer are correct to hold that it is the habitual residence of the characteristic performer that normally presents the closest territorial relationship with a commercial contract. No sufficient justification has been provided for attributing special significance to the habitual residence of the party who effects the characteristic performance as satisfying the requirement of proximity. It might be that it is because the habitual residence of the characteristic performer is the place where it acquires technical know-how on effecting the substantial performance obligation, and thus gives that place a legitimate claim to being the law that is most closely connected to the contract in commercial and economic terms. On this ground, it might be argued that the triumph of the law of the professional is consistent with the principle of proximity.

If the applicable law in commercial contracts is also concerned with locating the country or legal system that is most closely connected to a contract, then it is opined that the place where the contract is performed is deserving of special significance. If the principal historical concern was the problem of identifying the place of performance, the place where the characteristic obligation is performed is a better rule in determining the country or legal system that is most closely connected with the contract, and at the same time addressing the concerns of predictability, certainty, simplicity, uniformity and stability of commercial contracts. In other words, the place of characteristic performance would better reconcile the goals of certainty on the one hand, and flexibility and proximity on the other hand.

[122] ibid 219.

[123] G Güneysu-Güngör, 'Article 4 of Rome I Regulation on the Applicable Law in the Absence of Choice – Methodological Analysis, Considerations' in P Stone and Y Farah (eds), *Research Handbook on EU Private International Law* (Cheltenham, Edward Elgar Publishing, 2015) 170, 172. See also R Fentiman, *International Commercial Litigation* 2nd edn (Oxford, Oxford University Press, 2015) 207, 209.

The Paris Court of Appeal's approach to applying the concept of characteristic performance is better on the basis that it held that:

> The place with which the contractual transaction has its closest connection is the place where the specific acts of performance of the contract, in the execution of the obligation that is characteristic of that type of contract, must be performed … [T]he law of the country where this obligation is executed still has a stronger claim to govern the contract where the party on whom his obligation rests has his domicile in the same country.[124]

The Paris Court of Appeal is right because it gives principal significance to the place where the characteristic obligation is performed rather than the place of business of the characteristic performer in determining the country or legal system that a contract is most closely connected with. It then submits that if the domicile of the characteristic performer coincides with the place of characteristic performance, the place of characteristic performance has a stronger claim to determining the country or legal system that a contract is most closely connected with. In other words, the idea that the place of business of the characteristic performer has a stronger claim to determining the country that is most closely connected to a contract because it is the true socio-economic source and power house of the performance is easy to accept where the place of the performance of the characteristic obligation coincides with the place of business of the characteristic performer.

The place of performance better satisfies the requirement of proximity when compared to the place of business of the characteristic performer. The place of performance of an international commercial transaction is one of principal commercial significance. It constitutes a very important component, if not decisive element, of a commercial transaction. Parties who enter into a commercial transaction are principally concerned with the performance in a contract. The seller is primarily concerned with the money the buyer would pay and the buyer is concerned with the goods the seller is willing to supply, and the service provider is concerned with payment it would receive for providing a service and the other party is concerned with the services the service provider would render. The obligation is the crux of a commercial contract. This explains why domestic legal systems provide for consequences where a party totally or partially fails, neglects or threatens not to perform its obligation in a commercial contract. This includes the remedies of damages (or compensation) and specific performance.

A major reason why the habitual residence of the characteristic performer does not generally satisfy the requirement of proximity is that it elevates and gives undue significance to an element that belongs to one of the parties and not the commercial contract itself.[125] Since each commercial contract has by definition

[124] *Sociètè Jansen v Sociètè Heurty*, [January 27, 1955], cited in Blom (n 92) 243.

[125] See also G Cuniberti, 'L'incertitude du lieu d'exécution sur la loi applicable au contrat. La difficile cohabitation des articles 4-2 et 4-5 de la Convention de Rome du 19 juin 1980' (2003) *Juris-Classeur Pèriodique* (general edition) 153.

several co-contracting parties, the same element will frequently designate with a comparable force another country or legal system, that of the habitual residence of one of the parties to the contract, so that, from this point of view, the contract will be connected to each of the countries concerned.[126]

However, it is important to stress that a key element that makes the place of performance satisfy the requirement of proximity is that a commercial contract is geared towards execution.[127] Though the place of business of the parties, place of negotiation and conclusion of a contract, language a contract is expressed in, and currency of payment are significant factors the parties might take into account when entering into an international commercial transaction, these factors are not as important as the performance which constitutes the crux of a commercial contract. To justify this proposition, an example may be given relating to a comparison between the place of business of the parties and the performance of an international commercial transaction as connecting factors the parties might take into account before entering into an international commercial transaction. Assume A, who is the buyer of goods, habitually resident in country X, enters into a transaction with B, who is the seller of goods, with his place of business in country Y, for the supply of medicinal products that purportedly cure cancer. B requests for payment in advance from A before the goods can be supplied. A subsequently discovers that the claim that B has products that can cure cancer is false. It is very unlikely that B would pay for the goods or even continue with the transaction because in reality B cannot perform its own part of the transaction by supplying the goods. On the other hand, the fact that B habitually resides in country Y is likely to be immaterial or less significant to A as a factor to take into account in entering into the international commercial transaction, if B in reality can supply the appropriate goods to A.

Thus, it might be that international businesspersons sometimes expect that, where the parties do not make a choice of law, the law of the country where the contract was performed would govern their commercial transactions.[128] Collins submits that the:

> place of business … is only really workable when the place of residence or business and the place of performance are the same place. If they are not the same, it would lead to the odd result if, for example, in an agency contract the agent was a resident of State X who was to perform all his duties in State Y it would be the law of State X which would govern the contract. In commercial contracts, where individuals are concerned, the state of residence is not a suitable or appropriate connecting factor. Nor is the test of the principal or subsidiary establishment a suitable test in the case of contracts concluded by companies.[129]

[126] ibid.
[127] ibid.
[128] Fentiman (n 123) 210–12.
[129] Collins (n 71) 46.

In summation, the place of performance generally satisfies the requirement of proximity when compared to the habitual residence of one or the other parties to an international commercial contract, or indeed any other potential connecting factor. In relation to the place of performance, at the very least, the characteristic performance is obviously the most appropriate and relevant criterion in the search for the country or legal system in which the commercial contract is most closely connected with.

C. Country-of-Origin Principle

The habitual residence of the characteristic performer is the country-of-origin of the goods and services. Thus, some scholars have linked the doctrine of the habitual residence of the characteristic performer to the country-of-origin principle.

In this section, first, the country-of-origin principle will be discussed from the perspective of EU constitutional federalism; second, from the perspective of economic development; and third, in the final analysis, a vigorous critique will be offered on the country-of-origin principle.

i. European Union Constitutional Federalism

Applying the concept of habitual residence of the characteristic performer might be regarded as a form of country-of-origin principle. The logic is that the law of the place from which the professional carries out his business should apply to every country of destination (the place of performance) in relation to clients the professional does business with. In effect, the law of the professional which 'originates' from his home country or business establishment is applied uniformly to several clients in cross-border transactions.

One may ask: is this a European doctrine, and one that has legitimacy under the EU choice of law rules? If this is a legitimate European doctrine in choice of law rules, does it sit comfortably with the logic of the principle of proximity, which is in the foundation of the EU choice of law rules in determining the applicable law in the absence of choice? Assuming it is a legitimate European doctrine, does it betray the claim that the EU choice of law rules apply universally, and not only within Member States? These issues are addressed in this section.

The 1957 Treaty of Rome is the EU constitutional document which is the backbone of EU integration.[130] The Treaty of Rome is what gave legal legitimacy to the European Economic Community, which eventually became the EU. In effect, the EU operates as an internal, single or common market, and the Treaty of Rome seeks to guarantee four fundamental freedoms: free movement of persons, goods,

[130] Now Treaty on European Union and the Treaty on the Functioning of the European Union (TFEU) [Official Journal C 326, 26/10/2012].

services and capital ('fundamental freedoms').[131] The EU private international law instruments, including choice of law rules, are mandated to give expression to these fundamental freedoms. Indeed, in relation to the Rome I, the European legislator mandates the EU 'to adopt measures relating to judicial cooperation in civil matters with a cross-border impact to the extent necessary for the *proper functioning of the internal market*'.[132] Thus, the logic is that the EU choice of law rules must give expression to these fundamental freedoms. This explains why some scholars view the EU choice of law rules as vehicle of EU integration.[133]

Some scholars also argue that historically, there is implicit support for the country-of-origin principle as a choice of law rule in the EU choice of law rules for contractual obligations.[134] Thus, Article 20 of the Rome Convention provides that:

> This Convention shall not affect the application of provisions which, in relation to particular matters, lay down choice-of law-rules relating to contractual obligations and which are or will be contained in the acts of the institutions of the European Communities or in national laws harmonized in implementation of such acts.[135]

Article 22(c) of the Rome I Proposal[136] also provides that:

> This Regulation shall not prejudice the application or adoption of acts of the institutions of the European Communities which … lay down rules to promote the smooth operation of the internal market, where such rules cannot apply at the same time as the law designated by the rules of private international law.[137]

Historical support is also drawn from the case law of the European Court of Justice (ECJ). The leading ECJ case that lays foundation for the doctrine of country-of-origin principle is *Rewwe-Zentral*.[138] The central issue in that case was whether a French claimant who had complied with the rules of its country-of-origin (France) on the minimum alcohol content that can be produced and marketed (in France), could be prohibited in Germany from marketing its alcoholic products in its territory (Germany) on the basis that the alcohol content is

[131] Article 26(2) of the TFEU.

[132] Recital 1 to Rome I (emphasis added).

[133] R Michaels, 'EU Law as Private International Law? Reconceptualising the Country-of-Origin Principle as Vested-Rights Theory' (2006) 2 *Journal of Private International Law* 195, 236 (citing others).

[134] ibid 199–201.

[135] See also The Green Paper on the Conversion of Rome Convention of 1980 on the law Applicable to Contractual Obligations into a Community Instrument and its Modernisation, COM (2002) 654 final, 14 January 2003, 5; Proposal for a Regulation of the European Parliament and the Council on the Law Applicable to Non-Contractual Obligations (Rome II), 22 July 2003, COM (2003) 427 final.

[136] Proposal for a Regulation of the European Parliament and the Council on the Law Applicable to Contractual Obligations (Rome I) presented by the Commission), 15 December 2005, Com (2005) 650 final (Rome I Proposal).

[137] See also Article 3(d) of the Rome II Regulation proposal (Proposal for a Regulation of the European Parliament and the Council on the Law Applicable to Non-Contractual Obligations (Rome II), 22 July 2003, COM (2003) 427 final).

[138] C-120/78, *Rewwe-Zentral AG v Bundesmonopolverwaltung für Branntwei*, EU:C:1979:42.

below the fixed limit as prescribed by German law. The ECJ held in the negative. In the words of the ECJ:

> There is therefore no valid reason why, provided that they have been lawfully produced and marketed in one of the Member States, alcoholic beverages should not be introduced into any other Member State; the sale of such products may not be subject to a legal prohibition on the marketing of beverages with an alcohol content than the limit set by the national rules.[139]

Another ECJ case law that supports the doctrine of country-of-origin principle is the ECJ's jurisprudence on freedom of establishment of companies within the EU.[140] In this connection, the leading case is *Centros*.[141] The central issue in *Centros* was whether Denmark was legally obligated to register the subsidiary of a corporation that two Danish citizens had registered under English law, although their only reason for using UK law had been to avoid the registration fees for Danish companies under Danish law. The facts of the case

> concerned a secondary establishment in Denmark, the host Member State, of a company, Centros Ltd, which was validly incorporated in the United Kingdom where it had its registered office but did not carry on business. Centros Ltd wished to set up a branch in Denmark in order to carry on its main business activities there. The Danish authorities did not question the company's existence under English law but denied it the right to exercise its freedom of establishment in Denmark by setting up a branch there, since it was not disputed that that form of secondary establishment was intended to avoid Danish rules on company formation, in particular the rules relating to the paying-up of a minimum share capital.[142]

The ECJ held that:

> a Member State (the host State) must allow a company validly incorporated in another Member State where it has its registered office to register another establishment (in that case, a branch) in the host State, from which it may develop its entire business. On that basis, the host Member State cannot impose on a company which has been properly formed in another Member State its own substantive company law, in particular the rules on share capital.[143]

There have been very few scholars (at least in English language) who have explicitly linked the country-of-origin principle to the doctrine of habitual residence of the characteristic performer in the EU choice of law rules, and in particular drawn inspiration from the principle of EU constitutional federalism. Cuniberti is one of such scholars who summarises clearly this analysis.[144] His explanations are worth quoting.

[139] ibid [14].

[140] See generally C-212/97, *Centros Ltd v Erhvervs- og Selskabsstyrelsen*, EU:C:1999:126; C-208/00, *Überseering BV v Nordic Construction Company Baumanagement GmbH*, EU:C:2002:632; C-167/01, *Kramer van Koophandel en Fabrieken voor Amsterdam v Inspire Act Ltd* EU:C:2003:512.

[141] *Centros* (ibid).

[142] *Überseering* (n 140) [42].

[143] ibid [43].

[144] G Cuniberti, *Conflict of Laws: A Comparative Approach* (Cheltenham, Edward Elgar Publishing, 2017) 68–72, 414.

Cuniberti submits that:

> certain fundamental principles of federalism can influence, and sometimes even command, the solution to the choice of law problem.
>
> One of the essential goals of federal systems is to maintain or build an internal market where residents of the different states can circulate and trade freely. Any obstacle which might hinder the exercise of such rights, including rules and indeed choice of law rules, is thus to be eliminated.[145]

He then applies the above reasoning to submit that the:

> argument supporting the choice of the habitual residence of one party is that it leads to the application of the law of origin of the product or the service (where the manufacturer or service provider is based). The European Union is a federal system, and one of its most fundamental principles is the four freedoms of movement: persons, products, services and capital. Like any other rule, a choice of law rule could restrict freedom of movement. By providing in effect for the application of the law of origin of products and services, Art. 4 prevents the issue from arising.[146]

One might challenge the proponents of the country-of-origin principle to the effect that the foundation of the EU choice of law rules in determining the applicable law in the absence of choice is based on the principle of proximity. In effect, where the country-of-origin does not coincide with the place of performance, the principle of proximity might not be satisfied. The rebuttal offered by proponents of the country-of-origin principle is that the [country of origin] principle is an EU fundamental freedom[147] of the professional, so that the Rome I must be regarded as secondary law. In effect, EU constitutional federalism which is a vehicle of European integration embodies the supremacy of EU law,[148] over other goals such as proximity (including the place of performance). In other words, the principle of proximity is not in the same class as the country-of-origin principle, but subordinates to the principle of country-of-origin. In addition, given that the country-of-origin is not in the same class as the principle of proximity, the country-of-origin principle is really not concerned with impacting on the principle of proximity.

One might also challenge the proponents of the country-of-origin principle to the effect that the Rome I applies the doctrine of habitual residence of the characteristic performer universally,[149] so that for example the logic fails where a Luxembourgish professional (habitually resident in Luxembourg) provides goods or services to a Nigerian client (habitually resident in Nigeria). Again, the response of the proponents of the country-of-origin principle is that the

[145] ibid 68–69.
[146] ibid 414.
[147] ibid 68–72 citing C-353/06, *Grukin and Paul*, EU:C:2008:559.
[148] C-6/64, *Costa v Enel*, EU:C:1964:66. See also G Beck, *The Legal Reasoning of the Court of Justice of the EU* (Oxford, Hart Publishing, 2012) for a detailed discussion on principles of EU law.
[149] Article 2 of Rome I.

country-of-origin principle is an EU fundamental freedom of the professional, so that the professional should have very minimum impediments in universally applying his law in relation to transactions within and outside the EU. Indeed, this logic of universality of the EU country-of-origin principle is supported by some American scholars who reconceptualise the country-of-origin principle as a form of vested rights theory.[150] In effect, the law of the professional is 'acquired' in his country-of-origin, 'vested' in him, and this law 'travels' with the professional universally, with little or no impediments, and must be 'validly applied' in relation to the transaction the professional has with clients all over the world (within and outside the EU).[151]

In summation, some proponents argue that EU constitutional federalism, which gives form to the country-of-origin principle is linked to the doctrine of habitual residence of the characteristic performer under EU choice of law rules. Indeed, in the eyes of some scholars, the country-of-origin principle is an EU fundamental freedom of the professional, which overrides any other choice of law goal of proximity or universality.

ii. Economic Development

The country-of-origin principle is also seen as a vehicle to promote economic development particularly in the EU. Thus, the logic is that applying the law of the habitual residence of the characteristic performer with little or no impediments fosters economic integration and prosperity in the free flow of persons, goods, services and capital.

The 1957 Treaty of Rome set out a programme which primarily focused on integration of EU community markets, which was effected by the removal of restrictions, in the free movement of persons, goods, services and capital. Professionals could thus freely do business in the EU with little or no barriers. Professionals were also to not to be imposed with additional burdens or impediments that are not prescribed by their country-of-origin. In effect, the country-of-origin principle is regarded as the vehicle of European economic integration,[152] so that any choice of law of rule of proximity or universality is a less important or subsidiary goal.

In the context of the EU, some scholars submit that the country-of-origin principle 'ensures the full expression of economic freedoms within the internal market'.[153] This logic is also applied and extended to transactions conducted by professionals outside the EU, so that the country-of-origin principle is viewed as promoting a form of globalisation of international trade and commerce.[154]

[150] See generally Michaels (n 133).

[151] ibid 221–22.

[152] See generally J Basedow, 'A Common Contract Law for the Common Market' (1996) 33 *Common Market Law Review* 1169.

[153] H Muir Watt, 'Choice of Law in Integrated and Interconnected Markets: A Matter of Political Economy' (2003) 7 *Electronic Journal of Comparative Law* 1, 11.

[154] ibid at 12–13.

In reality, the country-of-origin principle favours the economy of developed countries, whose professionals' export goods and services to other countries (whether developing or developed). Mankowski puts it in the following words:

> the principle of characteristic performance carries a certain level of friendliness to exporters. Thus it favours exporting oriented economies. In turn States might feel tempted to protect their national industry by legislative means, by subsidizing it and by leaning towards public choice. In substance, the principle is a kind of 'country-of-origin' principle. This applies to the export of goods and services alike.[155]

In effect, the professional can freely conduct his business in many countries with little or no impediment arising from the obstacles that might be posed by choice of law rules, such as applying the law of the place of performance. The professional would have his transaction regulated by his own law rather than the law of a foreign country, so he has the confidence to freely export goods and services worldwide.

In the context of the country-of-origin principle promoting economic development, there are three points worthy of note.

First, the professional is not to be discriminated against in doing business in other countries, so that if the country of destination (the place of performance) imposes additional burdens or impediments on the professional, this would be seen as a violation of the fundamental freedom of the professional. Thus, some scholars submit that the country-of-origin principle is 'designed to prevent discrimination in the form of a double regulatory burden imposed on goods and services entering a foreign market'.[156]

Second, and flowing from the above, the professional must not be subjected to additional rules or measures not imposed by the country-of-origin that would make it difficult for him to compete with professionals (at the country of destination or place of performance) in other Member States or countries outside the EU. The idea that the professional must be allowed to compete favourably with other professionals in other countries is brilliantly elucidated by Muir Watt in the following words:

> the combined effect of deregulation and mobility leads to competition between Member States to attract business … Indeed, an essential part of European integration seems to be that former monopolistic States are transformed into locations that must compete with others for goods and services. The regulatory competition for public goods creates incentives to improve performance and ensures that governmental initiative really responds to citizens preferences.[157]

If the above logic is applied on a global scale (within and outside the EU), the implication would be that competition among professionals due to less regulation

[155] Mankowski (n 92) 458–59 (footnotes in the quotation omitted).
[156] Muir Watt (n 153) 11.
[157] ibid 11–12.

and liberalisation of the market economy would lead to better service delivery for consumers and clients.

Third, the professional must be insulated from the risk of having the law of the country of destination (the place of performance) apply to him, where the law of the place of performance is hostile to his commercial transaction, or not sophisticated enough to meet the needs of his commercial transaction. In effect, foreign substantive law (of the law of the place of performance) may erode the commercial incentive of foreign trade.[158] In addition, if the professional is unfamiliar with the choice of law rules of a foreign country, and is unable to insist on a choice of law clause that protects its interest, it could lead to 'psychological trade barriers'.[159]

If the professional is in a position where he must do business in the country of destination (place of performance), and envisages that his law would not be applied, the professional may have to further insure himself from any potential legal or commercial risk of applying the law of the place of performance. This increase in transaction costs would ultimately have to be borne by the clients in other countries. In effect, the application of the law of the professional would forestall such a problem from arising. In this connection, the country-of-origin principle is also linked to a form of welfare economics that reduces the prices of goods and services for clients and consumers.[160]

In summation, the country-of-origin rule is a form of liberalisation of the free market economy both within and outside the EU, so that professionals can conduct their business freely, with little or no impediments that might arise from applying a choice of law rule that selects a foreign law to govern his transaction.

iii. Critique

The logic of the doctrine of country-of-origin principle as the basis for applying the doctrine of habitual residence of the characteristic performer is not without its weaknesses.

Before offering a critique of the country-of-origin principle, it must be noted that there has been very little academic attention devoted to the issue of the habitual residence of the characteristic performer (in EU choice of law rules) being a country-of-origin principle, at least in English language. For example Cuniberti and Mankowski, who explicitly draw this link, address the issue in not more than two pages. Other scholars who extensively draw the link between choice of law rules and the country-of-origin principle, do not expressly focus on the doctrine of habitual residence of the characteristic performer.[161] So one is found in an unenviable position where one has to critique a doctrine that has not been fully developed.

[158] Basedow (n 152) 1182.
[159] ibid 89.
[160] See s II.B.i of this chapter.
[161] Michaels (n 133); Muir Watt (n 153); Basedow (n 152).

A starting point for critiquing the country-of-origin principle is that the relationship between the EU law principle of country-of-origin and Article 4 of Rome I, and how any possible conflict between both provisions is to be resolved, is not so clear, and firmly established.[162] If the logic of the country-of-origin principle is regarded as valid, it would mean that Member State courts that have applied the escape clause under EU choice of law rules have actually been violating EU law. If the country of origin is an expression of the supremacy of EU law, then a corresponding rationale must be provided to justify why the escape clause should be allowed to apply, where the habitual residence of the characteristic performer is not sufficiently connected with the contract. In other words, if the goal of proximity is less subordinate to the country-of-origin rule, then another equally important EU norm must be generated as a justification for applying Article 4(3) of Rome I. Scholars who support the doctrine of country-of-origin principle do not provide an answer to this problem.

Classifying the doctrine of habitual residence of the characteristic performer as one that is based on the country-of-origin principle appears to abusively conflate two concepts that are not the same. The country-of-origin principle does not appear to be a private international law rule that designates the applicable law, as is the case of the doctrine of habitual residence of the characteristic performer.[163] As Michaels rightly submits 'The country-of-origin principle does not simply designate the applicable law. Rather, it restricts applicability of the law designated by traditional private international law rules if they are more restrictive than those of the country of origin.'[164] More importantly, the legitimacy of the doctrine of country-of-origin in the context of the doctrine of the habitual residence of the characteristic performer as a choice of law rule is open to question, despite its conceptually seductive appeal to the eyes of some scholars. Given that the theory has a Swiss origin, it is not consistent with the idea that it aims at satisfying EU federal ideals, since Switzerland is not a Member of the EU, and Schnitzer wrote before the EU even existed.

It must be asked: to what extent was the country-of-origin principle a guiding factor in utilising the concept of the habitual residence of the characteristic performer in EU choice of law rules? The answer is that legislative history is silent on this. It is trite that legislative history, including the explanatory memorandum and discussions of the expert group is a legitimate way to ascertain the intention of the EU legislator.[165]

In particular, the Guiliano-Lagarde report which provides a rationale for the application of the concept of habitual residence of the characteristic performer does not mention the country-of-origin principle.[166] In addition, some scholars

[162] See generally Michaels (n 133).
[163] Ibid 207.
[164] ibid 208. See also 211–12.
[165] See M McParland, *The Rome I Regulation on the Law Applicable to Contractual Obligations* (Oxford, Oxford University Press, 2015) 129–32, [3.68]–[3.78] for a detailed treatment.
[166] (n 6) 20–21.

who conducted a thorough and detailed analysis of the legislative history of the Rome Convention and Rome I do not mention the country-of-origin principle as the reason why the EU legislator opted for the doctrine of the habitual residence of the characteristic performer.[167]

Given that the country-of-origin principle is such an important issue in EU law, it would have been so easy for the EU legislator to explicitly provide for it, at least in the Recitals to Rome I. In effect, there should be no room for speculation as to whether such an important principle is the overriding goal of Article 4 of Rome I. In reality, it might be that the country-of-origin principle was not in the mind of the EU legislator or those who negotiated the drafting of the EU choice of law rules in determining the applicable law in the absence of choice.

The country-of-origin principle might have legitimacy in other fields of EU law such as freedom of establishment of companies, and the directive on electronic commerce,[168] but its legitimacy under Article 4 does not rest on solid grounds. The EU choice of law rules in determining the applicable law in the absence of choice is historically founded on the principle of proximity.

Assuming for the purpose of argument that the country-of-origin principle has legitimacy in Article 4 of Rome I, there are problems that arise.

First, the logic of the country-of-origin principle does not sit comfortably with the principle of proximity.[169] A professional in a tax haven with little or no connections with the country of destination (the place of performance) would have his law applied. As some scholar aptly observes:

> For example, the Court of Justice in *Centros* obliged Denmark to recognise a company as English although, indisputably, all relevant connections pointed to Denmark: the company had been set up by two Danes for their Danish business, the only contact to England, apart from the registration, was the formal address for the company as a friend's place.[170]

If the goal of Article 4 of Rome I is the country-of-origin principle, then the principle of proximity should be done away with since the country-of-origin is not consistent with the principle of proximity.

Second, if the country-of-origin principle is such an important goal that the European legislator must give effect to it in the EU choice of law rules, there are a number of provisions which do not fit, such as consumer contracts. Under Article 6 of the Rome I, it is the habitual residence of the consumer that applies, rather than that of the professional. It must be queried: does this provision violate the EU country-of-origin principle then? Or does it show that the country-of-origin principle is not essential enough to control?

[167] McParland (n 165) [10.01]–[10.410].

[168] e-commerce directive of 2000 – Directive 2000/31/EC of the European Parliament and of the Council of 8 June 200 on certain legal aspects of information society services, in particular electronic commerce, in the Internal Market (Directive on electronic commerce), [2002] OJ L178/1.

[169] Michaels (n 133) 208, 232, 238.

[170] ibid 232.

Third, most international commercial contracts (such as contracts of sale and provision of services), which are the vehicle of freedom of movement will contain choice of law clauses. Such choice of law clauses would not always be the law of the professional. It must thus be queried: in cases where the parties choose a neutral law, and that law impedes the interest of the professional in legal proceedings, would the EU country-of-origin principle be applied to trump the principle of party autonomy? Or, again, does this show that the country-of-origin principle is not essential enough to control?[171]

Fourth, the idea that the country-of-origin principle leads to economic development also contains arguments that mirror the triumph of the law of the professional, which has been vigorously challenged and refuted in this chapter.[172] However, some points are worthy of mention here.

It should be queried: why should the law of the professional be arbitrarily chosen? The country-of-origin principle is inconsistent with the weaker party philosophy contained in the EU choice of law rules.[173] Moreover, the EU Member States do not operate a form of unbridled capitalism. In reality, the economy of EU States also implement social welfare policies for consumers, employees, and other categories of weaker parties. Thus, 'Critics of the country-of-origin principle point to a vital state interest in protecting the (social) welfare of its own citizens against individual interests of suppliers; they oppose what they see as undue emphasis on market liberalism over the social welfare state.'[174] In addition, the place of performance should normally play a better role in protecting the interest of its inhabitants (especially consumers) against sub-standard goods and services that might originate from exporters of goods and services.

The emphasis on the country-of origin principle strips the place of performance of its regulatory function in international commercial transactions. Arguments that the professional should not be deprived of an advantage he acquires from the law of his home country, so as to enhance competition among professionals, underlies an approach that supports under-regulation. This approach might impinge on the interest of local professionals located in the country of destination (the place of performance), if a foreign professional is allowed to take benefit of his own law, rather than the law of the place of performance. This state of affairs could be regarded as unfortunate especially for developing countries whose local professionals are at a disadvantage, when compared to the exporter of goods and services from a developed foreign country. Local professionals in developing

[171] Indeed, it is worth noting that, where secondary legislation specifically endorses the country of origin principle, it then goes on to create an exclusion for choice of law rules promoting freedom of choice: see, e.g., Annex to the Directive on electronic commerce, which creates a specific exception to the principle contained in Article 3(1) of Rome I for 'the freedom of the parties to choose the law applicable to their contract'. A similar exception applies to 'contractual obligations concerning consumer contracts'.

[172] See s II.B.i of this chapter.

[173] See s II.B.iii of this chapter.

[174] Michaels (n 133) 232.

countries might thus find it difficult to thrive against foreign professionals of developed countries that export goods and services. In the long run, this hurts the economic interests of developing countries.

Finally, the idea that applying the law of the professional leads to economic development is one that requires empirical evidence to prove. Admittedly, free movement of persons, goods, services and capital enhances economic development and free trade. However, the idea that the application of the law of the place of performance would be an impediment to economic development is a rather bold and extravagant claim that must be proved by empirical evidence. On the contrary, some scholars have submitted, inter alia, based on empirical evidence that in England, the deployment of the escape clause to displace the rule of the habitual residence of the characteristic performer is one that economically promotes England as a centre for international commercial litigation, and also does not frustrate the aims of EU choice of law integration.[175] In effect, even if the country-of-origin is such an important EU principle, it should be able to tolerate the application of the law of the place of performance.

III. Escape Clause and the Place of Performance

One may ask: if the principal proposal in this book is accepted, should the escape clause under a revised Article 4(3) of Rome I be deleted or dispensed with? In the alternative, would it be acceptable to retain the current rule, and explicitly give the place of performance special significance under a revised Article 4(3) of Rome I?

Chapter 2 of this book included a historical analysis on the tension between Article 4(2) and 4(5) of the Rome Convention, especially in the context of the significance of the place of performance as a connecting factor.[176] It is not the purpose of this chapter to repeat what was said in chapter two.

In this chapter what will be considered is first, whether, the escape clause should be retained in a revised version of Article 4 of Rome I, if the principal proposal in this book is accepted; and second, whether in the alternative special significance should be explicitly given to the place of performance under a new recital that interprets Article 4(3) of Rome I.

A. Should the Escape Clause be Retained under a Revised Version of Article 4 of Rome I Regulation?

The escape clause in Article 4(3) of Rome I provides that where 'it is clear from all the circumstances of the case that the contract is manifestly more closely

[175] See generally Fons (n 103).
[176] See ch 2, s III.

connected with a country other than that indicated in paragraphs 1 or 2, the law of that other country shall apply'.

In this section, three issues will be discussed. First, a theoretical exposition will be made on the significance of the escape clause. Second, it will be discussed why the logic of the current rule does not sit well with application of the escape clause, and why the place of characteristic performance is a preferred principal connecting factor. Third, and more importantly, a justification will be made to retain the escape clause despite the principal proposal in this book.

It is important to make a theoretical exposition on the significance of the escape clause. This is important because it would lead one to consider whether it is necessary to retain the escape clause if the principal proposal in this book is accepted, or whether the current rule could be retained, but the place of performance should then be given special significance under a revised Article 4(3) of Rome I Regulation.

Ideally the European legislator would have wished that there was a connecting factor that perfectly and absolutely determined the applicable law in the absence of choice for commercial contracts. In other words, the European legislator would have preferred a connecting factor that solves choice of law issues for international commercial contracts perfectly without the need of an escape clause.[177] Such a connecting factor would perfectly and absolutely satisfy the goals of certainty, predictability and that of proximity at the same time. In addition, it would always be easy to determine and apply. Does such a connecting factor exist? Is the place of characteristic performance a perfect connecting factor? Why do we need an escape clause?

An escape clause is a provision inserted in a legal instrument to supplement or cure the defect in the principal connecting factor, especially where the law designated by the principal connecting factor has little or no connection with the dispute to be resolved before the court. Escape clauses honour the claim that no legal instrument is perfect and strive to improve the instrument by giving the court the discretion to locate the law of a country that is more or most closely connected with the subject-matter. In effect, escape clauses exist in choice of law because there is no connecting factor that is a perfect answer to the determination of the applicable law in the absence of choice.

The escape clause honours the claim that rigid choice of law rules would not always satisfy the requirement of proximity. In effect, the role of the escape clause is to introduce flexibility in the settlement of the conflict of laws and to best designate the country or legal system with the closest connection to the dispute in commercial contracts: usually the place where the commercial contract is geographically most concentrated.

Despite the advantage of flexibility and proximity offered by the escape clause, it has been demonstrated that if the escape clause is not properly tamed, it could

[177] See Rome I Proposal (n 136) 6.

breed uncertainty, as was the case in the relationship between Article 4(2) and 4(5) of the Rome Convention.[178]

In reality, the rules in Article 4(1) and (2) of Rome I designate the habitual residence of the characteristic performer for most commercial contracts. If as it has been opined in this book, that the habitual residence of the characteristic performer, without a corroboration of other significant connecting factors, does not satisfy the requirement of proximity, then there is a failure in the logic in relation to the connection between the rules in Article 4(1) and (2), and Article 4(3) of Rome I. We have a situation where the principal connecting factor, usually the habitual residence of the characteristic performer, does not result in proximity, and the escape clause is directed to the principle of proximity.

One of the conditions for the proper functioning of the European choice of law rules is that the general criterion or connecting factor used in determining the applicable law should on its own have sufficiently strong connection to the dispute.[179] In fact, if this criterion or connecting factor is most often sufficient to designate the country or legal system having the closest links with the dispute, in theory and practice, it will only be rarely displaced by the application of the escape clause.[180] But if the criterion or connection factor turns out to be generally weak, the danger is that the escape clause is utilised very often, and the escape clause which should normally be an exception, becomes the rule.[181] In other words, if the principal connecting factor or criterion is generally weak in indicating the principle of proximity, the escape clause would frequently be applied to determine the applicable law in the absence of choice.

This is another good reason why it is advocated that the principal connecting factor under a revised Article 4 of Rome I should be the place of characteristic performance. Given that the place of characteristic performance, on its own, generally satisfies the criteria of proximity, and is a more suitable connecting factor for international commercial contracts when compared to other connecting factors, if the proposal in this book is accepted, the escape clause would rarely be applied because the application of the place of characteristic performance would frequently satisfy the requirements of proximity. In other words, the escape clause would rarely be invoked to cure any potential defect of the place of characteristic performance in the search for the country or legal system that is most closely connected to a commercial contract.

It must be stressed that the escape clause is a necessity and should not be dispensed with despite the principal proposal made in this book. Though this book has strongly advanced the view that the place of characteristic performance should be the principal connecting factor for commercial contracts under a revised

[178] See s III of ch 2.
[179] Cuniberti (n 125).
[180] ibid.
[181] ibid.

Rome I, it is by no means perfect. In unusual cases, the place of characteristic performance might not appropriately satisfy the requirement of proximity.

There are at least three scenarios where the place of characteristic performance becomes a weak connecting factor. First, if the professional in an unusual case equally[182] carries out his obligations in several countries, it would be difficult to identify the main place of performance. If the main place of performance is identified in such a case, it would likely be a weak connecting factor because the performance is spread across different countries, and also connected to such countries. By way of comparative analysis, in the United States' conflict of laws, Section 188(2) of the Second Restatement[183] rightly provides that 'the place of performance can bear little weight in the choice of the applicable law when … performance by a party is to be divided more or less equally among two or more states …'[184]

Second, if other connections point to another country other than the place of characteristic performance, it would be obvious that the place of characteristic performance does not satisfy the requirement of proximity. Assuming for example in an unusual case, the professional and client are both nationals of country X and habitually resident in country X as well, for a contract to be performed in country Y. The place of negotiation and conclusion of the contract, the currency of payment, and business language of the contract are all connected exclusively to country X. In effect, all the connections are with country X except the place of characteristic performance which is connected to country Y. This would be an obvious case where the place of characteristic performance in country X does not appropriately satisfy the requirement of proximity when compared to country Y.

Third, if the contracts are very closely related, the place of characteristic performance might be displaced in favour of another law that is very closely related to the commercial contract in question. A classic example is a contract of guarantee, where the guarantor undertakes to perform the obligation of another party under the principal contract. If the place of characteristic performance of the guarantee obligation leads to a law that is inconsistent with the applicable law (in the absence of choice) governing the main contract, this would be an ideal situation where the court can apply the law governing the main contract to the contract of guarantee, so as to reach a coherent solution between the parties.[185] This is where

[182] More often than not in situations where the professional carries out his obligations in several countries, there would usually be a country where his principal obligations are concentrated in.

[183] Restatement (Second) Conflict of Laws, 1971 (commentary section).

[184] It also provides that the place of performance can bear little weight if 'at the time of contracting it is either uncertain or unknown'. While I agree with this statement of the law, on the basis that the place of performance would be a weak connecting factor in such circumstances, it is submitted that this statement of the law is divorced from reality. In other words, situations where the place of performance would be unknown or uncertain at the time of contracting hardly ever arises in practice.

[185] See generally *M Serge Fourez v SA Residence Le Verseuil* cited in V Parisot, 'Note sous Civ 1ère 12 octobre 2011, no 10-19517' (2012) *Journal de Droit International*, Comm 20, 1335 (Convention de Rome du 19 juin 1980 sur la loi applicable aux obligations contractuelles – loi applicable au cautionnement). See also CSA Okoli, 'The Significance of the Doctrine of Accessory Allocation as a Connecting Factor under Article 4 of Rome I Regulation' (2013) 9 *Journal of Private International Law* 449.

the current Recital 20 to Rome I would be useful in displacing the place of characteristic performance. In effect, a single law should be applied decisively to a very closely related contract(s) where the application of the law of place of characteristic performance leads to an incoherent solution.

In summation, despite the proposal in this book, the escape clause should not be dispensed with, but retained to cater for unusual situations where the place of characteristic performance does not appropriately satisfy the requirement of proximity.

B. Alternative Proposal: Giving Special Significance to the Place of Performance under Article 4 of Rome I Regulation

A potential counter-argument to the principal proposal is that the approach of the European legislator under Article 4(3) of Rome I makes the conditions for the application of the escape clause stringent, by inter alia replacing the phrase '*more* closely connected' (under Article 4(5) of the Rome Convention), with '*manifestly* more closely connected'. Thus, the escape clause would be applied rarely. In effect, the counter submission would be that the argument advancing the view that the escape clause would be rarely applied, if the place of characteristic performance, is utilised as the principal connecting factor crumbles.

This counter-argument necessitates a consideration of two issues. First, it would be necessary to consider whether the operation of the escape clause under Article 4(3) of Rome I, and the significance of the place of performance in relation thereto is clear. Second, it would be considered whether in the alternative, the current rules could be retained, and the place of performance explicitly given special significance under a new recital to Rome I.

i. Operation of Article 4(3) of Rome I Regulation

The conditions for the operation of Article 4(3) of Rome I are not so straightforward. There have been varied interpretations of Article 4(3), at least, in academic literature.[186] The approach to interpreting Article 4(3) would remain a matter of academic and judicial controversy until the CJEU makes a clear pronouncement on the conditions for the operation of Article 4(3). Certainly, the CJEU has interpreted

[186] J Fraser, 'Escape from Uncertainty: Article 4(3) of Rome I Regulation' (2017) 7 *Southampton Student Law* Review 10; A Arzandeh, 'The Law Governing International Contractual Disputes in the Absence of Express Choice by the Parties' (2015) 4 *Lloyd's Maritime and Commercial Law Quarterly* 525; Fons (n 103); CSA Okoli and GO Arishe, 'The Operation of the Escape Clauses in the Rome Convention, Rome I Regulation and Rome II Regulation' (2012) 8 *Journal of Private International Law* 513; A Dickinson, 'Rebuttable Assumptions (*ICF* v *Balkenende*)' (2010) *Lloyd's Maritime and Commercial Law Quarterly* 27; Magnus (n 68); Z Tang, 'Law Applicable in the Absence of Choice – The New Article 4 of the Rome I Regulation' (2008) 71 *Modern Law Review* 785.

the relationship between Article 4(2) and 4(5) of the Rome Convention,[187] but in view of some changes in the structure and language of Article 4(3) of Rome I, a new interpretation by the CJEU is definitely desired.

It is submitted that there are four ways in which the relationship between the relationship between Article 4(1) and (2) and Article 4(3) of Rome I can be interpreted.[188]

The first approach is that the relationship between Article 4(1) and (2) and Article 4(3) favours a functionally weak presumption approach that gives weight to other significant connecting factors such as the place of performance in displacing the principal connecting factor of the habitual residence of the characteristic performer. The opinion is premised on the fact that it is only the structure of Rome I that has changed and not really its content – it is substantially similar to the Rome Convention. Thus, some English judges still regard the fixed rules under Article 4(1) and (2) as functionally weak because it is liable to be displaced by other significant connecting factors such as the place of performance.[189] If the weak presumption theory is applied, it might be argued that the place of performance should be given special significance and could easily trump Article 4(3) in practice because the habitual residence of the characteristic performer without a corroboration of other connecting factors is liable to be easily displaced. In other words, the place of performance would better designate the country that is manifestly more closely connected to a commercial contract. Thus, Collins et al submit that:

> It is likely that the escape clause in the Regulation may most usefully be employed in those cases where the place of performance differs from the habitual residence or place of business of the party who is identified in the specific cases in Art 4(1), or who is required to effect the characteristic performance of the contract in the context of Art 4(2).[190]

The second approach is that the relationship between Article 4(1) and (2) and Article 4(3) favours the doctrine of commercial expectations, which gives significant weight to connecting factors such as the place of performance. Emphasis is also placed on Recitals 20 and 21 to Rome I, which provide that in order to determine the law of the country with which the contract is most closely connected, account should be taken, among other things, of 'whether the contract in question has a very close relationship with another contract or contracts'. Fentiman submits that the 'reason is important. It avoids the commercially detrimental result that related contracts are governed by different laws. Implicitly commercial effectiveness animates the search for the applicable law.'[191] If doctrine of commercial

[187] *Intercontainer* (n 67); C-305/13, *Haeger & Schmidt GmbH v Mutuelles du Mans assurances IARD (MMA IARD) and others*, EU:C:2014:2320.

[188] For the relationship between Article 4(2) and 4(5) of the Rome Convention, see ch 2, s III.

[189] *Bill Kenwright Ltd v Flash Entertainment FZ LLC* [2016] EWHC 1951 (QB) [38].

[190] Collins (n 66) 1826-3, [32-080].

[191] R Fentiman, 'The Significance of Close Connection' in J Ahern and W Binchy (eds), *The Rome II Regulation on the Law Applicable to Non-Contractual-Obligations: A New International Litigation Regime* (The Hague, Martinus Nijhoff 2009) 85, 95.

expectations is applied, it could be argued that the expectation of the parties is that a commercial contract is geared towards performance, so that the fixed rules in Article 4(1) and (2) might be displaced where it does not coincide with the place of performance.

For reasons earlier advanced on the inappropriateness of using the weak presumption approach and theory of commercial expectations in the Rome Convention, it is opined here that their textual legitimacy in Rome I is open to question.[192]

The third approach is that the intermediary approach is favoured under Rome I, and strong reasons are advanced for this opinion.[193] First, the rules in Articles 4(1) and 4(2) are aimed at legal certainty and foreseeability in the relationship between parties to a commercial transaction, while the escape clause in Article 4(3) retains a degree of flexibility to displace the rules in Articles 4(1) and 4(2) where the country is manifestly more closely connected with the contract. Thus, it represents a balance between requirements of legal certainty and flexibility as handed down by the CJEU, which is what the intermediary approach aims at. Second, Article 4 of Rome I is said to honour the claim contained in Recital 16 to Rome I which has the objective of legal certainty and foreseeable rules, while retaining 'a degree of discretion to determine the law that is most closely connected' to the contractual relationship in the absence of a choice made by the parties. Third, it is also argued that the strong presumption approach is

> not even consistent with the much tighter wording of the Rome I Regulation because it is possible for the law indicated by the presumption (rule under Rome I) to have 'real significance' and yet for another law to be 'manifestly' more closely connected to the contract.[194]

If this approach is applied, the place of performance might retain some special significance depending on the circumstances of the case.

Given the history surrounding the abuse of the escape clause under the Rome Convention by some Member State courts, it is likely that a form of strong presumption approach has been favoured by the European legislator, with some limited flexibility. Thus, it has been held that 'Article 4(3) deliberately places a high hurdle in the way of a party seeking to displace the primary rule.'[195] Second, it might be that the escape clause does not need to be resorted to very often as Articles 4(1) and 4(2) may often have sufficient connection to the dispute, if it is corroborated by other connecting factors that are not the place of performance, to justify its application. Third, the use of the phrases 'clear from all the circumstances of the case' and 'manifestly more closely connected' in Article 4(3) indicate that the

[192] See ch 2, s III.
[193] O Lando and PA Nielsen, 'The Rome I Proposal' (2007) 3 *Journal of Private International Law* 29, 38; Tang (n 186) 798; Beaumont and Mc Eleavy (n 116) 475.
[194] Beaumont and Mc Eleavy (n 116) 475.
[195] *BNP Paribas SA v Anchorage Capital Europe LLP & Ors* [2013] EWHC 3073 (Comm) [64].

escape clause is an exceptional remedy that is to be rarely utilised in determining the law of a country that applies to a contract between the parties in the absence of choice.[196] As Popplewell J holds:

> The text and architecture of Article 4 of the Rome I Regulation is very different from that of the Rome Convention. In particular, the test is no longer expressed as one of closest connection; the test is that contained in the rules set out in Article 4.1 and 4.2, which are no longer expressed as presumptions or as being subject to the closest connection test; and the closest connection test has become an 'escape clause' to be applied only where it is *clear* that the connection is *manifestly* closer to a country other than that dictated by the tests in Article 4.1 and 4.2, so that they are to be disregarded. The word 'clear' reflects what the ECJ had already said was the effect of Article 4.5 of the Rome Convention in the Interfrigo case, but the word 'manifestly' suggests a more stringent standard than before, as does the elevation of the criteria in Article 4.1 and 4.2 to tests from mere presumptions of closest connection. The new language and structure suggests a higher threshold, which requires that the cumulative weight of the factors connecting the contract to another country must clearly and decisively outweigh the desideratum of certainty in applying the relevant test in Article 4.1 and 4.2.[197]

Furthermore, the CJEU has interpreted the word 'manifestly' to mean that it 'ought to operate only in exceptional cases'.[198] It is possible that the CJEU might interpret Article 4(3) the same way.[199]

Thus, it is likely that the position under Article 4(3) is that the escape clause should not be utilised if the connecting factors with the law of another country are of similar weight to those indicated by the rules in Articles 4(1) or 4(2). The preponderance of other connecting factors required in displacing the rules in Articles 4(1) or 4(2) must be overwhelming or very significant. If this approach is adopted, the place of performance under Article 4 would have marginal significance when compared to the fixed rules under Article 4(1) and (2).[200]

In summation, it is not quite clear what interpretation would be given to the relationship between Article 4(1) and (2) and Article 4(3). Assuming, a form of strong presumption approach is favoured by the CJEU, it would mean that the place of performance has marginal significance under Article 4(3).

[196] See the Explanatory memorandum from the Commission, accompanying the Proposal for Rome II, COM (2003) 427 final (Explanatory Memorandum) 12.

[197] *Molton Street Capital LLP v Shooters Hill Capital Partners LLP, Odeon Capital Group LLC* [2015] EWHC 3419 [94]. In the context of Article 4(3) of Rome II, (which is similar to Article 4(3) of Rome I) it has also been held that the escape clauses therein is an exceptional remedy: *Fortress Value Recovery Fund I LLC & Ors v Blue Skye Special Oppurtunities Fund L.P & Ors* [2013] EWHC 14 (Comm) [47]; *Stylianou v Toyoshima* [2013] EWHC 2188 (QB) [61], [64]; *Moreno v The Motor Insurer's Bureau* (2015) EWCA Civ 379 [47] (Gilbart J) – 'not generally be disapplied'; *OPO v MLA* [2014] EWCA Civ 1277 [112] – 'high standard'; *Winrow v Hemphill* [2014] EWHC 3164 (QB) [42].

[198] C-78/95, *Hendrikman v Magenta Druck & Verlag*, EU:C:1996:380 [23]. See also C-7/98, *Krombach v Bamberski*, EU:C:2000:164 [44]. The ECJ in these cases was concerned inter alia with interpretation of the phrase 'manifestly contrary to public policy' under Article 27(1) of the Brussels Convention (now Article 45(1)(a) of Brussels Ia).

[199] See also Recital 7 to Rome I.

[200] See also *First Laser Ltd v Fujian Enterprises (Holdings) Co* [2012] HKCU 1397 [55]–[56].

This state of affairs begs the question: if a commercial contract, without more, generally has no significant connection with the country or legal system of the habitual residence of the characteristic performer, in the alternative, why should there not be a clearer indication as to what 'manifestly more closely connected' means, such as giving special significance to the place of performance under Article 4(3)? This issue is addressed in the next section.

ii. Alternative Proposal

This section is an alternative proposal to the main proposal of this book, and it is that: if the present connecting factor must be kept, that the place of performance should be explicitly given special significance under a revised Article 4(3) of Rome I (through the recitals).

If the relationship between Article 4(1) and (2) and Article 4(3) of Rome I is very clear to the effect that it supports a form of strong presumption approach, then it might be a good reason (though not conclusive or decisive) to accept the view that the principal proposal in this book should not be accepted. Even if the principal argument in this book crumbles, given the considerable significance of the place of performance in commercial contracts, it would be considered whether the place of performance should have special significance under Article 4(3). The implication would thus be that an alternative argument can be made for the place of performance to be explicitly given special significance under a revised Article 4(3) (through the recitals).

The current Article 4(3) does not explicitly give special significance to the place of performance in displacing Article 4(1) and (2). The only connecting factor that is explicitly given special significance is the doctrine of accessory allocation or infection.[201]

Given that the place of performance best indicates the principle of proximity when compared to the habitual residence of the characteristic performer, this necessitates an alternative consideration of whether express significance should be given to the place of performance under a revised Article 4(3). If this alternative proposal is accepted, it would mean that the place of performance plays a subsidiary role under Article 4(3) – a way of confirming whether or not the principal connecting factors in Article 4(1) and (2) sufficiently satisfy the principle of proximity on the facts of the case.

If the current position is that the place of performance has marginal significance when interpreting Article 4(3), such a position does not tally with the principle of proximity.

In this connection, the idea that the rule of the habitual residence of the characteristic performer leads to certainty because the escape clause is applied stringently is deceptive. The 'certainty' is really a dubious one. It is a situation where the

[201] Recital 20 to Rome I.

European legislator mandates the decision maker to apply the principal connecting factor of the habitual residence of the characteristic performer even though it would generally not satisfy the requirement of proximity when compared to the place of performance. Since the habitual residence of the characteristic performer is a weak but is not an irrelevant connecting factor, such a situation might lead the decision maker to apply the escape clause very narrowly. It would lead to an unfortunate state of affairs where the place of performance might better indicate the country or legal system with a manifestly closer connection to a commercial contract, but the decision maker is inclined to preserve the principle of legal certainty, predictability and uniformity in applying Article 4(1) and (2).

In addition, Article 4 appears to expressly focus on legal certainty in judicial proceedings.[202] However, commercial certainty for international commercial actors is important as well.[203] It does not appear that the European legislators exclude the goals of commercial certainty.[204] International commercial persons might draft some of their contracts in a hurry, or not document their contracts properly, by not specifying for a choice of law clause. In such situations, it might generally be that if you ask an international business person what law should govern, he might expect that the law of the place where the characteristic performance is effected should govern, given that such performance is the relative crux of the contract. The law of the place of performance might generally give business efficacy to the parties' contract. Some of such international commercial persons would thus be surprised and disappointed that the habitual residence of one of parties, which might not have a genuine connection to the commercial contract, is the governing law.

Considering the significance the place of performance occupies in commercial transactions, it is surprising that the European legislator, in the alternative, did not explicitly give the place of performance special significance under Article 4(3) of Rome I. Thus, it is alternatively proposed that the fixed rules under Article 4(1) and (2) of Rome I could be retained, including the rule of the habitual residence of the characteristic performer as a connecting factor, and explicitly make the place of performance a special connecting factor that can be taken into account in displacing the fixed rules.

As earlier stated in chapter two, during the period of negotiations for a Rome I, the Financial Markets Law Committee (FMLC), and UK proposed that the place of characteristic performance should be explicitly given special significance under Article 4(3), but the European legislator did not accept this proposal.[205] It is thus opined (in the alternative) that under a revised Article 4(3), a recital

[202] See Recital 6 and 16 to Rome I.

[203] Financial Markets Law Committee, 'Legal Assessment of the Conversion of the Rome Convention to a Community Instrument and the Provisions of the Proposed Rome I Regulations' – European Commission Final Proposal for a Regulation on the Law Applicable to Contractual Obligations (Rome I) (2006) 121(3) 12–14 www.fmlc.org/Documents/April06Issue121.pdf.

[204] Fons (n 103).

[205] See ch 2, s IV.

should be included, which expressly takes into account the place of characteristic performance.

A potential counter-argument might be that Recital 20 to Rome I already provides sufficient indication on how Article 4(3) should be interpreted. This counter-argument is simplistic.

Recital 20 is not really aimed as satisfying the requirement of geographical proximity.[206] The principal aim of Recital 20 is to apply a single law to commercial contracts that are very closely related, which leads to a coherent solution in determining the rights and obligation of the parties. In effect, it avoids a form of judge-made *dépeçage* so that different laws are not applied to very closely related commercial contracts. Recital 20 thereby leads to legal and commercial certainty in applying a single law to disputes, and at the same time combines flexibility by giving the decision maker the discretion to apply Article 4(3) in appropriate circumstances. It is a rule that suits the convenience of judges and lawyers, so that they don't have to worry about reconciling potentially conflicting laws to commercial contracts that are very close, which leads to sound administration of justice. At best, Recital 20 satisfies the requirement of commercial (not geographical) proximity, by applying a single law to ensure that the risks of the parties are allocated consistently, and their transaction costs are reduced.

Moreover, there would be a significant number of cases where very closely related contracts are not in issue, and in such cases, the place of performance might be a suitable candidate to specially consider in deciding whether or not to displace Article 4(1) and (2).

In subscribing to this alternative proposal, this book has been guided by the following questions: is the place of performance to be simply taken into account in interpreting the escape clause or is it one of special significance? If the place of performance is simply one of the factors to be taken into account in interpreting the escape clause would the goals of proximity and flexibility be met in determining the country or legal system that is manifestly more closely connected to a commercial transaction? If the place of performance is given special significance in displacing Article 4(1) and (2), would the goal of legal certainty, predictability and uniformity in judicial proceedings be met in determining the applicable law in the absence of choice under Article 4? Would attributing the place of performance with special significance make the escape clause truly exceptional?

It is opined that this alternative proposal would be better than the current law because decision makers would be more courageous to apply the law of the place of performance, where the rules in Article 4(1) and (2) are not manifestly more closely connected to a commercial contract than the place of performance. The current rule might make decision makers timid or unsure whether to apply the law of the place of performance, if it is manifestly more closely connected to a contract. In effect, under the current rule, decision makers might substantially interpret

[206] cf Okoli (n 185) 478–79.

Article 4(3) to mean that the only condition on which Article 4(3) should apply is where Article 4(1) and (2) does not have a genuine connection to the commercial contract, thereby making the escape clause and the potential significance of the place of performance extinct.

In addition, the alternative proposal in this book would make the escape clause one that truly balances the requirement of legal and commercial certainty and flexibility, as the current rule appears to tilt too much on the side of legal certainty. The goals of proximity would also be met and clearly articulated. The decision maker would be in a better position to weigh the significance of the principal connecting factor in Article 4(1) and (2) and satisfy himself as to whether or not a genuine case has been made for applying the escape clause, (which might be the place of performance) in order to satisfy the requirement of proximity.

Another alternative argument could be that a more pragmatic way to make the place of performance have special significance under Article 4(3) is that the CJEU, if the issue arises, should make a pronouncement that also takes into account the significance to be given to connecting factors in interpreting Article 4(3), such as the place of performance. Thus, pending a potential revision of Article 4, the CJEU might specifically address this issue and fill the gap, by giving special significance to the place of performance. Arguments which might persuade the CJEU to give special significance to the place of performance under the current Article 4(3) might include: the place of performance is objective, satisfies the requirement of legal and commercial proximity; it is of absolute significance under Article 9(3) of Rome I in respect of foreign country overriding mandatory rules; it is of special significance under Article 7(1) of Brussels Ia; it is of special significance in Article 4(1)(c) of Rome I; it is of special significance under Article 5(1) of Rome I; it is of special significance under Article 8(1) of Rome I; and it is also of special significance under Article 12(2) of Rome I. These reasons might motivate the CJEU to give special significance to the place of performance under Article 4(3) of Rome I. The CJEU would then hold that the place of performance under Article 4(3) may have special significance, if it is exclusively or substantially performed in one country; if Article 4(1) and (2) is of no real significance in the circumstances of the case, or is not corroborated by other connecting factors.

Despite the attractive views advanced on the CJEU giving special significance to the place of performance under the current Article 4(3), such a decision would amount to usurping the powers of the European legislator. Given the history of Article 4, particularly the fact that the UK, during the negotiation period, expressly made a suggestion to give the place of performance special significance under Article 4(3) of Rome I Proposal, but the proposal was not included in the final version of Article 4(3), it is apparent that the place of performance under the current rule should be considered alongside other connecting factors, without generally having any special weight.

In summation, it is alternatively proposed that the European legislator expressly gives the place of performance special significance under a revised Article 4(3) of Rome I.

IV. Moving Towards the Place of Characteristic Performance: Some Issues

The principal proposal in the preceding sections demonstrated why the weaknesses of the place of performance as a connecting factor can be remedied by relying on the characteristic obligation. The idea is that it is preferable to isolate the characteristic obligation, and designate it as the principal connecting factor for commercial contracts, rather than the habitual residence of the characteristic performer. In other words, utilising the solution of the place of characteristic performance is a better way to remedy the defect of the place of performance as a connecting factor, when compared to utilising the habitual residence of the characteristic performer.

If the principal proposal in this book is accepted, one cannot ignore the possibility that issues might arise in practice relating to how the concept of characteristic obligation applies as a choice of law rule.

It might be argued that the problem of identifying the characteristic obligation exists under the current rule, that is irrespective of the proposal to rely on the place of characteristic performance rather than the habitual residence of the party providing the characteristic performance. Thus, focusing on the concept of the place of characteristic performance is not so significant.

In reality, given that the concept of *habitual residence* of the characteristic performer is the main focus of Article 4(1) and (2) of Rome I, rather than the *place* of characteristic performance, the individual determination of the characteristic obligation may have been neglected more by lawyers and judges under the current rule.[207] In effect, if the principal proposal in this book is accepted, in practice the determination of the concept of place of characteristic performance might arise before the court more often when interpreting a revised Article 4 of Rome I. It is thus significant to address some issues that might arise from the concept of place of characteristic obligation.

A. Identifying the Characteristic Obligation

Identifying an autonomous and uniform definition of the meaning of 'characteristic obligation' would likely reduce the problems of uncertainty, and lack of uniformity. Also, utilising the concept of characteristic obligation helps to reduce the problems of determining the performance of the obligation in question and the *place* where the performance is effected. If Member State courts were to adopt their domestic or substantive private international law approaches in defining the concept of characteristic obligation, there would be the potential threat of uncertainty and lack of uniformity.

[207] Collins (n 66) 1822; Güneysu-Güngör (n 123) 179.

Given the fact that the concept of characteristic obligation for commercial contracts has been in existence under the EU choice of law rules since 1980, there is no good reason why it should cause so much controversy as to its application in practice. It has also been rightly submitted that 'The difficulties surrounding the notion of characteristic performance may, however, be overstated. The vast majority of contracts are simple contracts of sale or contracts for the provision of services in return for money', where the characteristic performer is easy to determine.[208] Some other scholars similarly submit that:

> One should not allow the ten percent of cases where the principle of characteristic performance does not provide a solution to become inefective [*sic*] with regard to the 'remainder', *ie* not less than 90% of the cases where the principle provides a solution[209]

Notwithstanding, for the purpose of being exhaustive, it is significant to address the concept of the identification of the characteristic performance.

In determining the concept of characteristic obligation, guidance may generally be sought from the Giuliano-Lagarde Report to the effect that:

> Identifying the characteristic performance of a contract obviously presents no difficulty in the case of unilateral contracts. By contrast, in bilateral (reciprocal) contracts whereby the parties undertake mutual reciprocal performance, the counter-performance by one of the parties in a modern economy usually takes the form of money. This is not, of course, the characteristic performance of the contract. It is the performance for which the payment is due, ie depending on the type of contract, the delivery of goods, the granting of the right to make use of an item of property, the provision of a service, transport, insurance, banking operations, security, etc., which usually constitutes the centre of gravity and the socio-economic function of the contractual transaction.[210]

However, the Report should only be utilised as a guide. In other words, the Report should not be followed slavishly. The idea that payment of money *cannot* constitute characteristic performance is open to question.[211] In other words, the idea that the party who provides counter-performance for which payment is due is the characteristic performer is at best a general rule. There might be cases where the payment of money constitutes the characteristic performance of the contract. Thus, it has been held that where one is concerned with a settlement agreement,

> the mere payment of money by A to discharge a debt or sums due by way of compensation to B with no obligation on B save for forbearance to sue, the '*characteristic*

[208] J Hill, 'Jurisdiction in Matters Relating to a Contract under the Brussels Convention' (1995) 44 *International and Comparative Law Quarterly* 591, 612.

[209] Mankowski (n 92) 443.

[210] (n 6) 20.

[211] See also Hoffmann (n 92) 8; K Lipstein, 'Introduction: Conflicts Convention' in K Lipstein (ed), *Harmonization of Private International Law by the EEC* 1st edn (London, University of London Institute of Advanced Legal Studies, 1978) 8–9; Vischer (n 64) 28–29; Jaffey (1984) (n 92) 550–51; AE Von Overbeck, 'Contracts: The Swiss Draft Statute Compared with the EEC Convention' in P North (ed), *Contract Conflicts, The EEC Convention on the Law Applicable to Contractual Obligations: A Comparative Study* (Amsterdam, North-Holland Publishing Company, 1982) 269, 277; d'Oliviera (n 96) 306, 309–11, 326–27; Torremans (n 71) 734.

performance' of the settlement agreement may properly to be regarded as the payment of money.[212]

Also, some scholars have submitted that in instalment contracts the obligation of the buyer might be regarded as the characteristic performance.[213]

Also, utilising the test of 'centre of gravity' and 'socio-economic function' of the contract in identifying the characteristic performer is not very easy to understand and apply in practice. They are very esoteric terminologies. The 'centre of gravity' test inter alia looks more suited to the concept of principle of closest connection than that of identifying the characteristic performer.[214] The 'socio-economic' function test might require additional expertise in sociology and economics to determine who the characteristic performer is.[215]

Some of the identified weaknesses in the Report have led some scholars to conclude that identifying the characteristic performer is an arbitrary exercise.[216] This arbitrary exercise appears to be evident in *Atlantic Telecom GmbH, Noter*.[217] In that case a Scot's Court (Outer House, Court of Session) was faced with the determination of what was the characteristic performance for a loan contract advanced by Party A for repayment by Party B. The Court embarked on extensive research on the existing judicial and academic authorities on the subject at the time. On the one hand some of the authorities argued that it was the borrower that provided the characteristic performance because it performed the 'essence of the obligation', while other authorities argued that it was the lender that provided the characteristic performance because it provided a service in advancing a loan for which payment was due. In effect, excellent arguments were presented by both sides which demonstrated that the characteristic performance of a loan contract could either be that of the lender or the borrower. In the final analysis, Lord Brodie regarded the obligation of the lender as the characteristic performance but conceded some difficulty in reaching his decision thus:

> In favouring the view that the socio-economic function of loan has more to do with the provision of capital rather than its eventual return and payment for its use, I have not ignored junior counsel for the noter's argument to the effect that because it is the commercial activity of the recipient of the loan, promoted by the loan, that will generate the wherewithal to permit repayment, the socio-economic function of the loan should be regarded as falling within the borrower's jurisdiction rather than that of the lender. I pause to note that junior counsel acknowledged the lender's role as promoting the commercial activity of the borrower, but why I am not persuaded to adopt his analysis is that it appears to me that what junior counsel was describing and relying upon, was not the borrower's commercial activity as borrower under the loan, but rather his activities,

[212] *Bill* (n 189) [37] (italics in the original quotation).

[213] Hoffmann (n 92) 8; Vischer (1982) (n 64) 28; Jaffey (1984) (n 92) 550–51.

[214] Though Recital 19 to Rome I utilises the test of centre of gravity, it is submitted here that it is quite vague, given that it does not offer a clear guidance on how to identify the characteristic performer.

[215] See also d'Oliveria (n 96) 313.

[216] Lipstein (n 211) 8–9, d'Oliveria (n 96) 309, 326–27.

[217] *Atlantic Telecom GmbH, Noter* [2004] SLT 1031.

> as entrepreneur, when, financed by the loan, he has entered the market to do whatever he does in order to earn his profits. That will typically involve him in other contracts. For example, the borrower's activities may take the form of establishing the means to provide telecommunication services and providing these services. This may require the purchase of equipment, the acquisition of rights from regulatory authorities and the maintenance of transmission facilities. These activities will require the borrower to enter into a variety of contracts. The borrower's obligations under these contracts may constitute 'the centre of gravity' and the predominant 'socio-economic function of these contractual transactions'. However, I am not persuaded that one can attribute these activities which are likely to occur within a network of different contracts, to the initial contract of loan for the purpose of discovering what is its socio-economic function. The editors of Cheshire and North describe the report's assertion that 'the concept of characteristic performance essentially links the contract to the social and economic environment of which it will form part' as grandiose and hard to understand … I would not demur. Nevertheless, the Act points to the report as an aid to construction of the Convention. As I have already observed, it cannot be ignored. Agreeing with what I understand to be said by Professor Morse, when it comes to the contract of loan, it does not appear to me to be self-evident that it is either the lender or the borrower whose performance of his obligations is characteristic of the contract. I accept that the borrower's obligation of repayment can be said to be what it is that distinguishes loan from donation and in that sense may be said to be characteristic. On the other hand, if one wished to distinguish loan from, for example, hire, the obligation to repay (or return) might be a less useful criterion.[218]

There might be two ways to better identify the characteristic performance under a commercial contract. The first is to ask: who is the true professional? The second is to ask: who performs the relatively more important or complex obligation? The decision maker might find it easier to identify the characteristic obligation by first determining who the true professional under the contract is. In this connection, the true professional could be regarded as the person who does the obligation under the contract that gives the contract its name.[219] The emphasis on the word '*true*' professional underscores the point that in a commercial arrangement the contracting parties may all be professionals, but it is the party that performs the obligation that gives the contract its name that is the *true professional*.

However, the term 'professional' should not be given a rigid legal meaning, but a liberal commercial meaning that takes into account persons who are not officially licensed by law to carry out a particular obligation. In effect, the professional who does the 'job' under the contract could also be a private person,[220] and does

[218] ibid [52].

[219] P Lagarde, 'The European Convention on the Law Applicable to Contractual Obligations: An Apologia' (1981–82) 22 *Virginia Journal of International Law* 91, 97.

[220] '*Frequently the characteristic performance is the typical professional conduct of the party who carries it out.* This is however no prerequisite of the characteristic performance. A private person can also effect the characteristic performance, for instance by letting a car to another or by selling a right.' (Emphasis added) – U Magnus, 'Article 4 of Rome I Regulation' in U Magnus and P Mankowski, *European Commentaries on Private International Law* vol II (Munich, Sellier European Law Publishers, 2017) 315, [176].

not have to be officially licensed by law to carry out his obligations. In other words, the professional's performance constitutes the essence of the contract. It would usually be the professional that carries out the relatively more important, complex or complicated obligation. It is important to stress the word 'relatively', because the other party's obligation is by no means denigrated or downplayed. What is being done is that the contending parties' obligations have been compared and one is regarded as the characteristic obligation because its obligation is relatively more important, complex or complicated.

Thus, in *Atlantic Telecom*[221] instead of the difficulties identified in following the Giuliano-Lagarde report, the court may have regarded the lender as the professional because it is the lender's 'job' to loan money, and it is his profession that gives the contract its name. The criteria suggested in this book on identifying the characteristic obligation may also be applied to other contracts of sale, services, agency and guarantee contracts etc.

Fortunately, the seller and service provider are widely regarded as the characteristic performer, and the European legislator adopts this position under the Brussels regime and Rome I regime. Thus, in this regard, the place of performance of the characteristic obligation for a contract of sale is the place where the goods are delivered, or agreed to be delivered under the contract;[222] and the place of performance of the characteristic obligation for a contract for the provision of services is the place where the services are provided or agreed to be provided.[223]

The test of 'who is the professional' and 'who performs the relatively more important and complex obligation' could also be applied to complex contracts, where identifying the characteristic performance is controversial. For example in a distributorship and franchise contract, identifying the characteristic performance under the contract is controversial.[224]

The European legislator under Article 4(1)(e) and (f) of Rome I designates the applicable law as both the habitual residence of the franchisee and distributor

[221] (n 217).
[222] Article 7(1)(b) of Brussels Ia.
[223] Article 7(1)(b) of Brussels Ia.
[224] The CJEU in C-9/12 *Corman-Collins SA v La Maison Du Whisky SA*, EU:C:2013:860 [37] recently went as far as classifying an exclusive distributorship contract as a contract for the provision of services since the distributor is remunerated for distributing the goods of the manufacturer. For academic controversy on this subject see Collins 'Practical Implications in England of the EEC Convention on the Law Applicable to Contractual Obligations' in P North (ed), *Contract Conflicts, The EEC Convention on the Law Applicable to Contractual Obligations: A Comparative Study* (Amsterdam, North-Holland Publishing Company, 1982) 205, 209–10; Collins (n 71) 47–48; O Lando (1987) (n 4) 204; Lando (1996–97) (n 94) 68; PA De Miguel Asensio, 'Applicable Law in the Absence of Choice to Contracts Relating to Intellectual or Industrial Property Rights' (2008) 10 *Year Book of Private International Law* 199, 203; LG Gutierrez, 'Franchise Contracts and the Rome I Regulation on the Law Applicable to International Contracts' (2008) 10 *Year Book of Private International Law* 233, 234–36; M-E Ancel, 'The Rome I Regulation and Distribution Contracts' (2008) 10 *Year Book of Private International Law* 221, 225–27; A Bonomi, 'The Rome I Regulation on the Law Applicable to Contractual Obligations – Some General Remarks' (2008) 10 *Year Book of Private International Law* 165, 174; Magnus (n 68) 33–34; R Plender and M Wilderspin, *European Private International Law of Obligations* 3rd edn (London, Sweet & Maxwell, 2009) 177–86.

respectively. Rome I gives no indication as to whether this designation is based on the concept of characteristic obligation. At best, Recital 17 to Rome I states that

> As far as the applicable law in the absence of choice is concerned, the concept of 'provision of services' and 'sale of goods' should be interpreted in the same way as when applying Article 5 of Regulation (EC) No 44/2001 in so far as sale of goods and provision of services are covered by that Regulation. Although franchise and distribution contracts are contracts for services, they are the subject of specific rules.

The Rome I Proposal states that the designation of the habitual residence of the franchisee and distributor are based on the protection of weaker parties.[225] This justification is however open to question. Admittedly, it is arguable that the franchisor who grants the franchisee permission or a licence to use its business name to sell a product or provide a service could dictate the terms of the contract. The grantor in a distribution contract who provides the goods to the distributor could also dictate the terms of the contract. However, this proposition is counterbalanced by the fact that the franchisor is dependent on the franchisee for the success of the business franchise just as the grantor is dependent on the distributor for the success of the distribution contract.

Identifying the characteristic obligation of a franchise contract is controversial.[226] On the one hand, it could be argued that it is the franchisor that does the 'job' by granting the licence or permission to the franchisee to use its business name which constitutes the essence of the contract for which the franchisee provides corresponding payment. On the other hand, it could be argued that the obligation of the franchisee is much more than payment on the basis that it does the 'job' under the franchise contract by utilising the business name of the franchisor, which is critical and fundamental to the franchise and thus constitutes the essence of the contract. This book subscribes to the latter idea on the basis that the franchisee does the relatively more important and complex works of utilising the business name of the franchisor, and making the business a success.

In the case of a distribution contract, the same controversy arises as to who is the characteristic performer.[227] On the one hand it could be argued that it is the grantor that is the professional because it is he who supplies the goods for which the distributor pays for, and this constitutes the essence of the obligation. On the other hand, it could be argued that it is the distributor that is the professional because the distributor's obligation is not merely that of payment for the goods, as the distributor by selling the grantor's products also builds up the market and advertises the goods and this constitutes the essence of the obligation. This book subscribes to the latter idea on the basis that the distributor does the relatively

[225] Rome I Proposal (n 136) 7.

[226] See also *J S Swan (Printing) Limited v Kall Kwik UK Limited* [2009] CSOH 99.

[227] See also *Print Concept GmbH v GEW (EC) Limited* [2001] EWCA CIV 352 [34]; *Waeco International Gmbh v Cardon* [2007] IPlr 38 [6]; *Societe Cecil v Societe Wolman* [2008] IPlr 41 [5]–[6]. cf *Societe ND Conseil SA v Societe Le Meridien Hotels et Resorts World Headquarters* [2007] ILpr 39 [4]; *Nestorway Ltd t/a Electrographic International v Ambaflex BV* [2006] IEHC 235.

more important and complex works, in distributing the goods, as the grantor is dependent on the distributor for the success of the distribution contract.

In this connection, it is suggested that for distribution and franchise contracts, the European legislator could provide under a revised Article 4 of Rome I that the place of performance of the characteristic obligation for a distribution contract is the place where the distributor distributes or sells the goods of the grantor or agrees to distribute or sell the goods of the grantor; and the place of performance of the characteristic obligation for a contract of franchise is the place where the franchisee promotes the business of the franchisor, or agrees to promote the business of the franchisor.

Some scholars have submitted that the concept of characteristic obligation would be impossible to identify in complex contracts such as barter, cooperation agreements, and joint venture agreements.[228] It is opined on the contrary that court might still identify the characteristic obligation under such contracts by looking for the true professional, weighing the obligation of the contending parties in the contract, and singling out the performance which is relatively more important. For example assuming A, habitually resident in Austria is in the business of exchanging valuable gold for cars. B habitually resident in Germany delivers gold to A in Austria, while A delivers a car to B in Germany. If there is a dispute inter alia as to the applicable law, the fact that A is the true professional in the arrangement between the parties could tilt in favour of his performance being regarded as the characteristic obligation. He is also the party that does the business and complex work as the professional under the contract.

Cases where the courts have been unable to identify the characteristic performer under the EU choice of law rules have been relatively few, and in such cases the courts did not explicitly take into account other criteria suggested in this book for identifying the characteristic performer – particularly the criteria of the party that performs the relatively more important obligation.[229] It is suggested that the criteria of the party who performs the relatively more important obligation would work well for complex contracts involving mutual obligations of the parties.

This criteria must not be regarded as arbitrary because in almost every contractual arrangement one party's obligation is usually relatively more important than the other, so that the legal relationship can be concentrated in one place. In effect, the concept of 'relatively more important obligation' aims to cure the defect of

[228] Hoffmann (n 92) 8–9; Jeunger (n 101) 301; Lando (1987) (n 4) 197, 203–4; Lando (1996–97) (n 94) 67; GM McGuiness, 'The Rome Convention: The Contracting Parties' (2000) *San Diego International Law Journal* 127, 147; J Hill and M Ni Shèilleabhain, *Clarkson & Hill's Conflict of Laws* (Oxford, Oxford University Press, 2016) 230, [4.59]. cf MR Badykov, 'The Russian Civil Code and the Rome Convention: Applicable Law in the Absence of Choice by the Parties' (2005) 1 *Journal of Private International Law* 269, 271–81.

[229] See for example *Apple Corps Limited v Apple Computers Incorporated* [2004] 2 CLC 720; *Golden Ocean Group Limited v Salgaocar Minining Industries Ltd, Mr Anil Salgaocar* [2012] EWCA Civ 265; *Scott v West & Mackie v Baxter* [2012] EWHC 1890 (Ch); *Golden Brownlie v Four Seasons Hotel Inc* [2014] EWHC 273 (QB); *Alexey Bazhanov, Morrins Commercial Inc v Arkadiy Fosman, Olga Fosman, Akvilon LLC* [2017] EWHC 3404 (Comm) [64].

the concept of characteristic obligation as it relates to complex contracts involving mutual obligations. Thus in a partnership between two persons resident in different countries and a dispute arises between such persons, generally, the principal, managing or senior partner's obligation is relatively more important, and the legal relationship should be concentrated in the place where the principal, managing or senior partner carries out his obligations. In addition, if courts of Member States were able to identify the country that is most closely connected to a contract, without the aid of presumptions, in cases where the connecting factors were evenly balanced,[230] there is no good reason why the criteria of 'relatively more important obligation' cannot be used to identify the characteristic performance in complex contracts involving mutual obligations.[231]

For example, in *Apple*,[232] the determination of what law applied to govern a settlement trademark agreement under Article 4(2) of the Rome Convention was in issue.[233] The claimant was a well-known music record company and the defendant was a well-known producer of computers and software. The claimant alleged that the defendant had broken, and intended to break, the settlement agreement made between the two companies in October 1991 which regulated the use of their respective trademarks in respect of various areas of activity or proposed activity. The parties' solicitors keenly negotiated the terms of the contract and inter alia deliberately did not include a choice of law or forum clause.

Mann J held that the characteristic performance in the contract could not be identified because the substance of the contract required the parties to mutually perform negative obligations in the settlement agreement. In the eyes of Mann J, none of the negative obligations of the parties was less significant, subsidiary or central to the other party.

However, he observed that 'If anyone was providing additional elements of performance which somehow tilted the balance so as to create a characteristic performance',[234] it was the claimant, 'which had extended the area affected by its negative obligation and thus (if anyone did) had provided the characteristic performance',[235] though he did not accept this type of analysis as the correct one.

It is opined that Mann J would have been able to identify the characteristic obligation of the parties in this case by focusing and comparing the *relative* importance or significance of the obligation of the parties under the settlement agreement. This is because he appears to concede that the *relatively* more important obligation in this case was that of the claimant.

In the alternative, given the controversy concerning the concept of characteristic obligation in the case of complex contracts, a compromise could be reached

[230] *Apple* (n 229).
[231] See also Badykov (n 228) 271–81.
[232] (n 229).
[233] It was however an ancillary issue used as a basis to determine whether or not the English court should assume jurisdiction in the case.
[234] *Apple* (n 229) [69].
[235] ibid at [69].

among Member States by looking into what constitutes the place of performance of the characteristic obligation for other commercial contracts, which are in their nature complex, and likely to arise in practice. For example in a letter of credit transaction which is a complex contract, the English commercial approach which regards the place where the seller receives payment against compliant documents (or should have received payment against complaint documents) could be classified as the place of performance of the characteristic obligation.[236] It is a commercially sensible approach on the basis that a letter of credit transaction is primarily concerned with the security of the seller's payment.[237] For contracts of intellectual property, it could be proposed that the place of performance of the characteristic obligation is the place where the intellectual property rights were granted or registered.[238] In respect of other complex contracts, the criteria of closest connection should be retained if the characteristic obligation cannot be identified by compromise.

B. Agreement on the Place of Characteristic Performance

A standard choice of law clause in an international commercial contract would normally be drafted as: 'This contract is governed by the law of X.' This is perhaps the best way to invoke Article 3 of Rome I. This section is not concerned with situations where the parties draft their choice of law clause in this manner. The main focus is: first, whether an agreement on the place of characteristic performance can be utilised as a form of party autonomy? And second, in situations where the place of characteristic performance is not utilised as a form of party autonomy, how an agreement on the place of characteristic performance can be utilised in determining the applicable law in the absence of choice.

Case law has demonstrated that in highly contested international commercial transactions parties (through their solicitors) are aware during contractual negotiations of the significance connecting factors play in determining the applicable law (in the absence of choice) in the EU choice of law rules.[239] Connecting factors could therefore be manipulated to suit a particular purpose in choice of law.[240]

In theory it is possible for parties to expressly or implicitly agree on the designation of connecting factors before their contract is executed. Parties, without more, can agree in advance to choose the language of the contract, currency of payment, place of negotiation and conclusion of contract, and the place where

[236] *Bank of Baroda v Vysa Bank Limited* [1994] CLC 41, 49; *Marconi Communications International v PT Pan Indonesia Bank Ltd* [2005] EWCA 422 [69].

[237] ibid (all).

[238] TK Graziano, 'Jurisdiction under Article 7 No. 1 of the Recast Brussels I Regulation: Disconnecting the Procedural Place of Performance from its Counterpart in Substantive Law' (2015) 16 *Year Book of Private International Law* 167, 215. See also De Miguel Asensio (n 224) 210–12.

[239] See generally *Apple* (n 229).

[240] ibid.

performance is effected under their contract. This would not be categorised as a form of party autonomy in the context of Article 3 of Rome I, if the parties do not make it clear that the agreement on the connecting factor shall be the governing law. In other words, an agreement on the designation of connecting factors, without indicating that the connecting factor should be used as the governing law for the parties' transaction is not a form of party autonomy under Article 3. Assuming A and B in a contract for the provision of services expressly agree that B would provide services to A, in A's country of habitual residence. This is simply an express agreement designating the connecting factor of the place of characteristic performance, without any indication that it shall be the governing law, so it is not a form of party autonomy in the eyes of Article 3.

However, where the parties agree that their contract shall be governed by the law of the place of characteristic performance (or any other connecting factor), there is no good reason why the court should normally not give effect to the express wishes of the parties. An agreement on the place of characteristic performance in this context constitutes a form of party autonomy under Article 3. This is because the parties in this case have agreed that the law of the place of characteristic performance shall govern their contract. If for example A and B in a contract for the provision of services expressly agree that the governing law is the place where B provides services to A, this is an express agreement designating the connecting factor of the place of characteristic performance, with a clear indication that it shall be the governing law. This is a form of party autonomy in the context of Article 3.

By way of analogy, under Brussels Convention the CJEU initially made it clear that there was a clear distinction between an agreement on the place of performance under Article 5(1) of the Brussels Convention (now Article 7(1) of Brussels Ia) and a choice of jurisdiction clause under Article 17 of the Brussels Convention (now Article 25 of Brussels Ia).[241] In the context of a proposed Rome I (as stated earlier), a similar distinction would likely arise as to the difference between an agreement on the place of characteristic performance in determining the applicable law in the absence of choice and an agreement that expressly designates the place of characteristic performance as the governing law, amounting to a form of party autonomy.

In addition, by way of analogy, the CJEU held that the Brussels Convention must be interpreted as meaning that an oral agreement on the place of performance which is designed not to determine the place where the person liable is actually to perform the obligations incumbent upon him, but solely to establish that the courts for a particular place have jurisdiction, is not governed by Article 5(1) of the Convention, but by Article 17. Whilst the parties are free to agree on a place of performance for contractual obligations, they are nevertheless not entitled, having regard to the system established by the Brussels Convention, to designate, with the sole aim of specifying the courts having jurisdiction, a place of performance having no real connection with the reality of the contract at which the obligations

[241] C-56/79, *Siegfried Zelger v Sebastiano Salinitri* EU:C:1980:15.

arising under the contract could not be performed in accordance with the terms of the contract.[242] In the context of the present and a proposed Rome I (as stated earlier), an oral or written agreement on the place of performance which is used as a basis for designating the applicable law has the same effect as a standard choice of law clause under Article 3 of Rome I. In such circumstances the chosen law which is designated by the place of performance generally does not have to have a connection to the reality of the parties' contract.[243]

In reality, an agreement on the designation of the place of characteristic performance by the parties is likely to arise where the determination of the applicable law in the absence of choice is before the court. Assuming the place of performance of the characteristic obligation is utilised as the principal connecting factor for commercial contracts what would be the significance of an agreement on the place of characteristic performance in determining the applicable law in the absence of choice?

It is submitted that parties should be allowed to retain the right to determine the place of the performance of the characteristic obligation under their contract.[244] In order to verify whether the parties have agreed on a place of performance of the characteristic obligation under their contract, the Member State court seised should take into account all the relevant terms and clauses of the parties' contract which are capable of clearly identifying that place, including terms and clauses which are generally recognised and applied through the usages of international trade or commerce, such as incoterms.[245]

If that cannot be done because the contract is either silent or provides for several places of performance, the court should look to where the characteristic obligation has in fact for the most part been carried out (provided this is not contrary to the parties' intentions, as it appears from the contract). For that purpose, the factual aspects of the case may be taken into consideration, in particular, the time spent in those places and the importance of the activities carried out there.[246]

C. Where the Place of Performance of the Characteristic Obligation Cannot be Identified

In the event the place where the characteristic obligation was principally carried out proves impossible or very controversial for the court to identify, a resort should

[242] C-106/95, *Mainschiffahrts Genossenschaft eG (MSG) v Les Gravieres Rhenanes Sarl*, EU:C:1997:70.

[243] Article 3 of Rome I. See also C-54/16, *Vinyls Italia SpA v Mediterranea di Navigazione SpA*, EU:C:2017:433.

[244] C-381/08, *Car Trim GMBH v Key Safety Systems Srl*, EU:C:2010:90; C-87/10, *Electrosteel Europe SA v Edil Centro SPA*, EU:C:2011:375.

[245] They are created and approved by the International Chamber of Commerce (ICC) for the purpose of addressing the obligations between commercial parties. See 'Incoterms@2010 – ICC rules for the use of domestic and international trade terms', *ICC Publications* number 715, 1–263.

[246] *Wood Floor* (n 78) [40]; C-386/05, *Color Drack* (n 73) [41]. *See also JEB Recoveries LLP v Binstock* [2016] EWCA 1008.

be made to the doctrine of the habitual residence of the characteristic performer, instead of an immediate resort to the principle of closest connection. Applying the test of the habitual residence of the characteristic performer as a residual connecting factor further promotes the aims of reconciling the aims of legal certainty and flexibility.

By way of analogy, this approach appears to be similar to the CJEU's decision under Brussels I on the allocation of jurisdiction for commercial contracts, in respect of a commercial agency, where the CJEU held that resort should be had to the domicile of an agent where (the agent's) services are performed in different Member States, and the principal place of provision of the services cannot be identified.[247]

The principal reason why the habitual residence of the characteristic performer is advanced as an alternative connecting factor where the place of performance of the characteristic obligation cannot be identified is that the habitual residence of the characteristic performer plays a subsidiary role to the place where characteristic performance is effected. Again, as earlier submitted, the habitual residence of the characteristic performer was invented because of the difficulties that could arise with identifying the place of performance.

An alternative solution might be to use the criteria of the last place of performance. This solution was utilised by the CJEU (under Brussels I on the allocation of jurisdiction for commercial contracts) in respect of contract for the sale of goods involving the carriage of goods, where the CJEU held in that case that the place of delivery for the purpose of the first indent of Article 5(1)(b) was to be taken as the place where the goods were or should have been physically transferred to the purchaser at their final destination, as a result of which the purchaser obtained or should have obtained actual power of disposal over the goods at the final destination of the sales transaction.[248] By way of analogy, one has also advocated this solution in respect of contract of carriage of goods in the event the principal place of delivery cannot be determined under the proviso to Article 5(1) of Rome I.[249] However, at the moment, it appears unsafe to recommend the approach of the last place of performance as a blanket solution for general commercial contracts. For example in a commercial contract, where a party performs a contract in various countries, and it is difficult to identify the principal place of performance, the last place of performance may have tenuous connections to the commercial contract, so that it is preferable to utilise the habitual residence of the characteristic performer as a residual connecting factor.[250] More importantly, there might be no *last* place of performance, when performance occurs simultaneously in various countries.

[247] *Wood Floor* (n 78); C-64/17, *Saey Home & Garden NV/SA v Lusavouga-Máquinas e Acessórios Industriais SA*, EU:C:2018:173 [45]–[46].

[248] *Car Trim* (n 244).

[249] Okoli (n 91) 521.

[250] See also *Lawlor* (n 49).

V. Conclusion

This chapter opined that the place of performance should be given special significance under a revised Article 4 of Rome I.

A critical analysis was made on why the concept of habitual residence of the characteristic performer was chosen as the principal connecting factor under the EU choice of law rules. The three main reasons are the difficulties of identifying or classifying the place of performance, the triumph of the law of the professional, and the country-of-origin principle. In this connection, factors that could weigh against the place of performance of the characteristic obligation as the principal connecting factor were raised and addressed. In the final analysis, it was opined that the arguments against the place of performance as a connecting factor is not a justifiable or sufficient reason to strip the place of performance of special significance.

It was then proposed that the place of characteristic performance should be the principal connecting factor under a revised Article 4 of Rome I as a means of remedying the defects of the place of performance as a connecting factor. Notwithstanding this proposal, it was opined that the escape clause should not be dispensed with, given that the concept of place of characteristic performance, though very suitable, is not a perfect connecting factor. In such unusual cases where the place of characteristic performance is unsatisfactory, the escape clause should be resorted to in determining the applicable law.

In the alternative, it was opined that the current rule could be retained and in a revised Article 4(3) of Rome I, the place of performance should be explicitly given special significance in interpreting the escape clause. The justification for this proposal was that the place of performance under the current Article 4(3) of Rome I may at best have marginal significance, and there would be cases where the place of performance best satisfies the test of proximity, but the decision maker might be timid to apply it.

Considering the principal proposal in this book, the application of the concept of the place of characteristic performance was also considered. First, it was opined that the courts should take into account the criteria of who is the true professional, and who performs the relatively more important obligation in determining the concept of characteristic obligation. Second, it was opined that parties can make an agreement on the place of characteristic performance, which the court should give effect to. Third, where the place of characteristic performance cannot be identified, a resort should be made to the habitual residence of the characteristic performer, rather than an immediate resort to the principle of closest connection.

4

Article 9(3) of Rome I Regulation: Place of Performance as an Expression of the Principle of Proximity

I. Introduction

A core aspect of this chapter is to opine that the place of performance in a foreign country overriding mandatory rules under Article 9(3) of Rome I is actually an expression or embodiment of the principle of proximity. This chapter is one of the principal arguments that advances the central theme of this book that the place of performance should be explicitly given special significance under a revised Article 4 of Rome I.

Article 9(3) of Rome I did not fall from the sky. In reality Article 9(3) was in particular shaped by historical experiences of the domestic conflict of law rules of some Member State courts pre-Rome Convention, Article 7(1) of the Rome Convention and Article 8(3) of the Rome I Regulation Proposal.

It is important to address the history of what led to Article 9(3) of Rome I in a comparative and analogous way. In particular, contending doctrines that implicitly or expressly challenge or contrast with the view that the place of performance under Article 9(3) is an expression of the principle of proximity, must be confronted, addressed and discredited.

In section II, the pre-Rome Convention experience on the place of performance in foreign country overriding mandatory rules would be critically analysed, and it would be opined inter alia that the place of performance was applied by some courts of Member States because it best satisfied the requirement of proximity.

In section III, it will be opined that under Article 7(1) of the Rome Convention, though the place of performance was not explicitly given special significance in determining foreign country mandatory rules, it was obvious that the place of performance was the connecting factor that best satisfied the test of 'close connection.'

In section IV, it will be opined that under Article 8(3) of the Rome I Proposal, restricting the scope of 'close connection' was at the heart of the negotiation process, and it was obvious that it was the place of performance that best satisfied the requirement of 'close connection.'

In section V, it will be opined inter alia that Article 9 of Rome I is also concerned with proximity (not only State interests), and based on the historical analysis undertaken in this chapter the place of performance is an expression of the principle of proximity under Article 9(3) of Rome I.

In section VI, it will be opined that despite the proposal in this book, Article 9(3) should not be suppressed, but made to apply against the excesses of party autonomy.

Section VII concludes.

II. A Historical and Comparative Analysis: Pre-Rome Convention

Prior to the enactment of the Rome Convention, it appears some Member State courts had applied or took into account foreign mandatory rules, albeit in diverse theoretical or doctrinal packages, that did not precisely fit into the methodology of Article 9(3). It appears that the place of performance had always been of considerable significance in foreign country overriding mandatory rules. As Dickinson aptly states, the

> impression of the practice in … Member States is that third country mandatory rules are most commonly invoked in situations where the mandatory rule prohibits conduct in the third country which constitutes, or is a necessary prerequisite to, performance of a contract.[1]

This section takes the position that the principal reason why some Member State courts, prior to the Rome Convention, gave considerable significance to the place of performance in applying a form of foreign country mandatory rules (better described as 'foreign illegality' at the time) was based on the fact that the *place* where the contract was performed served a regulatory function for international commercial contracts.

However, it will be contended that whatever justification or theory that might be advanced to the contrary, the place of performance was also a factor of considerable significance because it usually had the closest or at least a substantial connection to an international commercial contract.

A. Paying Tribute to AV Dicey

During the period of the eighteenth to the early twentieth century, it was very controversial in English case law whether foreign illegality (including the law

[1] A Dickinson, 'Third Country Mandatory Rules in the Law Applicable to Contractual Obligations: So Long Farewell, Auf Wiedersehen, Adieu?' (2007) 3 *Journal of Private International* 53, 87. See also A Bonomi, 'Note – Article 7(1) of the European Contracts Convention: Codifying the Practice of Applying Foreign Mandatory Rules' (2000–01) 114 *Harvard Law Review* 2462, 2471–72.

of the place of performance) rendered the contract unenforceable.[2] Alexander records the reasons for the English approach at the time, in the following words:

> The English doctrine of foreign illegality has evolved from an earlier era when considerations of international comity were far less important than the unfettered pursuit of the British national interests so that contracts governed by English law involving a UK national and which required an act to be performed in a foreign country in violation of that country's laws were held valid and enforceable against the party whose breach was alleged.[3]

Thus, in 1734 the then Lord Chief Justice, Lord Hardwicke, in *Boucher*[4] upheld the enforcement of a contract governed by English law, even though the export of gold from Portugal to England was prohibited by Portuguese law. Lord Hardwicke rationalised that:

> if it should be laid down, that because goods are prohibited to be exported by the laws of any foreign country from whence they are brought, therefore the parties should have no remedy or action here, it would cut off all benefit of such trade from this kingdom, which would be of very bad consequence to the principal and most beneficial branches of our trade; nor does it ever seem to have been admitted.[5]

Indeed, in the early twentieth century, Lord Wrenbury declared that: 'Illegality according to the law of another country does not affect the merchant.'[6]

However, in the late nineteenth century, Dicey postulated that: 'A contract is, in general, invalid in so far as … the performance of it is unlawful by the law of the country where the contract is to be performed.'[7] In reality, though Dicey was not the first scholar (even in England) to formulate this kind of idea,[8] his postulation proved to be very influential around the world.

Dicey's rule was first expressly endorsed by the English Court of Appeal in *Ralli Brothers v Compania Naviera Sota Y Aznar* ('*Ralli Bros*'),[9] and later recognised and applied in a significant number of English cases.[10] Dicey's formulation has also

[2] *Boucher v Lawson* [1734] Eng Rep 53, 125; *British & Foreign Marine Insurance v Samuel Sanday & Co* [1916] 1 AC 650, 672. cf *De Wutz v Hendriks* [1824] 2 Bing 314.

[3] K Alexander, 'Civil Liability on the Periphery: Third Country Transactions in Violation of United States Economic Sanctions' (1999) 10 *European Business Law Review* 314, 322 (footnotes omitted).

[4] (n 2).

[5] ibid 125.

[6] *British & Foreign Marine Insurance v Samuel Sanday & Co* [1916] 1 AC 650, 672.

[7] AV Dicey, *Conflict of Laws* 1st edn (London, Sweet and Maxwell, 1896) 560. What is usually cited particularly by English judges is AV Dicey, *Conflict of Laws* 2nd edn (London, Sweet and Maxwell, 1908) 553.

[8] For an earlier and similar academic view see J Westlake, *A Treatise on Private International Law* (London, W Maxwell & Son, 1880) 176–77, [192].

[9] *Ralli Brothers v Compania Naviera Sota Y Aznar* [1920] 2 KB 287 (CA) 291 (Lord Sterndale MR).

[10] See for example *Foster v Driscoll* [1929] 1 KB 470 (CA), 520 (Sankey LJ); *Kleinwort, Sons & Co v Ungarische Baumwolle AG* [1939] 2 KB 678, 694 (Mackinnon LJ), 697 (Du Parcq LJ), 700 (Atkinson J); *Kahler v Midland Bank Ltd* [1950] AC 25, 36 (Lord Normand); *Zivnostenska Banka National Corporation v Frankman* [1950] AC 57, 71–72 (Lord Simonds); *Euro-Diam Ltd v Bathurst* [1987] 2 WLR 1368, 1378; *Lemenda Trading Co Ltd v African Middle East Petroleum Co Ltd* [1986] QB 448, 454–56.

been recognised and applied in some Commonwealth African countries,[11] and other Commonwealth countries such as Canada,[12] Singapore,[13] Australia[14] and Hong Kong.[15] His formulation might also have influenced an aspect of United States' conflict of laws.[16]

In the context of Rome I, Beaumont and McEleavy expressly credit the intellectual contribution of Dicey by submitting that his statement 'has an uncanny similarity to the new Article 9(3) of Rome I Regulation'.[17] Indeed, it is opined that Dicey's influence on Article 9(3) is apparent.

The principal reason why emphasis has been placed on Dicey's intellectual contribution to Article 9(3) is that under English case law, there is no precise theory or principle for the application of Dicey's formulation.[18] Some English or common law scholars have even questioned whether Dicey's formulation, and in particular, the English cases that have applied it, can be truly classified as one of conflict of laws.[19] This explains why some English scholars have been very critical of Dicey's formulation, by describing it as a 'misleading and unnecessary generality'.[20]

[11] See generally R Oppong, *Private International Law in Commonwealth Africa* (Cambridge, Cambridge University Press, 2013) 146–48.

[12] See generally *Montreal Trust Co v Stanrock Uranium Mines Ltd* 1965 CarswellOnt 215, [1966] 1 OR 258, 53 DLR (2d) 594; Supreme Court [Court of Appeal] [62]; *Frischke v Royal Bank* 1977 CarswellOnt 281, [1977] 2 ACWS 615, 17 OR (2d) 388, 4 CPC 279, 80 DLR (3d) 393; *R v Spencer* 1982 CarswellOnt 2283, 8 WCB 111; *Gillespie Management Corp v Terrace Properties* 1989 CarswellBC 169, [1989] BCWLD 2416, [1989] CLD 1249, [1989] BCJ No 1768, 17 ACW. (3d) 522, 39 BCLR (2d) 337, 62 DLR (4th) 221; *Cardel Leasing Ltd v Maxmenko* 1991 CarswellOnt 633, [1991] OJ No 2163, 2 PPSAC (2d) 302, 30 ACWS (3d) 502, 3 WDCP (2d) 20; *Arab Banking Corporation c Wightman* 1996 CarswellQue 1681, [1996] RJQ 1715, JE 96-1439, EYB 1996-88038.

[13] *Patriot Pte Ltd v Lam Hong Commercial Co* [1980] 1 MLJ 135; *Singapore Finance Ltd v Soetanto* [1992] 2 SLR 407; *Shaikh Faisal Bin Sultan Al Qassim t/a Gibca v Swan Hunter Singapore Pte Ltd.* [1995] 1 SLR 394. See generally TK Sing, 'Illegal Contracts in the Conflict of Laws: Some Recent Developments in Singapore' (1993) *Singapore Journal of Legal Studies* 214–25; DCG Sian, 'Contractual Illegality and Conflict of Laws' (1995) 7 *Singapore Academy of Law Journal* 303.

[14] See generally *Attorney-General (UK) v Heinemann Publishers Australia Pty Ltd* [1987] 75 ALR 353, 459; *Fullerton Nominees Pty Ltd T/A Western Refrigeration* 74 *V Darmago* [2000] WASCA 4.

[15] See generally *Ryder Industries Ltd v Chan Shui Woo* [2016] 1 HKC 323.

[16] See Section 202(2) of the Restatement (Second) of Conflict of Laws 1971 which provides that: 'When performance is illegal in the place of performance, the contract will usually be denied enforcement.'

[17] PR Beaumont and PE McEleavy, *Private International Law AE ANTON* 3rd edn (Edinburgh, W Green, 2011) 517, [10.302]. See also A Bonomi, 'Article 9 of Rome I Regulation' in U Magnus and P Mankowski, *European Commentaries on Private International Law* vol II (Munich, Sellier European Law Publishers, 2017) 634, [129], fn 148.

[18] See generally P Kaye, *The New Private International Law of Contract of the European Community* 1st edn (Aldershot; Brookfield, Dartmouth Publishing Company, 1993) 70; J Collier, *Conflict of Laws* 2nd edn (Cambridge, Cambridge University Press, 1994) 212–13; R Fentiman, *Foreign Law in English Courts* 1st edn (Oxford, Oxford University Press, 1998) 109; FMB Reynolds, 'The Enforcement of Contracts involving Corruption or Illegality in other Countries' (1997) *Singapore Journal of Legal Studies* 371, 391. See also Bonomi (n 1) 2472.

[19] ibid (all).

[20] Reynolds (n 18) 394.

This criticism of Dicey is unwarranted and misplaced. To my mind, Dicey was a scholar who was centuries ahead of his time on the significance of the law of the place of performance in the context of foreign country overriding mandatory rules; he should not be blamed for the manner in which English judges and scholars have interpreted his formulation.

The true rationale of Dicey's rule (and the English cases that applied it) lies in the fact that the law of the place of performance is generally one of considerable significance in international commercial transactions.[21] This view point, inter alia, also lends support to the idea that the place of performance generally satisfies the requirement of proximity in international commercial contracts, and indeed does it better than other connecting factors.

i. The Fallacious English Domestic Law of Contract Theory

The argument that Dicey's formulation is one that is also based on proximity as regards the significance of the place of performance in foreign country overriding mandatory rules faces a very significant hurdle. It is a fallacious argument advocated and perpetuated by many English (or common law) scholars that Dicey's formulation as applied in the first case of *Ralli Bros* is simply based on English domestic law of contract relating to frustration of the obligation in an English contract, and has nothing to do with conflict of laws. The underlying or 'invisible' reason why many English scholars hold this view might be that in reality, the concept of foreign mandatory rules was 'unknown' to English conflict of laws at the time, 'at least not under that name'.[22]

The true genesis of this problem begins with the decision in *Ralli Bros*.[23] In *Ralli Bros*,[24] an English firm in July 1918 chartered a Spanish steamship from the owners, who were a Spanish firm, to carry a cargo of jute from Calcutta to Barcelona at a freight of £50 per ton, one half to be paid to the owners in London on the vessel sailing from Calcutta and the balance to be paid at Barcelona by the receivers of the cargo, as to one half on arrival of the steamship and the remainder concurrently with the discharge. The freight payable at Barcelona was to be

[21] See also JHC Morris, 'The Eclipse of the Lex Loci Solutionis – A Fallacy Exploded' (1952–53) 6 *Harvard Law Review* 505, 509–12, 531; D Jackson, 'Mandatory Rules and Rules of 'Ordre Public' in P North (ed), *Contract Conflicts, The EEC Convention on the Law Applicable to Contractual Obligations: A Comparative Study* (Amsterdam, North-Holland Publishing Company, 1982) 59, 61 fn 6; Reynolds (n 18) 391; Dickinson (n 1) 78.

[22] P Torremans et al, *Cheshire, North and Fawcett, Private International Law* 15th edn (Oxford, Oxford University Press, 2017) 743. See also S Viejobueno, 'Private International Law Rules Relating to the Validity of International Sales Contracts' (1993) 26 *Comparative and International Law Journal of South Africa* 172, 194; W Tetley, 'Evasion/*Fraude à la loi* and Avoidance of the Law' (1993–94) 39 *McGill Law Journal* 303, 312–13; J Hill and A Chong, *International Commercial Disputes: Commercial Conflict of Laws in English Courts* 4th edn (Oxford, Hart Publishing, 2010) 533, [14.3.5].

[23] 'The underlying basis of the *Ralli Bros* … decision has been a matter of controversy for most of the 95 years since it was decided.' – *Ryder* (n 15) [46].

[24] (n 9). The facts of the case as stated here draw heavily from the headnote of the report.

paid in cash or approved bills at charterers' option at the current rate of exchange for bankers' short bills in London. The charterparty, which was made in London, was in English and on the charterers' own form, contained an arbitration clause under which disputes were to be decided by commercial men in London. The steamship sailed from Calcutta and half the freight was duly paid. She arrived at Barcelona on 28 December 1918, and a sum of money was paid in sterling by the receivers of the cargo. A subsequent Spanish law was set which made it illegal for the freight on jute to Spain to exceed 875 pesetas per ton. Owing to alterations in the rate of exchange the freight reserved by the charterparty was, at the date of the arrival of the steamship at Barcelona, largely in excess of 875 pesetas per ton. The receivers of the cargo at Barcelona refused to pay the balance of the freight reserved by the charterparty. The Spanish owners thereupon claimed to recover the balance of the freight from the charterers in England, notwithstanding that it exceeded the freight limited by Spanish law. The English Court of Appeal held that on the facts of the case the charterparty was governed by English law, but the owners could not recover the balance of the freight from the charterers in England to the extent that it was illegal according to the law of the place of performance (Spain).

The prevailing[25] or preponderant[26] academic view is that the *Ralli Bros* case is one that is based on English domestic law of contract relating to frustration of performance. This is labelled in this book as the 'mainstream English academic view' because it is a view supported and advocated by a considerable number of leading English (or common law) academics,[27] including prominent academic disciples of Dicey. The academic disciples of Dicey record this mainstream view in the following words:

> The prevailing academic view was that supervening illegality according to the law of the place of performance did not prevent an English court from enforcing the contract, unless it were governed by English law. The principle in *Ralli Bros*, on this view, was not

[25] *Ryder* (n 15) [43]; L Collins et al, *Dicey, Morris & Collins, The Conflict of Laws* 15th edn (London, Sweet and Maxwell, 2012) 1838, [32-100]; A Chong, 'The Public Policy and Mandatory Rules of Third Countries in International Contracts' (2006) 2 *Journal of Private International Law* 27, 63.

[26] Sian (n 13) 336.

[27] FA Mann, 'Proper Law and Illegality in Private International Law' (1937) 18 *British Yearbook of International Law* 97, 107–13; JD Falconbridge, *Essays on the Conflict of Laws* (Toronto, Canada Law Book Co., Ltd., 1947) 330–34; GC Cheshire, *International Contracts* 1st edn (London, Jackson, Son & Company, 1948) 71–74; GC Cheshire, *Private International Law* 4th edn (London; Oxford, Clarendon Press; Oxford University Press, 1952) 225–27; Morris (n 21) 509–12, 531; E Rabel, *The Conflict of Laws: A Comparative Study* (Michigan, University of Michigan Law School, 1947) 535; L Collins, 'Practical Implications in England of the EEC Convention on the law Applicable to Contractual Obligations' in P North (ed), *Contract Conflicts, The EEC Convention on the Law Applicable to Contractual Obligations: A Comparative Study* (Amsterdam, North-Holland Publishing Company, 1982) 205, 211–12; FA Mann, 'The Proper Law in the Conflict of Laws' (1987) 36 *International and Comparative Law Quarterly* 437, 449; GC Cheshire and P North, *Private International Law* 11th edn (Oxford, Oxford University Press, 1987) 487–89; TC Hartley, 'Mandatory Rules in International Contracts: The Common Law Approach' (1997) 266 *Recueil des Cours* 341; Reynolds (n 18) 379–95; Beaumont and McEleavy (n 17) 517–18, [10.303]; Collins (2012) (n 25) 1838, [32-100].

> a principle of conflict of laws at all, but merely an application of the English domestic principles with regard to the discharge or suspension of contractual obligations by supervening illegality, and the illegality of performance under the *lex loci solutionis* was no more than a fact to be taken into account by an English court in judging whether performance had become impossible.[28]

The principal rationale for this view point was that the applicable law was meant to generally govern the whole contract including the performance. In other words, it was already established authority that the law of the place of performance does not simply govern performance if it is not the *lex causae*.[29] The implication of this was that the rule in *Ralli Bros* only applied to English contracts (that is contracts governed by English law), and not contracts governed by foreign law. A contrary interpretation of this view point would give the law of the place of performance undue importance in displacing the *lex causae* or governing law. This point is well amplified by Morris, in the following words:

> the question has been discussed whether the Exception is part of the English conflict of laws at all. It has been strenuously argued that it is merely a rule of the English domestic law of contracts and does not apply unless the proper law of the contract is English. According to this argument, if the proper law of the contract is not English, it does not necessarily follow that illegality by the *lex loci solutionis* furnishes an excuse for non-performance; whether it does so or not is a matter for the domestic rules of the proper law. This argument is undoubtedly attractive. The proper law has better claims than the law of the place of performance to regulate the effects of illegality, which are very different in different systems of domestic law. Illegality and its effects are clearly matters which concern the substance of the obligation, and the law of the place of performance has nothing to do with it.[30]

Indeed, some English (or common law) scholars[31] and judges[32] submit that *Ralli Bros* has been cited in well-known English law of contract textbooks, relating to the concept of frustration in English law of contract.[33] In addition, some other common law scholars supporting this English mainstream academic view submit that Dicey's formulation or the *Ralli Bros* case has never been applied in a case where it was recognised that foreign law was the governing law of the contract.[34]

[28] Collins (2012) (n 25).

[29] *Jacobs v Crèdit Lyonnais* [1884] 12 QBD 589.

[30] Morris (n 21) 509–10 (footnotes omitted). For a strong approval of this view point see also Mann (1987) (n 27) 449.

[31] Mann (1937) (n 27) 111; Reynolds (n 18) 379–80 (citing others).

[32] *Eurobank Ergasias SA v Kalliroi Navigation Company Limted* [2015] EWHC 2377 (Comm.) [36]; *Ryder* (n 15) [43].

[33] In particular, these leading texts on English law of contract state that '*Ralli Bros* … established a principle of the domestic law of contract relating to discharge by supervening illegality and does not establish a rule of the conflict of laws': H Beale et al, *Chitty on Contracts* 32nd edn (London, Sweet & Maxwell, 2015) [30-360].

[34] H Smith, 'Enforcement of Foreign Mandatory Rules' (2000) 1 *Hibernian Law Journal* 305, 308.

To my mind, this English mainstream academic view is puzzling. It really begs the questions: what is conflict of laws or private international law? Was Dicey a recognised expert in English domestic law of contract? Could it be that Dicey, who was writing a text on conflict of laws, formulated a principle suited only to English domestic law of contract?

Dicey was known for his considerable influence first in English constitutional law,[35] and then, English conflict of laws.[36] He was really not known for his expertise in English domestic law of contract, and it is strongly doubted whether Dicey was simply or only concerned with English domestic law of contract when he made his formulation.

Dicey's formulation and its application in *Ralli Bros* can be categorised as one of conflict of laws. In this connection, Lord Wright is correct in construing *Ralli Bros* as a conflict of laws principle in the following words:

> The proper law of the contract does indeed fix the interpretation and construction of its express terms and supply the relevant background of statutory or implied terms. But *that part of the English law which is commonly called the conflict of laws requires, where proper, the application of foreign law*; eg, English law will not enforce a performance contrary to the law of the place of performance in circumstances like those existing in *Ralli Bros v Compania Naviera Sota y Aznar* and the law of the place of performance, though it will not be effective to affect the construction of the contract in regard to its substance (which must be ascertained according to the rule of the proper law, as was held in Jacobs, Marcus & Co. v Credit Lyonnais) will still regulate what were called in that case the incidents and mode of performance in that place. English law will in these and sometimes in other respects import a foreign law, but the contract is still governed by its proper law.[37]

Teare J also holds that *Ralli Bros* case 'is so well-known a principle of the English conflict of laws …'[38]

Conflict of laws deals with claims within a national legal system which involve a foreign element. In *Ralli Bros*, the ultimate application of Spanish law (the law of the place of performance) made this case one of conflict of laws.[39] It is difficult to understand how Spanish law was applied to govern an aspect of the performance in the contract, and yet it is claimed that this is simply based on English domestic law of contract. Is *Ralli Bros* rule not a form of judge made *dépeçage*?

[35] AV Dicey, *Introduction to the Study of the Law of the Constitution* 1st edn (New York, Macmillan and Company Limited, 1885).

[36] Dicey (1896) (n 7) 560.

[37] *Vita Food Products Inc v Unus Shipping Co Ltd (In Liquidation)* [1939] AC 277, 291 (emphasis added and footnotes omitted).

[38] *Deutsche Bank AG and others v Unitech Global Limited, Unitech Limited* [2013] EWHC 2793 (Comm) [99].

[39] 'I think on principle and on authority the charterers are not bound to perform that part of the contract, that is, the payment of freight above the maximum *allowed by Spanish law, which has become illegal by the law of the place of its performance.*' – *Ralli Bros* (n 9) 292 (Lord Sterndale MR).

Is the rule in *Ralli Bros* not similar to Article 9(3)?[40] Indeed, it is trite that one of the reasons that facilitated the UK opting into Rome I, despite initial hesitation, was because of the similarity between the *Rallis Bros* and Article 9(3).[41] As Vischer brilliantly submits:

> The influence of the English practice and doctrine is obvious. The reservation of the overriding mandatory provisions of the *lex loci solutionis* under the exclusion of other 'third laws' was first retained in the famous English case *Ralli Bros. v. Compana Naviera Sota Y Aznar … By inserting the rule into the Rome I Regulation, the old dispute of whether the Ralli Bros. principle is a conflict of laws rule or a principle of English domestic law seems to be settled; it is now definitely a conflict rule.*[42]

Moreover, the view that *Ralli Bros* applies only when the contract is governed by English law is not supported by the statements or decisions of English judges, especially from the House of Lords at the time, in a significant number of cases. In *Adelaide Electric Supply Co Ltd v Prudential Assurance Co Ltd*,[43] Lord Wright held that:

> It is established that prima facie, *whatever is the proper law of the contract* regarded as a whole, the law of the place of performance should be applied in respect of any particular obligation which is performable in a particular country other than the country of the proper law of the contract.[44]

[40] O Lando, and PA Neilsen, 'The Rome I Proposal' (2007) 3 *Journal of Private International Law* 29, 46; O Lando and PA Nielsen, 'The Rome I Regulation' (2008) 45 *Common Market Law Review* 1687, 1722–23; S James, 'Rome I: Shall we Dance?' (2008) 2 *Law & Financial Market Review* 113, 117; Ministry of Justice, 'Should the UK opt in? *Response to Consultation* CP05/08CP(R), January 2009, [74]; J Harris, 'Mandatory Rules and Public Policy under the Rome Convention' in F Ferrari and S Leible (eds), *The Law Applicable to Contractual Obligations in Europe* (Munich, Sellier European Law Publishers, 2009) 299–306; V Marazopoulou, 'Overriding Mandatory Provisions of Article 9(3) of Rome I Regulation' (2011) 64 *Revue Hellènique de Droit International* 779, 791–92; A Briggs, *Private International Law in English Courts* 1st edn (Oxford, Oxford University Press, 2014) 593, 7.251; R Plender and M Wilderspin, *European Private International Law of Obligations* 4th edn (London, Sweet & Maxwell, 2014) 365, [12-035]; J Hill and M Ní Shúilleabháin, *Clarkson & Hill's Conflict of Laws* (Oxford, Oxford University Press, 2016) 242, [4.99]; Bonomi (n 17) 639, [129]–[130]. See also A Philip, 'Mandatory Rules, Public Law (Political Rules) and Choice of Law in the EEC Convention on the Law Applicable to Contractual Obligations' in P North (ed), *Contract Conflicts, The EEC Convention on the Law Applicable to Contractual Obligations: A Comparative Study* (Amsterdam, North-Holland Publishing Company, 1982) 105; AJE Jaffey, 'The English Proper Law Doctrine and the EEC Convention' (1984) 33 *International and Comparative Law Quarterly* 531, 544; Tetley (n 22) 329; O Lando, 'Dicey and Morris: A Review' (1998) 47 *International and Comparative Law Quarterly* 394, 406–07; Chong (n 25) 35. For a contrasting view see *Eurobank* (n 32) [36].

[41] Ministry of Justice (n 40); Bonomi (n 17) 639, [129].

[42] F Vischer, '"Revolutionary Ideas" and the Swiss Statute on Private International Law' in K Boele-Woelki et al (eds), *Convergence and Divergence in Private International Law: Liber Amicorum Kurt Siehr* (The Hague, Schultess and Eleven International Publishing, 2010) 101, 108.

[43] *Adelaide Electric Supply Co Ltd v Prudential Assurance Co Ltd* [1934] AC 122.

[44] ibid 151 (emphasis added). However, it is conceded that Lord Wright's statement is contrary to the English Court of Appeal's decision in *Jacobs* (n 29), which held that the *lex causae* and not the place of performance generally governs matters related to the performance. In this connection, I generally agree with Morris' criticism of Lord Wright's statement to the extent that: 'The fatal objection to it as a principle is that it is wide enough to cover almost any question that can arise under a valid contract.

Lord Normand held after referring to *Ralli Bros*, that:

> The principle on which they were decided is that the courts of this country will not compel the fulfilment of an obligation when performance includes the doing in a foreign country of something which *the laws of that country* make it illegal to do.[45]

Lord Simonds, in regard to a contract which was governed by the law of Czechoslovakia, held that:

> The fulfilment of the contract therefore involves the doing of an act in Czechoslovakia … which is *by the law of Czechoslovakia*, itself the law of the contract, illegal. It is, I think, clear that the courts of this country will not enforce such performance.[46]

Similarly, Lord Reid in the same case held that:

> it is now settled that, *whatever be the proper law of the contract*, an English court will not require a party to do an act in performance of a contract which would be an offence under the law in force where the act has to be done.[47]

Diplock LJ also held in another case that:

> the English courts will not enforce performance or give damages for non-performance of an act required to be done under a contract, *whatever be the proper law of the contract*, if the act would be illegal in the country it is required to be performed.[48]

Assuming for the purpose of argument, that these very-well respected and experienced English judges are wrong for contrasting with the mainstream English academic view that *Ralli Bros* only applies when the contract is governed by English law, it is also opined that it still makes *Ralli Bros* principle one of conflict of laws. Again, the principal reason for this view is that it is foreign law that ultimately applies.[49] As Harris aptly remarks: 'Nonetheless, the foreign law is the trigger and it is that law which is ultimately taken into account. It may be thought better to describe this as the application of third state's mandatory rules.'[50]

Jackson also submitted that:

> this explanation ends with the English rule that where English law is the governing law the law of the place of performance is applied to adjudge the legality or otherwise of the contract. And that is to *assess 'illegality' by the law of the place of performance* even though it is not the law of the forum nor the governing law.[51]

Its adoption would restrict the scope of the proper law of the contract almost entirely to matters of formation' – Morris (n 21) 531.

[45] *Kahler* (n 10) 36 (emphasis added).

[46] *Zivnostenska* (n 10) 71 (emphasis added).

[47] ibid 79 (emphasis added).

[48] *Mackender and Others v Feldia AG and Others* [1967] 2 QB 590, 601 (emphasis added).

[49] See also Chong (n 25) 41–42.

[50] Harris (n 40) 301. Harris in this quotation actually makes reference to *Foster* (n 10) and *Regazzoni v KC Sethia* [1958] AC 301.

[51] Jackson (n 21) 61 (emphasis added).

Similarly, Briggs appears to be very critical of this English mainstream academic view when he submits that:

> One misinterpretation of the few cases which vouched for the rule deduced that as the contracts in the cases had English law as their proper law, the principle was confined to such contracts and did no more than illustrate the domestic contractual doctrine of frustration. Such a reading of the cases was only possible by being deaf to the language and tone in which the judgments were expressed …[52]

To submit that what was applied in the *Ralli Bros* case (to render the contract unenforceable) was simply domestic English law on frustration of contracts rather than Spanish law is fallacious or at best a legal fiction. It is just as fallacious as the logic behind the vested rights theory. As Juenger rightly notes the vested rights theory is

> one of several theories that attempt to explain why judges in conflict cases may resort to foreign law instead of applying those they are sworn to uphold. The vested rights theory deals with the problem by denying its existence: it teaches that courts never apply foreign law, but that they merely enforce foreign created rights. That explanation had been exposed by … scholars as sophistry and circular reasoning …[53]

In summation, the idea that Dicey's rule as applied in the first case of *Ralli Bros* is simply one of English domestic law of contract and not conflict of laws is fallacious.

ii. The Law of Place of Performance and the Principle of Proximity

Proximity in this context literally means nearness or closeness. In the context of private international law, the concern is with a country or legal system that has substantial connection to a dispute. The concept of proximity occupies a special place in the field of private international law in a significant number of jurisdictions around the world, encompassing matters of jurisdiction, choice of law and, recognition and enforcement of foreign judgments.[54] Historically, the principle of proximity in choice of law became dominant in the jurisprudence of some Member State courts of the EU in the twentieth century.[55]

As a matter of policy, the law of the place of performance has the greatest interest in regulating an international commercial transaction extra-territorially because it usually has substantial connection to the dispute. The place of performance would usually be the centre of activity for an international commercial contract and thus its law might legitimately lay claim to applying extra-territorially, though it might not be the governing law.

[52] Briggs (n 40) 593, paragraph 7.251.

[53] FK Juenger, 'Conflict of Laws: A Critique of Interest Analysis' (1984) 32 *The American Journal of Comparative Law* 1.

[54] See generally P Lagarde, 'Le Principle de Proximitè dans le Droit International Privè Contemporian' (1986) 196 *Recueil des Cours* 1.

[55] Giuliano-Lagarde Report [1980] OJ C282 19.

Prior to the enactment of the Rome Convention, the application of the law of the place of performance in relation to foreign illegality (or third country mandatory rules) in the context of the case law of some Member State courts, might lend support to the implicit idea that the law of the place of performance was applied in these cases either because it was generally the country of closest connection or at least one that had substantial connection to the parties' international commercial dispute. In other words, the idea that the international commercial contract should not be illegal according to the law of the place of performance, might be another way of saying that the country that generally has the closest or at least substantial connection to the international commercial contract, particularly from a regulatory perspective, should not be violated. Admittedly, this view point is not explicitly endorsed in these judicial decisions, but it is a view point this book subscribes to.

There are some scholars who also support this view point.[56] Jaffey who does not agree that *Ralli Bros* is simply a matter of English substantive law that subsequent illegality excuses a party from performance, submits that 'the justification for applying the Spanish invalidating rule would be that the contract was *closely connected* with Spain in that regard'.[57]

Alexander also submits that:

> A number of factors will be considered, namely whether the foreign contract has *a connection with England* or has implications which directly affect English policy. For example, an English court will refuse to enforce a foreign contract that requires acts to be performed in England that are criminal at either common law or by statute, notwithstanding the contract's legality under its governing law.[58]

Mills also shares Alexander's view, as he stresses the point that English case law on, inter alia, the significance of the place of performance relating to public policy, which led to the application of domestic or foreign law, can be justified on the basis of the principle of proximity.[59]

Chong is also right when she submits that the English cases on the place of performance relating to foreign illegality are based on the principle of proximity.[60] In this connection, she rightly submits that the place of performance is generally the strongest connecting factor in determining the concept of 'close connection' for foreign country overriding mandatory rules – it is stronger than other factors such as the *lex loci contractus* and the residence of the parties.[61]

[56] AJE Jaffey, 'Essential Validity of Contracts in the English Conflict of Laws' (1974) 23 *International and Comparative Law Quarterly* 1, 29; Alexander (n 3) 325; A Mills, 'The Dimensions of Public Policy in Private International Law' (2008) 4 *Journal of Private International Law* 201–36; Chong (n 25) 45–47, 69.

[57] Jaffey, ibid 29 (emphasis added).

[58] Alexander (n 3) 325 (emphasis added).

[59] Mills (n 56).

[60] Chong (n 25) 45–46.

[61] ibid.

At the expense of prolixity, one quotes her views on the place of performance satisfying the requirement of proximity in foreign country overriding mandatory rules. She submits that: '[T]he performance obligation forms the heart of the contract and thus it has long been recognized that the *lex loci solutionis* has the necessary "close connection" with a contract such that it has a legitimate interest in having its law applied.'[62] She then submits: '[T]he third country that would most obviously be considered to have a legitimate interest in having its law applied by the forum is the place of performance.'[63] She also submits: 'Of all potentially applicable laws of third countries, it is well established that the *lex loci solutionis* has a legitimate interest in being applied to an international contract.'[64]

Moreover, the fact that English case law appeared to apply foreign illegality only if it violated the law of the place of performance, implicitly confirms the view that the place of performance was generally one of closest or substantial connection to an international commercial contract.[65] This explains why the English practice did not give effect to other connecting factors such as the residence of the parties and the *lex loci contractus* as it relates to foreign illegality, if these connecting factors did not coincide with the place of performance. The reason for this approach might be that these factors are of marginal significance when compared to the country of the place of performance.

Thus, in *Kleinwort*:[66]

> The plaintiffs, who were bankers carrying on business in London, accepted three bills of exchange drawn on them by a Hungarian company and payable in three months in London. The bills were sent to the plaintiffs on April 4, 1938, by a Hungarian bank together with a letter from the Hungarian company undertaking to provide cover for the bills in London one day before maturity and a guarantee by the Hungarian bank. On the same day the Hungarian bank wrote to the plaintiffs under separate cover drawing the attention of the plaintiffs to the fact that both the drawers and they would only be in a position to provide cover at maturity if the exchange regulations prevailing in Hungary at that date enabled them to do so. At that date legislation in Hungary made it illegal for Hungarian subjects to pay money outside Hungary without the consent of the Hungarian National Bank. No consent was obtained for payment of the bills in question. Cover not having been provided at maturity, the plaintiffs brought an action against the Hungarian company and the Hungarian bank claiming payment of the amount of the bills and interest.[67]

[62] ibid.

[63] ibid 47.

[64] ibid 69.

[65] See also *De Beeche v South American Stores Ltd* [1935] AC 148, 156; *Rex v International Trustee for the Protection of Bondholders AG* [1937] AC 500, 519; *Toprak v Finagrain* [1979] 2 Lloyd's Rep 38; *Euro-Diam Ltd* (n 10) 1378; *Libyan Arab Foreign Bank v Bankers Trust Co* [1989] QB 728: *Abuja International Hotels Ltd v Meridien SAS* [2011] EWHC 87 (Comm) [27]; *Golden Ocean Group Ltd v Salgaocar Mining Industries Pvt Ltd* [2011] 1 CLC 125 [144]; *Spleithoff's Bevrachtingskantoor BV v Bank of China Ltd* [2015] 1 CLC 651 [202].

[66] (n 10).

[67] Facts quoted from the headnote.

The English Court of Appeal held inter alia that the proper law of the contract was English law and that, since the contract was to be performed in England, it was enforceable in the English Courts, though its performance might involve a breach by the defendants of the law of their residence (Hungarian law). Mackinnon LJ held thus:

> Here it is said that to pay this money in London is unlawful by the law of Hungary. If this contract had been to pay money in Budapest, no doubt that principle would have applied, and the law of Hungary would have been the lex loci solutionis, but the payment of the money was to be made in England, and the law of England is the lex loci solutionis. Therefore the exception where the performance is unlawful by the law of the country where the contract is to be performed does not arise ...[68]

Oppong, a leading authority in African private international law (and the academic godfather of private international law in Commonwealth Africa), also confirms that the place of performance is given absolute significance in determining foreign illegality by the courts of some Commonwealth African countries.[69] He states the position very lucidly thus:

> What is certain is that the courts will not enforce a contract which is illegal under *lex loci solutionis* ... On the other hand, the mere fact that performance is illegal under the laws of any other country which has some connection with the contract, such as the place of residence, business, nationality or domicile of one party, will not prevent enforcement of the contract ... This is an appropriate stance because it prevents a situation arising where one party can rely on their own independent connections with a system of law to defeat performance under the contract.[70]

A basis for justifying the decision in *Kleinwort* might be that Hungary did not have substantial connection to the dispute (when compared to the place of performance) because it was the residence of the defendant. If Hungary was the place of performance, the situation would have been different because it would have substantial connection to the claim relating to payment on a bill of lading, and thus have a legitimate basis to regulate the transaction extra-territorially.

Again, what is missing in Oppong's statement of the law in some Commonwealth African countries, is that the implicit reason why the place of performance is given absolute significance in determining matters of foreign illegality is because the place of performance usually has the closest connection to an international commercial contract, and thus the place of performance is in the best position to regulate a commercial transaction extra-territorially even though it is not the governing law.

[68] *Kleinwort* (n 10) 694. See also K Lipstein, 'Introduction: Conflicts Convention' in K Lipstein (ed), *Harmonization of Private International law by the EEC* 1st edn (London, University of London Institute of Advanced Legal Studies, 1978) 11.

[69] Oppong (n 11) 147–48.

[70] ibid.

iii. The Law of the Place of Performance and Regulatory Function in International Commercial Contracts

It is trite that the law of the place of performance serves a regulatory function in international commercial transactions, though it might not be the chosen law. Where an international commercial contract is illegal or constitutes a criminal offence according to the law of the place of performance, it is obvious that such a country would normally have an interest in wanting to regulate such a transaction extra-territorially. Indeed, in the eyes of some US conflict of laws:

> The state where performance is to occur under a contract has an obvious interest in the nature of the performance and in the party who is to perform. *So the state where performance is to occur has an obvious interest in the question whether this performance would be illegal.*[71]

The idea that the law of the place of performance serves as a regulatory function in international commercial transactions implicitly supports the view that the place of performance is normally one of closest or substantial connection.[72] The reason is simple. A State should not want to have an interest in regulating an international commercial transaction extra-territorially, if such a State does not have at least a reasonable or substantial connection to the dispute. This view point appears to be supported by Lorenzo who submits that:

> the application of mandatory rules of the place of performance is due to a generally accepted system or principle, doubtlessly connected to the respect of sovereignty, which compels the parties to comply with some peremptory norms of the country where the contract must be performed related to competition, environment, healthcare, natural resources, etc. However, *such a consideration … of such rules is rooted in a close territorial connection that makes application predictable, rather than its public character.*[73]

Moreover, the idea that the place of performance in the context of the application of foreign illegality is simply (or only) one that yields to State or public interests is questionable. In other words, the interest of the parties must not be overlooked, as they are the persons seeking remedies in an international commercial contract. This explains why this book uses the label 'regulatory function' because it aptly captures the significance of the place of performance in international commercial transactions, without the excessive or absolute use of 'public' law language. In other words, the expectations and interests of the parties are not overlooked when this terminology is employed.

[71] Section 188(2) Restatement (Second) of Conflict of Laws, 1971 (commentary section) (emphasis added). See also *Panama Processes SA v Cities Service co.* (Supreme Court of Oklahoma) July 17, 1990 796 P.2d 276 1990 WL 98171 71,598.

[72] Section 188(2) Restatement (Second) of Conflict of Laws, 1971 (commentary section) also rightly provides that, 'When both parties are to perform in the state, this state will have so close a relationship to the transaction …'

[73] SS Lorenzo, 'Choice of Law and Overriding Mandatory Rules in International Contracts after Rome I' (2010) 12 *Yearbook of Private International Law* 67, 88 (emphasis added). Though this submission was made in the context of arbitral proceedings, it also applies to judicial proceedings.

This section explores other theoretical labels used by judges and scholars in applying the law of the place of performance as a regulatory function in the context of foreign illegality. It also considers the practical significance of the law of the place of performance, particularly in the context of recognition and enforcement of foreign judgments and arbitral awards.

a. Regulatory Function: What is in a Name?

Various labels have been used to justify why the place of performance serves a regulatory function in international commercial transactions. These labels include international comity, public international law and public policy. Again, the principal objection to these theories is the excessive or absolute use of public law language, so that 'regulatory function' might be a better expression. These labels are reviewed below.

International Comity

One of the oldest rationales for applying the law of the place of performance in the context of foreign illegality is based on international comity.[74]

Comity is a term that is difficult to define because it is imprecise. In addition, comity may have varied meanings or interpretation in the context of jurisdiction, choice of law and, recognition and enforcement of foreign judgments.

In the context of the recognition and enforcement of foreign judgments, the US Supreme Court in the late nineteenth century held that:

> 'Comity,' in the legal sense, is neither a matter of absolute obligation, on the one hand, nor of mere courtesy and good will, upon the other. But it is the recognition which one nation allows within its territory to the legislative, executive or judicial acts of another nation, having due regard both to international duty and convenience, and to the rights of its own citizens or of other persons who are under the protection of its laws.[75]

In the context of choice of law, Briggs submits inter alia that comity is derived from territoriality, which 'requires a court to respect and not to question, the laws of a foreign State in so far as those apply to persons, property, and events located within the territorial jurisdiction of a foreign State'.[76] He clarifies this position in the eyes of common law by submitting that:

> The instructive answer of the common lawyer would be that the common law has a fierce, almost fundamentalist, view of the role of territoriality. It has and may exercise jurisdiction over defendants who are present within its territorial jurisdiction, simply because they are present; it recognizes and enforces judgments given by the courts of

[74] On the subject of comity in private international law see generally JK Bleimaier, 'The Doctrine of Comity in Private International Law' (1978–79) 24 *Catholic Lawyer* 327; DE Childress, 'Comity as Conflict: Resituating International Comity as Conflict of Laws' (2010) 44 *UC Davis Law Review* 11; A Briggs, 'Principle of Comity in Private International Law' (2011) 354 *Recueil Des Cours* 77.

[75] *Hilton v Guyot* 159 US 113, 163–64 (1895).

[76] Briggs (n 74) 181.

> the place in which the defendant was present, simply because he was present; and it acknowledges the role of the lex situs in determining whether a transfer – voluntary or involuntary makes not the slightest difference – of property was effective in law, simply because the property was there. Such an adherence to territorialism can be made to appear as though it is vouched for by the doctrine of comity.[77]

The above definitions offered by the US Supreme Court and Briggs do not specifically vouch for why international comity is used as a basis for applying the law of the place of performance to regulate matters of foreign illegality. To one's mind, in the context of applying the law of the place of performance to matters of foreign illegality, international comity means that as a matter of courtesy, the court of one State should take into account and apply the law of the place of performance, if the international commercial contract is illegal or constitutes a criminal offence according to that law. In this connection, international comity means that the forum applies the law of the place of performance to regulate an international commercial contract not simply as a matter of international obligation or reciprocity, but principally as a matter of courtesy. Given that the place of performance, in matters of foreign illegality, usually has the greatest interest in regulating an international commercial contract extra-territorially, it might be regarded as hostile to smooth international relations for the forum not to give effect to the law of the place of performance without good justification.

This principle was applied in the early part of the nineteenth century in the case of *De Wutz*[78] where an English court refused to enforce an English contract for the loan of money to assist a rebellion by subjects of Crete, which was recognised at the time as a foreign friendly state. The court held that contracts 'to raise money to support the subjects of a government in amity with our own, in hostilities against their government are void'.[79] In this case, resorting to comity was understandable and made the case very special, as the issue was a rebellion against the foreign state. Refusing to give effect to the law of the place of performance may have been considered as a hostile act by the government of that place, and would likely disrupt smooth diplomatic relations with the forum.

Dicey also justified his formulation on the basis that the English court should not enforce an illegal contract that violates the law of the place of performance of 'a foreign and friendly country'.[80] Lord Wright also held that Dicey's formulation 'is based on the principle that it is contrary to the comity of nations that the Court of one country should seek to enforce the performance of something in another country which is forbidden by the law of that country'.[81]

[77] ibid at 111.

[78] (n 2).

[79] Noted in Alexander (n 3) 322; Bonomi (n 1) 2471–72.

[80] Dicey (1908) (n 7) 553. See also JJ Fawcett, 'Evasion of Law and Mandatory Rules in Private International Law' (1990) 49 *Cambridge Law Journal* 44, 55; Alexander (n 3) 322; Chong (n 25) 34.

[81] *Rex* (n 65) 519.

The principle of international comity was explicitly endorsed and applied in the famous cases of *Foster*[82] and *Regazzoni*.[83] The manner in which this cases were decided implicitly supports the view that courtesy is used as a basis to vouch for the application of international comity in the context of the law of the place of performance regulating foreign illegality.

In *Foster*, the parties formed a partnership or syndicate to import whisky into the United States of America with the aim of making a huge profit from the enterprise. At the material time, the sale of alcoholic beverages was illegal in the United States. The parties subsequently had a dispute arising from the transaction. The majority of the Court of Appeal declared the transaction to be void on grounds of violating the law of the place of intended performance.[84] Lawrence LJ in the majority leading judgment held that:

> I am clearly of the opinion that a partnership formed for the main purpose of deriving profit from the commission of a criminal offence in a foreign and friendly country is illegal, even although the parties have not succeeded in carrying out their enterprise, and no such criminal offence has in fact been committed; and none the less so because the parties may have contemplated that if they could not successfully arrange to commit the offence themselves they would instigate or aid and abet some other person to commit it. The ground upon which I rest my judgment that such a partnership is illegal is that its recognition by our Courts would furnish a just cause for complaint by the United States Government against our Government (of which the partners are subjects), and would also be contrary to our obligation of international comity as now understood and recognized, and therefore would offend against our notions of public morality.[85]

In *Regazzoni* the defendants agreed to sell and deliver to the claimants jute bags, both parties contemplating that they should be shipped from India to Genoa for resale in South Africa. The parties were also aware that the export of jute from India to South Africa was prohibited by Indian law (due to apartheid that was existing at the time in South Africa). English law was the governing law of the contract. The defendants repudiated the contract. The (then) House of Lords unanimously held that the contract was unenforceable since an English court will not enforce a contract, or award damages for its breach, if its performance would involve doing an act in a foreign and friendly State which violates the law of that State. Again this principle was said to be based on inter alia international comity.

[82] (n 10).

[83] (n 50). See also *United City Merchants (Investments) Ltd v Royal Bank of Canada (The American Accord)* 1982] QB 208, 242; *Lilly Icos LLC v 8PM Chemists Ltd* [2009] EWHC 1905 (Ch) [263]–[265]; *Ispahani v Bank Melli Iran* [1998] Lloyd's Rep Bank 133, 140.

[84] Scrutton LJ dissented because he was not of the view that performance of the contract involved a breach of American law. He would probably have agreed with the majority if he was of the view that performance of the contract involved a breach of American law. In this connection Scrutton LJ said 'I have no doubt that if seller and buyer agreed to ship the whisky into the United States contrary to the laws of that country the contract would not be enforced here …' – *Foster* (n 10) 496.

[85] ibid 510.

The idea that the application of the law of the place of performance, in the context of foreign illegality, is simply based on international comity is open to question.[86] Why should considerable or decisive significance be given to whether a country is 'friendly' in order to apply its laws as the place of performance? It is opined that undue emphasis should not be placed on whether the country is friendly, or whether the forum is applying a foreign mandatory rule as a matter of courtesy.

Furthermore, States typically do not care about the fate of private disputes (remedies in particular), except if their strongest interests are at stake, such as in the case of a rebellion. States are more likely to be concerned with expressing their interest extra-territorially in matters that are fundamental to its political, economic or social welfare.

Public/Customary International Law

Public international law is another very old rationale for the application of the law of the place of performance in the context of foreign illegality. The justification for this approach is that the court of one State should not assist in breaking the laws of another sovereign State. Westlake appears to be one of the earliest scholars who advanced this view, when he submitted inter alia that one sovereign cannot enjoin the performance of an act that is illegal in a foreign country.[87]

In reality, though international comity is used in private international law, it could also be argued that it is a sub-category of public international law. Thus some scholars submit that:

> English and American courts often refer to 'international comity' in situations to which there ought more properly to be applied the term 'international law'. It is probable that many a present rule of international comity will in future become one of international law.[88]

In contrast, some scholars simply view the typology of cases based on *Foster* and *Regazzoni* as one that is based on public international law, rather than international comity. Thus, Sian submits that 'the rationale for the rule is not comity but the prevention of an attack upon the legal integrity of the foreign country where performance of the contractual obligation was to have taken place'.[89]

Mann submits that the cases applying Dicey's formulation is:

> … probably a general principle, evidenced by the practice of all civilised nations, and therefore a principle of customary international law, that no one is required to do an act

[86] See also Dickinson (n 1) 77; Harris (n 40) 279.
[87] Westlake (n 8) 176–77, [192].
[88] R Jennings and A Watts (eds), *Oppenheim's International Law* vol I, 9th edn (Oxford, Oxford University Press, 1992) 51. See also Alexander (n 3).
[89] Sian (n 13) 338 (citing others).

which at the material time and place is unlawful, illegal or criminal and for this reason in law impossible.[90]

Reynolds also submits that: '[t]he basis of the rule should be sought in public international law, or at least in the common understanding of nations'.[91] He again submits that: 'It is obvious that the increased amount and sophistication of international commerce (and hence also on international law-breaking) may well lead to this doctrine being invoked with continuing frequency, if its scope can be established.'[92]

The use of the 'public international law' terminology is open to question. In reality, these international commercial cases such as *Foster* and *Regazzoni*, were concerned with disputes between private parties and not States. As Philip aptly notes, 'the borderline between public and private law becomes difficult to draw, as public regulations pervade the life of individuals to an increasing extent'.[93]

The remedies sought in *Foster* and *Regazzoni* were compensatory or restitutive in nature between private individuals. In *Foster*, the US was not a party to the dispute, and it is open to question whether the breach of US law on the prohibition of the distribution of alcohol is one that attracts the general application of public international law principles. At best, the public policy of the United States was offended. In *Regazzoni*, India was not a party to the dispute and it is open to question whether the breach of India's law on sale of goods to South Africa is one that attracts the general application of public international law principles. Again, at best, the public policy of India was offended.

While one does not undermine or ignore the underlying 'public international law' significance in these cases, it should not be overstated. On the contrary, this might simply be a convergence or confluence between public and private international law.[94] In other words, 'private international law, therefore, needs to determine the legitimate interests of individuals and states in one single dispute'.[95] In the cases of *Foster* and *Regazzoni*, private international law was directly determining the legitimate interest of private individuals and indirectly determining the interests of the States which might want their law to apply extra-territorially

[90] FA Mann, *Foreign Affairs in English Courts* (Oxford, Oxford University Press, 1986) 155. See also FA Mann, *Further Studies in International Law* (Oxford, Oxford University Press, 1990) 155–58.

[91] Reynolds (n 18) 382.

[92] ibid 373.

[93] Philip (n 40) 89.

[94] See generally A Mills, *The Confluence of Public and Private International Law: Justice, Pluralism and Subsidiarity in the International Constitutional Ordering of Private Law* 1st edn (Cambridge, Cambridge University Press, 2009). In particular see HW Baade, 'The Operation of Foreign Public Law' (1995) 30 *Texas International Law Journal* 431; M Wojewoda, 'Mandatory Rules in Private International Law' (2000) 7 *Maastricht Journal of European and Comparative Law* 183, 194–96; M Bagheri, 'Conflict of Laws, Economic Regulations and Corrective/Distributive Justice' (2007) 28 *University of Pennsylvania Journal of International Law* 113, 133; B Verschraegen, 'Austrian Report' (2012) 20 *European Review of Private Law* 51, 58.

[95] Bagheri, ibid 133 (citing others).

having regard to the fact that such States were the place of performance, and the activities of the parties were aimed at hurting a fundamental legal norm of such States.

Public Policy

Public policy is another rationale for the application of the law of the place of performance in the context of foreign illegality. However, the major objection to this label is that it is difficult to ascertain or define,[96] and could thus lead to uncertainty.[97] Is it domestic, foreign, transnational or international public policy? Or is it a combination of these? How is public policy determined? The questions are endless. This explains why one English judge famously remarked that public policy 'is a very unruly horse and when once you get astride it you never know where it will carry you'.[98]

Nevertheless, some Member State courts have utilised public policy as a basis for applying the law of the place of performance in relation to foreign illegality. In this connection, Bonomi does a fantastic job in recording the pre-Rome Convention case law in Germany and France concisely and succinctly.[99]

In relation to the German practice, he states that:

> The German Federal Court, for example, has consistently rejected claims brought pursuant to sales and carriage contracts that intended to infringe on foreign customs laws or to transgress foreign prohibitions on importing and exporting. In one such case concerning the importation of cocaine into British India, the German court acknowledged that although German law applied and would uphold the validity of the contract at issue, the general notion of the 'public welfare' of India prohibited the court from enforcing the contractual claim. Likewise, the German Supreme Court took foreign mandatory rules into account when it invalidated an insurance contract involving the exportation of art objects from Nigeria to Germany. Although the contract was governed by German law, the court cited Nigerian mandatory rules forbidding the exportation of art objects and declared the contract void as against public morality.[100] Using analogous reasoning, the German Supreme Court also refused to honor loans to finance the smuggling and sale of alcohol deliverable on the high seas near the territorial waters of Sweden and Finland.[101]

[96] Mills (n 56). See also A De Lotbinière Mcdoughall, 'International Arbitration and Money Laundering' (2004–05) 20 *American University International Law Review* 1021, 1043; H Yu, 'Choice of the Proper Law Vs Public Policy' (2008) 1 *Contemporary Asia Arbitration Journal* 107; L Villiers, 'Breaking in the "Unruly Horse": The Status of Mandatory Rules of Law as a Public Policy Basis for the Non-Enforcement of Arbitral Awards' (2011) 18 *Australian International Law Journal* 155, 162.

[97] *Kuwait Airways Corporation v Iraqi Airways Co & Anor* [2002] UKHL 19 [17]–[18] (Lord Nichols).

[98] *Richardson v Mellish* [1824] 2 Bing 229, 252. *Cf. Enderby Town Football Club Ltd v The Football Association Ltd* [1971] 1 All ER 215 at 219 (Lord Denning).

[99] Bonomi (n 1) 2471–72.

[100] It is uncertain if this particular case would be qualified as the place of performance in relation to the country of origin of the goods under Article 9(3) of Rome I. See K Siehr, 'Private International Law and the Difficult Problem to Return Illegally Exported Cultural Property' (2015) 20 *Uniform Law Review* 503, 509. cf Reynolds (n 18) 382–86.

[101] Footnotes omitted in the quotation.

In relation to the French practice, he states that:

> French appeals courts used similar rationales to take into account the 'public policies' of foreign states regardless whether the applicable law was the forum law, the law of another state as chosen by the parties, or the law of another state as provided for by the conflicts rules employed in the absence of party choice. For example, French courts have invalidated contracts that provide for smuggling, citing the strong interest of the smugglers' destination state in regulating such activities. Also relying on the mandatory rules of a foreign state, the Tribunal de la Seine invalidated a loan governed by French law that would have supported a revolution in Venezuela.[102]

In the examples cited by Bonomi, it is not so clear whether these German and French courts were applying domestic, foreign, international or transnational public policy. This could be contrasted with the English approach which has applied transnational public policy in a double-barrelled way, in relation to foreign illegality. In other words, the public policy of the forum and the foreign country must militate against the enforcement of the international commercial contract.

Thus, in *Lemenda*[103] the defendants in August 1984 entered into an agreement with the national oil corporation of Qatar, for the supply to the defendants of 750,000 barrels of crude oil per month. At the time of the execution of the supply contract the defendants signed a side letter in which they confirmed that the supply contract had been negotiated without agents or brokers, and without the payment of commission to anyone. The parties agreed that the supply contract was governed by Qatar law, and under that law contracts which were contrary to public policy were void. Early in 1985 the plaintiffs entered into an agreement with the defendants under which, if the plaintiffs procured the renewal of the supply contract, they would be paid commission of 30 US cents a barrel. Both parties conceded that the commission contract was governed by English law. The High Court per Philip J held thus:

> In my judgment, the English courts should not enforce an English law contract which falls to be performed abroad where: (i) it relates to an adventure which is contrary to a head of English public policy which is founded on general principles of morality, and (ii) the same public policy applies to the country of performance so that the agreement would not be enforceable under the law of that country.[104]

Lemanda's case was another way of applying the law of the country of closest connection, the place of performance, to render the contract unenforceable.[105] In the German and French cases discussed above, the law of the place of performance was also one of closest connection or at least substantial connection to the international commercial contract. Thus, the better view is that the place of performance in these cases might be regarded as serving a regulatory function in international commercial transactions.

[102] ibid (footnotes omitted). The interest of the foreign state is admittedly strong in such a case.
[103] (n 10).
[104] ibid 461.
[105] Mills (n 56) 207, 215.

b. The Law of the Place of Performance: Enforcement of Foreign Arbitral Awards and Judgments

The law of the place of performance is of immense practical significance in international commercial transactions. The regulatory function served by the law of the place of performance is such that a foreign judgment or arbitral award that disregards or violates the law of performance would face practical difficulties at the stage of recognition and enforcement. It is trite that a foreign judgment or arbitral award, no matter how well written, is a useless piece of paper if it cannot be recognised and enforced.

In this connection, the significance of the law of the place of performance has been engaged by other scholars particularly in the context of international commercial arbitration. Though it is controversial[106] as to whether arbitrators are bound to take into account and apply mandatory rules of a foreign country, in order to avoid the enforcing forum from refusing the recognition and enforcement of the award based on public policy,[107] most scholars accept the view that as a minimum, international arbitral practice respects mandatory rules of the country where a contract is to be performed.[108] The principal rationale for this view is that the country where the contract is to be performed normally has the closest connection with the contract.[109]

If the law of the place of performance is violated, the practical difficulty the award creditor may experience during enforcement is evidenced in the arbitral decision in *Krupp v Kopex*[110] where it was observed that:

> Krupp's deliveries were in the last moment before the transportation by railway to Poland, affected by General Jaruzelki's Decree issued on 21 December 1981, prohibiting

[106] See generally O Lando, 'The Law Applicable to the Merits of the Dispute' in P Sarcevic (ed), *Essays on International Commercial Arbitration* (Amsterdam, Springer, 1989) 129, 157; De Lotbinière Mcdoughall (n 96) 1049–51; J Hill, 'Some Private International Law Aspects of the Arbitration Act 1996' (1997) 46 *International and Comparative Law Quarterly* 274, 305; Yu (n 96) 108–10; CS Gibson, 'Arbitration, Civilisation and Public Policy: Seeking Counterpoise between Arbitral Autonomy and the Public Policy Defense in View of Foreign Mandatory Public Law' (2008–09) 113 *Penn State Law Review* 1227, 1247–54; Villiers (n 96). See also B Yuksel, 'The Relevance of the Rome I Regulation to International Commercial Arbitration in the European Union' (2011) 7 *Journal of Private International Law* 149–78.

[107] See Article V(2) of the Convention on the Recognition and Enforcement of Foreign Arbitral Awards 1958 (New York Convention).

[108] MR Baniassadi, 'Do Mandatory Rules of Public Law Limit Choice of Law in International Commercial Arbitration?' (1992–93) 10 *International Tax and Business Law* 59, 70; H Daniel, 'Choice of Law and Foreign Mandatory Rules in International Arbitration' (1994) 11 *Journal of International Arbitration* 57, 69, 86; M Blessing, 'Mandatory Rules of Law *versus* Party Autonomy in International Arbitration' (1997) 14 *Journal of International Arbitration* 23, 34; Hill (n 106) 305 (citing others); AFM Maniruzzaman, 'Choice of Law in International Contracts – Some Fundamental Conflict of Laws Issues [article]' (1999) 16 *Journal of International Arbitration* 141, 166; De Lotbinière (n 96) 1049–51; V Pavic, 'Bribery and International Commercial Arbitration – The Role of Mandatory Rules and Public Policy' (2012) 43 *Victoria University Wellington Law Review* 661, 676.

[109] ibid (all).

[110] Decided by an arbitral tribunal sitting in Zurich, Switzerland on 09/09/1983. Cited in Blessing (n 108) 34.

> all further industrial imports (amounting to many billions of Dollars) essentially because of the unavailability of foreign currency. Nevertheless, the industrial equipment already manufactured by Krupp had to be paid for. As a consequence, the Polish party was well advised to see to it that import could nevertheless take place on the basis of a special permit, so that, for the benefit of the Polish economy, the facility could be erected for the price it had to pay to Krupp anyway.[111]

In relation to judicial proceedings, in *Soleimany v Soleimany*,[112] the English Court of Appeal refused to enforce a foreign arbitration award in England that was based on a claim by one Iranian national against another for damages arising out of a contract where the parties had smuggled carpets out of Iran in violation of its export control and excise laws. The Court of Appeal stated the principle to the effect that:

> An English court will not enforce a contract governed by English law, or to be performed in England, which is illegal by English domestic law. Nor will it enforce a contract governed by the law of a foreign and friendly state, or which requires performance in such a country, if performance is illegal by the law of that country … The rule applies as much to the enforcement of an arbitration award as to the direct enforcement of a contract in legal proceedings.[113]

By way of analogy, foreign judgments that violate the mandatory rules of the law of the place of performance might also face practical difficulties at the stage of recognition and enforcement of the judgment.[114] Thus, it has been held by a Canadian court that 'an Ontario Court should decline to give judgment requiring performance of an act in a foreign jurisdiction if the performance there was illegal'.[115] In the United States, Section 202(2) of the Second Restatement[116] provides that: 'When performance is illegal in the place of performance, the contract will usually be denied enforcement.'[117]

Even in the EU, where the enforcement of foreign judgments is expedited with little or no legal impediments among Member State courts,[118] failure to take into account the mandatory rule of the law of the place of performance of a Member State might result in practical difficulties for the recognition and enforcement of such foreign judgment.

Admittedly, non-compliance with Article 9(3) per se cannot result in another Member State court refusing to recognise and enforce the foreign judgment.[119]

[111] ibid.
[112] *Soleimany v Soleimany* [1999] QB 785.
[113] ibid 803–04.
[114] See also Marazopoulou (n 40) 794–95.
[115] *Montreal* (n 12) [60].
[116] Restatement (Second) of Conflict of Laws 1971.
[117] See also *Panama* (n 71); *Wood Bros Homes Inc v Walker Adjustment Bureau* (Supreme Court of Colorado, En Banc) October 22, 1979 198 Colo. 444 601 P.2d 1369.
[118] See generally Section 36 to 44 of Brussels Ia. See also Recitals 26–27 to Brussels Ia.
[119] For a detailed analysis see generally Bonomi (n 17) 599, 614 [44], 660–61, [207]–[212].

But where the non-compliance with Article 9(3) is manifestly contrary to the public policy of the forum of enforcement, there is no good reason why recognition and enforcement should not be denied.[120] The reason is simple. The EU principle of mutual trust and uniformity cannot sensibly be applied to the domestic public policy of the forum. In other words, a Member State court that is recognising and enforcing a foreign judgment is not bound by the manner in which the originating court interprets Article 9(3). If the originating court gives Article 9(3) an interpretation that hurts the legal order of a Member State that is recognising and enforcing the foreign judgment, it might be denied recognition and enforcement.

For example, assume A and B normally domiciled in the Netherlands enter into an agreement for B to become an agent for A, for the sale of Indian hemp in the United Kingdom. The contract is perfectly legal in the Netherlands, but illegal in the UK, the place of performance. A dispute arises between A and B, because B has refused to declare all the profits he made to A. A sues B in the Netherlands. B does not challenge the courts' jurisdiction and both parties agree that Dutch law should apply. A gets judgment in the Netherlands against B, despite B's objection that Article 9(3) of Rome I should be applied to invalidate the obligation under the contract. A decides to enforce the judgment in Germany because B now has most of his assets there. It is likely that Germany would decline enforcement on grounds of public policy, since the contract is also illegal in the eyes of UK law – the place of performance.[121]

iv. The Law of the Place of Performance and Party Expectations

Parties who enter into an international commercial contract should reasonably expect that if their transaction violates the law of the place of performance, it would not be enforced. The expectation of the parties in this context is one that also yields to proximity because the obligation is usually the most crucial element for the parties in a contract. The idea that the parties' expectation of respecting the law of the place of performance in the context of foreign illegality yields to the principle of proximity, also lends support to discrediting the excessive or absolute use of 'public' law or State interests.

Moreover, this idea is not new. Westlake who appears to be the intellectual godfather of this idea submits that 'a contract that is illegal in the country

[120] See generally Section 45 to 51 of Brussels Ia, and C-7/98 *Dieter Krombach v André Bamberski*, EU:C:2000:164.

[121] In the context of the relationship between Article 9 and 21 of Rome I, see Harris (n 40) 275, 284, 320; Siehr (n 100) 824; M McParland, *The Rome I Regulation on the Law Applicable to Contractual Obligations* (Oxford, Oxford University Press, 2015) 177, [15.112]; Bonomi (n 17) 614, [42]–[44]; 629, [95]; 660–61, [207]–[212].

in which it is to be performed cannot have raised any expectations as to its performance'.[122]

Jaffey submits that: 'contractors should reasonably anticipate that the laws of a country will in the interests of that country regulate or attach legal consequences to things done within its territory'.[123]

Chukwumerije submits that: '[t]he parties should be presumed to act on the understanding that the contract would be performed in accordance with the rules of the country where performance is required'.[124]

Chong rationalises the cases applying Dicey's formulation to the effect that 'the parties' expectations in this situation is that the contract would not be enforced as enforcement would expose the party who has to carry out that particular performance to sanctions in the place of performance'.[125]

This idea has also been recognised and applied in an arbitral decision of the International Chamber of Commerce in the following words:

> Since the contract must be performed in Lebanon, Syria and Jordan, it is a sure fact that the Lebanese importer was obliged to comply with the mandatory rules of the countries of importation and that the Japanese party cannot now claim that those rules cannot be raised against him.
>
> Any merchant of a country who attempts to sell his products in another country is bound to respect the mandatory rules of the country of reception and cannot claim to be unaware of or not respect police laws or the regulation governing the importation of his goods, particularly when this law or regulation or regulation existed at the time of the performance of the contract.[126]

In summation, given that the parties regard the performance in a contract as its most important element, there is an expectation that such parties would not do anything illegal or unlawful in the place of performance, even though the law of the place of performance is not the governing law.

v. The Law of the Place of Performance and Essential Validity

The significance of the law of the place of performance in the context of foreign illegality might be one that is concerned with the essential or material validity of a contract. Indeed, Dicey regarded illegality according to the law of the place of performance as one of the exceptions to the rule that the proper law of the contract governs the validity of a contract.[127] In reality, the cases applying Dicey's

[122] Westlake (n 8) 176–77, [192] quoted with approval in M Hellner, 'Third Country Overriding Mandatory Rules in the Rome I Regulation: Old Wine in New Bottles?' (2009) 5 *Journal of Private International Law* 447, 449.

[123] Jaffey (n 56) 11.

[124] O Chukwumerije, 'Mandatory Rules of Law in International Commercial Arbitration' (1993) 5 *African Journal of International and Comparative Law* 561, 574.

[125] Chong (n 25) 65.

[126] *ICC Case No 1859*, 1973 Rev Arb 122. Cited in Chukwumerije (n 124) 574.

[127] Dicey (1908) (n 7) 553.

rule might be regarded as using the law of the place of performance to determine the essential validity of a contract.[128]

The fact that the place of performance was a very significant factor in the context of the essential validity lends support to the idea that the place of performance is normally the connecting factor that best embodies the principle of proximity or close connection. As Lord Simon aptly remarked: the 'criterion of a real and substantial connection seems to be to be useful and relevant in considering the choice of law for testing, if not all questions of essential validity, at least the questions of quintessential validity …'[129]

The fact that the place of performance was the *only*[130] connecting factor that was utilised as an exception to the *lex causae*, in English practice to determine essential validity confirms the view that the place of performance is a factor of considerable significance in international commercial transactions. Moreover, the importance English case law at the time attached to law of the place of performance in the context of foreign illegality, raised questions as to whether the law of the place of performance was a rule (rather than an exception) to determine essential validity of contract.[131]

In this connection, the only connecting factor that *attempted* to challenge the absolute significance of the place of performance was the *lex loci contractus*. Some judges[132] and scholars[133] had expressed the 'highly controversial'[134] view at the time that a contract that is illegal by the *lex loci contractus* would not be enforced in English courts. Other scholars[135] rightly regarded such a view as erroneous, as it was not a view supported by the practice of English case law.[136]

[128] See generally *Ralli Bros* (n 9) 304 (Scrutton LJ); *Kleinwort* (n 10) 693 (Mackinnon LJ), 696 (Du Parcq LJ); *Toprak* (n 65) 105. See also Jaffey (n 56); Sian (n 13) 2472. In the context of Article 10(1)(e) of the Rome Convention and 12(1)(e) of Rome I see O Lando, 'The EEC Convention on the Law Applicable to Contractual Obligations' (1987) *Common* 24 *Market Law Review* 159, 205–11.

[129] *Vervaeke v Smith* [1983] 1 AC 145, 166. See generally Mills (n 56).

[130] See also *Libyan* (n 65); *Libyan Arab Foreign Bank v Manufacturer Hanover Trust Co (No 2)* [1989] 1 Lloyd's Rep 608.

[131] 'when I had the privilege of being taught by Professor Dicey he was always anxious to insist on this, that students of law heard so much about exceptions to rules and, comparatively speaking, so little about the rules themselves, that they were apt to think that the law was to be found rather in the exceptions than in the rules.' – *Kleinwort* (n 10) 696 (Du Parcq LJ). For a detailed academic analysis see also Morris (n 21) 505.

[132] Greer LJ in *The Torni* [1932] 78, 88.

[133] PM North, *Cheshire and North's Private International Law* 10th edn (Oxford, Oxford University Press, 1979) 230–33; JHC Morris, *Dicey and Morris on the Conflict of Laws* 8th edn (London, Sweet & Maxwell, 1976) 756–57; JHC Morris, *The Conflict of Laws* 2nd edn (London, Sweet & Maxwell, 1980) 233–34; Viejobueno (n 22) 207.

[134] L Collins, Dicey & Morris, *The Conflict of Laws* 11th edn (London, Sweet &Maxwell, 1987) 1219.

[135] KD Untiedt, 'International Contracts under the Conflict of Laws Rules of Great Britain and Japan' (1984) 7 *Loyola of Los Angeles International and Comparative Law Journal* 193, 212; Sian (n 13) 306, 345; AM Sinclair, 'Conflict of Law Problems in Admiralty' (1961) 15 *Southwestern Law Journal* 207, 254–55; L Collins, 'Contractual Obligations – The EEC Preliminary Draft Convention on Private International Law' (1976) 25 *International and Comparative Law Quarterly* 35, 38.

[136] See generally *Euro-Diam* (n 10) 190. See also Untiedt (n 135) 212.

III. Article 7(1) of the Rome Convention: The Principle of Proximity and the Place of Performance

Article 7(1) of the Rome Convention[137] provides that:

> When applying under this Convention the law of a country, effect may be given to the mandatory rules of the law of another country with which the situation has a close connection, if and in so far as, under the law of the latter country, those rules must be applied whatever the law applicable to the contract. In considering whether to give effect to these mandatory rules, regard shall be had to their nature and purpose and to the consequences of their application or non-application.[138]

Article 7(1) of the Rome Convention is similar to Article 9(3) of Rome I, save that the phrase 'close connection' has been excised from Article 9(3). It is thus important to discuss Article 7(1) of the Rome Convention, in order to demonstrate inter alia why the place of performance under Article 9(3) of Rome I is an expression of the principle of proximity.

The *true* historical origin of Article 7(1) of the Rome Convention is debatable, in particular as to whether it is of German or Dutch heritage. Lord Collins et al submit that:

> Its historical origin probably lies with the German theory that foreign public laws (especially exchange control and import or export restrictions) should apply if the interests of the forum or of a third country are not unduly violated.[139]

[137] It was substantially worded in a similar way as Article 7 of the 1972 Preliminary Draft Convention on the Law Applicable to Contractual and Non-Contractual Obligations (1972 Draft Convention).

[138] cf Article 13 of the Benelux Treaty concerning Uniform Law on Private International Law of July 3, 1969; Section 187(2)(b) of the U.S Restatement (Second) of Contracts 1981; Article 3079 of the Civil Code of Quèbec of 1991; Article 16 of the Hague Convention of 1 July 1985 on the Law Applicable to Trusts and on their Recognition; Article 19 Swiss Private International Law Act 1987; Article 9(2) Basel Resolutions of the Institute of International Law 1991; Proposed Section 9(10) of Australian Law Reform Commission (Choice of Law (Report No 58) (Canberra, Australian Government Publishing Service, 1992); Article 11 Mexico City Convention 1994. For a comparative analysis of Article 7(1) of the Rome Convention with these statutes see generally P Lagarde, 'The European Convention on the Law Applicable to Contractual Obligations: An Apologia' (1981) 22 *Virginia Journal of International Law* 91; GR Delaume, 'The European Convention on the Law Applicable to Contractual Obligations: Why a Convention' (1981) 22 *Virginia Journal of International Law* 105; F Meisel, 'Harmonisation of Contracts, Jurisdiction and Conflicts of Laws in the European Community' (1988) 13 *Holdsworth Law Review* 46; JP Fletcher, 'An Argument for Ratification: Some Basic Principles of the 1994 Inter-American Convention of the Law Applicable to International Contracts' (1999) 27 *Georgia Journal of International and Comparative Law* 477; G Fouchard in E Gaillard and J Savage (eds), *Goldman on International Commercial Arbitration* 354 (Leiden, Kluwer International, 1999) 852; Chong (n 25) 36, 65 (fn 26); Plender and Wilderspin (n 40) 363, [2-032]; Bonomi (n 17) 637.

[139] Collins (2012) (n 25) 1830, 32-085.

Plender and Wilderspin also express the view held by some other scholars that Article 7(1) has its origins in the *Sonderhaust* theory that:

> [d]eveloped in Germany during the Second World War as a defence to proceedings brought in the United States against German borrowers of United States bonds which ceased to be serviced after the introduction of exchange controls in 1931.[140]

In contrast, a preponderant number of scholars[141] express the view that it is of Dutch origin and by citing the famous dictum in the Dutch Supreme Court's decision in *Alnati*.[142] The Giuliano-Lagarde report records it as follows:

> although the law applicable to contracts of an international character can, as a matter of principle, only be that which the parties themselves have chosen, 'it may be that, for a foreign State, the observance of certain of its rules, even outside its own territory, is of such importance that the courts must take account of them, and hence apply them in preference to the law of another State which may have been chosen by the parties to govern their contract'.[143]

In addition, Hellner claims that de Winter's work[144] actually influenced the Dutch Supreme Court's decision in *Alnati* because AG Minkenhoff in that case cited de Winter's article with approval and the Dutch Supreme Court's decision was phrased in similar terms as de Winter's article.[145]

Article 7(1) is a form of escape clause. As Philip rightly submits, 'Article 7 is a rule which in *various ways* constitutes an escape clause, making it possible in certain circumstances to avoid the application of the rules of the Convention.'[146] He also rightly submits that:

> It is general in nature and covers all international mandatory rules of third countries with which there is a close connection. It may partly be read as an escape clause from the general choice of law rules of the Convention.[147]

[140] Plender and Wilderspin (n 40) 363, [12-032]. See also FK Juenger, 'American and European Conflicts Law' (1982) 30 *American Journal of Comparative Law* 117, 123.

[141] Delaume (n 138) 113; Philip (n 40) 104; O Lando, 'New American Choice-of-Law Principles and the European Conflict of Laws of Contracts' (1982) 30 *American Journal of Comparative Law* 19, 33; J Schultsz, 'Dutch Antecedents and Parallels to Article 7 of the EEC Contracts Convention of 1980' (1983) 47 *Rabels Zeitschrift* 267, 276–77; Lando (1998) (n 40) 406; Reynolds (n 18) 381; HLE Verhagen, 'The Tension between Party Autonomy and European Union Law: Some Observations on *Ingmar GB LTD v EATON LEONARD TECHNOLOGIES INC*' (2002) 51 *International and Comparative Law Quarterly* 135, 135–36; Chong (n 25) 44; Beaumont and McEleavy (n 17) 538, [14.3.14]; Bonomi (n 17) 635–36, [121].

[142] Decided 13 May 1966.

[143] (n 55) 26.

[144] LL de Winter, 'Dwingend recht bij international overeenkomsten' (1964) 11 *Nederlandse Tijdschrift voor International Recht* 329.

[145] Hellner (n 122) 449.

[146] Philip (n 40) 100 (emphasis added). See also Lando (1982) (n 141) 33 – 'art. 7(1) of the Convention is only an exception to the operation of the traditional conflict rule.' cf Harris (n 40) 290.

[147] Philip (n 40) 104.

The fact that Article 7(1) of the Rome Convention is a form of escape clause is an important point that would be returned to in the context of Article 9(3) of Rome I.[148]

Article 7(1) of the Rome Convention was a statutory provision that embodied a very flexible form of judicial discretion, and aroused significant controversy among some Member States.[149] In fact, the UK, Germany, Luxembourg, Ireland, Portugal, Latvia and Slovenia entered a reservation not to apply Article 7(1).[150] The UK's reason to enter a reservation was even more forceful. North, a leading English private international law scholar at the time brilliantly records the reason in the following words:

> It was felt by the United Kingdom that Article 7(1) was a recipe for *confusion*, in that a judge might feel obliged to steer his way through three possibly mutually inconsistent sets of mandatory rules; for *uncertainty*, an uncertainty which freedom to choose the applicable law is intended, in the business community, to avoid; for *expense*, in that proof of the mandatory rules for all relevantly connected foreign laws might be called for; and for *delay*, in that Article 7(1) might provide the means of delaying litigation inordinately, with a fear that it might frighten potential arbitration and litigation away from the United Kingdom.[151]

The reasons for entering into a reservation by some Member States, particularly the UK, attracted divergent responses from scholars. For those in support of the reservation, they regarded Article 7(1) as a 'dangerous',[152] 'most unfortunate provision',[153] 'incongruous and even immoral',[154] because it could lead to 'unpredictable results',[155]

[148] See s VI of this chapter.

[149] Giuliano-Lagarde (n 55) 27; P North (ed), *Contract Conflicts, The EEC Convention on the Law Applicable to Contractual Obligations: A Comparative Study* (Amsterdam, North-Holland Publishing Company, 1982) 17; Bonomi (n 1) – Article 7(1) 'engenders significant controversy' citing E Jayme, 'The Rome Convention on the Law Applicable to Contractual Obligations (1980)' in P Sarcevic (ed), *International Contracts and Conflict of Laws: A Collection of Essays* (London, Graham & Trotman/Martinus Nijhoff, 1990) 36, 46 (describing Article 7(1) as containing the 'most controversial conflicts rule of the Rome Convention'); BV Hoffmann, 'Assessment of the EEC Convention from a German Point of View' in P North (ed), *Contract Conflicts: The EEC Convention on the Law Applicable to Contractual Obligations: A Comparative Study* (Amsterdam, North-Holland Publishing Company, 1982) 221, 229 (characterising Article 7 as the 'most revolutionary and highly debated article' in the Convention); AG Szpunar in C-135/15, *Hellenic Republic v Nikiforidis* EU:C:2016:281 [2], [79].

[150] The reservation was entered pursuant to Article 22(1)(a) of the Rome Convention.

[151] North (n 149) 19–20 (emphasis added).

[152] Reynolds (n 18) 382; Wojewoda (n 94) 198.

[153] L Collins, *Essays in International Litigation and the Conflict of Laws* (Oxford, Clarendon, corrected edition 1996) 425.

[154] FA Mann, 'Contracts: Effect of Mandatory Rules' in P North (ed), *Contract Conflicts: The EEC Convention on the Law Applicable to Contractual Obligations: A Comparative Study* (Amsterdam, North-Holland Publishing Company, 1982) 31 (citing others).

[155] Delaume (n 138) 113. See also Jackson (n 21) 73–75; Philip (n 40) 103; CGJ Morse, 'Contracts of Employment and the EEC Contractual Obligations Convention' in P North (ed), *Contract Conflicts, The EEC Convention on the Law Applicable to Contractual Obligations: A Comparative Study* (Amsterdam, North-Holland Publishing Company, 1982) 143; Reynolds (n 18) 382; GM McGuinness, 'The Rome Convention: The Contracting Parties' Choice' (2000) 1 *San Diego International Law Journal* 127, 159–60; C Tillman, 'The Relationship between Party Autonomy and the Mandatory Rules in the Rome

'injustice',[156] and 'create practical problems'[157] such as frustrating 'party expectations'.[158]

For those against the reservation, they regarded Article 7(1) as 'its main advantage'[159] and 'one of the most useful rules'[160] on the ground that inter alia it enhanced 'the international harmony of decisions since, regardless of which State Court's hearing the case, an instrument is created which makes it possible to give a uniform decision',[161] thereby reducing forum shopping,[162] and also promoted 'international co-operation and solidarity'[163] among States. Thus, some scholars regarded the reasons against the reservation as 'not very convincing'[164] and 'regrettable'.[165]

It is important to note that there were two main factors in the exercise of flexible judicial discretion under Article 7(1) that caused this controversy. The first, and perhaps more important, was the meaning of the term 'close connection'. The second was the interpretation of the phrase 'regard shall be had to their nature and purpose and to the consequences of their application or non-application'. These factors are considered below.

A. Close Connection

In relation to the first factor, 'close connection', it is clear that it included factors that would be considered under the current Article 4 of Rome I.[166] However it was unclear whether 'close connection' was to be given a strict or broad interpretation – a position comparable in some ways to the then Article 4(5) of the Rome Convention.[167] The Giuliano-Lagarde report records it in the following words:

> The former text did not specify the nature of the 'connection' which must exist between the contract and a country other than that whose law is applicable. Several experts

Convention' (2002) *Journal of Business Law* 45, 70; MM Hakki, 'Choice of Law, Contracts and The EC's 1980 Rome Convention: A Re-evaluation in the 21st Century' (2003) *Australian Law Journal* 156, 165; Chong (n 25) 39, 57; Beaumont and Mc Eleavy (n 17) 514, 10.292; AG Szpunar in *Hellenic Republic* (n 149) [79].

[156] FA Mann, 'Effect of Mandatory Rules' in K Lipstein (ed), *Harmonisation of Private International Law by the EEC* (London, University of London Institute of Advanced Legal Studies, 1978) 36.

[157] Collins (1982) (n 27) 206.

[158] Delaume (n 138) 119–20. See also Chong (n 25) 44.

[159] D Lasok and P Stone, *Conflict of Laws in the European Community* (London, Professional Books, 1987) 377.

[160] ibid 378.

[161] AG Szpunar in *Hellenic Republic* (n 149) [80] (citing others).

[162] See also PR Williams 'The EEC Convention on the Law Applicable to Contractual Obligations' (1986) 35 *International and Comparative Law Quarterly* 1, 24.

[163] AG Szpunar in *Hellenic Republic* (n 149) [80] (citing others).

[164] Lando (1998) (n 40) 408.

[165] Tetley (n 22) 329.

[166] See also Hellner (n 122); Bonomi (n 17) 599, 640, [136].

[167] See also Fawcett (n 80) 61; Bonomi (n 1) 2475; Lorenzo (n 73) 83 (fn 66).

> have observed that this omission might oblige the court in certain cases to take a large number of different and even contradictory laws into account. This lack of precision could make the court's task difficult, prolong the proceedings, and lend itself to delaying tactics. Accepting the force of these observations, the Group decided that it is essential that there be a genuine connection with the other country, and that a merely vague connection is not adequate. For example, there would be a genuine connection when the contract is to be performed in that other country or when one party is resident or has his main place of business in that other country. Among the suggested versions, the Group finally adopted the word 'close' which seemed the most suitable to define the situation which it wished to cover.[168]

The Report was ambivalent on the meaning of 'close connection'. On the one hand, it could be said that the Report favoured a restrictive interpretation because it required a 'genuine' connection. However, in reality, the term 'genuine connection' as used in the context of the Report allowed any relevant geographical factor to be taken into account, including that of the forum.[169]

Other scholars were very clear in suggesting a very narrow interpretation to Article 7(1) of the Rome Convention. Philip submitted that:

> The requirement in the original draft of 1972 was 'any connection'. That was changed during the renegotiations first into 'significant connection' and then, finally to 'close connection'. In both cases the intention was further to sharpen the requirement.[170]

Williams suggested that it should be used 'very rarely'.[171] Tillman submitted that it 'supposes more than a minimal and just connection between the foreign country and the contract as a whole. A substantial connection in the light of their nature and purpose is necessary.'[172] Bonomi also interpreted 'close connection' to mean *significant* connection.[173] In addition, some scholars argued that 'close connection' should be restricted to one or at most two countries.[174]

Indeed, during the period of negotiation of the then Article 7(1) of the 1972 Draft Convention, some scholars, drawing from the *Ralli Bros* cases, had already advocated narrowing the scope of 'close connection' to a specific connecting factor of the place of performance.[175]

[168] (n 55) 27.

[169] Williams (n 162) 23. See also Tillman (n 155); J Erauw, 'Observations about Mandatory Rules Imposed on Transatlantic Commercial Relationships' (2003–2004) 26 *Houston Journal of International Law* 269.

[170] Philip (n 40) 103.

[171] Williams (n 162) 22.

[172] Tillman (n 155) 77 (citing inter alia Jackson (n 21) 73.

[173] Bonomi (n 1) 2475.

[174] U Drobing, 'Comments on Art. 7 of the Draft Convention' in O Lando et al (eds), *European Private International Law of Obligations Acts and Documents of an International Colloqium on the European Preliminary Draft Convention on the Law Applicable to Contractual and Non-Contractual Obligation* 1st edn (Berlin, Mohr, 1975).

[175] Lipstein (n 68) 11.

Of particular significance to this book is that scholars agreed that the place of performance would best or obviously satisfy the requirement of 'close connection', when compared to other connecting factors. Bonomi submitted that:

> It seems clear that for a genuine connection with the situation to exist, the contract must be associated with a foreign country in such a manner that makes it appropriate to safeguard the operation of specific foreign mandatory rules. For example, if a foreign country maintains mandatory rules regarding the performance of contracts, the situation may be held to have a close connection with that country if that country is the *locus solutionis* but not if it is merely the *locus contractus* ...[176]

Harris also submits that:

> It is notable that only two examples were given by Giuliano and Lagarde of countries of close connection whose mandatory rules might be invoked under Article 7(1) of the Convention. Although, this was only intended to be illustrative, the fact remains that the situation where performance is to be effected in a state where it has become unlawful was, is and always has been the obvious, paradigmatic case for giving effect to a third state's overriding mandatory rules.[177]

Indeed, Lando expressly considered whether '[T]he place of performance of the contract may be a more precise concept than that with which the situation has a close connection ...'[178] In other words, the place of performance was the factor that normally or best embodied the concept of 'close connection' in foreign country overriding mandatory rules, and could thus limit the scope of judicial discretion. In this connection, this explains why some scholars have seriously raised the question as to whether there is a significant difference between Article 9(3) of Rome I, and Article 7(1) of the Rome Convention in the sense that the place of performance had always been considered a factor that best represents the idea of close connection.[179]

Moreover, though there is very scanty case law from Member State courts on Article 7(1) of the Rome Convention, the place of performance was the connecting factor that triggered its application in a French case. In *Moller Maersk c Viol*,[180] the Cour de Cassation in applying Article 7(1) of the Rome Convention quashed a judgment of an Appeal Court that had not taken account of an embargo of French goods imposed by the law of Ghana, the country to which the goods were to be delivered.[181]

[176] Bonomi (n 1) 2475.
[177] Harris (n 40) 320. See also Chong (n 25) 43.
[178] Lando (n 40) (1998) 408.
[179] Hellner (n 122).
[180] Judgment no 330 of March 16, 2010.
[181] cf Plender and Wilderspin (n 40) 367, [12-037]: 'The judgment is not particularly strong authority on the application art.7(1) since the decision of the Cour d'appel was annulled not because the court of appeal had wrongly interpreted that provision but because it had failed to even consider its application.'

B. Governmental Interest Analysis[182]

In relation to the second factor, the phrase 'regard shall be had to their nature and purpose and to the consequences of their application or non-application' has rightly been interpreted by many scholars as a form of governmental interest analysis.[183]

The significance of this governmental interest analysis provision in Article 7(1) of the Rome Convention must not be overstated.[184] This provision can only be considered if the contract has a close connection with a country. In other words, the close connection factor which is in reality a jurisdictional selecting rule (like Article 4 of Rome I), must be satisfied before the governmental interest analysis can be engaged or trigerred. This point is stressed to demonstrate the view that the idea of proximity should not be overlooked in the context of Article 7(1) of the Rome Convention (and Article 9(3) of Rome I), while undue or exaggerated significance is given to the concept of State interests. In other words, Article 7(1) of the Rome Convention also satisfies the requirement of proximity.

This book is indebted to Guedj who appreciates this view point when he extensively compares mandatory rules in Europe to the governmental interest analysis in the US.[185] In relation to Article 7(1) of the Rome Convention he rightly submits that:

> Like choice-of-law rules, the lois de police contain spatial criteria which operate partly as connecting factors … Indeed, the lois de police are both jurisdiction-selecting and rule-selecting. This clearly distinguishes them from recent American theories.[186]

[182] For the foundation of this theory in the United States see B Currie, 'The Constitution and the Choice of Law: Governmental Interests and Judicial Function', in *Selected Essays on the Conflict of Laws* – https://chicagounbound.uchicago.edu/cgi/viewcontent.cgi?article=11636&context=journal_articles. See also SC Symeonides, 'The Choice-Of-Law Revolution Fifty Years after Currie: An End and a Beginning' (2015) 2 *University of Illinois Law Review*, 1847.

[183] Lagarde (n 138) 93 (fn.12), 103; Delaume (n 138) 119–20; FK Juenger, 'The European Convention on the Law Applicable to Contractual Obligations: Some Critical Observations' (1981–82) 22 *Virginia Journal of International Law* 123, 136; Williams (n 162) 22; F Vischer, 'The Principle of The Typical Performance in International Contracts and the Draft Convention' in P North (ed), *Contract Conflicts, The EEC Convention on the Law Applicable to Contractual Obligations: A Comparative Study* (Amsterdam, North-Holland Publishing Company, 1982) 25, 26, 29; Jackson (n 21) 68, 75; Philip (n 40) 103; Lasok and Stone (n 159) 377–78; S Cohen, 'The EEC Convention and U.S Law Governing Choice of Law for Contracts, with particular emphasis on the Restatement Second: A Comparative Study' (1988–89) 13 *Maryland Journal of International Law and Trade* 223; TG Guedj, 'The Theory of the Lois de Police, A Functional Trend in Continental Private International Law – A Comparative Analysis with Modern American Theories' (1991) 39 *American Journal of Comparative Law* 661, 697; HM Horlacher, 'The Rome Convention and the German Paradigm: Forecasting the Demise of the European Treaty on the Law Applicable to Contractual Obligations' (1994) 27 *Cornell International Law Journal* 173, 179–80; Fletcher (n 138) 499; Tillman (n 155); Chong (n 25) 36; Dickinson (n 1) 57–59. See also Lando and Nielsen (n 40) 326; Hill and Chong (n 22) 538, [14.3.14]; Marazopoulou (n 40) 789–90.

[184] cf Tillman (n 155) 68.

[185] Guedj (n 183) 661.

[186] ibid 676-7. See also Tillman (n 155) 68.

He also rightly submits that:

> Lois de police are jurisdiction *and* rule-selecting. The spatial criterion has two functions: 1) The criterion delineates the scope of application of the rule which embodies it; 2) it operates as a connecting factor. When the conditions set by the purpose and the content of the rule are met, the lois de police forces the jurisdiction of that legal order irrespective of the law designated by the choice of law rule.[187]

He then concludes that 'the concept of policy in the theory of the lois de police is revealed by the purpose and the content of the very rule which embodies it. *Beyond that rule, it has no significance.* No attempt is made to generalize a given policy.'[188]

In summation, first the State's policy is a pre-requirement to identify mandatory rules, and second, proximity is then required to conclude to its application. Under Article 7(1) of the Rome Convention, the substance of the policy of a State can only be taken into account if such a State has a close connection, or is proximate to the situation involved.

IV. Article 8(3) of the Rome I Proposal: The Principle of Proximity and the Place of Performance

During the conversion of the Rome Convention into Rome I, the European Commission drafted Article 8(3) of the Rome I Proposal in the following words:

> Effect may be given to the mandatory rules of the law of another country with which the situation has a close connection. In considering whether to give effect to these mandatory rules, courts shall have regard to their nature and purpose in accordance with the definition in paragraph 1 and to the consequences of their application or non-application for the objective pursued by the relevant mandatory rules and for the parties.[189]

Article 8(3) of the Rome I Proposal was in reality a substantial re-enactment of Article 7(1) of the Rome Convention.[190] The UK comprising of inter alia stakeholders such as international commercial entities (particularly in the city of London) and some academics were very hostile to Article 8(3) of the Rome I Proposal, and thus the UK was initially hesitant to opt in.[191] In essence, the principal reason for

[187] Guedj (n 183) 679 (emphasis in the original).
[188] ibid 687 (emphasis added).
[189] For a detailed history on Article 8(3) of Rome I Regulation Proposal see Hellner (n 122); McParland (n 121) 697–705, [15.57]–[15.90].
[190] See also Hellner (n 122); Harris (n 40) 272–73.
[191] See generally Financial Markets Law Committee, 'Legal Assessment of the Conversion of the Rome Convention to a Community Instrument and the Provisions of the Proposed Rome I Regulations' – European Commission Final Proposal for a Regulation on the Law Applicable to Contractual Obligations (Rome I) (2006) 121(3) 12–14. www.fmlc.org/Documents/April06Issue121.pdf; Letter from Baroness Ashton of Upholland, Parliamentary under Secretary of State of State,

the objection was that it was a threat to the economic and commercial interest of the UK, in the sense that parties who for example expressly choose English law would not be guaranteed the stability of their contractual bargain, due to the potential application of foreign overriding mandatory rules.[192] This could in turn lead to increased transaction costs as regards investigating the content of the potential application of foreign overriding mandatory rules, so that international commercial parties may seek alternative competing forums such as New York and Singapore, where party autonomy would be guaranteed more protection.[193]

This time the UK (as other Member States) did not have the option to enter a reservation as was the case under the Rome Convention.[194] It was either in or out. This led to a series of intense negotiations among Member States as to what compromise package would get the UK to opt into Rome I.

During this period of negotiation some scholars seized the opportunity to make contributions that could shape the discourse on Article 8(3) of the Rome I Proposal. The two scholars worth mentioning are Chong[195] and Dickinson.[196]

Chong was critical about the official UK position on Article 8(3), particularly the claims that it could lead to uncertainty because of the use of vague terminology 'close connection', as was the case under Article 7(1) of the Rome Convention.[197] She countered, as other scholars in the past, that 'close connection' should be given a narrow construction. She then submitted by particularly drawing from English pre-Rome Convention case law to the effect that the place of performance should be the ideal connecting factor that should normally be invoked under Article 8(3), when compared to other potential connecting factors, such as the residence of the parties and place of contracting. In her view, the place of performance whether from the perspective of party expectations or State interests, was one that normally yielded to proximity. At the expense of prolixity, one would quote her views chronologically.

She submits that:

> if performance subsequently becomes illegal according to the law of the place of performance, non-application of the mandatory rule would expose the party carrying out performance to sanctions in the place of performance if the contract is enforced. In this situation, the parties' legitimate expectations would probably be that the performance should be abandoned and the court should take account of this.[198]

to Lord Grenfell, Chairman of the HL Select Committee on European Union, 16 May 2006. See also Council Doc 13035/06, Add 4 [22.9.2006], 'Annex B setting out in detail the UK Government's objections to the proposed Art 8.3'; S Dutson, 'A Misguided Proposal' (2006) *Law Quarterly Review* 374, 377; Dickinson (n 1); Harris (n 40); Beaumont and Mc Eleavy (n 17) 514–15, [10.292]–[10.295]; Plender and Wilderspin (n 40) 364, [12-034]. See also James (n 40) 117; Lando and Nielsen (n 40) 1721; Marazopoulou (n 40) 780.

192 ibid (all).

193 ibid (all).

194 Ministry of Justice (n 40); Hellner (n 122) 451.

195 Chong (n 25).

196 Dickinson (n 1).

197 Chong (n 25) 60–70.

198 ibid 61. In the context of Article 9(3) of Rome I, see also Lorenzo (n 73) 88.

She also submits that 'the body of common law cases whereby English courts have indirectly given effect to the *lex loci solutionis* contains principles that can inform and guide courts as to the future application of Article 8(3)'.[199]

She then finally submits that '[T]he classic example of a third country that has a legitimate interest in having its laws applied in an international contract is the place of performance.'[200]

In contrast to the position taken by Chong, Dickinson was very critical of the concept of 'close connection' under Article 8(3). Interestingly, he inter alia drew parallels to the escape clause under Article 4(5) of the Rome Convention (now Article 4(3) of Rome I) and submitted thus:

> From a legal certainty viewpoint, however the rules of displacement in Article 4 of the Convention as it stands is considerably less problematic than the proposed Article 8(3) in that the former is framed as an exception to a series of presumptions and expressly fixes the standard ('the contract is more closely connected with another country') by reference to which the judge must choose between two alternative governing laws. The judge has no choice as to the legal test to be applied. In contrast, although the proposed Article 8(3) stipulates certain criteria to which the judge must have regard, it does not otherwise prescribe or describe the process by which the judge is to determine whether or not to apply a third-country mandatory rule which meets the threshold of 'close connection' test.[201]

However, Dickinson also subscribed to the pragmatic view that the place of performance was of considerable significance in foreign country overriding mandatory rules as regards defining the concept of 'close connection', and suggested that it should be taken into account under a revised Article 8(3).[202]

It is important to note that during the period of negotiation, the principal focus of the delegations representing different Member States of the EU was on defining the scope of 'close connection' rather than the governmental interest analysis provision.[203] This point is important because it was Article 8(3) of Rome I Proposal that directly gave birth to Article 9(3) of Rome I. Again, this is to stress the point that the principle of proximity should not be ignored or overlooked under Article 9(3) of the Rome I, whilst giving undue emphasis to its governmental interest analysis or State interests provision. As Hellner observes:

> The criterion of 'close connection' in the Rome Convention has been the subject of much criticism since it is admittedly rather vague and might make the task of a court difficult. This was one of the *main points* of criticisms against the rule and the narrowing of scope was … intended to make the rule more acceptable to those Member States that had previously entered a reservation against Article 7(1).[204]

[199] Chong (n 25) 61.
[200] ibid 62.
[201] Dickinson (n 1) 64–65. cf Harris (n 40) 290.
[202] Dickinson (n 1) 87–88.
[203] See generally Hellner (n 122); McParland (n 121) 697–705, [15.57]–[15.90].
[204] (n 122) 464.

Indeed, this book is indebted to Hellner, a Member of the Swedish delegation, who brilliantly records the negotiation process in a published article.[205] Hellner notes that the Dutch,[206] Swedish[207] and Danish[208] delegation had all proposed the place of performance as the absolute connecting factor under a revised Article 8(3) of the Rome I Proposal.[209] He records that '[T]he aim of the proposal was to clarify the meaning of "close connection", which in and by itself could mean virtually anything …'[210] He also records inter alia that: 'To those delegations that favoured Article 8(3) it could be said that the key content was preserved since the most important case of a 'close connection' is when the contract is performed in a country …'[211]

As regards justifying why the place of performance was given absolute significance among other potential connecting factors, he records that:

> At the meeting of 3–4 July 2007 it was decided to delete the text referring to the habitual residence of the parties, since the only example that anyone could imagine of when this connecting factor would be relevant would be in cases of trade embargoes, economic sanctions and the like. Such cases were not considered sufficiently relevant to be included in the text. And at any rate, if one wanted to cover such cases one would probably have to include nationality as well and that would have lead [sic] to too much uncertainty.[212]

It is common knowledge that the compromise package of giving significance to the place of performance as the absolute connecting factor in narrowing the scope of 'close connection' under a new Article 9(3) of Rome I is what persuaded the UK to eventually opt in to Rome I.[213] Moreover, Article 9(3) is similar to English case law on the significance of the place of performance applying to foreign illegality.

V. Article 9 of Rome I Regulation

This section is concerned with three matters. First, it will define the concept of overriding mandatory rules under Article 9(1) of Rome I, and opine that the principle of proximity is not excluded from the scope of Article 9 of Rome I. Second, it will opine that the place of performance under Article 9(3) of Rome I is an expression of the principle of proximity. Third, it will consider whether

[205] ibid 447–70.
[206] Council document 8789/07 of 23 April 2007.
[207] Council document 9208/07 of 4 May 2007.
[208] Council document 9765/07 of 22 May 2007.
[209] (n 122) 451–55.
[210] ibid 453.
[211] ibid 454.
[212] ibid.
[213] ibid. See also Harris (n 40) 290; Hill and Chong (n 22) 536, [14.3.11]–[14.3.12]; Lorenzo (n 73) 84; Beaumont and McEleavy (n 17) 516, [10.297]; Plender and Wilderspin (n 40) 364, [12-034]; Bonomi (n 17) 637–38, [127]–[128].

foreign overriding mandatory rules other than that of the place of performance can be taken into account.

A. Definition of Overriding Mandatory Provisions

Article 9(1) of Rome I provides that:

> Overriding mandatory provisions are provisions the respect for which is regarded as crucial by a country for safeguarding it public interests, such as its political, social or economic organisation, to such an extent that they are applicable to any situation falling within their scope, irrespective of the law otherwise applicable to the contract under this Regulation.

On the face of Article 9(1), it appears it is only concerned with State interests and has nothing to do with satisfying the principle of proximity. This view might also be reinforced by the strong use of 'public law' language in Article 9(1) and Recital 37 to Rome I. Recital 37 provides that:

> Considerations of public interest justify giving the courts of the Member States the possibility, in exceptional circumstances, of applying exceptions based on public policy and overriding mandatory provisions. The concept of 'overriding mandatory provisions' should be distinguished from the expression 'provisions which cannot be derogated from by agreement' and should be construed more restrictively.

The use of the term 'public interests' should not be interpreted too literally or strictly. Indeed, some well-respected European scholars are very critical (and rightly too) of the 'public law' language used in Article 9(1), which creates the wrong impression that it is not in any way concerned with the interest of the parties.[214] Some of these scholars also express the correct view that, in reality, Article 9(1) was inspired by a dictum of the CJEU in *Arblade*,[215] a case that was also concerned with the protection of the private interests of employees as weaker parties. The implication of this is that Article 9 should be interpreted to the effect that it does not apply to protect *purely* private interests.[216]

[214] Hellner (n 122) 458–59; Harris (n 40) 294–96; Lorenzo (n 73) 91; Beaumont and McEleavy (n 17) 509–10, [10.277]–[10.280]; Plender and Wilderspin (n 40) 354–59, [12-012]–[12023]; Bonomi (n 17) 621–49, [71]–[170]. For a contrasting view see generally U Magnus and P Mankowski, 'Joint Response to the Green Paper on the Conversion of the Rome Convention of 1980 on the Law Applicable to Contractual Obligations into a Community Instrument and Its Modernisation' COM(2002) 654 final 33. In the context of Article 7(1) of the Rome Convention see Jackson (n 21) 84–94. In this connection some of these scholars also note that the strict public law or State interests approach is mainly German. cf For literature supporting the view that foreign overriding mandatory rules are strictly of a public law nature in the context of Article 7(1) of the Rome Convention see also Verhagen (n 141) 144; Hakki (n 155) 167.

[215] C-369/96; *Arblade*, EU:C:1999:575 [30]. It appears this decision was principally influenced by the publication: P Francescakis, 'Quelques precisions sur les lois d'application immediate et leurs rapports avec les règles de conflit de lois' (1966) 55 *Revue critique de droit international privé* 1–18.

[216] Hellner (n 122) 458–59; S Winnard, 'Is it Mandatory? State Interests, General Words and International Contracts' (2014) 20 *New Zealand Business Law Quarterly* 244, 256.

The above opinion is not made to undermine the obvious significance of State or public interests under Article 9. The opinion is only made to stress the point that Article 9 is also meant to satisfy other requirements – in particular that of proximity.

The idea that Article 9(1) satisfies the requirement of proximity is also supported by some highly regarded European scholars. In this connection, Bonomi rightly submits that:

> a close connection is implicitly required for the purpose of Article 9. This follows from the condition, established by Art. 9(1), that an overriding provision is to be, 'regarded as crucial by a country for safeguarding its public interest.' This condition can only be satisfied when situations falling within that provision's scope are somehow connected to the State that has enacted the provision at hand. Furthermore, the need for a genuine connection also follows from public international law, which limits the scope of a State's 'jurisdiction to prescribe' to situations having a genuine connection with the enacting State.[217]

In summation, Article 9 of Rome I also aims to satisfy the requirement of proximity.

B. Is the Place of Performance an Expression of the Principle of Proximity under Article 9(3) of Rome I Regulation?[218]

Article 9(3) of Rome I provides that:

> Effect may be given to the overriding mandatory provisions of the law of the country where the obligations arising out of the contract have to be or have been performed, in so far as those overriding mandatory provisions render the performance of the contract unlawful. In considering whether to give effect to those provisions, regard shall be had to their nature and purpose and to the consequences of their application or non-application.[219]

The phrase 'close connection' is not expressly mentioned in Article 9(3). The principal question is: does this mean Article 9(3) has nothing to do with proximity? In particular, does the absolute significance given to the place of performance under Article 9(3) also imply that it is meant to satisfy the requirement of proximity?

Having regard to a detailed account of the history that gave birth to the current Article 9(3), the place of performance is meant to embody the concept of close connection. In addition, Rome I is a continuation of the Rome Convention, so that

[217] Bonomi (n 17) 629, [96]. See also Marazopoulou (n 40) 794; Siehr (n 100) 824.

[218] Italics are used in this section to indicate the proposed reform to the existing law.

[219] This section is not really concerned with the scope or *full* interpretation of Article 9(3) of Rome I. For a detailed analysis see Hellner (n 122); Harris (n 40); Beaumont and McEleavy (n 17) 514–19, [10.292]–[10.304]; Marazopoulou (n 40); Plender and Wilderspin (n 40) 367–71, [12-038]–[12-045]; McParland (n 121) 367–71, [12-038]–[12-045]; Bonomi (n 17).

Article 9(3) should not be interpreted without paying attention to its history under the Rome Convention.

This opinion is not intended to undermine the obvious significance of State interests or in particular the regulatory function the place of performance plays in international commercial transactions. As Harris rightly submits:

> It is clear that the mischief behind Article 9(3), in particular, is to prevent a contracting party from having to perform in a state where performance is illegal. That party might not be, or need not be, present in that state in order to do so, as where, for instance, he or she uses another party to deliver goods to the buyer, or where performance consists of the transfer of intangible property. This, of course, does not alter the fact that to perform in that state would be unlawful.[220]

Bonomi also holds the view that 'the reference to the place of performance may be justified because this connecting factor gives legitimacy to a country's assertion of its own overriding interests'.[221]

However, the significance of place of performance as a jurisdictional-selecting rule which satisfies the requirement of proximity under Article 9(3) must not be ignored or overlooked. In reality, under Article 9(3) the substantive law of a State can only be invoked after establishing that that State is the *place of performance*. Implicitly, the absolute significance given to the place of performance as a jurisdictional selecting rule is meant to satisfy the requirement of proximity. In other words, its principal intendment is to create certainty in determining what 'close connection' means.[222]

This is a viewpoint that is subscribed to by some other scholars. In this connection, Hellner submits that:

> The main question that begs an answer is whether 'the country where the obligations arising out of the contract have to be or have been performed' significantly differs from 'a country with which the situation has a close connection.' Without doubt, the place of performance is the most important connecting factor for overriding mandatory rules. Most such rules require for their applicability that there is a performance of the contract in the legislating state. As it is the concept of performance will usually overlap with other connecting factors such as location of property and effect of a market. Currency is a connecting factor that would not necessarily involve performance in the state of the currency ... What is more, connecting factors such as (habitual) residence or nationality of one of the parties are highly unusual in practice. Rules that spring to mind of this author would be trade embargoes and the like-rules that are relatively uncommon these days.[223]

[220] Harris (n 40) 294.

[221] Bonomi (n 17) 641, [40].

[222] Whether this would lead to certainty in practice is beyond the scope of this work. In particular see AG Szpunar in *Hellenic Republic* (n 149) [83]–[84]. For a detailed analysis see Harris (n 40); Plender and Wilderspin (n 40) 367–71, [12-038]–[12-045]; Bonomi (n 17) 640, paragraphs 134–35, cf Ministry of Justice (n 40) [69].

[223] Hellner (n 122) 467.

Marazopoulou expresses the view that:

> '*close connection*' prerequisite was deleted in the final version of the article, and, hereafter, only the overriding mandatory provisions of the place of performance are to be given effect. The law of the place of performance was preferred as one of the closest-connected laws, while it also has the advantage of providing legal certainty as well.[224]

Siehr is also emphatic when he concludes that:

> Every case, either falling under Article 9 or 21 of Rome I Regulation, has to have some contact with the situation of the case in dispute. This principle of proximity, *proximité* or *Inlandsbeziehung* or – for purposes of Article 9(3) of Rome I Regulation a connection of the case with the foreign country providing the mandatory rule – is well accepted in European conflict of laws. There is hardly any real case in which a foreign overriding mandatory provision with no connection with the situation in dispute wanted to be applied.[225]

Given the fact that the place of performance would normally meet the requirement of proximity under Article 9(3), some scholars have seriously questioned whether Article 9(3) is a case of 'old wine in new bottles'.[226] In other words is there a significant difference between Article 9(3) of Rome I and, Article 7(1) of the Rome Convention and Article 8(3) of the Rome I Proposal? This book answers the question in the positive.[227]

While this book does not subscribe to the extreme or rather misleading view held by some scholars that the place of performance under Article 9(3) of Rome I is 'totally different from the term close "connection"',[228] it holds the view that the place of performance is not necessarily equivalent to the concept of 'close connection'.

In unusual cases the place of performance would not satisfy the requirement of proximity. For example, the place of performance might not satisfy the requirement of proximity especially in cases where the obligation takes place in many countries.[229] In addition, as Harris also submits:

> it is tempting to suggest that in cases where the place of performance is somewhat arbitrary, as in the case where payment is to be made by internet transfer, or access to software for downloading is to be granted, then the case for invoking the overriding

[224] Marazopoulou (n 40) 782–83 (emphasis added). See also Harris (n 40) 319.

[225] Siehr (n 100) 826.

[226] See generally Hellner (n 122).

[227] See also AG Szpunar in *Hellenic Republic* (n 149) [25], [81]–[82]; C-135/15, *Hellenic Republic* (CJEU decision), EU:C:2016:281 [45].

[228] W Lei, 'Mandatory Rules of the Rome I Regulation: Not 'Old Wine in New Bottles' (2011) 7 *Canadian Social Science* 166, 170. Moreover, Lei in the same line (or context) makes a preceding contradictory statement to the effect that 'the place of performance can be seen as one of the most important close connecting factors'.

[229] For the view that Article 9(3) might apply to different places of performance, see in particular AG Szpunar in *Hellenic Republic* (n 149) [93]–[94] (citing others). For a detailed academic analysis see generally Plender and Wilderspin (n 40) 367–71, [12-038]–[12-045]. See also Hellner (n 40) 464–67.

mandatory provisions of the place of performance under Article 9(3) is rather less strong.[230]

Thus, the better view is expressed by Bonomi to the effect that Article 9(3)

> is intended to specify, in a restrictive sense, the connection required between the situation and the State that enacted a mandatory norm: whereas the Convention simply required the existence of a 'close connection', without any further specification, the Regulation refers only to norms of the country, 'where the obligations arising out of the contract have to be or have been performed.[231]

Furthermore, given that the application of Article 9(3) is not mandatory but discretionary, Article 9(3) should not be applied in such unusual cases where the place of performance does not satisfy the requirement of proximity. As stated earlier, a clear example where the place of performance may not satisfy the requirement of proximity are cases where the contract is to be performed in many countries. Of course in situations where the contract is performed in many countries, some of such countries might have a close connection to the situation, and in such cases Article 9(3) could be applied despite the fact that performance takes place in many countries. However, for countries where the performance is rather slight or insignificant, Article 9(3) as a matter of discretion should not be applied.

This opinion is also supported by the fact that the place of performance under Article 9(3) was utilised to give form to the vague concept of close connection (in a restrictive sense) that was previously utilised under Article 7(1) of the Rome Convention and Article 8(3) of Rome I Proposal. Moreover, given that Article 9(3) is a successor to Article 7(1) of the Rome Convention, in the spirit of continuity of European private international instruments,[232] it should not deviate from the

[230] Harris (n 40) 317.

[231] Bonomi (n 17) 638, [128].

[232] C-533/07, *Falco Privatstiftung and another v Weller-Lindhorst*, EU:C:2009:257 [7], [48]–[57]; C-167/08, *Draka NK Cables Ltd and others v Omnipol Ltd*, EU:C:2009:263 [20]; C-180/06, *Ilsinger v Dreschers*, EU:C:2009:303 [58]; C–111/08, SCT *Industri AB (in Liquidation) v Alpenblume AB*, EU:C:2009:419 [6], [22]–[24]; C-189/08, *Zuid-Chemie BV v Philippo's Mineralenfabriek NV/SA*, EU:C:2009:475 [18]–[19]; C-533/08, *TNT Express Nederland BV v AXA Versicherung AG*, EU:C:2010:243 [36]; C-585/08 and C-144/09 (Joined Cases), *Pammer v Reederei Karl Schlüter GmbH & Co KG Hotel Alpenhof GesmbH v Heller* EU:C:2010:740 [8], [56]; C-406/09, *Realchemie Nederland BV v Bayer Cropscience AG*, EU:C:2011:668 [5], [38]; C-514/10, *Wolf Naturprodukte GMBH v SEWAR SPOL. SRO*, EU:C:2012:367 [4], [20]; C-616/10, *Solvay SA v Honeywell Fluorine Products Europe BV and Others*, EU:C:2012:445 [6], [42]–[43]; C-133/11, *Folien Fischer AG v Ritrama SPA*, EU:C:2012:664 [7], [31]–[32]; C-456/11, *Gothaer Allgemeine Versicherung AG v Samskip GmbH*, EU:C:2012:719 [34]; C-645/11, *Land Berlin v Sapir*, EU:C:2013:228 [31]–[32]; C-147/12, *Öfab, Östergötlands Fastigheter AB v. Koot*, EU:C:2013:490 [28]–[29]; C-49/12, *Revenue and Customs Commissioners v Sunico APS*, EU:C:2013:545 [32]–[33]; C-386/12, *Re Schneider*, EU:C:2013:633 [4], [21]; C-469/12, *Krejci Lager & Umschlagbetriebs GMBH v Olbrich Transport und Logistik GMBH*, EU:C:2013:788 [6]; C-297/14, *Hobohm v Benedikt Kampik Ltd & Co KG and others*, EU:C:2015:844 [4], [31]; C-12/15, *Universal Music International Holding BV v Schilling*, EU:C:2016:449 [4], [22]–[23]; C-322/14, *El Majdoub v CarsOnTheWeb.Deutschland GmbH*, EU:C:2015:334 [6], [27], [28].

historical and philosophical goal of proximity enshrined under Article 7(1) of the Rome Convention. It is thus proposed that a revised Article 9(3) of Rome I should read as follows:

> Effect may be given to the overriding mandatory provisions of the law of the country *or legal system* where the obligations arising out of the contract have to be or have been performed, in so far as those overriding mandatory provisions render the performance of the contract unlawful. In considering whether to give effect to those provisions, regard shall be had to their nature and purpose and to the consequences of their application or non-application.
>
> *Notwithstanding the foregoing, effect should not be given to the overriding mandatory provisions of the law of the country or legal system where the obligations arising out of the contract have to be or have been performed, if the country does not have a close connection with the situation of the case.*

In summation, Article 9(3) is an expression of the principle of proximity, and the courts of Member States should not apply the law of the place of performance if it does not satisfy the test of 'close connection' to a situation.

C. Taking into Account of Foreign Country Overriding Mandatory Rules Other than Those of the Place of Performance

Article 9(3) restricts the application of foreign overriding country mandatory rules to the place of performance. However, Article 9(3) does not expressly provide whether the foreign overriding mandatory rules of another country other than the place of performance *can be taken into account* or *recognised*. Is there a distinction between *applying* and *taking into account* foreign country overriding mandatory rules?

In *Hellenic Republic*,[233] the CJEU was for the first time confronted with the interpretation of Article 9 (3), and had to address the issue of taking into account the foreign overriding mandatory rules of another country other than the place of performance. In this connection, the issue raised was:

> Does Article 9(3) of the Rome I Regulation exclude solely the direct application of overriding mandatory provisions of another country in which the obligations arising out of that contract are not to be performed, or have not been performed, or does that provision also exclude indirect regard to those mandatory provisions in the law of the Member State the law of which governs the contract?[234]

In this case, the claimant was a Greek national employed as a teacher at a Greek primary school in Germany. His contract of employment commenced in 1996.

[233] (n 227).
[234] ibid [24].

It was agreed that the contract had since been amended and that it was governed by German law. In response to the economic crisis in Greece, from the period beginning October 2010 to December 2012, Greece reduced the claimant's gross remuneration (previously calculated in accordance with German law) on account of Greek Laws implementing agreements that Greece had concluded with the European Commission, the European Central Bank and the International Monetary Fund (UN). The claimant started proceedings in the German courts seeking to recover his loss in salary on the grounds that his employment relationship was conducted in Germany and subject only to German law.

The German Federal Labour Court observed that whilst classifying the Greek laws mentioned reducing the claimant's gross remuneration as 'overriding mandatory provisions' within the meaning of private international law, the outcome of the case in the main proceedings turned on whether those Greek mandatory laws could apply – directly or indirectly – to an employment relationship conducted in Germany and subject to German law, which did not permit such reductions.

Furthermore, German law permits a court to take into account the overriding mandatory provisions of any other State (here, the overriding provisions of Greece), whereas it was open to question whether under Article 9(2) and (3) of the Rome I, account can only be had to the mandatory provisions of the *lex fori* (here, Germany) or of the legal order where the contract has to be performed (which the German courts held to be connected solely with German, the *lex loci laboris*).

The CJEU began with the premise that for the purpose of determining the scope of Article 9 of Rome I, it should be stressed that party autonomy is the general principle under Rome I, which was enshrined in Article 3 and 8 of Rome I, applicable to this case.[235] Since Article 9 of Rome I derogated from the principle of party autonomy, it had to be applied exceptionally and strictly.[236]

The CJEU observed from the drafting history of Article 7(1) of the Rome Convention, the concept of 'close connection' was excised in order to 'restrict disturbance to the system of conflict of laws caused by the application of overriding mandatory provisions other than those of the State of the forum'.[237]

Thus, to allow the court to apply overriding mandatory rules other than that specified in Article 9(2) and (3) 'would be liable to jeopardise full achievement of the regulation's general objective, which, as stated in recital 16, is legal certainty in the European area of justice'.[238] The provisions of Article 9(2) and (3) must therefore be regarded as exhaustive.[239]

[235] ibid [42].
[236] ibid [43]. Applying C-184/12, *Unamar*, EU:C:2013:663 and Recital 37 to Rome I.
[237] (n 226) [45].
[238] ibid [46].
[239] ibid [49].

In the final analysis, the CJEU held that:

> Article 9 of the Rome I Regulation must therefore be interpreted as precluding the court of the forum from applying, as legal rules, overriding mandatory provisions other than those of the State of the forum or of the State where the obligations arising out of the contract have to be or have been performed. Consequently, since, according to the referring court, Mr Nikiforidis's employment contract has been performed in Germany, and the referring court is German, the latter cannot in this instance apply, directly or indirectly, the Greek overriding mandatory provisions which it sets out in the request for a preliminary ruling.
>
> On the other hand, Article 9 of the Rome I Regulation does not preclude overriding mandatory provisions of a State other than the State of the forum or the State where the obligations arising out of the contract have to be or have been performed from being taken into account as a matter of fact, in so far as this is provided for by a substantive rule of the law that is applicable to the contract pursuant to the regulation.
>
> The Rome I Regulation harmonises conflict-of-law rules concerning contractual obligations and not the substantive rules of the law of contract. In so far as the latter provide that the court of the forum is to take into account, as a matter of fact, overriding mandatory provisions of the legal order of a State other than the State of the forum or the State of performance of the contractual obligations, Article 9 of the regulation cannot prevent the court seised from taking that matter of fact into account.[240]

The decision of the CJEU that a Member State court can take into account foreign overriding mandatory rules as a matter of fact, other than the place of performance as specified under Article 9(3), if the *lex causae* so allows, seems curious. The language of Article 9(3) already specifies that 'effect may be given'[241] to foreign overriding mandatory rules. It is not so clear why there is a need to create a distinction between *taking into account* and *applying*, or *recognition* and *enforcement* of foreign overriding mandatory rules. What value does this distinction add to Article 9(3)?[242] In other words, if there is a distinction between *taking into account* and *applying* foreign overriding mandatory rules, so what?

It may be counter-argued that the way in which the CJEU's decision may be rationalised might be that Article 9(3) must be read in context with Article 9(2), which only provides for the *application* of overriding mandatory rules of the forum. Thus, by restricting the 'giving effect' of foreign overriding mandatory rules, it seems that Article 9(3) restricts *both* the *application* and *taking into account* as a fact to foreign overriding mandatory rules. In addition, the editors of Cheshire, North, and Fawcett rationalise the CJEU's decision on the basis that:

> For example, it may be taken into account on the level of substantive contract law e.g. under the doctrine of illegality or the doctrine of impossibility, that the contract

[240] ibid at [50]–[52].

[241] See generally McParland (n 121) 711, [15.113]–[15.116].

[242] S Rammeloo, '"From Rome to Rome" – Cross-border Employment Contract. European Private International Law: Intertemporal law and Foreign Overriding Mandatory Laws – Case C-135/15 *Greek Republic v Grigorios Nikiforidis*, EU:C:2016:774' (2017) 24 *Maastricht Journal of European and Comparative Law* 298, 320.

violates an overriding mandatory provision of the law of a country other than the forum State or the State where performance is to take place.[243]

It is opined here that the approach of the CJEU is surprising because it paid due attention to the history of what led to Article 9(3). Foreign overriding mandatory rules had historically been a matter of controversy particularly because of the uncertainty it generated. Article 9(3) created a strict operation on the concept of foreign country overriding mandatory rules. Allowing the *lex causae* to *take into account* foreign overriding mandatory rules, if the substantive law so allows as a matter of fact, does not appear to be what the drafters of Rome I may have intended. The CJEU in effect carved out a new exception to Article 9(3), which amounts to a form of judicial legislation.

Second, it is not so clear whether *taking into account* or *recognising* foreign country overriding mandatory rules as a matter of fact (other than the place of performance) as prescribed by the substantive law governing the contract, might allow the *indirect* application of a foreign overriding mandatory rule that is not the place of performance. If a foreign overriding mandatory rule (that is not the place of performance) is *taken into account* and *indirectly applied* as a matter of fact under substantive law, it might not have a close connection or satisfy the requirement of proximity. As stated earlier, the principal historical reason why place of performance was given absolute significance as a connecting factor under Article 9(3) was because it best embodied the principle of proximity in matters of foreign country overriding mandatory rules and did it better than other connecting factors. The application of a foreign mandatory rule is justified by the close connection the country has with the situation, which is best satisfied by the place of performance. In this case before the CJEU, the only connection the claimant had with Greece was nationality; the case was substantially and most closely connected with Germany, where the obligations took place.

Third, the concern of certainty and predictability is another important issue. The CJEU in this case did not address the delicate task of how the German Labour Court should reconcile the fact that in *taking into account* German substantive law, the claimant would be entitled to his claim, but in *indirectly applying* Greek law as a foreign overriding mandatory rule as a matter of fact through German substantive law, the claimant would be denied his claim. It is not enough to say that the discretion lies in the court while *applying* the *lex causae* to determine how to *take into account* the Greek overriding mandatory provisions.

The implication of the foregoing is that the CJEU's decision in this case needs to be carefully re-evaluated. In particular, the distinction between *taking into account* and *applying* foreign overriding mandatory rules have to be clearly and precisely articulated as regards the practical significance it has on the operation of Article 9(3).

[243] Torremans (n 22) 752.

VI. Should Article 9(3) of Rome I Regulation be Suppressed?

The core argument in this chapter is that the place of performance under Article 9(3) embodies the principle of proximity, so that this is a good reason why Article 4 of Rome I should be revised. The question might thus arise: does it mean Article 9(3) should be suppressed? This question arises because there would normally be a coherence between Article 9(3) and Article 4, if the place of performance is made the principal connecting factor under a revised Article 4. Some might argue on this basis that Article 9(3) should be made redundant. In this connection, if one thinks Article 9(3) should be suppressed, it might be stressed that such an approach has an important gain for legal certainty in two respects. First, generally, there would be no more application of foreign overriding mandatory rules. Second, there would be no need to coordinate between foreign overriding mandatory rules, and the law governing the contract under Article 4.

It is opined here that Article 9(3) should remain despite the proposal in this book, because freedom of choice allows the parties to choose a law other than the law of the place of performance. The implication of this is that if the proposal in this book is accepted, Article 9(3) would mainly operate to displace, disregard or derogate from Article 3 of Rome I rather than Article 4. In effect, there would be a coherence between Article 4 and 9(3).

For example, if the proposal in this book is accepted, in a case such as *Foster*[244] where the parties planned to commit an illegal act in the US, the applicable law under Article 4 would be US law (of a particular State), since US is the place of delivery of the illegal goods. There would be no need to apply Article 9(3) because the *lex causae* is already US law. But if the parties in *Foster* expressly choose the law of Utopia to govern their obligations, Article 9(3) can then be utilised.

This point is important because the current Article 9(3) operates as a form of escape clause to the traditional choice of law rules under Articles 3 and 4.[245] Article 9(3) is a type or form of escape or exceptional clause because it chooses and applies a particular law in circumstances which are an exception to party autonomy, or the usual or traditional choice-of-law-process.[246] 'It is also exceptional because it is a choice-of-law rule that is attentive to the substantive content of the

[244] (n 10).

[245] Philip (n 40) 105.

[246] See also Lando (1982) (n 141) 33; Mills (n 56) 209. In this book, traditional choice of law rules mean the law applicable under both Article 3 and 4 of Rome I. It should be noted that there is a distinction between mandatory rules operating as an escape clause to party autonomy – 'ordinary' mandatory rules' (contained in Articles 3(3) and (4), 6 and 8 of Rome I), and mandatory rules operating as an escape clause to the traditional choice of law rules – 'overriding' mandatory rules (Article 9 of Rome I). Thus Recital 37 to Rome I provides that '[T]he concept of 'overriding mandatory provisions' should be distinguished from the expression 'provisions which cannot be derogated from by agreement' and should be construed more restrictively'.

applicable law.'[247] Of course, this is not to say Article 9(3) performs exactly the same function as the escape clause in Article 4(3) of Rome I.

The point being made is that where the current Article 9(3) is applied as a matter of flexible judicial discretion, it *displaces*, *disregards* or *derogates* from the traditional applicable law, which is virtually a similar function performed by an escape clause.

If the proposal in this book is accepted, when Article 9(3) applies, it would only *modify* or *limit* party autonomy. It would not *entirely displace*, *disregard* or *derogate* from party autonomy. The reason is that it is only an *aspect* or *issue* in the contract that is *displaced*, *disregarded* or *derogated* from; other aspects or issues in the contract remain validly governed by the chosen law. This explains why the application of overriding mandatory rules usually leads to a form of judge made *dépeçage*, in the sense that it leads to the application of more than one law to govern the whole contract. In other words, where Article 9(3) is applied to an *aspect* or *issue* in a contract, the traditional choice of law rule of party autonomy is retained to govern the other *aspects* or *issues* in the contract, that are not affected by the application of Article 9(3).

In summation, despite the proposal in this book, Article 9(3) should not be suppressed, but utilised to checkmate the excesses of Article 3.

VII. Conclusion

This chapter contained another principal argument justifying why the place of performance should be given special significance under a revised Article 4 of Rome I. The central idea of this chapter is that the place of performance is also an expression of the principle of proximity under Article 9(3) of Rome I. If this is correct, then this is a good reason why the place of performance should be explicitly given special significance under a revised Article 4 of Rome I.

In section II, a historical and comparative approach was used to justify why the place of performance is also an expression of the principle of proximity under Article 9(3) of Rome I. It was argued that under pre-Rome Convention case law, one of the reasons why the place of performance was of considerable significance in the context of foreign illegality (as it was then) was because there was an implicit idea that the place of performance was normally one of closest or substantial connection to an international commercial contract.

In section III, in the context of Article 7(1) of the Rome Convention, it was argued that undue significance should not be given to its governmental interest

[247] Mills (n 56) 209. It should be noted that Mills made this submission in the context of public policy. It is however submitted that this also applies in the context of mandatory rules because matters of mandatory rules and public policy are very similar. They can even overlap in practice. See for example, AG Szpunar in *Hellenic Republic* (n 149) [68]. For academic literature supporting this view see also Chong (n 25) 32–35; Harris (n 40) 297.

analysis provision, while ignoring the principle of 'close connection' expressly enshrined therein. The governmental interest analysis provision can only be considered if there is a 'close connection' with the foreign country. It was then opined that there was (or is) academic consensus that the place of performance is the connecting factor that obviously and normally satisfied the requirement of proximity under Article 7 of the Rome Convention.

In section IV, in the context of Article 8(3) of Rome I Proposal, it was demonstrated that the issue of 'close connection', and not its governmental interest analysis provision, was at the heart of the negotiation process to get the UK to opt into Rome I. There was a consensus that the place of performance would best satisfy the requirement of proximity in foreign country overriding mandatory rules, which explains why absolute significance was given to the place of performance under a new Article 9(3) of Rome I.

In section V, in the context of defining overriding mandatory rules, it was opined that Article 9(1) of Rome I is not only concerned with State interests, but is also concerned with satisfying the requirement of proximity.

In the context of Article 9(3) of Rome I, it was opined that it could not be interpreted without its history, particularly in Article 7 of the Rome Convention and Article 8(3) of the Rome I Proposal. It was again opined that the governmental interest analysis provision in Article 9(3) of Rome I must not be exaggerated, as it can be considered *only* in the context of the law of the place of performance. This makes Article 9(3) a form of jurisdictional selecting rule as well. It was then opined the place of performance is also an expression of the principle of proximity under Article 9(3). It was however, conceded that the place of performance is not necessarily the same thing as 'close connection', and would not best satisfy the requirement of proximity in unusual cases.

In section VI, it was opined that Article 9(3) should not be supressed despite the proposal in this book, rather it should operate against the excesses of party autonomy.

5

Coherence between Jurisdiction and Choice of Law: Implications for the Place of Performance

I. Introduction

One of the principal grounds, it is argued that the place of performance should be expressly given special significance under a revised Article 4 of Rome I, is that the place of performance is given special significance under the EU rules in the allocation of jurisdiction for commercial contracts. This opinion is inspired by the coherence between some matters of jurisdiction and choice of law in civil and commercial matters.

The principal question is: should the European legislator amend Article 4 of Rome I, to explicitly give special significance to the place of performance, on the basis that the place of performance is given special significance under Article 7(1) of Brussels Ia?

The formidable challenge the above question faces is that matters of jurisdiction and choice of law are conceptually different and are separate processes in private international law. This is also a position that is widely accepted internationally.

This counter-argument is not strong enough to outweigh the proposal made in this book. The idea that there is a fundamental distinction between matters of jurisdiction and choice of law is not absolute. Indeed, a significant number of scholars in the past have rightly expressly or implicitly discredited the idea that the distinction between matters of jurisdiction and choice of law is absolute, by drawing attention to some 'interrelationship',[1]

[1] P Hay, 'The Interrelation of Jurisdiction and Choice-of-law in United States Conflicts Law' (1979) 28 *International and Comparative Law Quarterly* 161; J Fawcett, 'The Interrelationship of Jurisdiction and Choice of Law in Private International Law' (1991) 44 *Current Legal Problems* 39; C Forsyth and P Moser, 'The Impact of the Applicable Law of Contract on the Law of Jurisdiction under the European Convention' (1996) 45 *International and Comparative Law Quarterly* 190; Z Tang, 'The Interrelationship of European Jurisdiction and Choice of Law in Contract' (2008) 4 *Journal of Private International Law* 35; F Pocar, 'Some Remarks on the Relationship between the Rome I and Brussels I Regulations' in F Ferrari and S Leible (eds), *The Law Applicable to Contractual Obligations in Europe* (Munich, Sellier European Law Publishers, 2009) 343.

'convergence',[2] 'synergy'[3] and 'coherence, connection and consistency'[4] between matters of jurisdiction and choice of law in civil and commercial matters.[5]

In particular, in a previous work, I have already submitted (based on the coherence between matters of jurisdiction and choice of law) that the place of performance 'occupies a special place in the scheme of European PIL rules applicable to contracts'[6] and 'it could be said that the place of performance is of considerable significance as a connecting factor'[7] for matters of commercial contracts in the EU choice of law rules. The aim of this book inter alia is to justify this claim.[8]

Section II discusses the types of coherence between jurisdiction and choice of law in the EU rules for civil and commercial contracts, in order to present the arguments in this chapter. Section III critically analyses the historical connection between the EU jurisdiction and choice of law regime for commercial contracts. Section IV discusses the existing coherence between jurisdiction and choice of law in commercial contracts, as it relates to the place of performance. Section V discusses the differences between jurisdiction and choice of law, which might militate against resolving them in the same manner. Section VI contains the arguments that support the central claim in this book. In particular, it is opined in section VI that the coherence of the principle of proximity, connecting factors and interpretation support the view that the place of performance should be given special significance under a revised Article 4 of Rome I. Section VII concludes.

II. Types of Coherence between Jurisdiction and Choice of Law

The classification of the types of coherence between jurisdiction and choice of law is utilised in this book to clearly present the arguments on justifying the

[2] J Meeusen et al (eds), *Enforcement of International Contracts in the European Union. Convergence and divergence between Brussels I and Rome I* (Antwerp-Oxford-New York, Intersentia, 2004).

[3] E Lein, 'The New Rome I/Rome II/Brussels I Synergy' (2008) 10 *Yearbook of Private International Law* 177.

[4] EB Crawford and JM Carruthers, 'Connection and Coherence between and among European Instruments in the Private International Law of Obligations' (2014) 63 *International and Comparative Law Quarterly* 1.

[5] Though I use the word 'coherence', it is synonymous with 'interrelationship', 'convergence', 'synergy', 'connection' or 'consistency' as used by other scholars.

[6] CSA Okoli, 'The Significance of the Doctrine of Accessory Allocation as a Connecting Factor under Article 4 of Rome I Regulation' (2013) 9 *Journal of Private International Law* 449, 454, fn 18.

[7] ibid.

[8] In the article, it was not necessary to justify this claim (on the place of performance), because the published article was focused on another connecting factor called 'accessory allocation.'

proposal. The classification is derived mainly from the EU rules on jurisdiction and choice of law.

It should however be noted that some of the types of coherence between jurisdiction and choice of law might actually overlap when applied in practice. Thus, the classification utilised in this book is not intended to categorise the coherence between matters of jurisdiction and choice of law into strict compartments.[9]

Coherence between jurisdiction and choice of law in private international law is an area that has not received exhaustive academic attention and treatment. This might be because it challenges the dogma created by some academics that jurisdiction and choice of law are conceptually distinct and separate.[10]

Tang who wrote on the topic over 10 years ago submitted that: 'Compared with scholarship in other conflicts topics, less attention has been paid to the interrelationship of jurisdiction and choice of law.'[11] She also submitted in relation to the European Regulations on jurisdiction and choice of law that:

> although the legislators claimed a willingness to create a systematic and congruent conflicts system, a close scrutiny of the texts of both regimes suggests insufficient consideration has actually been given to the implications of the development of one upon the other.[12]

Given the insufficient attention that has been paid by academics in this area of conflict of laws, one is not surprised that very few scholars have managed to provide their suggestions on how they classify the coherence between matters of jurisdiction and choice of law. This might also be explained on the basis that some of the early and leading scholars who addressed the topic from an American[13] and English[14] common law perspective were more concerned with the practice, than matters of conceptual analysis and theoretical formulations.

The EU private international law in civil and commercial matters presents the coherence between jurisdiction and choice of law in a very unique way when compared with what occurs in other countries or legal systems of the world. This might also explain why previous scholarship did not specifically address the classification of the coherence between matters of jurisdiction and choice of law in EU private international law.

Tang appears to have been the first to suggest a classification in the context of EU private international law. She classified what she labelled as 'the interrelationship' between jurisdiction and choice of law in matters of contract into

[9] Moreover, the idea that legal concepts can be classified into *strict* legal categories is not a view this book subscribes to.

[10] Fawcett (n 1).

[11] Tang (n 1).

[12] ibid 36.

[13] Hay (n 1).

[14] Fawcett (n 1).

three broad categories. The first was the consistency between jurisdiction and choice of law in the area of classification and the prerequisites of party autonomy. The second was the influence choice of law might have on jurisdiction, with a particular focus on the impact of the ECJ's decision in *Tessili*.[15] The third was the influence jurisdiction might have on choice of law, with a particular focus on the fact that public policy and overriding mandatory rules of the forum could limit the effect of an otherwise applicable law.[16]

In the same year, Lein's article classified what she labelled as 'the synergy' between the Brussels I, Rome I and Rome II Regulations into three categories. The first was the synergy of fundamental principles, which included the principles of freedom of choice, principle of proximity and protection of weaker parties. The second was the synergy of structure and solutions. The third was the synergy of interpretation.[17]

In this chapter, it is sufficient to classify the coherence between matters of jurisdiction and choice of law into three categories: coherence of principles, coherence of connecting factors and coherence of interpretation.[18] This classification is mainly utilised to present the arguments and justify the proposal in this chapter.

Coherence of principles means that matters of jurisdiction and choice of law share some principles, so that the idea that the place of performance in commercial contracts best satisfies the requirement of the principle of geographical proximity in matters of EU jurisdiction rules is a good reason to hold the view that the place of performance is also the connecting factor that best satisfies the requirement of geographical proximity in matters of EU choice of law.

Coherence of connecting factors means that matters of jurisdiction and choice of law sometimes utilise identical connecting factors, which usually leads to the forum applying its own law, as would usually be the case if the place of performance of the characteristic obligation is made the principal connecting factor for commercial contracts under a revised Article 4 of Rome I.

Coherence of interpretation means that some concepts in matters of jurisdiction can also be interpreted equivalently (or uniformly) with that of choice of law (and vice versa) so that Member State courts in interpreting a revised Article 4 of Rome I can carefully draw inspiration from the jurisprudence of the CJEU that has equivalently interpreted the concept of place of performance of the characteristic obligation.

[15] C-12/76, *Industrie Tessili Italiana Como v Dunlop AG*, EU:C:1976:133 [15].

[16] Tang (n 1) 58–59.

[17] Lein (n 3).

[18] In doing so, the classification I adopt is similar to that of the approach of Lein only in the context of coherence of interpretation and coherence of principles.

III. Historical Connection between the EU Jurisdiction and Choice of Law Regimes for Commercial Contracts: A Critical Analysis

In chapters two and three, some of the weaknesses of the place of performance were identified in relation to determining the applicable law in the absence of choice for commercial contracts. Despite the identified weaknesses of the place of performance, it was argued that the habitual residence of the characteristic performer is usually not a suitable connecting factor, when compared to the place of performance. It was then opined that the criteria of place of characteristic performance would better remedy the defect of the place of performance as a connecting factor.

By way of analogy, the place of performance initially faced some challenges in the EU regime for the allocation of jurisdiction for commercial contracts. Despite the identified weaknesses of the place of performance for commercial contracts under the Brussels Convention regime, the place of performance was not done away with completely – the place of performance was revised. Thus, the solution to remedying the defects of the place of performance as a connecting factor can also be found in a brief historical analysis of the Brussels regime jurisprudence, and the lessons than can be drawn from its history. The analysis of the Brussels regime jurisprudence leads one to conclude that the place of performance of the characteristic obligation is a pragmatic and promising solution if it is utilised as the principal connecting factor for commercial contracts, under a revised Article 4 of Rome I. It also leads one to conclude that the problems of identifying the place of performance can be remedied.

The Brussels Convention regime which utilised 'the place of performance of the obligation in question' as a connecting factor, for the allocation of jurisdiction for commercial contracts, was the first European private international law instrument that exposed the weaknesses of the place of performance as a connecting factor.[19]

[19] For authoritative commentary on this see AG Lenz in C-288/92, *Custom Made v Satwa*, EU:C:1994:86; AG Ruiz-Jarabo Colmer in C-440/97, *Group Concorde and others v The Master of the Vessel Suhadiwarno Panjan, Pro Line Ltd and, others*, EU:C:1999:146 [48]–[51]; K Takashi, 'Jurisdiction in Matters Relating to Contract: Article 5(1) of the Brussels Convention' (2002) *European Law Review* 530, 541–43; PR Beaumont, 'The Brussels Convention Becomes a Regulation: Implications for Legal Basis, External Competence and Contract Jurisdiction' in J Fawcett (ed), *Report and Development of Private International Law: Essays in Honour of Sir Peter North* (Oxford, Oxford University Press, 2002) 16 and 17; P Mankowski in U Magnus and P Mankowski (eds), *Brussels I Regulation* (Munich, Sellier European Law Publishers, 2007) 153 [131]; B Punt, 'Heading for a more Characteristic Jurisdiction?' (2009) *International Business Law Journal* 51, 56; B Ubertazzi, 'Licence Agreements Relating to IP Rights and the EC Regulation on Jurisdiction' (2009) 40 *International Review of Intellectual Property and Competition Law* 912, 922; U Grusic, 'Jurisdiction in Complex Contracts Under the Brussels I Regulation' (2011) 7 *Journal of Private International Law* 321, 329–30; P Shine, 'The Problem of Place of Performance in Contract under Brussels I Regulation: Can One Size Fit All?' (2011) *International Company and Commercial Law Review* 20, 25.

In *De Bloos*,[20] the European Court of Justice (ECJ) in interpreting Article 5(1) of the Brussels Convention held that the obligation to be taken into account is that which corresponds to the contractual right on which the plaintiff's action is based, so that in a case where the plaintiff asserts the right to be paid damages or seeks the dissolution of the contract by reason of wrongful conduct of the other party, the obligation referred to in Article 5(1) is still that which arises under the contract and the non-performance of which is relied upon to support such claims.[21] In other words, the ECJ held that the performance is based on the contested obligation before the court of a Member State.

In *Tessili*,[22] the ECJ in interpreting Article 5(1) of the Brussels Convention found itself unable to provide an independent, autonomous and uniform definition of the place of performance, nor clearly classify what the obligation was (as was the case in *De Bloos*), on the basis that at the time there were differences obtaining between national laws on contractual obligations and absence of legal development of any unification in the substantive applicable law.[23]

The decision in *De Bloos* and *Tessili* created uncertainty by making the concept of place of performance of the obligation in question uncertain, imprecise, and thereby threatening uniformity.[24]

In *Ivenel*,[25] the ECJ regarded the decision in *De Bloos* as a general rule which should not be applied to employment contracts. The ECJ held that in the case of a claim based on different obligations arising from a single contract for commercial representation which had been described by the national court as a contract of employment, the obligation to be taken into consideration for the purposes of Article 5(1) of the Brussels Convention was the obligation which characterised the contract and the obligation to carry out the work.[26] Interestingly, the ECJ, by way of analogy, borrowed from Article 6 of the Rome Convention (now Article 8 of Rome I), which in reality utilised the concept of place of characteristic performance for employment contracts.

Ivenel was the first time the ECJ was applying the concept of place of characteristic performance, though it was applying it to employment contracts, rather than commercial contracts. The decision in *Ivenel* was a welcome development as it created certainty in determining the place of performance for an employment contract, when compared to the criteria utilised by the ECJ in *De Bloos* and *Tessili* for commercial contracts. In addition, the ECJ's decision in *Ivenel* was a classic example of the coherence between jurisdiction and choice of law, as it borrowed from the EU rules on the determination of the applicable law in the absence of choice for employment contracts. It remained to be seen whether the criteria

[20] C-14/76, *A De Bloos SPRL v Bouyer SA*, EU:C:1976:134.
[21] ibid.
[22] (n 15).
[23] ibid [13]–[14].
[24] (n 19) all.
[25] C-133/81, *Ivenel v Schwab*, EU:C:1982:199.
[26] ibid.

of place of characteristic performance as applied by the ECJ in *Ivenel* would be extended to commercial contracts under the Brussels Convention rule on the allocation of jurisdiction for commercial contracts.

In *Shenavai*,[27] the ECJ was called upon by the UK Government to apply the exception in *Ivenel* by way of analogy to all contracts for the provision of professional services (which was a commercial contract) on the basis that it would be easier to locate a *single* obligation, than the criteria adopted in *De Bloos*. The ECJ rejected the argument of the UK. It justified the approach taken in *Ivenel* on the basis that:

> contracts of employment, like other contracts for work other than a self-employed basis, differ from other contracts – even those for the provision of services – by virtue of certain peculiarities: they create a lasting bond which brings the worker to some extent within the organizational framework of the business of the undertaking or employer, and they are linked to the place where the activities are pursued, which determines the application of mandatory rules and collective agreements. It is on account of those peculiarities that the court of the place in which the characteristic obligation of such contract is to be performed is considered best suited to resolving the disputes to which one or more obligations under such contracts may give rise.[28]

The decision in *Shenavai* was perhaps regrettable. It was an opportunity for the ECJ to make the concept of place of performance more precise and certain, by utilising the concept of place of characteristic performance, at least in the case of contracts for the provision of services. It might be that the invisible or underlying reason why the ECJ did not extend the decision in *Ivenel* to commercial contracts, was that it did not want to reach a decision that was inconsistent with *De Bloos* and *Tessili*, which applied the concept of contested obligation in commercial contracts, rather than the place of characteristic performance.[29] If this was a principal concern for the ECJ, it might have had a rethink on its decision in *De Bloos* and *Tessili*, by restricting its decision in those cases to complex commercial contracts, where the characteristic obligation cannot be identified.

The problems of determining the place of performance from the case law in *De Bloos* and *Tessili* gave rise to various suggestions and solutions as to how the concept of 'place of performance of the obligation in question' could be reformed. These suggestions were proffered to the ECJ in *Groupe Concorde*[30] which concerned the determination of the place of performance of the obligation in question for a contract of carriage of goods by sea.

The German Government supported an autonomous interpretation of 'the place of performance of the obligation'. The German Government argued that since there are many different types of contracts, the place of performance should

[27] C-266/85 *Shenavai v Kreischer*, EU:C:1982:199.

[28] ibid [14].

[29] This appears evident from a later decision of the ECJ which maintained the status quo in C-440/97, *Groupe Concorde*, EU:C:1999:456.

[30] ibid.

be determined by reference to each type of contract. This would have required an exhaustive determination for the place of performance for most types of contracts through the national case law.

Furthermore, the German Government suggested that to maintain the necessary equilibrium between the parties, the place of performance of a contract should be determined in each case according to the particular obligation in question. Thus, in the case of contracts for the sale or use of property in return for consideration, the place of performance could be determined to be the place where the immovable property is situated or where the movable property is located, depending on the stipulations of the contract. In contracts for services, the place of performance could be deemed to be the place where the service in question is to be mainly carried out.

The UK Government also advocated an autonomous interpretation of 'place of performance'. It argued that an autonomous interpretation would result in legal certainty, uniformity and also reduce the potential for forum shopping.

The UK added that the practical application of an independent definition should be effected on a case by case basis. Thus in the present case before the ECJ, since the action arose from the delivery of damaged goods on the basis of a contract of carriage, the UK government suggested (in the case) that the place of performance of the obligation is the place at which it was agreed that those goods were to be delivered.

The European Commission also supported an independent determination of the place of performance on the basis that the place of performance of the obligation to deliver goods without damage under a contract for the international carriage of goods by sea, is 'the place where the goods have been or are to be delivered'.

The French and Italian Government on the contrary argued that to permit the national court to designate the place of performance according to the circumstances of each of these relationships would give rise to unforeseeability and, therefore, legal uncertainty. They also pointed out that the finding an autonomous concept of place of performance would work in very few simple contracts and would therefore lead to unsatisfactory results in majority of cases having regard to the constant evolution of contractual practice in international trade.

AG Ruiz-Jarabo Colomer, in his opinion suggested that:

> the place of performance of a contractual obligation means the place designated by reference to the circumstances of the case, taking account of the nature of the legal relationship in question, it being understood that it is presumed that that place is the same as the place where the obligation characterising the legal relationship in question was or is to be performed. If more than one place is designated, that having the closest connection with the dispute must be chosen.[31]

[31] ibid [109].

Again, the ECJ in its judgment preferred to maintain the status quo but acknowledged that a review of the concept of place of performance of the obligation in question was being carried out with several proposals for reforms and suggestions. It was thus evident that the only way the weakness of the place of performance could be remedied in the case of commercial contracts, was by legislative reform. In effect, under the Brussels Convention regime, the intervention of the European legislator was needed to cure the defect of the place of performance in the allocation of jurisdiction for commercial contracts.

Under the Brussels I (which replaced the Brussels Convention), the European legislator retained the criteria of 'the place of performance of the obligation in question' in allocating jurisdiction for commercial contracts.[32] However, the European legislator provided uniform and autonomous criteria for defining the meaning of 'place of performance of the obligation in question' for a contract of sale and a contract for the provision of services.[33] This solution adopted by the European legislator was a product of compromise among Member States, and was also influenced by experience of the Brussels Convention regime.[34] In effect, the European legislator under the Brussels I regime moved to the concept of place of performance of the characteristic obligation as a way of replacing the concept of place of performance of the contested obligation for commercial contracts of sale of goods and provision of services.

Given that contracts of sale and provision of services are the type of transactions that usually arise in practice, the criteria utilised by the European legislator was at least a satisfactory solution. However, the decision by the European legislator to restrict the concept of place of characteristic performance to contracts of sale and provision of services was perhaps regrettable. The concept of place of characteristic performance should have been made the general rule in the allocation of jurisdiction for commercial contracts under the Brussels I. Given that the concept of characteristic obligation (though operative through the concept of habitual residence) was the presumptive connecting factor for commercial contracts under Article 4(2) of the Rome Convention – an instrument that came into force 1 April 1991 – the European legislator under Brussels I should have made the concept of place of characteristic performance the principal connecting factor, and the concept of contested obligation restricted to unusual cases where the characteristic obligation cannot be identified. Thus, the decision of the European legislator to restrict Article 5(1)(b) of the Brussels I (now Article 7(1)(b) of the Brussels Ia) to contracts of sales and provision of services is a missed opportunity that does not fully take advantage of the concept of characteristic obligation, which is principally utilised for commercial contracts under the EU choice of law rules.

[32] Article 5(1)(a) of Brussels I; Article 7(1)(a) of Brussels Ia.

[33] Article 5(1)(b) of Brussels I; Article 7(1)(b) of Brussels Ia.

[34] Beaumont (n 19) 16 and 17; AG Trstenjak in *Falco Privatsfitung and another v Weller-Lindhort*, EU:C:2009:34 [94].

In summation, by way of analogy, applying the Brussels Convention and Brussels I regime experience to Article 4 of Rome I, at the expense of being prolix, it is proposed that the place of performance of the characteristic obligation should be used as the principal connecting factor for general commercial contracts under a revised Article 4 of Rome I. In effect, the concept of place of characteristic performance could also be extended to include other commercial contracts, which are not contracts of sale and provision of services.

IV. Choice of Law as a Determinant of Jurisdiction under Article 7(1)(a) of Brussels Ia

Establishing a coherence between matters of jurisdiction and choice of law in the context of the place of performance for commercial contracts is really not new. In the context of the place of performance as a connecting factor, there is already a form of coherence between jurisdiction and choice of law in commercial contracts under EU private international law. Currently, there is a connection between Article 7(1)(a) of Brussels Ia and Article 4 of Rome I. Admittedly, the current form of coherence between Article 7(1)(a) of Brussels Ia and Article 4 of Rome I is not satisfactory and requires reform.

At the time the European legislators created the old Brussels Convention, there were no uniform choice of law rules in the law of obligations for Member State courts. The idea that the coherence between the subject-matter of jurisdiction and choice of law would later arise was perhaps unthinkable at the time. The ECJ decisions in 1976, which came prior to the enactment of the Rome Convention, changed the tide. Article 5(1) of the Brussels Convention provided that a person domiciled in a Member State may, in another Member State, be sued in matters relating to a contract, in the courts for the place of performance of the obligation in question.

In *De Bloos*[35] the ECJ in interpreting Article 5(1) of the Brussels Convention held that the meaning of place of performance of the obligation in question was based on the contested obligation before the court of a Member State.[36]

On the same day, in *Tessili*,[37] the ECJ held that the 'place of performance of the obligation in question' within the meaning of Article 5(1) of the Brussels Convention is to be determined in accordance with the law which governs the obligation in question according to the rules of conflict of laws of the court before which the matter is brought.[38]

[35] (n 20).
[36] ibid [13]–[14].
[37] (n 15).
[38] (n 15) [15]. For a critique of this decision see the Opinion of AG Lenz in *Custom Made* (n 19).

When Brussels I came into force, Article 5(1)(b) (now Article 7(1)(b) of Brussels Ia) made the decision in *Tessili* inapplicable to contracts for the sale of goods and provisions of services, in which case the Member State courts uniformly had to identify the place of performance of the characteristic obligation for such contracts, based on the place of delivery of the goods and provision of services respectively.[39] However, in accordance with the principle of continuity, the ECJ's decision in *Tessili* equally applies to both Article 5(1)(a) of Brussels I and Article 7(1)(a) of Brussels Ia.[40]

The implication of the above is that Member State courts have applied both the Rome Convention and Rome I in determining the place of performance of the obligation in question in determining the allocation of jurisdiction for commercial contracts under Article 5(1) of the Brussels Convention and Article 5(1)(a) of Brussels I (now Article 7(1)(a) of Brussels Ia).[41] In this connection, the applicable law as determined under the EU choice of law rules directly influences and determines the allocation of jurisdiction under Article 7(1)(a) of Brussels Ia.

The ECJ's case law in *Tessili* and some Member State court's jurisprudence that have applied it in practice demonstrates that choice of law directly influences jurisdiction under Article 7(1)(a) of Brussels Ia. It is also opined on this basis that Article 7(1)(a) somewhat influences the determination of the applicable law, since the Member State court has to reach a finding on the applicable law in order to determine whether it has jurisdiction. Viewed from this perspective, in the context of the place of performance for commercial contracts, the reality of the relationship between jurisdiction and choice of law could be regarded as symbiotic.

This point is better appreciated and illustrated by looking at the decisions of some Member State Courts. In *Definitely Maybe v Marek Lieberberg*,[42] the defendant applied to set aside the service of claim for breach of contract on the ground that under Article 5(1) of the Brussels Convention the English court had no jurisdiction to hear the case. The plaintiff, an English company, had commenced the claim against the defendant, a German company, for the unpaid balance of two performances by the plaintiff's music band, which had taken place in Germany. Morison J (on appeal) correctly appreciated the ECJ's case in *Tessili* and observed that the jurisdiction of the English High Court was in reality dependent on the applicable law as determined by the Rome Convention. He observed thus:

> the place of performance of an obligation … in this case does, depend upon which system of law governs the contract. Under German law the place of performance of an

[39] See generally C-381/08, *Car Trim GmbH v KeySafety Systems Srl*, EU:C:2010:90.

[40] See Recital 19 to Brussels I and Recital 34 to Brussels Ia. See also C-533/07, *Falco*, EU:C:2009:257 [46]–[57].

[41] See Recital 19 to Brussels I and Recital 34 to Brussels Ia. See also *Falco* (n 40) [46]–[57].

[42] *Definitely Maybe v Marek Lieberberg* [2001] 1 WLR 1745. See also *Dinkha Latchin T/A Dinkha Latchin Associates v General Mediterranean Holdings SA & or* [2002] CLC 330 (QB); *Kenburn Waste Management Ltd v Heinz Bergmann* [2002] EWCA Civ 98; *Commercial Marine Piling Ltd v Pierse Contracting Ltd* [2009] EWHC 2241; *BNP Paribas SA v Anchorage Capital Europe LLP & Ors* [2013] EWHC 3073 (Comm).

> obligation to pay is the domicile of the debtor, namely Germany. Under English law the place of performance of the defendant's obligation to pay is England, the place where the money is to be received. Thus, the question as to whether these proceedings can continue in this jurisdiction is dependent upon the answer to the question: what is the governing law of the contract? If the answer is English law, then the proceedings can continue here and the appeal must be allowed.[43]

The High Court determined under Article 4(5) of the Rome Convention that German law was applicable and consequently held that the lower court was right in declining jurisdiction.

Thus, the decision in *Tessili* confirms that, in the context of the place of performance, there is already a form of coherence between matters of jurisdiction and choice of law. In effect, the central argument in this chapter which is based on the coherence between jurisdiction and choice of law in supporting the central claim in this book should not be regarded as revolutionary, or too radical from the existing law.

However, the problem with the decision in *Tessili* is that if the place of performance is made the principal connecting factor for commercial contracts under Article 4 of Rome I, it could lead to circularity if applied in conjunction with Article 7(1)(a) of Brussels Ia, which uses the applicable law to determine the place of performance for jurisdictional purposes.[44]

The decision in *Tessili* also probably leads to forum shopping. Under Article 4 of Rome I, it remains a matter of controversy as to when the principal connecting factor (usually the habitual residence of the characteristic performer) or the escape clause is to be invoked.[45] Given this state of affairs, it would not be surprising for potential litigants to sue, under Article 7(1)(a) of the Brussels Ia, in a court that would likely select a law favourable to that litigant in designating jurisdiction based on how the court usually construes Article 4 of Rome I.[46]

The solution to this problem might be to considerably reduce the scope of Article 7(1)(a) of Brussels Ia.[47] This could be done by applying the principle

[43] *Definitely Maybe* (n 42) [4].

[44] A Summers, 'Interpreting Article 4(3) of Rome I' www.academia.edu/1998215/Interpreting_Article_4_3_of_the_Rome_I_Regulation. P. 30.

[45] See ch 3, s III.B.i.

[46] See also Tang (n 1) 52–55.

[47] Tang (n 1) 58; Grusic (n 19) 340; TK Graziano, 'Jurisdiction under Article 7 No. 1 of The Recast Brussels I Regulation: Disconnecting the Procedural Place of Performance from its counterpart in Substantive Law' (2015) 16 *Yearbook of Private International Law* 167, 214. Interestingly, the CJEU in C-9/12 *Corman-Collins SA v La Maison du Whisky SA*, EU:C:2013:860 qualified an exclusive distribution contract as one for the provision of services despite the fact that Recital 17 to Rome I creates a distinction between service contracts and distribution contracts. In effect, it appears the CJEU 'pragmatically' squeezed an exclusive distribution contract into Article 5(1)(b) of Brussels I in order to avoid the problems of applying Article 5(1)(a) of Brussels I. For a strong critique of this innovative approach by the CJEU see P Beaumont and B Yüksel 'Cross-border Civil and Commercial Disputes Before the Court of Justice of the European Union' in P Beaumont et al, *Cross-border Litigation in Europe* 1st edn (Oxford, Hart Publishing, 2017) 499, 522–23.

of place of characteristic performance in a blanket way to commercial contracts. Alternatively, the scope of Article 7(1)(b) could explicitly provide for commercial contracts (including complex contracts) that are likely to arise in practice and, also, expressly determine the characteristic performance under the contract.

In addition, Member State courts might find it easier to determine the characteristic performance even in complex contracts by asking the questions: who is the true professional under the contract that does the job that gives the contract its name? Who performs the relatively more important or complex obligation? The decision maker could thus seek to ascertain who really does the job under the contract and compare the obligations of the parties, and reach a conclusion in its view as to which obligation of the parties is relatively more important or complex.[48]

V. What are the Differences between Choice of Law and Jurisdiction which Militate against Resolving them in the Same Manner?

The fact that it is argued in this book, that the coherence between matters of jurisdiction and choice of law is a good reason to justify the proposal, does not in any way suggest that matters of jurisdiction and choice of law must be resolved in the same manner.

It must be cautioned that this coherence should not be applied absolutely or blindly so as not to obscure the traditional distinction between matters of jurisdiction and choice of law.

Resolving matters of jurisdiction and choice of law in the same way might increase the danger of forum shopping and threaten international uniformity.[49]

Matters of EU jurisdiction rules usually involve litigational convenience, the interest of the parties and the forum.[50] One of the reasons why the domicile of the defendant is the main rule under Article 4 of Brussels Ia might be to protect the interest of the defendant. Suing the defendant in its forum generally favours the interest of the defendant because such a party is being sued in its forum, and would probably incur less costs when compared to the claimant who travels to the forum of the defendant to institute legal proceedings. Moreover, apart from the interests of legal certainty and predictability in legal proceedings,[51] an underlying rationale for generally founding jurisdiction at the forum of the defendant might

[48] See ch 3, s IV.A.
[49] See also Hay (n 1) 162.
[50] See also Fawcett (n 1) 58; Lein (n 3) 196.
[51] Recital 15 to Brussels Ia.

be that since the defendant is the one being sued, such a party should not generally be subject to the inconvenience and cost of litigating in a foreign forum, especially where the claimant's case is vexatious and frivolous.

In the same vein, one of the reasons why the Brussels Ia, as an exception, allows the claimant to sue the defendant in an alternative forum that has a close link (based on fixed connecting factors), is to take into account the interest of the resolution of the dispute, such as the proximity of the evidence, given that the defendant's domicile might not always satisfy the requirement of proximity of evidence.[52]

On the contrary, choice of law is mainly concerned not only with connecting factors to determine the most closely connected law, but with such matters as mandatory rules and public policy.[53]

In addition, while the European jurisdiction rules might allow litigation in more than one fora, the European choice of law rules usually support a single law to apply.[54]

In essence, this book is aware of the danger of conflating matters of jurisdiction with choice of law, but argues on the contrary that these problems would not significantly be an impediment to the central claim in this chapter.

VI. Why do European Jurisdiction Rules Support the Claim on the Significance of the Place of Performance of the Commercial Contract in Choice of Law Matters?

The fact that there are certain differences between matters of jurisdiction and choice of law, which militates against resolving them in the same way, does not diminish the strength of the proposal.

It is of very little significance in the context of what is classified in this book as 'coherence of principles', 'coherence of connecting factors' and 'coherence of interpretation' because the rationale or philosophical foundation is quite similar between matters of jurisdiction and choice of law (in these types of coherence), so that concerns of the distinction between matters of jurisdiction and choice of law being blurred, may arise only in unusual or exceptional cases. In addition, there is a far reaching coherence of other principles, between Brussels Ia and Rome I, including party autonomy[55] and protection of weaker parties.[56] The only real

[52] Recital 16 to Brussels Ia.

[53] See also Fawcett (n 1) 58; Lein (n 3) 196. cf Article 24 of Brussels Ia.

[54] See also Lein (n 3) 196.

[55] See Recital 12 to Rome I. See also Article 3 of Rome I and Article 25 of Brussels Ia.

[56] See generally Recital 18 to Brussels Ia, and Recital 23 to Rome I. For consumer contracts see Article 18(1), 19(1)–(3) and 26(1) of Brussels I Recast, and Article 6 and 11(4) of Rome I Regulation.

exception is that of commercial contracts, where the parties do not make a choice of law.

In effect, the coherence between jurisdiction and choice of law supports the claim in this chapter from the perspective of coherence of principles, coherence of connecting factors and coherence of interpretation.

A. Coherence of the Principle of Proximity

A connecting factor could particularly be very useful in determining the principle of proximity both for matters of jurisdiction and choice of law. This is a form of coherence because a single connecting factor is recognised as generally satisfying the requirement of proximity in both matters of jurisdiction and choice of law.

This idea is evident in matters of jurisdiction and choice of law for contracts of immovable property, employment contracts and non-contractual obligations. In other words, in these obligations, the same connecting factor used for determining matters of jurisdiction, as generally satisfying the requirement of proximity, is also used for choice of law.

However, this form of coherence is missing in commercial contracts. What this section seeks to address is: whether in matters of commercial contracts, it is justifiable to have the place of performance determine proximity for jurisdiction issues, and on the other hand have the habitual residence of the characteristic performer as the connecting factor that generally determines proximity for choice of law issues.

In effect, it is argued that jurisdiction and choice of law in civil and commercial matters share some common principles in identifying the connecting factor that generally designates the principle of proximity in a given dispute. In particular, it is argued that the place of performance best satisfies the requirement of geographical proximity, when compared to other connecting factors, both from the perspective of jurisdiction and choice of law in commercial contracts.

It is important to stress that applying the concept of coherence of geographical proximity in matters of jurisdiction to choice of law is not done blindly. The reference to geographical proximity is used to stress the *close link* between the country and dispute (contract or tort).

i. Place where the Property is Located for Immovable Property

Article 24(1) of Brussels Ia (previously Article 22(1) of Brussels I, and Article 16(1) of Brussels Convention) provides that in proceedings which have

For employment contracts see Article 21(1)(b), 23, 26(1) of Brussels Ia, and Article 8 of Rome I. For insurance contracts see Article 11(1)(b), 12, 15 and 26 of Brussels Ia, and Article 7(2) of Rome I.

as their object rights *in rem* in immovable property or tenancies of immovable property, the courts of the Member State in which the property is situated shall have exclusive jurisdiction. The Jenard Report,[57] the CJEU,[58] Advocate Generals (AGs)[59] and some Member State courts[60] have consistently (and rightly) justified this rule as satisfying the requirement of geographical proximity on the basis that these courts are best placed to ascertain the facts and to apply the relevant rules and practices, for the efficacious conduct of proceedings and sound administration of justice. In addition, AG Poiares Maduro also justified the requirement of exclusive jurisdiction for such courts on the grounds that:

> It is also closely linked to a normative legal principle: the traditional sovereignty of each contracting state to control, adjudicate and protect real rights of private individuals upon immovable property located in its territory. The area of property law relating to immovable property is a typical area where for mandatory political and economic reasons the State where the property is located retains a legislative authority that naturally extends to an exclusive jurisdiction for actions in rem.[61]

By way of analogy, Article 4(1)(c) of Rome I[62] (which is similar to Article 24 of Brussels Ia) provides that a commercial contract relating to a right in rem in immovable property or to a tenancy of immovable property shall be governed by the law of the country where the property is situated. The rule under Article 4(1)(c) of Rome I can also be justified on the basis that (inter alia) it satisfies the requirement of geographical proximity.

The idea that the place where the property is situated is utilised in determining proximity in both matters of EU jurisdiction and choice of law rules does not obscure the distinction between jurisdiction and choice of law. It demonstrates that the place where the property is situated is the appropriate connecting factor that suitably and coherently determines the concept of proximity for both EU matters of jurisdiction and choice of law.

[57] [1979] OJ C59/1, 35.

[58] C-241/83, *Erich Rösler v Horst Rottwinkel*, EU:C:1985:6 [20]; C-158/87, *Scherrens v Maenhout and others*, EU:C:1988:370 [10]; C-115/88, *Reichert and others v Dresdner Bank* EU:C:1990:3 [10]; C-8/98, *Dansommer A/S v Andreas Götz*, EU:C:2000:45 [27]; C-280/90, *Hacker v Euro-Relais GmbH*, EU:C:1992:92 [9]; C-4/03, *Gesellschaft für Antriebstechnik mbH &amp Co. KG v Lamellen und Kupplungsbau*, EU:C:2006:457 [9]; C-73/04, *Klein v Rhodos Management Ltd*, EU:C:2005:205 [16]; C-343/04, *Land Oberösterreich v ČEZ A.S*, EU:C:2009:660 [28]–[29]; C-438/12, *Weber v Weber*, EU:C:2014:212 [41]; C-417/15, *Schmidt v Schmidt*, EU:C:2014:6 [29].

[59] AG Lenz in C-220/84, *AS-Autoteile Service GmbH v Pierre Malhe*, EU:C:1985:302 [1]; AG La Pergola, in C-8/98, *Dansommer A/S*, EU:C:1999:398 [7]–[10]; AG Darmon in C-280/90, *Hacker* [15]; AG Geelhoed in C-4/03, *Gesellschaft*, EU:C:2004:539 [27]; AG Geelhoed in C-73/04 *Klein*, EU:C:2005:205 [5], [30], [39]; AG Poiares Maduro in C-343/04, *Land Oberösterreich*, EU:C:2009:242 [33]–[39]; AG Kokott in C-420/07, *Apostolides v David Charles Orams and Linda Elizabeth Orams*, EU:C:2008:749 [83]; AG Jääskinen in C-438/12, *Weber*, EU:C:2014:43 [27]; AG Kokott in C-417/15, *Schmidt*, EU:C:2013:540 [37], [48].

[60] C-9 O 62/95, *Re A Claim for Payment for A Timeshare* [1997] ILPr 524 (District Court, Germany); C-XII ZR 28/01, *Re a Contract Concerning a Usufructory Right* [2008] ILPr 8 [10] (German Federal Supreme Court); *Sauchiehall Street Properties one Limited v E M I Group* 2015 GWD 1–3 [48].

[61] *Land Oberösterreich* (n 59). Footnotes omitted.

[62] Previously Article 4(3) of the Rome Convention.

More importantly, the connecting factor of the place where the property is situated is also justified, as Maduro expressly says, by sovereignty. One would therefore submit that the connecting factor is justified by two rationales (proximity and sovereignty), and that these two rationales result in the use of the same connecting factor for both jurisdiction and choice of law.

Furthermore, the place where the property is situated is the crux of a contract relating to a right in rem in immovable property or to a tenancy of immovable property. In reality, the place where the property is situated would normally be the place of performance of the contract. The place where the property is situated is the place where the landlord or owner of the immovable property effectively performs his obligations (such as delivering the property and maintaining it) to the tenant or client. In the same vein, the place where the property is situated would usually be the place where the tenant pays the landlord or owner of the immovable property. This justifies why the criteria of the place where the property is situated is an appropriate connecting factor for both matters of jurisdiction and choice of law.

ii. Place of Performance of the Characteristic Obligation for Employment Contracts

In matters of employment contract, there is the principal concern of protecting weaker parties in the context of jurisdiction and choice of law.[63] However, it must be noted that the protection of weaker parties in EU private international law is not excessive or unbridled so as not to frustrate commercial and economic efficacy in employment relationships. Excessive protection of employees in private international law might frustrate commercial and economic efficacy in employment relationships. This might explain why EU private international law utilises the principle of proximity, via the place where the employee habitually carries out its work, as a means of generally protecting the employee in matters of jurisdiction and choice of law.

In matters of jurisdiction for employment contracts, Article 21(1)(b) of the Brussels Ia (previously Article 19(2)(a) of the Brussels I and Article 5(1) of the Brussels Convention) provides that the employee (as an exception to Article 4 of the Brussels Ia) can sue its employer in the courts for the place where or from where the employee habitually carries out his work. In reality, this criteria (Article 21(1)(b) of the Brussels Ia) is the place of performance of the characteristic obligation for an employment contract.[64] The CJEU has consistently (and rightly) held that the place of performance of the characteristic obligation for employment contracts satisfies the requirement of geographical proximity (for ease of taking of evidence, sound administration of justice and efficacious conduct of proceedings), which is mainly suited to protecting the employee as a weaker party, given that

[63] See also Recital 23 to Rome I.

[64] *Ivenel* (n 25) [14].

this is the place where it is usually least expensive for the employee to commence, or defend himself against, court proceedings.[65] Some Advocate Generals in their Opinion to the CJEU have also endorsed this view.[66]

By way of analogy, in matters of choice of law for employment contracts, Article 8(2) of Rome I (which is similar to Article 21(1)(b) of the Brussels Ia) provides (as an exception to Article 3(1) and 8(1) of Rome I) that the law that applies is law of the country in which or, failing that, from which the employee habitually carries out his work in performance of the contract. In reality, Article 8(2) of Rome I (previously Article 6(2)(a) of the Rome Convention) also utilises the criteria of the place of performance of the characteristic obligation for employment contracts. The CJEU[67] and some Advocate Generals in their Opinion[68] have rightly justified the rule in Article 6(2)(a) of the Rome Convention (and Article 8(2) of Rome I) as satisfying the requirement of geographical proximity, which is mainly suited to protecting the employee as a weaker party.

Under Article 8(2) of Rome I, the connecting factor of the place where the employee habitually carries out its work for his employer (which is in reality the place of performance of the characteristic obligation) is the principal connecting factor. It is indeed possible to displace this principal connecting factor, but it is submitted that the circumstances in which it can be displaced are usually very clear on the basis that: generally the place where an employee carries out its work for its employer most closely connects an employment contract with a particular country.[69]

The idea that in EU private international law, the place of performance of the characteristic obligation is used as a connecting factor in both matters of jurisdiction and choice of law for employment contracts in order to inter alia satisfy the requirement of proximity does not obscure the distinction between jurisdiction and choice of law. It demonstrates that the place where the employee habitually carries out its work is affected by the business and political environment of any given State by reason of their work in that State,[70] which makes such place usually the most closely connected to the employment contract, from the perspective of jurisdiction and choice of law.

Furthermore, the key element of an employment contract is the performance of the employee. The employee's performance is the crux of the contract. Thus, from

[65] *Ivenel* (n 25) [15]; C-125/92, *Mulox IBC Ltd v Geels*, EU:C:1993:306 [18]–[19]; C-383/95, *Rutten v Cross Medical Ltd*, EU:C:1997:7 [22]; C-37/00, *Weber v Universal Ogden Services Ltd*, EU:C:2002:122 [40]; C-437/00, *Pugliese v Finmeccanica SpA*, EU:C:2003:219 [18]; C-154/11, *Mahamdia v People's Democratic Republic of Algeria*, EU:C:2012:491 [41], [44] and [46].

[66] AG Jacobs in C-383/95, *Rutten*, EU:C:1996:417 [39]; AG Jacobs in C-37/00, *Weber*, EU:C:2001:554 [44]–[46]; AG Jacobs in C-437/00, *Pugliese*, EU:C:2002:511 [43], [57].

[67] C-29/10, *Koelzch v Etat du Grand Duchy of Luxembourg*, EU:C:2011:151 [42]; C-64/12, *Schlecker v Boedeker*, ECLI: EU:C:2013:551 [34].

[68] AG Trstenjak in C-29/10, *Koelzch*, EU:C:2010:789 [44], [50]; AG Trstenjak in C-384/10, *Voogsgeerd v Navimer, SA*, EU:C:2011:564 [52]; AG Wahl in C-64/12, *Schlecker v Boedeker*, EU:C:2013:241 [26], [32], [56], [59].

[69] See generally *Schlecker* (n 67).

[70] AG Trstenjak in *Voogsgeerd* (n 68) [52]; C-384/10, *Voogsgeerd v Navimer, SA*, EU:C:2011: 842 [51].

the perspective of jurisdiction and choice of law, the place where the employee generally performs its duties to his employer is the country or legal system that has the closest connection to an employment contract.

iii. Place of Direct Damage for Non-Contractual Obligations

In matters of jurisdiction for non-contractual obligations, Article 7(2) of the Brussels Ia provides that the place where the harmful event occurred or may occur has jurisdiction (as an alternative to Article 4 of Brussels Ia). The place of harmful event has been justified (under Article 5(3) of both the Brussels Convention and Brussels I) as having a close link between the contract and the court called on to hear and determine the case. In other words, the place where the harmful event occurred is usually the most appropriate for deciding the case, in particular on the grounds of proximity and ease of taking evidence, is equally relevant whether the dispute concerns compensation for damage which has already occurred or relates to an action seeking to prevent the occurrence of damage.

From a jurisdictional perspective, it (the place of harmful event) aids the facilitation of evidence (including witnesses), efficacious conduct of proceedings and sound administration of justice. These views have been widely endorsed by the Jenard Report,[71] the CJEU in decided cases,[72] Advocate Generals in their Opinions[73] and some Member State courts.[74]

[71] (n 57) 25–26.

[72] C-21/76, *Bier v Mines de Potasse d' Alsace*, EU:C:1976:166 [11]; C-220/88, *Dumez France SA & Tracoba SARL v Hessische Landesbank & others*, EU:C:1990:8 [17]; C-68/93 *Shevill, Ixora Trading Inc, Chequepoint SARL and Chequepoint International Ltd v Presse Alliance SA*, EU:C:1995:6 [19]; *Antonio Marinari contre Lloyds Bank plc v Zubaidi Trading Company*, EU:C:1995:289 [10]; C-167/00, *Verein für Konsumenteninformation v Karl Heinz Henkel*, EU:C:2002:555 [46]; C-18/02, *Danmarks Rederiforening, acting on behalf of DFDS Torline A/S v LO Landsorganisationen i Sverige, acting on behalf of SEKO Sjöfolk Facket för Service och Kommunikation*, EU:C:2004:74 [27]; C-189/08, *Zuid-Chemie BV v Philippo's Mineralenfabriek NV/SA*, EU:C:2009:475 [24]; C-133/11, *Folien Fischer AG v Ritrama SPA*, EU:C:2012:664 [36]–[38]; C-228/11, *Melzer v MF Global UK Ltd*, EU:C:2013:305 [27]; C-147/12, *Öfab, Östergötlands Fastigheter AB v Koot*, EU:C:2013:490 [50], [57]; C-45/13, *Kainz v Pantherwerke AG*, EU:C:2014:7 [27]; C-572/14, *Austro-Mechana Gesellschaft zur Wahrnehmung mechanisch-musikalischer Urheberrechte GmbH v Amazon EU Sàrl, Amazon Services Europe Sàrl, Amazon.de GmbH, Amazon Logistik GmbH, Amazon Media Sàrl*, EU:C:2013:515 [31]; C-352/13, *Hydrogen Peroxide SA v Akzo Nobel NV (Re Cartel Damage Claims-CDC)*, EU:C:2015:335 [40]; C-47/14, *Holterman Ferho Exploitatie BV v Spies von Büllesheim*, EU:C:2015:574 [74]; C-12/15, *Universal Music International Holding BV v Schilling*, EU:C:2016:449 [27].

[73] AG Léger in C-68/93, *Shevill*, EU:C:1994:303, [8], [55]; AG Darmon in *Fiona* [57], [71]; AG Jacobs in C-18/02, *Danmarks*, EU:C:2003:182 [40]; AG Cruz Villalón in C-523/10 *Wintersteiger AG v Products 4U Sondermaschinenbau GmbH*, EU:C:2012:90 [17]; AG Jääskinen in C-133/11, *Folien*, EU:C:2012:226 [57]–[58]; AG Jääskinen in C-228/11, *Melzer*, EU:C:2012:766 [56]; AG Szpunar in C-375/13, *Kolassa v Barclays Bank Plc*, EU:C:2014:2135 [56]; AG Wahl in C-350/14, *Lazar v Allianz SpA*, EU:C:2015:586 [51]; AG Jääskinen in C-352/13, *Hydrogen*, EU:C:2014:2443 [45]; AG Saugmandsgaard Øe in C-572/14, *Austro-Mechana*, EU:C:2016:90 [93]; AG Szpunar in C-12/15, *Universal Music*, EU:C:2016:161 [28]; AG Wahl in C-102/15, *Gazdasagi Versenyhivatal v Siemens Aktiengesellschaft Osterreich*, EU:C:2016: 225 [59].

[74] *AMT Futures v Marzillier* [2014] EWHC 1085 [4]–[5] (Comm) [appeal allowed by the English Court of Appeal in *Marzillier, Dr Meier & Dr Guntner Rechtsanwaltsgesellschaft mbH v AMT Futures*

By way of analogy, in matters of choice of law, Article 4(1) of Rome II applies the law of the place of direct damage, which is similar to the place of harmful event under Article 7(2) of Brussels Ia.[75] The place of (direct) damage is the connecting factor that best meets the requirement of geographical proximity (as is the situation under a similar Article 7(2) of Brussels Ia). Interestingly, AG Wahl appears to also subscribe to this view in his opinion to the CJEU, in a case on Rome II, where he applied a similar analogy by relying on a previous CJEU decision interpreting Article 5(3) of the Brussels Convention.[76]

The significance of the foregoing is that in matters of jurisdiction and choice of law, EU private international law identifies the place of direct damage as generally satisfying the requirement of proximity in non-contractual obligations. This approach does not obscure the distinction between matters of jurisdiction and choice of law, but recognises that based on the principle of coherence of geographical proximity, the place of direct damage works well for both matters of jurisdiction and choice of law in non-contractual obligations.

Furthermore, matters of non-contractual obligations are usually focused on the damage in order to ascertain liability of the tortfeasor. Matters of the non-contractual obligations are geared towards the damage that has occurred. The damage constitutes the main element of the tort, and therefore generally satisfies the requirement of geographical proximity in matters of jurisdiction and choice of law.

iv. Place of Performance for Commercial Contracts

Whereas in the case of contracts of real property, employment contracts and torts, there is coherence in the EU rules in utilising the same connecting factor to satisfy the principle of proximity, Article 7 of Brussels Ia and Article 4 of Rome I do not have this form of coherence for commercial contracts, which is a very important obligation. It is submitted that this is unfortunate.

The place of performance of the *characteristic obligation* is given absolute significance as a connecting factor for commercial contracts (of contracts of sale and provision of services) under Article 7(1)(b) of Brussels Ia. The place of performance of the *obligation in question* is also given absolute significance as a connecting factor under Article 7(1)(a) for commercial contracts that are not contracts of sale or provision of services. The place of performance (under Article 5(1) of the Brussels Convention and Article 5(1)(a) and (b) of Brussels I)[77] has been justified on

Ltd [2015] EWCA Civ 143[2015] ILPr 20 [32] without challenging this statement]; *XL Insurance Co SE (formerly XL Insurance Co Ltd) v AXA Corporate Solutions Assurance* [2015] EWHC 3431 (Comm) [75].

[75] However, it should be noted that Article 7(2) of Brussels Ia also grants jurisdiction to the place where the event giving rise to the damage occurred. See generally *Bier* (n 72).

[76] *Lazar* (n 73) [77], [80]. He relies on the CJEU's decision (at [77] of his opinion) interpreting Article 5(3) of the Brussels Convention in *Dumez* (n 72) [21].

[77] Now Article 7(1)(a) and (b) of Brussels Ia.

the basis of satisfying the requirement of geographical proximity, on the basis that (the place of performance) has a close link between the contract and the court called on to hear and determine the case. From a jurisdictional perspective, the geographical proximity of the place of performance aids the facilitation of evidence (including witnesses), efficacious conduct of proceedings and sound administration of justice. These views have been widely endorsed by the Jenard Report,[78] the CJEU in decided cases,[79] Advocate Generals in their Opinion[80] and some Member State courts.[81]

Where a valid choice of law has not been made, Article 4(1) of Rome I provides for (commercial contracts) fixed connecting factors to determine the applicable law in the absence of choice.[82] Article 4(2) of Rome I also provides that the law of the habitual residence of the characteristic performer would apply (to commercial contracts) where: first, it does not fall within the category of contracts mentioned in Article 4(1) of Rome I, and second, where it falls within more than one of the sub-categories mentioned in Article 4(1)(a)–(h) of Rome I.[83] The principal connecting factors (under Article 4(1) and (2) of Rome I) are principally aimed at satisfying the requirement of legal certainty, predictability and foreseeability.[84]

[78] (n 57) 23–24.

[79] *Tessili* (n 15) [13]; *Shenavai* (n 27) [6]; C-256/00, *Besix SA v Wasserreinigungsbau Alfred Kretzschmar GmbH*, EU:C:2002:99 [31]; C-386/05, *Color Drack GmbH v. Lexx International Vertriebs GmbH*, EU:C:2007:262 [22], [34], [42]; C–204/08, *Rehder v Air Baltic Corporation*, EU:C:2009:439 [22], [32]–[37], [44]–[45]; C-19/09, *Wood Floor Solutions Andreas Domberger GmbH v Silva Trade SA*, EU:C:2010:137 [22]–[27], [39]–[40]; C-9/12, *Corman-Collins* (n 47) [31], [39]; C-469/12, *Krejci Lager & Umschlagbetriebs GMBH v Olbrich Transport und Logistik GMBH*, EU:C:2013:788 [20]; C-196/15, *Granarolo SpA v Ambrosi Emmi France SA*, EU:C:2016:559 [38]–[40]. cf C-288/92, *Custom Made Commercial Ltd v Stawa Metallbau GmbH*, EU:C:1994:268 [16].

[80] AG Mancini in C-34/82, *Martin Peters Bauunternehmung GmbH v Zuid Nederlandse Aannemers Vereniging (South Netherlands Contractors' Association)* [1983] ECR 987; AG Tesauro in C-106/95 *Mainschiffahrts-Genossenschaft eG (MSG) v Les Gravières Rhénanes SARL*, EU:C:1996:361 [9]; AG Léger in C-420/97, *Leathertex Divisione Sintetici SpA v Bodetex BVBA*, EU:C:1999:483 [112], [115], [164]; AG Ruiz-Jarabo Colomer in *Groupe Concorde* (n 19) [56], [63]–[67], [86]–[87], [91], [106]; AG Geelhoed Fonderie in C-334/00 *Officine Meccaniche Tacconi SpA v Heinrich Wagner Sinto Maschinenfabrik GmbH (HWS)*, EU:C:2002:68; AG Trstenjak in *Falco* (n 34) [24]; AG Trstenjak in C-19/09, *Wood Floor*, EU:C:2010:6 [33], [65]; cf Opinion of AG Lenz in *Custom Made* (n 19).

[81] *Intersubsmagazine SA v Time Warner Publishing BV Before the Juzgado de Primera Instancia* No 8, Bilbao 20 September 1995 [1996] ILPr 240 [29] (Court of First Instance, Spain); C-4 Ob 165-07d, *Falco* [2008] ILPr 22 [15] (Austrian Supreme Court Reference to CJEU); C-CA164/08, *J S Swan (Printing) Limited v Kall Kwik UK Limited* [2009] CSOH 99 [23] (Outer House, Court of Session, Scotland); C-X ZR 76/07, *Re Place of Performance of a Passenger Flight* [2009] ILPr 30 [10], [17] (German Federal Supreme Court); *Car Trim* [2009] ILPr 33 [17], [23] (German Federal Supreme Court Reference to CJEU); *Jurisdiction in the Case of a Sale Involving the Carriage of Goods*, [2010] ILPr 29 [26] (German, Regional Court of Appeal, Stuttgart); C-2012 FOLIO, *Deutsche Bank AG London Branch v Petromena ASA* [2013] EWHC 3065 [57] (Commercial Court, England); *Canyon Offshore Ltd v GDF Suez E&P Nederland BV* [2014] EWHC 3801 (Commercial Court, England) [44]–[45], [52]–[53]; *Worldview Capital Management SA v Petroceltic International Plc* [2015] EWHC 2185 (Commercial Court, England) [32]–[34]; *JEB Recoveries LLP v Binstock* [2016] EWCA Civ 1008 (English, Court of Appeal) [51], [56].

[82] Recital 19 to Rome I.

[83] Recital 19 to Rome I.

[84] C-133/08, *Intercontainer Interfrigo SC (ICF) v Balkenende Oosthuizen BV*, EU:C:2009:617 [62].

In reality, the principal criteria under Article 4(1) and (2) is the habitual residence of the characteristic performer. The place of characteristic performance is certainly not the principal connecting factor.

Article 4(3) of Rome I reconciles the requirement of legal certainty with flexibility.[85] It provides as an escape clause,[86] that where there is another country that is manifestly more closely connected to the country, other than that indicated by the principal connecting factors under Article 4(1) and (2), the law of the country that is manifestly more closely connected would apply. This exception or escape clause is based on the principle of proximity,[87] but does not expressly give special significance to the place of performance.[88]

Article 4(4) of Rome I provides that where the applicable law cannot be determined under Article 4(1) and (2), the law that is most closely connected to the commercial contract should apply (otherwise known as 'the principle of closest connection'). The principle of closest connection is also based on the principle of proximity, but does not expressly give special significance to the place of performance.[89]

Thus, there is a failure in the logic between Article 7 of Brussels Ia and Article 4 of Rome I, given that in the former, the place of performance is given absolute significance in determining proximity, but in the latter the significance of the place of performance is marginal. As has been opined strongly in this book, generally, the place of performance would better satisfy the requirement of proximity for choice of law in commercial contracts, when compared to the habitual residence of the characteristic performer, or indeed any other connecting factor.

In effect, the idea that the place of performance best satisfies the requirement of geographical proximity in matters of jurisdiction for commercial contracts can by way of analogy be applied to matters of choice of law to the effect that the place of performance best satisfies the requirement of geographical proximity in matters of choice of law for commercial contracts. In reaching this conclusion, this book does not blindly apply the analogy derived from jurisdiction to choice of law. Indeed, it might be stressed that matters of jurisdiction are mainly procedural, tailored towards facilitation of evidence, and efficacious conduct of proceedings. These considerations do not apply to choice of law.

What is being said is that the analogy that can legitimately be applied from matters of jurisdiction to matters of choice of law is that the place of performance is the connecting factor that best embodies the *close link* between the *country* where the contract is performed and commercial contract in question. It is from this perspective, that it is opined that the place of performance best embodies the idea of geographical proximity. Indeed, the place of performance, rather than the

[85] Recital 16 to Rome I.
[86] Recital 20 to Rome I.
[87] See generally *Schlecker* (n 67).
[88] Recital 20 to Rome I.
[89] Recital 21 to Rome I.

habitual residence of the characteristic performer, is that place where the 'main action' or 'main element' in the contract takes place so that that country could legitimately want its law to apply on the grounds of geographical proximity.

Since the place of performance best satisfies the requirement of geographical proximity in commercial contracts (for the purpose of choice of law), it is open to question why the EU legislator does not explicitly give the place of performance special significance under Article 4 of Rome I. The place of performance deserves to be explicitly given special place under a revised Article 4 of Rome I.

B. Coherence of Connecting Factors

Under Article 4 of Brussels Ia, the principal foundation of European jurisdiction rules is based on the convenience and interest of the defendant, while under Article 7 of Brussels Ia the principle of proximity of the court to the dispute plays a complementary role. In the context of the European choice of law rules, party autonomy reigns supreme under Article 3 of Rome I, while the principle of proximity plays a subsidiary role under Article 4 of Rome I.

Where the parties have not provided for a forum selection and choice of law clause, and the claimant chooses to sue in the court that has proximity with the dispute under Article 7 of Brussels Ia, is it not a good thing for the designated court and applicable law to coincide? The English and Scottish law Commission,[90] in their drafted response to the 1972 Preliminary Draft Convention observed that:

> It may be noted that Article 5(1) of the Judgments Convention provides that a defendant domiciled in a Contracting State may, in another Contracting State, be sued in matters relating to a contract in the courts for the place where the contract has been, was to have been or is to be performed. If Article 4 were to be adopted in its present form there might therefore tend to be a divorce of jurisdiction and applicable law in the sense that a court assuming jurisdiction under the Judgments Convention would be required by the Convention now under consideration to apply a foreign law.[91]

In effect, there is a lack of coherence between Article 7(1) of Brussels Ia and Article 4 of Rome I because a Member State court would normally apply foreign law, rather than the law of the forum. If Article 7(1) of Brussels Ia and Article 4 of Rome I both utilise the connecting factor of the place of performance for commercial contracts, the Member State court seised with jurisdiction would usually apply its own law.

Furthermore, the EU legislator adopts an approach that lacks coherence between the concept of habitual residence of a company under Article 4(1)(a),

[90] www.scotlawcom.gov.uk/files/4413/1739/0072/Private_International_Law__Consultative_Document_on_EEC_Preliminary_Draft_Convention_on_the_Law_applicable_to_Contractual_and Non Contractual_Obligations.pdf.

[91] ibid.

(b), (e) and (f), and Article 4(2) of Rome I, and Article 63 of Brussels Ia.[92] Under Article 19 of Rome I, the habitual residence of a company is the place of central administration, unless the contract is concluded or is to be performed under a contract by a branch, agency or any other establishment of a company, in which case, the place where the branch, agency or any other establishment is located shall be treated as the place of habitual residence. Under Article 63 of Brussels Ia, the domicile of a company could either be its statutory seat, central administration or principal place of business. This lack of coherence might be a good reason to do away with the habitual residence of the characteristic performer as the principal connecting factor for commercial contracts in the European choice of law rules.

Insufficient scholarly attention has been devoted to the designated court and applicable law coinciding. Indeed, previous scholars who have specifically addressed the issue of coherence between matters of jurisdiction and choice of law in civil and commercial matters have not *specifically* carved out or labelled the 'coherence of connecting factors' as a form of coherence.

Admittedly, few scholars have noted the gap between the designated court and applicable law not coinciding in the context of Article 7(1)(b) of Brussels Ia and 4(1)(a) and (b) of Rome I. In this connection, Pocar submitted that 'the European harmonization appears to disregard the approach of making forum and jus coincide in order to assure the coherence of the system and predictability of its solutions …'[93] He also queries thus: 'Is it appropriate to renounce a priori an approach aimed at making the forum and jus coincide?'[94]

Crawford and Carruthers also submitted that there is a 'discord' and 'mismatch' between Article 7(1)(b) of Brussels Ia and Article 4(1)(a)–(b) of Rome I, such that the designated court and applicable law usually do not coincide.[95]

The issue of the court and applicable law coinciding is a significant issue. The EU private international law methodology in jurisdiction and choice of law is also one that is generally suited to the aims of international uniformity, harmony, and reduction of forum shopping. Unilateralism and protectionism are greatly reduced by not generally advancing the interests of the forum court in assuming jurisdiction and the application of the *lex fori*. Thus, the approach of the European jurisdiction rules and choice of law is not to unilaterally advance the aim of the court seised assuming jurisdiction and applying its own law. If a Member State court seised could always assume jurisdiction and apply its own law arbitrarily, the goal of EU integration in civil and commercial matters would be greatly jeopardised.

[92] Recital 39 to Rome I.

[93] Pocar (n 1) 344. cf GC Moss, 'Performance of Obligations as the Basis of Jurisdiction and Choice of Law (Lugano and Brussels Conventions Article 5(1) and Rome Convention Article 4) (1999) 4 *Nordic Journal of International Law* 379, 389–90.

[94] Pocar (n 1) 347.

[95] Crawford and Carruthers (n 4) 607–10.

However, the relevant question is: is it a good thing for the designated court and applicable law to coincide? Can the aims of international harmony and uniformity be reconciled with the designated court applying its own law? It would be demonstrated below that the answer to these questions is an emphatic yes.

i. *Is it a Good Thing for the Designated Court and Applicable Law to Coincide?*

Indeed, it is a good thing for the designated court to apply its own law, to the extent that the goals of uniformity and legal certainty are not threatened, as envisaged by the European legislator. The designated court is more familiar with its own law and is in the best position to apply its own law when compared to a foreign court. There is no language barrier for the designated court and the lawyers. It is more convenient and efficient for lawyers and judges in the designated court to apply the law of the forum, and the risk of the designated court wrongly applying its own law is greatly reduced. Litigation and transaction costs, and delays are greatly reduced since the lawyers in the designated court are normally experts in the application of the law of the forum and there would be no need to consult and pay foreign experts on the content of foreign law. Some scholars or jurists have also expressed similar views.[96]

Zweigert even put it more strongly, when he submitted that:

> The judge applying foreign law is a dilettante, a beginner; he is timid. The judge applying the *lex fori* is a learned expert; he is a sovereign, superior judge ... On the whole the judicial process has a lower quality where the judge applies foreign law than where he applies [the] *lex fori*.[97]

Thus, one of the ways to enhance the proper functioning of EU private international law is to craft the rules in such a way that the court assuming jurisdiction would usually apply its own law. In effect, making the place of performance of the characteristic obligation the principal connecting factor under a revised Article 4 of Rome I would fulfil this goal.

[96] AJE Jaffey, 'The English Proper Law Doctrine and the EEC Convention' (1984) 33 *International and Comparative Law Quarterly* 531, 532; Fawcett (n 1) 53; J Hill, 'Jurisdiction in Matters Relating to a Contract under the Brussels Convention' (1995) 44 *International and Comparative Law Quarterly* 591; O Lando, 'Some Issues Relating to the Law Applicable to Contractual Obligations' (1996–1997) 7 *Kings College Law Journal* 55, 66; O Lando, and PA Neilsen, 'The Rome I Proposal' (2007) 3 *Journal of Private International Law* 29, 35; P Rogerson, 'Problems of the Applicable Law of the Contract in the English Common Law Jurisdiction Rules: The Good Arguable Case' (2013) 9 *Journal of Private International Law* 387, 401; P Mankowski, 'Article 3 of Rome I Regulation' in U Magnus and P Mankowski, *European Commentaries on Private International Law* vol II (Munich, Sellier European Law Publishers, 2017) 143–46. See also *AMT Futures* (n 74) [43] (Popplewell J). *Cf.* G Ruhl, 'Methods and Approaches in Choice of Law: An Economic Perspective' (2006) *Berkeley Journal of International Law* 801, 807–15.

[97] K Zweigert, 'Some Reflections on the Sociological Dimensions of Private International Law or: What is Justice in the Conflict of Laws?' (1973) 44 *University of Colorado Law Review* 283, 293.

ii. Can the Aims of International Harmony and Uniformity be Reconciled with the Designated Court Applying its Own Law?

The designated court and applicable law can coincide if identical connecting factors are used for both regimes. This would not frustrate the aims of international harmony and uniformity because the same criterion that is used in assuming jurisdiction would usually produce the same result of the law of the designated court applying. In this connection, if the place of performance of the characteristic obligation is made the principal connecting factor for commercial contracts under a revised Article 4 of Rome I, it would create a coherence with Article 7(1)(b) of Brussels Ia, so that where the court assumes jurisdiction it would usually apply its own law.

A potential counter-argument is that in commercial contracts the courts of the domicile of the defendant would also have jurisdiction. Thus, the claimant can either sue the defendant in its domicile or the place of performance. In such situation the application of the *lex fori* where several courts have jurisdiction does not lead to international harmony and uniformity.

This counter-argument is not convincing. It would usually depend on the terms of the contract between the parties. In reality, the designation of the place of characteristic performance as the connecting factor for jurisdiction and choice of law in commercial contracts would frequently lead to the forum applying its own law. First, where performance takes place at the domicile of one of the parties, this party will rely on it to sue at home, and the other one must sue in that court too. Second, where performance takes place in a third state, both parties might rely on it to avoid suing in their opponent's home court.

Where the professional sues the client, under a revised Article 4 of Rome I and Article 7(1) of Brussels Ia, the same court would have jurisdiction and apply its own law. If the client is the one suing, the client has the option to sue the professional in (the professional's) domicile, or the place of characteristic performance. The place of characteristic performance would usually be the domicile or habitual residence of the client. The client is at a considerable and practical advantage suing in its own domicile or habitual residence. The obvious considerable and practical advantages are that client would save costs and his lawyers are familiar with the law of the forum and its procedural rules. Thus, it is highly unlikely that the client would sue the professional in (the professional's) domicile or habitual residence. In effect, the problem of a divorce between jurisdiction and applicable law in the context of the client suing the professional in its domicile or habitual residence is unlikely to occur.

In this connection, lets us assume a German service provider habitually resident and domiciled in Germany provides services in France, to a French person habitually resident and domiciled in France. The place of performance of the characteristic obligation in this case is France. The implication of this is that if the German company rightly sues the French person in France under Article 4 or Article 7(1)(b) of Brussels Ia, French law would ordinarily apply under a proposed revised Article 4(1)(b) of Rome I. In effect, in this case, the domicile of the defendant is also the place of characteristic performance. If the client is the one suing the professional, the client is likely to select the place of characteristic performance, which is the client's forum. In effect, the chances that the court and applicable law would coincide in this scenario are very high. Regrettably, under the current rules (Article 4(1)(b) of Rome I), German law would apply, and there would be a divorce between jurisdiction and the applicable law.[98]

In addition, in the example provided above, the forum has a legitimate claim to apply its law based on the principle of proximity, rather than the habitual residence of any of the parties. Applying German law under the current Article 4(1)(b) of Rome I simply as a result of the habitual residence of the German party does not seem appropriate.

The coherence of connecting factors also applies in relation to Article 24(1) of Brussels Ia (previously Article 22(1) of Brussels I, and Article 16(1) of Brussels Convention), which provides that in proceedings which have as their object rights *in rem* in immovable property or tenancies of immovable property, the courts of the Member State in which the property is situated shall have exclusive jurisdiction. By way of analogy, Article 4(1)(c) of Rome I provides that a contract relating to a right in rem in immovable property or to a tenancy of immovable property shall be governed by the law of the country where the property is situated.[99] The implication of this is that a Member State court assuming exclusive jurisdiction under Article 24(1) of Brussels Ia would usually apply its own law under 4(1)(c) of Rome I. This view has also been widely endorsed by the CJEU in some of its decisions,[100] the Advocate Generals in their Opinion to the CJEU,[101] and some Member State courts.[102]

In addition, the proviso to Article 24(1) of Brussels Ia (previously proviso to Article 22(1) of Brussels I), states that in proceedings which have as their object tenancies of immovable property concluded for temporary private use for a maximum period of six consecutive months, the courts of the Member State in which the defendant is domiciled shall also have jurisdiction, provided that the tenant is a natural person and that the landlord and the tenant are domiciled in the same Member State. By way of analogy, Article 4(1)(d) of Rome I provides that notwithstanding Article 4(1)(c) of Rome I, a tenancy of immovable property concluded for temporary private use for a period of no more than six consecutive months shall be governed by the law of the country where the landlord has his habitual

[98] This is assuming the escape clause under Article 4(3) of Rome I is not (exceptionally) utilised in favour of French law.

[99] Previously Article 4(3) of the Rome Convention.

[100] C-73/77, *Sanders v Van der Putte*, EU:C:1977:208; *Reichert* (n 58) [10]; *Dansommer* (n 58) [27]; *Hacker* (n 58) [9]; *Gesellschaft* (n 58) [9]; *Klein* (n 58) [16]; *Weber* (n 58) [41]; *Schmidt* (n 58) [29].

[101] AG Lenz in *AS Autoteile* (n 59) [1]; AG La Pergola in *Dansommer* (n 59) [7]; AG Darmon in *Hacker* (n 59) [15]; AG Geelhoed in *Klein* (n 59) [5], [30], [39]; AG Kokott in *Apostolides* (n 59) [83].

[102] (n 60) all.

residence, provided that the tenant is a natural person and has his habitual residence in the same country.[103] The implication of this is that a Member State court assuming jurisdiction under the proviso to Article 24(1) of Brussels Ia would usually apply its own law under 4(1)(d) of Rome I.

The idea that the coherence of connecting factors leads to the designated court applying its own law was also noted by AG Jacobs in the context of employment contracts in the EU, when he submitted that 'in a high proportion of cases the law governing the contract will be that of the State in which the work is performed …'[104] It has also been noted by AG Trstenjak in *Koelzsch*[105] in the context of employment contracts for the purpose of creating a coherence between Article 6(2)(a) of the Rome Convention (now Article 8 (2) of Rome I) and Article 5(1) of the Brussels Convention (now Article 21(1)(b)(i) of Brussels Ia). Her Opinion runs thus:

> The reason which, from the purposive viewpoint, suggests that the case-law relating to Article 5(1) of the Brussels Convention can be applied to the interpretation of Article 6(2)(a) of the Rome Convention is that consistency between *forum* and *ius* is desirable, which means that the court with jurisdiction to determine a case should apply the law of its own State. Ideally, the jurisdiction rule would confer jurisdiction on the court of the State the law of which will apply on the basis of the rules of private international law. In that way the court would apply the law with which it is most familiar, thereby reducing the possibility of erroneously applying (foreign) law and at the same time avoiding a confirmation of foreign law which proves to be exacting from the viewpoint of time and also cost.
>
> The uniform interpretation of 'the country' and 'the place where the employee habitually carries out his work' in Article 6(2)(a) of the Rome Convention and Article 5(1) of the Brussels Convention may therefore be conducive to consistency between *forum* and *ius*, because on the basis of uniform interpretation, the court for the place where the employee habitually carries out his work will generally have jurisdiction for disputes arising from contracts of employment, and that court will at the same time apply its own law (*lex loci laboris*).[106]

The coherence of connecting factors also works well with regard to the relationship between Article 4(1) of Rome II and Article 7(2) of the Brussels Ia.[107] For example, in practice, where a German court (like any other Member State court) assumes

[103] Indeed, it might be submitted that the proviso to Article 22(1) of Brussels I is what influenced the drafting of Article 4(1)(d) of Rome I. This is because Article 4(3) of the Rome Convention had no such proviso. This is another form of coherence between matters of jurisdiction and choice of law.

[104] AG Jacobs in *Pugliese* (n 66) [57].

[105] (n 68).

[106] ibid [80]–[81] (footnotes omitted).

[107] However, Article 4(1) of Rome II does not apply the principle of ubiquity in Article 7(2) of Brussels Ia. Thus, there would be no coherence where the place which gave rise to the damage is applied in Article 7(2) of Brussels Ia, since it would not coincide with the place where the damage actually manifests itself.

jurisdiction under Article 5(3) of the Brussels I, it usually applies the law of the forum under Article 4(1) of Rome II.[108]

The analogy drawn between the EU instruments on matters of jurisdiction and choice of law in relation to contracts of immovable property, employment contracts and non-contractual obligations, where coherence between identical connecting factors usually leads to the forum applying its own law, indicates that statutory reality supports the idea of making the designated court and applicable law coincide by utilising the identical connecting factor of the place of performance of the characteristic obligation under Article 7(1) of the Brussels Ia and a revised Article 4 of Rome I. In effect, if the coherence between jurisdiction and choice of law in relation to contracts of immovable property, employment contracts, and non-contractual obligations, leads to the forum applying its own law, this would also be a desired solution under a revised Article 7(1) of Brussels Ia and Article 4 of Rome I.

In summation, the coherence between the place of performance of the characteristic obligation under a proposed revised Article 4 of Rome I and Article 7(1) of the Brussels Ia would usually lead to the designated court applying its own law. This would be a good thing.

C. Coherence of Interpretation

If the place of performance is given special significance under a revised Article 4 of Rome I, the manner in which the concept of place of performance has been interpreted in the EU jurisdiction rules could be extended to apply to choice of law. In the same vein, the manner in which the concept of place of performance is interpreted under a revised Article 4 of Rome I could be extended to apply to the European jurisdiction rules. This is a form of coherence of interpretation. The coherence of interpretation in matters of jurisdiction and choice of law is thus an important issue that is worth considering in the context of the proposal in this book.

The coherence of interpretation between matters of jurisdiction and choice of law has statutory legitimacy in the EU, though it is contained in the recitals and not the main articles. The recitals in EU instruments of private international law are not binding,[109] but could be highly persuasive in guiding the court (CJEU or

[108] See for example BGH, 29.4.2010 – Xa ZR 5/09 (Germany, Third Instance); BGH, 9.7.2009 – Xa ZR 19/08 (Germany, Third Instance); LG Frankfurt aM, 29.03.2012 – 2-24 O 177/11 (Germany, First Instance); OLG Koblenz, 9.12.2011 – 10 U 108/11 (Germany Second Instance).

[109] C-429/07, *Inspector van De Belastingdienst v XBV* [2009] i-4833 [31], C-136/04, *Deutsches Milsch Kontor*, EU.C.2005:716; C 308/97, *Giuseppe Manfredi v Regione Puglia*, EU:C:1998:566 [31]. See further M McParland, *The Rome I Regulation on the Law Applicable to Contractual Obligations* (Oxford, Oxford University Press, 2015) 120–26, [3.39]–[3.56].

Member State courts) in reaching its decision. In addition, some recitals include original rules which have been subsequently endorsed by the CJEU.[110]

Recital 7 to Rome I explicitly states that:

> The substantive scope and the provisions of this Regulation should be consistent with Council Regulation (EC) No 44/2001 of 22 December 2000 on jurisdiction and the recognition and enforcement of judgments in civil and commercial matters (Brussels I) and Regulation (EC) No 864/2007 of the European Parliament and of the Council of 11 July 2007 on the law applicable to non-contractual obligations (Rome II).

Recital 7 to Rome II also explicitly provides that:

> The substantive scope and the provisions of this Regulation should be consistent with Council Regulation (EC) No 44/2001 of 22 December 2000 on jurisdiction and the recognition and enforcement of judgments in civil and commercial matters (5) (Brussels I) and the instruments dealing with the law applicable to contractual obligations.

Recital 7 to both Rome I and Rome II expressly legitimise the coherence of interpretation between jurisdiction and choice of law in civil and commercial matters in the widest sense.

There are other provisions of Rome I that legitimise the coherence of interpretation between Rome I and Brussels I (and Brussels Ia) in a specific sense. For example in relation to contract of sale and provision of services, Recital 17 to Rome I provides that:

> As far as the applicable law in the absence of choice is concerned, the concept of 'provision of services' and 'sale of goods' should be interpreted in the same way as when applying Article 5 of Regulation (EC) No 44/2001 in so far as sale of goods and provision of services are covered by that Regulation.

In relation to consumer contracts, Recital 24 to Rome I also provides that:

> *Consistency with Regulation (EC) No 44/2001 requires both that there be a reference to the concept of directed activity as a condition for applying the consumer protection rule and that the concept be interpreted harmoniously in Regulation (EC) No 44/2001 and this Regulation* bearing in mind that a joint declaration by the Council and the Commission on Article 15 of Regulation (EC) No 44/2001 states that 'for Article 15(1)(c) to be applicable it is not sufficient for an undertaking to target its activities at the Member State of the consumer's residence, or at a number of Member States including that Member State; a contract must also be concluded within the framework of its activities'. The declaration also states that 'the mere fact that an Internet site is accessible is not sufficient for Article 15 to be applicable, although a factor will be that this Internet site solicits the conclusion of distance contracts and that a contract has actually been concluded at a distance, by whatever means. In this respect, the language or currency which a website uses does not constitute a relevant factor.[111]

[110] See C-328/12, *Ralph Schmid v Lilly Hertel*, EU:C:2014:6 [21].

[111] Emphasis added.

There are two main questions that would be addressed here. The first is: why is coherence of interpretation between matters of jurisdiction and choice of law important? The second is: when should coherence of interpretation be utilised? These questions are very important and relevant to justifying the proposal in this chapter.

i. *Why is Coherence of Interpretation Important?*

A significant number of scholars, who have addressed the issue of coherence of interpretation, have not specifically provided reasons as to why the coherence of interpretation between jurisdiction and choice of law is important.[112]

The significance of the coherence of interpretation principally lies in pragmatism. It makes the task of national courts simpler and more convenient, since such courts can draw on the jurisprudence of the CJEU that has interpreted equivalent concepts in other European instruments, and apply it. In addition, it also reduces delay and costs that may be involved where the Member State court has to make a reference to the CJEU for preliminary ruling on an issue that is not *acte clair*, in the instrument itself. Thus, Member State courts can draw from European jurisdiction rules to interpret issues of choice of law, and vice versa. In this connection, Marazopoulou also rightly submits that 'From a more practical point of view, similar interpretation of concepts expressed in the same words in jurisdictional and substantive law instruments would facilitate the judges' task and hence further improve legal certainty.'[113] These points could be further justified by some decisions of some Member State courts.

In the English case of *Hillside (New Media) Ltd v Baasland*,[114] the court was concerned with the interpretation of place of damage under Article 4(1) of Rome II in the context of financial loss arising from gambling. In this case, the Norwegian defendant threatened to sue an English gambling company in Norway for the losses he (the defendant) suffered while gambling on the claimants' website. The claimants (an English gambling company) in response claimed against the Norwegian defendant in the English High Court for a declaration that it was not liable to the defendant in respect of any potential judgment the defendant obtains in Norway. One of the questions the High Court had to determine was whether the place where the damage occurred in respect of the gambling financial loss suffered by the defendant was in England or Norway. The High Court in essence held that the place where the damage occurred was in England.

[112] cf A Dickinson, 'Fatal Accidents – the Law Applicable to Claims by Family Members' (2016) 132 *Law Quarterly Review* 212.

[113] V Marazopoulou, 'Overriding Mandatory Provisions of Article 9(3) of Rome I Regulation' (2011) 64 *Revue Hellènique de Droit International* 779, 784.

[114] *Hillside (New Media) Ltd v Baasland* [2010] EWHC 3336 (Comm).

In reaching that decision (of the place where the damage occurred), the High Court made explicit reference to Recital 7 to Rome I and applied the coherence of interpretation, by applying the CJEU jurisprudence under Article 5(3) of the Brussels Convention and Brussels I to the effect that the 'place where the damage occurred' under Article 4 of Rome II, was equivalent to the place where it 'directly produced its harmful effects upon the person who is the immediate victim of that event' within the meaning of the CJEU's case law (under Article 5(3) of the Brussels Convention and Brussels I).[115]

Assuming the place of performance of the characteristic obligation is made the principal connecting factor for commercial contracts under a revised Article 4 of Rome I, national courts can draw inspiration from the jurisprudence of the CJEU under Article 5(1)(b) of Brussels I (now Article 7(1)(b) of Brussels Ia), that has applied the connecting factor. Through an abundance of case law, it might simplify the task of determining the place of performance of the characteristic obligation.

In addition, another practical benefit is that applying the connecting factor of the place of performance of the characteristic obligation (under a revised Article 4 of Rome I) to a wide range of commercial contracts would provide the necessary inspiration to expand the scope of Article 7(1)(b) of Brussels Ia (beyond contracts of sale and the provision of services), thereby reducing resort to Article 7(1)(a) of the Brussels Ia (which threatens the aim of uniformity).[116]

Indeed, there are scholars who have rightly argued for an expansion of the scope of Article 7(1)(b) of the Brussels Ia beyond contract of sale and provision of services, in order to enhance legal certainty, predictability, foreseeability of solutions.[117] This proposal might be a more pragmatic way of giving effect to their proposal.

ii. When Should Coherence of Interpretation be Utilised?

Though there is explicit statutory legitimacy on the coherence of interpretation between matters of jurisdiction and choice of law in the EU instruments on choice of law (in the law of obligations), the recitals do not explicitly state when or how it should be utilised. Does it apply absolutely? Is it a general rule? Is it an exception? What are the criteria for applying coherence of interpretation?

The CJEU, Advocate Generals, Member State courts and scholars have also not provided a *precise* formulation on when the coherence of interpretation should be utilised. Addressing this issue is important because an imprecise justification for applying the coherence of interpretation might lead to uncertainty in practice.

[115] ibid [28].

[116] See generally *Tessili* (n 15) [15]. For a critique of this decision see the Opinion of AG Lenz in *Custom Made* (n 19).

[117] Tang (n 1) 58; Grusic (n 19) 340; Graziano (n 47) 214.

Also, of particular importance to this book, it provides a rationale for the proper implementation of the proposal made in this chapter.

Sections a–d discuss the position taken by the CJEU, Advocate Generals, Member State courts and scholars on when the coherence of interpretation should be utilised. Given that these authorities have not articulated a 'precise criteria' or 'precise test' on when the coherence of interpretation should be utilised, section e is then devoted to a proposal on when the coherence of interpretation should be utilised.

a. The CJEU

The CJEU has referred to Recitals 7 to Rome I and Rome II, and Recitals 17 and 24 to Rome I in reaching some of its decisions, but has not articulated a precise criteria on how the concept of coherence of interpretation should operate.

In one case the CJEU generously utilised the coherence of interpretation, but the CJEU did not mention or discuss the criteria for applying the coherence of interpretation. Thus, in *Pammer*[118] the Austrian courts made a reference to the CJEU (which decided to hear the cases jointly) to give preliminary rulings on (i) whether a voyage by freighter constituted package travel for the purposes of Article 15(3) of Brussels I, and (ii) by what criteria a trader whose activity was presented on its website could be considered to be directing its activity to the Member State of the consumer's domicile, within the meaning of Article 15(1)(c) of Brussels I.

The facts (of the first case) was that the claimant who was domiciled in Austria, booked a voyage by freighter, as described on the internet, through a German intermediary company, with the defendant trader, who was also a German company. The claimant refused to embark on the ground that the description of the vessel on the intermediary's website did not correspond with the conditions on the vessel itself. He sought, through the Austrian courts, reimbursement of the sum paid, on the basis that the voyage contract was a consumer contract for package travel, and not simply a contract for carriage, because it provided for a combination of travel and accommodation for an inclusive price, within the meaning of Article 15(3) of Brussels I (now Article 17(3) of Brussels Ia).[119] The defendant disputed that the contract was a consumer contract and the Austrian court ruled in favour of the defendant.

[118] C-585/08 and C-144/09 (Joined Cases), *Pammer v Reederei Karl Schlüter GmbH & Co KG, and Hotel Alpenhof GesmbH v Heller*, EU:C:2010:740. See also C-191/15, *Verein für Konsumenteninformation v Amazon EU Sàrl*, EU:C:2016:612 [3], [10], [36]–[39]; C-249/16, *Kareda v Benko*, EU:C:2017:472 [12].

[119] Articles 15 and 16 of Brussels I (now Articles 17 and 18 of Brussels Ia) as an exception provides for special jurisdiction in relation to consumer (acting outside his profession) contracts, for the consumer to sue in his domicile or the domicile of the defendant. Article 15(3) (now Article 17(3) of Brussels Ia) provides this special jurisdiction shall not apply to a contract of transport other than a contract which, for an inclusive price, provides for a combination of travel and accommodation.

The facts of the second case was that the defendant who was domiciled in Germany, refused to pay a hotel bill for a stay, booked on the internet, with the claimant Austrian hotel, after finding fault with the hotel's services. The claimant claimed for the outstanding money in the Austrian courts. The defendant claimed that the Austrian courts lacked jurisdiction because the contract had not been concluded with a trader pursuing commercial activities with the Member State of the consumer's domicile, as required by Article 15(1) of Brussels I (now Article 17(1)(c) of Brussels Ia).

The CJEU in its judgment reached its decision on grounds of coherence of interpretation by making explicit reference to Recitals 7 and 24 to Rome I.[120] On the first question, the CJEU answered in the positive. It conceded that though the concept 'package travel' was not expressly mentioned in Article 15(3) of Brussels I, Article 6(4)(b) of Rome I expressly made mention of that concept in the context of consumer contracts (by making express reference to Directive 90/314) so that it was legitimate to make a parallel interpretation between both instruments.[121]

On the second question, the CJEU held that:

> In order to determine whether a trader whose activity is presented on its website or on that of an intermediary can be considered to be 'directing' its activity to the member state of the consumer's domicile, within the meaning of article 15(1)(c) of Regulation No 44/2001, it should be ascertained whether, before the conclusion of any contract with the consumer, it is apparent from those websites and the trader's overall activity that the trader was envisaging doing business with consumers domiciled in one or more member states, including the member state of that consumer's domicile, in the sense that it was minded to conclude a contract with them.[122]

The CJEU utilised the coherence of interpretation by holding that its decision was inter alia:

> also borne out by the joint declaration of the Council and the Commission at the time of the adoption of Regulation No 44/2001, reproduced in recital 24 in the Preamble to Regulation No 593/2008, according to which the mere fact that a website is accessible is not sufficient for article 15(1)(c) of Regulation No 44/2001 to be applicable.[123]

The CJEU has specifically addressed the issue of coherence of interpretation marginally in one decided case. In *Kainz*,[124] the CJEU made a pronouncement on the doctrine of the coherence of interpretation. The CJEU was concerned in this case with identifying the place of harmful event in respect of product liability for the purpose of applying Article 5(3) of Brussels I. In that case, the claimant who

[120] *Pammer* (n 118) [10], [11], [12], [42].
[121] ibid [39]–[46].
[122] ibid (second operative part of the CJEU's judgment). See also [75]–[93].
[123] ibid [74].
[124] C-45/13, *Kainz v Pantherwerke AG*, EU:C:2014:7. The CJEU decided, after hearing AG N Jääskinen, to proceed to judgment without an opinion.

was resident in Austria purchased in Austria a bicycle which had been manufactured by the defendant, a German company in Germany. The claimant, having been injured when falling from the bicycle in Germany, brought a claim for damages before the Austrian courts on the ground that the fall had been caused by a defect in the bicycle. The claimant relying on Article 5(3) of Brussels I (now Article 7(2) of Brussels Ia)[125] submitted that the place of the event giving rise to the damage was in Austria since the bicycle had been brought into circulation there. The defendant contested the international jurisdiction of the Austrian courts, contending that the place of the event giving rise to the damage was in Germany. The action was dismissed. On the claimant's appeal, the Austrian Supreme Court referred to the CJEU for a preliminary ruling a number of questions seeking clarification of the concept of the place of the event giving rise to the damage in relation to liability for defective products.

The CJEU in its judgment made express reference to Recital 7 to Rome II as a basis for its decision.[126] The CJEU held that Article 5(3) of Brussels I 'must be interpreted as meaning that, where a manufacturer faces a claim of liability for a defective product, the place of the event giving rise to the damage is the place where the product in question was manufactured'.[127] Though the CJEU made express reference to Recital 7 and Article 5 of Rome II as a basis for its decision, it expressed caution in the use of coherence of interpretation in its judgment when it stated as follows:

> It must be stated next that, although it is apparent from recital 7 in the preamble to Regulation 864/2007 that the European Union legislature sought to ensure consistency between Regulation 44/2001, on the one hand, and the substantive scope and the provisions of Regulation 864/2007, on the other, that does not mean, however, that the provisions of Regulation 44/2001 must for that reason be interpreted in the light of the provisions of Regulation 864/2007. The objective of consistency cannot, in any event, lead to the provisions of Regulation 44/2001 being interpreted in a manner which is unconnected to the scheme and objectives pursued by that Regulation.[128]

The CJEU's decision in *Kainz* on the coherence of interpretation only says two things. First, coherence of interpretation is not automatic. Second, coherence of interpretation should not be utilised in a manner that is unconnected with the scheme and objectives pursued by European jurisdiction or choice of law rules. The decision in *Kainz* and other CJEU decisions do not precisely articulate the criteria for applying the concept of coherence of interpretation. Perhaps, the

[125] Article 7(2) of Brussels Ia provides that a person domiciled in a Member State could be sued in another Member State in matters relating to tort, delict or quasi-delict, in the courts for the place where the harmful event had occurred, which is either the place where the damage had occurred or the place of event giving rise to the damage. See *Bier* (n 72); *Shevill* (n 72).

[126] *Kainz* (n 124) [8]. See also [9] of the judgment where express reference is made to Article 5 of Rome II.

[127] ibid [33].

[128] ibid [20].

reason why the CJEU has not made an exhaustive pronouncement on the coherence of interpretation is because the issue has not been specifically raised before it. In other words, there has been no recorded case where the determination of the criteria for the coherence of interpretation was in issue before the CJEU. Given that the CJEU only deals with live issues and not hypothetical or academic issues, the CJEU might not be faulted for not providing a precise criteria on how the coherence of interpretation should operate.

b. Advocate Generals

The Opinion of Advocate Generals, though having no binding legal value, appears to have some influence on the decision of the CJEU, and is thus worthy of consideration. The AGs have utilised the coherence of interpretation more often than the CJEU. Though it is not so clear from the Opinion of the AGs how liberal the coherence of interpretation should be utilised, there is an implicit consensus that it should not be used absolutely.

In practice, AG Trstenjak has applied the coherence of interpretation more often in her Opinion when compared to other AGs. In the first two cases, where she applied the concept of coherence of interpretation, she did not provide any criteria on how it should apply. Given the manner in which she generously utilised the concept of coherence of interpretation, it was initially uncertain if she favoured the view that coherence of interpretation should be applied as a general rule.

Thus in *Falco*,[129] the central question in that case was whether a contract under which the owner of an intellectual property right grants its contractual partner the right to use that right in return for remuneration is a contract for the provision of services within the meaning of the second indent of Article 5(1)(b) of Brussels I. AG Trstenjak in her Opinion[130] and the CJEU[131] both reached the same conclusion in answering the referred question in the negative.

However, AG Trstenjak's Opinion provided a more robust reasoning by virtue of the fact that she brilliantly applied the coherence of interpretation (unlike the CJEU) by stressing the significance of Recitals 7 and 17 to Rome I to the effect that the CJEU in interpreting the concept 'services' in the second indent of Article 5(1)(b) of Brussels I 'will have to avoid giving it a meaning that conflicts with the meaning and purpose of the Rome I Regulation.'[132]

She observed that:

> As pointed out by the German Government in its observations, the history of the adoption of the Rome I Regulation shows that the original proposal contained, in

[129] (n 40).
[130] (n 34) [75].
[131] (n 40) [44].
[132] (n 34) [68]. See also AG Bot in *Kareda* (n 118) [9].

> Article 4(1) relating to the applicable law in the absence of choice on the part of the parties, not only subparagraph (b) to determine the law applicable to a contract for the provision of services but also a subparagraph (f) on identification of the law applicable to a contract relating to intellectual or industrial property rights. It is apparent from the *travaux préparatoires* that subparagraph (f) was not included in the final version of the Rome I Regulation because consensus was not reached within the Council on the question of which contractual party was obliged to provide the service characteristic of that type of contract, not because it was necessary to classify such contracts in the category of contracts for the provision of services. If therefore, in interpreting the concept of 'services' in Regulation No 44/2001, the granting of licences were to be included within that term that would be to run counter to the meaning and purpose of the same concept used in the Rome I Regulation. This is therefore a further argument confirming that licence agreements are not contracts for the provision of 'services' within the meaning of the second indent of Article 5(1)(b) of Regulation No 44/2001.[133]

Also, in *Pammer*,[134] AG Trstenjak in delivering her Opinion to the CJEU made explicit reference to both Recitals 24 and 7 to Rome I as the legal bases for her Opinion.[135] She expressly relied on the coherence of interpretation in addressing the first issue before the court. Her Opinion is worthy of quotation:

> In the wider context of European Union legislation, however, account is to be taken of an analogy with the Rome Convention on the law applicable to contractual obligations ('the Rome Convention') or the Rome I Regulation, which has replaced that Convention. Article 5(5) of the Rome Convention provides for the same exception as in Article 15(3) of Regulation No 44/2001. Article 5 of the Rome Convention, which governs the question of which law is to apply to consumer contracts, provides in paragraph 5 that this special rule applies to contracts which, for an inclusive price, provide for a combination of travel and accommodation, although contracts of carriage are excluded from this special rule by Article 5(4)(a). The fact that the same terminology is used in the Rome Convention and in Regulation No 44/2001 that was adopted later undoubtedly indicates that it was the intention of the legislature that the phrase 'contract which, for an inclusive price, provides for a combination of travel and accommodation' should be afforded a uniform interpretation in the context of both provisions.
>
> This need for a uniform interpretation exists even after the adoption of the Rome I Regulation. Article 6(4)(b) of the Rome I Regulation provides that the special provisions applicable to consumer contracts do not apply to contracts of carriage other than contracts relating to package travel within the meaning of Directive 90/314. The Rome I Regulation therefore goes one step further than Regulation No 44/2001 which was adopted earlier, in which Directive 90/314 is not mentioned. However, regard should be had to two principles of interpretation … Although the Rome I Regulation makes express reference to Directive 90/314, both provisions are to be uniformly interpreted as

[133] (n 34) [69] (footnotes omitted).

[134] (n 118).

[135] *Pammer*, EU:C:2010:740 [7], [48], [55], [72] and [73]. cf Opinion of AG Cruz Villalón in C-190/11, *Mühlleitner v Yusufi*, EU:C:2012:542 [30].

> Directive 90/314 had not yet been adopted when the Rome Convention was concluded. Secondly, the need for a uniform interpretation of Regulation No 44/2001 and the Rome I Regulation also has to be heeded. The concept of a contract of carriage that falls within the scope of consumer contracts has to be uniformly interpreted in both provisions. Recital 7 in the preamble to the Rome I Regulation states that the substantive scope and the provisions of that regulation are to be consistent with Regulation No 44/2001.[136]

On the second question, she expressly reached her Opinion on the grounds of coherence of interpretation by making reference to both Recitals 7 and 24 to Rome I.[137] She opined that: 'When interpreting the concept of directing activities in 15(1) (c) of Regulation No 44/2001, … the Court of Justice will have to take care not to interpret this concept in a manner contrary to the spirit and purpose of the Rome I Regulation.'[138]

However, in the latter case of *Koelzch*,[139] AG Trstenjak provided some criteria on the concept of coherence of interpretation, by submitting inter alia that it should not be applied as a general rule. In *Koelzch* the Luxembourg Court of Appeal referred a question to the CJEU as to whether the conflict rule in Article 6(2)(a) of the Rome Convention was to be interpreted as meaning that, where the employee worked in more than one country but returned systematically to one of them, that country had to be regarded as the country in which the employee habitually carried out his work.

AG Trstenjak in her Opinion[140] to the CJEU and the CJEU in its decision,[141] both concluded that Article 6(2)(a) of the Rome Convention (now Article 8(2) of Rome I) must be interpreted as meaning that, in a situation in which an employee carries out his activities in more than one Contracting State, the country in which the employee habitually carries out his work in performance of the contract, within the meaning of that provision, is that in which or from which, in the light of all the factors which characterise that activity, the employee performs the greater (or essential) part of his obligations towards his employer.[142]

AG Trstenjak in delivering her Opinion to the CJEU made express reference to Recital 7 to Rome I as a legal basis for her Opinion.[143] She expressly took into account, inter alia, the coherence of interpretation to the effect that the 'case law relating to art. 5(1) of the Brussels Convention can be applied to the interpretation of art. 6(2)(a) of the Rome Convention'.[144] She labelled what one refers to

[136] *Pammer* (n 135) [47]–[48] (footnotes omitted).
[137] ibid [72]–[73].
[138] ibid.
[139] (n 67).
[140] (n 68) [91]–[100].
[141] (n 67) [50].
[142] The only difference (which is really not a material one) between the Opinion of AG Trstenjak and the CJEU's decision was that while the CJEU used the word 'greater', AG Trstenjak used the word 'essential'.
[143] *Koelzch* (n 68) [10].
[144] ibid [70]–[79], [99].

as 'coherence of interpretation' in this work, as 'systematic interpretation'. Two points she made on what she referred to as systematic interpretation are worth quoting.

She opined that:

> A systematic interpretation suggests parallel interpretation of article 6(2)(a) of the Rome Convention and article 5(1) of the Brussels Convention. This has two aspects. It is necessary to take account, first, of the fact that in the past the wording of article 6 of the Rome Convention has influenced the interpretation of article 5(1) of the Brussels Convention and, secondly, of the wording of article 8(2) of Rome I, which was adopted at a later date.[145]

She then held the Opinion that:

> For the purpose of systematic interpretation, mention must also be made of an additional ground in support of applying the case law on article 5(1) of the Brussels Convention to the interpretation of article 6(2)(a) of the Rome Convention, namely the fact that the Community legislature took account of that case law in the procedure for the adoption of Rome I which followed the Rome Convention. Article 8(2) of Rome I provides that, to the extent that the law applicable to the individual employment contract has not been chosen by the parties, the contract is to be governed by the law of the country in which or, failing that, from which the employee habitually carries out his work in performance of the contract.[146]

However, AG Trstenjak opined that the coherence of interpretation should not be applied absolutely. She expressed some caution in her Opinion thus:

> Nevertheless I should like to point out generally that a degree of caution is required in the parallel interpretation of identical or similar terms arising from conflict rules and rules for determining international jurisdiction because the two categories of rules have different aims. Whereas the purpose of conflict rules is to determine the law applicable to a contractual obligation (in the present case, a contract of employment), the purpose of rules for determining international jurisdiction is to identify the court having jurisdiction. Therefore the conflict rules (Rome Convention) generally lead to the determination of the law of a single country, but on the basis of the rules for determining the court with international jurisdiction it may be open to the claimant – at least in certain cases – to choose the forum before which he will be sued.
>
> Accordingly, I should like to say that in the present case I am not pleading in favour of general uniformity in the interpretation of all identical or similar terms in the Rome and Brussels Conventions. I must stress, in particular, that it is not possible to start from the general presumption that all identical or similar terms must be interpreted uniformly: on the contrary, the question of uniform interpretation must be considered in the context of each individual case. (See my opinion in Falco Privatstiftung v Weller-Lindhorst (Case C-533/07) [2010] Bus LR 210, paras 60 et seq.) Terms which are sometimes entirely appropriate to one field cannot be interpreted uniformly … However, it is true that in fields in which the provisions of the two instruments have

[145] ibid [70].
[146] ibid [74] (footnotes omitted).

> the same aim of protection (for example, the protection of employees or consumers) a uniform interpretation will be more likely.[147]

While this book agrees with AG Trstenjak that the coherence of interpretation should not be applied automatically or absolutely, it does not subscribe to the view that it should not be applied generally, in the case of similar and identical terms arising from EU jurisdiction and choice of law rules.[148]

Other AGs who have utilised the coherence of interpretation have also not provided a precise criteria on how it is to be utilised. At best, they opine that it should not be applied absolutely. There have been at least four other cases where the coherence of interpretation was utilised, but no clear guideline was provided on how it should operate. Thus, in *Cartel Damage Claims*,[149] one of the questions referred to the CJEU inter alia was whether Article 6(1) of Brussels I Regulation (now Article 8(1) of Brussels Ia)[150] applied in the case of an action for damages and disclosure, brought jointly against defendants which had participated in several Member States, at different places and at different times in a single and continuous infringement of EU competition rules, as found by a decision of the Commission, even where the applicant had withdrawn its action against the sole co-defendant domiciled in the same Member State as the court seised.

Suffice it to say that AG N Jääskinen[151] and the CJEU[152] reached a similar conclusion by answering the question posed in the affirmative, subject to a proviso that Article 6(1) of Brussels I does not apply where the Member State court finds that, at the time the proceedings were instituted, the applicant and that defendant had colluded to artificially fulfil, or prolong the fulfilment of, that provision's applicability.

AG N Jääskinen stressed the fact that if the defendants are sued in different Member States, there would inter alia be a risk of the court applying different legal regimes to the defendants which would lead to an incoherent solution in determining the liability of the defendants.[153] He also justified his Opinion by making express reference to the coherence of interpretation, and citing Recital 7.[154] His opinion runs thus:

> Like the commission, I note that such an interpretation has the not inconsiderable advantage of reflecting the intention expressed by the legislature in the Rome II

[147] ibid [82]–[83] (footnotes omitted).

[148] See s VI.C.ii.e of this chapter.

[149] C-352/13, *Cartel Damage Claims (CDC) Hydrogen Peroxide SA v Akzo Nobel NV and others*, EU:2015:335.

[150] Article 8(1) of Brussels Ia provides that a person domiciled in a Member State may also be sued 'where he is one of a number of defendants, in the courts for the place where any one of them is domiciled, provided the claims are so closely connected that it is expedient to hear and determine them together to avoid the risk of irreconcilable judgments resulting from separate proceedings'.

[151] *Cartel Damage Claims*, EU:C:2014.2443 [54]–[90].

[152] (n 149) [33].

[153] (n 151) [66]–[74].

[154] ibid [75]. See also fn 56 of his Opinion.

> Regulation, especially in article 6 entitled 'Unfair competition and acts restricting free competition', paragraph 3 of which sets out the possibility, for a claimant suing several defendants in the context of a dispute in this field, of centralising his claims before a single court 'in accordance with the applicable rules on jurisdiction' and of basing his claims on the law of that court. To my mind, due account should be taken of this legal guideline, in the interests of coherence between the instruments of Union law applicable to cross-border disputes, despite the fact that, as the defendants contend, the Rome II Regulation is not, ratione temporis, applicable in this case.[155]

In *Lazar*,[156] the central question referred to the CJEU for preliminary ruling by an Italian court was whether Article 4(1) of the Rome II had to, in order to determine the law applicable to a non-contractual obligation arising from a road traffic accident, be interpreted as meaning that the damage arising from the death of a person in such an accident, which occurred in the Member State of the court seised, sustained by close relatives of the deceased who resided in another Member State, had to be regarded as damage or as 'indirect consequences' of that accident, within the meaning of that provision.

Suffice it to say that in the Opinion of AG Wahl,[157] and decision of the CJEU,[158] they both classified (in their answer to) the above referred question as 'indirect consequences' of that accident, within the meaning of Article 4(1) of Rome II.

AG Wahl made express reference to Recital 7 to Rome II as a legal basis for his Opinion.[159] He relied on the Explanatory Memorandum to the Commission's Proposal for to Rome II,[160] which made express reference to the case law of Article 5(3) of both the Brussels Convention and Brussels I, to stress the point that both Article 4(1) of Rome II and Article 5(3) of Brussels I make a distinction between direct and indirect damage.[161] He then justified his reference to the case law of Article 5(3) of Brussels Convention and Brussels I on the basis of coherence of interpretation.[162] His Opinion runs thus:

> However, I consider that, although the objectives pursued by each of those legal acts are somewhat different, the concepts referred to in the Rome II Regulation must, as far as possible, be understood by reference to the interpretations adopted in connection with the Brussels Convention or the Brussels I Regulation. A degree of parallelism must be established in the interpretation of those notions in so far as the legal instruments all pursue an objective of the foreseeability of the solutions adopted.[163]

[155] ibid (footnotes omitted).

[156] C-350/14, *Lazar v Allianz SPA*, EU:C:2015:802.

[157] (n 73) [85].

[158] (n 156) [30].

[159] (n 73) [4], [49]. See also Joined Cases C-359/14 & C-475/14, *Ergo Insurance SE v If P&C Insurance AS*, EU:C:2015:630 [3], [43], [48]–[49], [56]–[58].

[160] Explanatory memorandum from the Commission, accompanying the Proposal for Rome II, COM(2003) 427 final 12.

[161] (n 73) [48]–[49].

[162] ibid [55]–[65].

[163] ibid [52].

In *Verein*,[164] AG Saugmandsgaard Øe in his Opinion, though applying a coherence of interpretation under both Recitals 7 to Rome I and Rome II Regulation,[165] cautioned that equivalent concepts used in Rome I, Rome II and Brussels I Regulations 'must not entirely overlap. Rather they should be interpreted not in an identical but in a parallel manner.'[166]

Also in *Gazdasági*,[167] the central question before the CJEU was whether an action for recovery of sums not due on the ground of unjust enrichment, which has its origin in the repayment of a fine imposed in a competition law proceedings falls within 'civil and commercial matters' within the meaning of Article 1 of Brussels I Regulation.

The Opinion of AG Wahl[168] and the CJEU's judgment[169] both answered the question in the negative.

AG Wahl (unlike the CJEU) inter alia reached his Opinion by both making express reference to Recital 7 to Rome II and utilising the coherence of interpretation thus:

> Indeed, in the first place, as argued by the German Government, it follows from Article 10(1) of Regulation (EC) No 864/2007 that, compared to contractual and non-contractual matters, in the default scenario, EU private international law regards unjust enrichment as being in a category of its own. Although Regulation No 44/2001 predates Regulation No 864/2007, the EU legislature has considered that the substantive scope and provisions of the one ought to be consistent with those of the other.[170]

In summation, the AGs have utilised the coherence of interpretation more often than the CJEU. This might indicate that the approach of the AGs on the coherence of interpretation is more liberal than that of the CJEU. However, some of the AGs have rightly cautioned that coherence of interpretation should not be applied absolutely. AG Trstenjak in *Koelzch*[171] even opines further that coherence of interpretation should not be applied as a general rule. The reason why this book does not agree with AG Trstenjak's Opinion that coherence of interpretation should not be applied as a general rule is addressed somewhere else in this chapter.[172]

c. Member State Courts

Though some of the Member State courts have held that the coherence of interpretation should not be applied absolutely, they do not appear to give a restrictive interpretation on the coherence of interpretation.

[164] (n 118).
[165] ibid, EU:C:2016:388 [45]–[48].
[166] ibid [47].
[167] C-102/15, *Gazdasági Versenyhivatal v Siemens Aktiengesellschaft Österreich*, EU:C:2016:607.
[168] ibid, EU:C:2016:225 [75].
[169] ibid [43].
[170] (n 168) [72] (footnote omitted). See also AG Kokott in C-185/15, *Kostanjevec v F&S Leasing GmbH*, EU:C:2016:397 [13], [47].
[171] (n 68).
[172] See s VI.C.ii.e of this chapter.

Thus, in *Allen v Deputy International Ltd*,[173] Stewart J in response to the caution expressed by the CJEU in *Kainz*,[174] correctly held that:

> The fact that the Kainz case … determines that the provisions of Regulation 44/2001 must not, for the reason of consistency, be interpreted in the light of Rome II, does not mean that the converse should not apply. There is good reason for recital (7) to Rome II. It refers to consistency in the 'substantial scope and *provisions*'. I accept that Rome II should not be a slave to the objective of consistency and that this objective should not lead to Rome II being interpreted in a manner unconnected to the scheme and objectives which it pursues. However, the court should where possible give effect to recital (7).[175]

In *Ertse Group Bank AG, London Branch v JSC 'VMZ' Red October & Ors*,[176] the English Court of Appeal was concerned with identifying the place of financial damage for the purpose of applying Article 4(1) of Rome II. The gist of the case was that the claimant made a claim for service out of jurisdiction on Russian defendants in respect of a loan agreement and guarantee that was subject to English law and jurisdiction. The claimant alleged that the Russian defendants conspired to put their assets beyond the reach of creditors. The place of payment in respect of the loan transaction was in New York. One of the questions before the court was to determine the place where the financial damage occurred within the meaning of Article 4(1) of Rome II.

Though the Court of Appeal conceded that Article 4 of Rome II and Article 5(3) of Brussels I were different in the sense that the 'latter contemplates that a claimant in tort may choose between the courts of the place where the harmful event occurred and the place where the damage was sustained. But the purpose of Rome II is to identify a single applicable law rather than a choice',[177] it held by expressly referring to Recital 7 to Rome II that 'the Rome II Regulation ought to be interpreted in a manner which is broadly in harmony with the jurisprudence and interpretation of similar provisions in the Judgments Regulation'.[178]

The Court of Appeal also applied the CJEU jurisprudence in Article 5(3) of Brussels I to the effect that both Article 4(1) of Rome II and Article 5(3) of Brussels I exclude the place where any indirect consequences of the event giving rise to the damage occur.[179] On this basis, the Court of Appeal held that the loss allegedly suffered within the meaning of Article 4(1) of Rome II was the conspiracy of the Russian defendants to damage the claimant's right to payment under the loan and guarantee agreement. On the contrary, the non-payment of the

[173] *Allen v Deputy International Ltd* [2014] EWHC 753(QB).
[174] (n 124).
[175] *Allen* (n 173) [13] (footnote omitted) (emphasis added).
[176] *Ertse Group Bank AG, London Branch v JSC 'VMZ' Red October & Ors* [2015] EWCA Civ 379.
[177] ibid [91].
[178] ibid [90].
[179] ibid [92]

facility agent to the claimant in London was merely an indirect consequence of the defendant's payment in New York.[180]

Thus, the approach of some Member State courts is to apply the doctrine of coherence of interpretation where the circumstance of the case warrants it. In particular, though the decisions of the English courts mentioned in this chapter support the view that coherence of interpretation should not be applied absolutely, these courts have refused to give the concept of coherence of interpretation a narrow meaning.

d. Scholars

Scholarly opinion that has addressed the issue of coherence of interpretation has not been exhaustive. Prior to the enactment of Rome I (which has some recitals that expressly favour coherence of interpretation), Briggs had strongly argued in favour of the concept of coherence of interpretation when he submitted that:

> It is inherently unlikely that those who drafted these instruments intended the central definitional terms to have divergent meanings: they were all drafted in Brussels, and comprise the jigsaw parts of what will one day soon be a private international legal code for the Member States.[181]

Tang, though supporting the idea of coherence of interpretation, rightly submits that the recitals on coherence of interpretation are not binding.[182] Lein, though supporting the idea of coherence of interpretation, rightly cautions that it should not be applied absolutely.[183] Dickinson, though supporting the idea of coherence of interpretation, also submits that 'a degree of independent interpretation may be no bad thing in the longer term'[184] on the basis 'that consistency does not demand complete fidelity'.[185] These scholarly views rightly state that coherence of interpretation is not absolute, but they don't go as far as stating whether it should be a general rule, an exception, or the criteria for applying the coherence of interpretation.

Some other scholars have argued that the coherence of interpretation should be applied contextually so that for example, Article 7(1)(b) of Brussels Ia should

[180] ibid [96]. See also *Committeri v Club Mediterranee Sa Generali Assurances Iard Sa* [2016] EWHC 1510 [33], [40]–[49].

[181] A Briggs and P Rees (P Rees as editor with no authorial role), *Civil Jurisdiction and Judgments* 4th edn (London, Informa/Lloyds of London Press, 2005) [2.124].

[182] Tang (n 1) 50. See also Marazopoulou (n 113) 784.

[183] Lein (n 1) 198.

[184] Dickinson (n 112) 212.

[185] ibid 214.

not be used to interpret Article 9(3) of Rome I).[186] Crawford and Carruthers put it lucidly, when they query thus:

> In this context one may consider interpretation of the critical phrase in Article 9.3 of the Rome I Regulation, viz. the 'law of the country where the obligations arising out of the contract have to be or have been performed'. In interpreting Article 9.3, that is, for the purposes of applicable law, is it legitimate to draw assistance from Regulation 1215, Article 7.1.b (ex-Brussels Regulation, Article 5.1.b), directing that unless otherwise agreed the place of performance of the obligation in question shall be, depending on the nature of contract, the place of delivery of goods or of provision of services?[187]

In response to the above query, they rightly submit that:

> It would seem perverse for a judge vested with special jurisdiction in contract under Article 7.1.b to conclude for choice of law purposes under Article 9.3 of Rome I, that 'the law of the country where the obligations arising out of the contract have to be or have been performed' was *other* than the place of delivery of goods, or provisions of services, as appropriate.[188]

Other scholars have submitted that the 'parallelity and correlation' between matters of jurisdiction and choice of law in the EU, 'requires that they should be uniformly interpreted as far as possible and as far as their purposes do not significantly differ'.[189] Similarly, some scholars appear to submit that it should be applied as a general rule, depending on the circumstances of the case.[190]

These scholarly views are all correct. In essence, if one is to sum up and reconcile the views of the scholars mentioned above, they submit that though coherence of interpretation is not binding or absolute, it should be applied as far as possible where the context so requires.

e. Way Forward

It is important to formulate what one considers should be the criteria for coherence of interpretation. It is opined that the coherence of interpretation

[186] J Harris, 'Mandatory Rules and Public Policy under the Rome Convention' in F Ferrari and S Leible (eds), *The Law Applicable to Contractual Obligations in Europe* (Munich, Sellier European Law Publishers, 2009) 269, 316; SS Lorenzo, 'Choice of Law and Overriding Mandatory Rules in International Contracts after Rome I' (2010) 12 *Yearbook of Private International Law* 67, 84–86; Marazopoulou (n 113) 783–87; A Bonomi, 'Article 9 of Rome I Regulation' in U Magnus and P Mankowski, *European Commentaries on Private International Law* vol II (Munich, Sellier European Law Publishers, 2017) 599, 645–48 [156]–[167]; AG Szpunar in C-135/15, *Hellenic Republic v Nikiforidis*, EU:C:2016:281 [91]–[94].

[187] Crawford and Carruthers (n 4) 8.

[188] ibid.

[189] U Magnus, 'Article 4 of Rome I Regulation' in U Magnus and P Mankowski, *European Commentaries on Private International Law* vol II (Munich, Sellier European Law Publishers, 2017) 328, [214].

[190] 'In our view, coordinated interpretation should be encouraged from a general aspect but the extent thereof should be considered on an *ad hoc* basis': Marazopoulou (n 113) 785 (emphasis in the original).

should generally be utilised, where the concepts used in one European instrument are equivalent to the other European instruments, and the context of the case so permits. In effect, if the concepts used in Brussels Ia is equivalent to Rome I (and vice versa), they should be given a parallel or uniform interpretation. Thus, it is important to provide a basis for justifying this opinion.

Why is it opined that coherence of interpretation should be a general rule, when matters of jurisdiction and choice of law are conceptually distinct? The reasons are two-fold. First, it is important to make the provisions between European jurisdiction and choice of law as consistent as far as possible given that they were drafted with the same philosophy in mind. In particular, the connecting factor of place of characteristic performance was utilised under the Brussels I to remedy the defect of the concept of place of performance of the obligation in question, so that the same philosophy applies with equal force to interpreting the proposed concept of place of characteristic obligation under a revised Article 4 of Rome I, which also aims to remedy the defect of the place of performance as a connecting factor.

Though the coherence of interpretation is not binding or absolute, refusing to give effect to its application, might in reality actually substantially subvert or violate the harmony between the European instruments on jurisdiction and choice of law in civil and commercial matters. In effect, the concept of coherence of interpretation should not be honoured in breach. An inconsistent or divergent interpretation between matters of jurisdiction and choice of law is not good for litigants and judges, particularly from the perspective of legal certainty in judicial proceedings. If the place of characteristic performance were to have an inconsistent meaning in matters of jurisdiction and choice of law, there would be legal uncertainty on how the concept should operate in the future. Conversely, a harmonious interpretation between matters of jurisdiction and choice of law would create certainty on how a concept should be interpreted in the future whether it arises in the context of jurisdiction or choice of law.

Second, if the coherence of interpretation is applied as an exception, it would frustrate the practical utility and effectiveness of the simplification of judicial task, convenience, reduction of legal and transaction costs and sound administration of justice.

If there is anything that can be learnt from the list of CJEU cases, Member State court decisions and Opinions of the AGs discussed in this work, it can be deciphered that the coherence of interpretation made the task of interpreting the law simpler. A concept in one European instrument, which is equivalent to another concept in another European instrument is interpreted uniformly. In effect, the concept in one European instrument could either serve as a form of guide or precedent on how the concept in issue before the court should be interpreted. If the coherence of interpretation is not utilised, the task of the decision maker is more difficult because he has to do a lot of work in developing or formulating a new interpretation to a concept in a European instrument. This difficulty would likely apply to the lawyers of the parties, if the coherence of interpretation is utilised exceptionally.

The decision maker enjoys convenience in utilising the coherence of interpretation. His task is less complicated. The decision maker saves considerable time in interpreting a concept in an EU instrument. Generally speaking, the parties are happier when their dispute has been resolved in a timely manner. If the coherence of interpretation was to be utilised exceptionally, more time might be expended in interpreting an EU concept, given that it would not be usually very convenient for a decision maker to make a speedy ruling on the interpretation of a concept in an EU instrument that has no guideline or precedent from another European instrument. This inconvenience would likely apply to the lawyers of the parties, if the coherence of interpretation is utilised exceptionally.

The legal and transaction costs of the parties are likely to increase if coherence of interpretation is utilised exceptionally. If the job of the lawyers of the parties are made more difficult and inconvenient because they cannot generally utilise the coherence of interpretation, their clients would have to bear the burden by paying their lawyers more money for the complicated task of advising on, or interpreting a concept in a European instrument. Of course, given that more time and resources are dedicated by lawyers to the complicated task of advising on, or interpreting a concept in an EU instrument without the aid of coherence of interpretation, the increase in legal and transaction costs for the clients is inevitable. Conversely, if the coherence of interpretation is utilised generally, the clients are likely to incur less legal and transaction costs because the job of their lawyers would be less complicated, and can be resolved in a timelier manner.

The sound administration of justice might not be satisfied if the coherence of interpretation is utilised exceptionally. If the task of the court and the lawyers of the parties is more difficult and inconvenient because the coherence of interpretation is not utilised, this does not aid the sound administration of justice. The sound administration of justice would be satisfied where the tasks of the decision makers and the lawyers of the parties are less complicated. Moreover, if in this situation, any of the parties cannot afford legal representation because of the increase in legal and transaction costs, arising from the complicated task of the lawyers, the aims of the sound administration of justice would be compromised.

Two criteria must be fulfilled before the coherence of interpretation is applied as a *general rule*. First, the principle of *equivalence* must be satisfied. Second, the *context* of the case must permit it.

On the first criterion, the principle of equivalence is satisfied where the concept used in a jurisdiction rule is *substantially similar* to the concept used in a choice of law rule (and vice versa). For example, the concept of sale of goods and provision of services have equivalent meanings in both Article 4(1)(a) and (b) of Rome I and Article 7(1)(b) of Brussels Ia.[191] Also, the concept of 'directed activity' or 'targeted activity' by a professional to a consumer's habitual residence has equivalent

[191] Recital 17 to Rome I.

meaning in both Article 6 (1) of Rome I and Article 17(1)(c) of Brussels Ia.[192] In effect, the place of characteristic performance for commercial contracts would also have an equivalent meaning from the perspective of EU jurisdiction and choice of law rules. The concept of place of characteristic performance should generally be interpreted uniformly in matters of jurisdiction and choice of law.

On the second criterion, the coherence of interpretation must be applied to suit the context of the case. It must not be applied in such a way that it produces absurd or unreasonable consequences. It must not violate the intendment of the European legislator, who honoured the conceptual and traditional distinction between matters of jurisdiction and choice of law, by creating separate instruments on jurisdiction and choice of law. Where the coherence of interpretation leads to absurd, or unreasonable, consequences, or produces an interpretation that the EU legislator did not intend, the coherence of interpretation must be discarded in such circumstances. Thus, it appears obvious that it is not proper to use Article 7(1)(b) of the Brussels Ia to analogously interpret Article 9(3) of Rome I (and vice versa), as their scheme and purpose are different. In other words, Article 9(3) of Rome I cannot be read in parallel or analogously with Article 7(1) of Brussels Ia (and vice versa). Article 7(1)(b) of Brussels Ia deals with allocation of jurisdiction for commercial contracts, while Article 9(3) of Rome I is concerned with the application of foreign overriding mandatory rules of the place of performance for general contractual obligations. Moreover, while Article 7(1)(b) of Brussels Ia is concerned with the concept of *place of characteristic performance*, Article 9(3) of Rome I is concerned with the place of performance of any obligation of the parties (not only the characteristic obligation).

For example, assuming A, habitually resident and domiciled in California, USA, agrees to deliver a certain class of drugs to B, habitually resident in the Netherlands. The place of delivery is in the Netherlands, but the place of payment is in California. Whereas that class of drugs is legal according to Dutch law, they are illegal in the eyes of Californian law. If a dispute subsequently arises between the parties in the Dutch court, and Article 9(3) of Rome I is in issue, it would be wrong for the Dutch Court to interpret Article 9(3) of Rome I, uniformly with Article 7(1)(b) of Brussels Ia to the effect that the place of performance of the parties can only be in Netherlands, because it is the place of delivery. Such a ruling would be wrong because it does not take into account the fact that California is also the 'place of performance', since it is the place of payment, and the parties' transaction is illegal according to Californian law.

Conversely, for example, a Member State court that interprets Article 4(1) of a revised Rome I can rightly draw inspiration from the decisions of the CJEU on how to identify both the place of performance of the characteristic obligation, and the distinction between a contract of sale and provision of services, in a contract for the supply of goods to be manufactured or produced, where the purchaser

[192] Recital 24 to Rome I.

specifies the quality and other requirements, but the seller supplying the materials is responsible for the quality.[193] In such a situation, the context permits that the coherence of interpretation should be utilised, so that the concept of place of characteristic performance is given a uniform interpretation in the EU jurisdiction and choice of law rules.

VII. Conclusion

This chapter has justified the proposal that the place of performance should explicitly be given special significance under a revised Article 4 of Rome I, based on the coherence between matters of jurisdiction and choice of law.

In section II, in order to justify the proposal, the coherence between matters of jurisdiction and choice of law were classified in civil and commercial matters into three categories: coherence of principles, coherence of connecting factors and coherence of interpretation.

In Section III, a historical analysis was made on how the concept of place of performance under the Brussels Convention evolved to place of characteristic performance under Brussels I. The lesson that could be learnt in the context of Rome I is that: instead of doing away completely with the concept of place of performance, the place of characteristic performance should be utilised as a way of remedying the defect of the place of performance in commercial contracts under a revised Article 4 of Rome I.

In Section IV, it was opined that, in the context of the place of performance for commercial contracts, there is already a form of coherence between the EU jurisdiction and choice of law rules, so that the opinion and proposal in this book should not be regarded as being too radical or revolutionary. However, it was admitted that the practice of Article 7(1)(a) of Brussels Ia and Article 4 of Rome I might lead to circularity, forum shopping and threaten international uniformity. It was then proposed that the scope of Article 7(1)(b) of Brussels Ia should be extended to include a vast majority of commercial contracts, so as to substantially restrict the scope of Article 7(1)(a) of Brussels Ia.

In Section V, it was conceded that some factors might militate against utilising jurisdiction and choice as uniform concepts, but such counter-arguments do not neutralise the proposal in this chapter.

In Section VI, it was opined that the coherence of principles, coherence of connecting factors and coherence of interpretation support the proposal made in this chapter, and thereby neutralises the counter-argument that jurisdiction and choice of law are distinct concepts.

[193] *Car Trim* (n 39) [31]–[33], [38]–[43]. See also C-196/15, *Granarolo SpA v Ambrosi Emmi France SA*, EU:C:2016:559.

In utilising coherence of principles, it was demonstrated that the idea that the place of performance satisfies the requirement of geographical proximity in commercial contracts for matters of jurisdiction is also a good reason to opine that the place of performance satisfies the requirement of geographical proximity for matters of choice of law for commercial contracts. This argument was inspired by making an analogy with contracts relating to immovable property, employment contracts, and non-contractual obligations, and on the basis that the (principal) connecting factors used for such obligations also satisfy the requirement of geographical proximity both from the perspective of jurisdiction and choice of law.

In utilising the coherence of connecting factors, it was stressed and demonstrated that if the place of characteristic performance is made the principal connecting factor for commercial contracts under a revised Article 4 of Rome I, it would lead to the designated court under Article 7(1)(b) of Brussels Ia applying (usually) its own law. It was strongly argued that this is a good thing. This opinion was reinforced and inspired by making an analogy with other provisions in the EU instruments on matters of jurisdiction and choice of law, such as contracts of immovable property, employment contracts, non-contractual obligations, where coherence between identical connecting factors usually leads to the designated court applying its own law.

In utilising the coherence of interpretation, it was stressed and demonstrated that if coherence of interpretation is utilised generally, where the circumstances of the case permit, it would simplify the task of Member State courts on the determination of the place of performance of the characteristic performance for commercial contracts both for jurisdiction and choice of law purposes, create convenience, reduce litigation and transaction costs and lead to the sound administration of justice.

In summation, the coherence between some matters of jurisdiction and choice of law in the EU private international law rules (in civil and commercial matters) is a good reason why the place of performance should be explicitly given special significance under a revised Article 4 of Rome I.

6

Legislative Proposal

I. Background

This chapter contains a synopsis of the legislative proposal in this book. It serves as a form of explanatory memorandum to the proposed model statute in this book. It only comments on the proposed changes or amendments to the existing law.[1]

Though this book is principally focused on legislative reform for the European legislator, the proposed model statute could be used by legislators, judges, arbitrators and other decision makers outside the EU in reforming their rules in relation to the law applicable in the absence of choice for international commercial contracts.

In the proposed model statute, there is the frequent use of 'country or legal system'. This is to take into account countries that practice a federal system (such as Nigeria, the United States, Canada and Australia), where a State or region might be regarded as a 'legal system' for the purpose of conflict of laws.

Section II discusses the principal proposal and the accompanying recitals to the principal proposal of this book. Section III discusses the alternative proposal of this book.

II. Proposed Model of a Revised Article 4 of Rome I Regulation and Accompanying Recitals

A. Principal Proposal

1. To the extent that the law applicable to the contract has not been chosen in accordance with Article 3 and without prejudice to Articles 5 to 8, the law governing the contract shall be determined as follows:

   (a) a contract for the sale of goods shall be governed by the law of the country *or legal system* where the seller; *mainly delivers the goods. Where the main place*

[1] Italics are used in this section to indicate the proposed reform to the existing law.

of delivery of the goods cannot be identified, the law of the country or legal system where the seller has his habitual residence shall apply;

(b) a contract for the provision of services shall be governed by the law of the country where the service provider; *mainly provides services. Where the main place of provision of services cannot be identified, the law of the country or legal system where the service provider has his habitual residence shall apply;*

(c) a contract relating to a right in rem in immovable property or to a tenancy of immovable property shall be governed by the law of the country *or legal system* where the property is situated;

(d) notwithstanding point (c), a tenancy of immovable property concluded for temporary private use for a period of no more than six consecutive months shall be governed by the law of the country or *legal system* where the landlord has his habitual residence, provided that the tenant is a natural person and has his habitual residence in the same country;

(e) a franchise contract shall be governed by the law of the country *or legal system* where the franchisee; *mainly promotes the business of the franchisor. Where the main place the franchisee promotes the business of the franchisor cannot be identified, the law of the country or legal system where the franchisee is habitually resident shall apply;*

(f) a distribution contract shall be governed by the law of the country where the distributor; *mainly distributes goods for the grantor or manufacturer. Where the main place where the distributor distributes goods for the grantor or manufacturer cannot be identified, the law of the country or legal system where the distributor is habitually resident shall apply;*

(g) *a contract of letter of credit shall be governed by the law of the country or legal system where the seller mainly receives payment against compliant documents;*

(h) *a contract of intellectual property shall be governed by the law of the country or legal system where the intellectual property right is mainly granted;*

(i) a contract for the sale of goods by auction shall be governed by the law of the country *or legal system* where the auction takes place, if such a place can be determined;

(j) a contract concluded within a multilateral system which brings together or facilitates the bringing together of multiple third-party buying and selling interests in financial instruments, as defined by Article 4(1), point (17) of Directive 2004/39/EC, in accordance with non-discretionary rules and governed by a single law, shall be governed by that law.

2. Where the contract is not covered by paragraph 1 or where the elements of the contract would be covered by more than one of points (a) to (h) of paragraph 1, the contract shall be governed by the law of the country *or legal system of the place where the characteristic performance is mainly effected. Where the main place of characteristic performance cannot be identified, the law of the country or legal system of the habitual residence of the party required to effect the characteristic performance shall apply.*

3. Where it is clear from all the circumstances of the case that the contract is manifestly more closely connected with a country other than that indicated in paragraphs 1 or 2, the law of that other country shall apply.
4. Where the law applicable cannot be determined pursuant to paragraphs 1 or 2, the contract shall be governed by the law of the country with which it is most closely connected.

i. Comment

The principal proposal is that the place of characteristic performance should be the principal connecting factor for commercial contracts. The criteria used is the main place of characteristic performance, so that in cases where the professional carries out his obligation to the client in more than one country, there shall be no doubt that the decision maker shall apply the law of the place where the professional mainly carries out his obligation to his client.

The habitual residence of the characteristic performer is used as a subsidiary connecting factor to cater for cases where the decision maker is unable to identify the main place of characteristic performance.

In order to give precision and clarity to the concept of characteristic performance, it is specifically determined for contracts of sales of goods, provision of services, franchise and distributorship. For contracts of sale, the place of characteristic performance is the main place of delivery. For contracts of provision of services, the place of characteristic performance is the main place of provision of services. The criteria of main place of delivery and provision of services corresponds with the criteria used for contracts of sale and provision of services under Article 7(1)(b) of Brussels Ia.

For contracts of franchise, the place of characteristic performance is the main place the franchisee promotes the business of the franchisor. For contracts of distributorship, the place of characteristic performance is the main place the distributor distributes the goods for the grantor or manufacturer.

Contracts of sale of goods, provision of services, franchise and distributorship constitute the vast majority of contracts that usually arise in real life adjudication matters. This explains why the concept of place of characteristic performance is given some precision and clarity in these cases.

In situations where the main place of characteristic performance cannot be identified for contracts of sale of goods, provision of services, franchise and distributorship, the law of the country or legal system of the habitual residence of the party effecting the characteristic performance shall apply. For contracts of sale of goods, the law of the country or legal system of the habitual residence of the seller shall apply. For contracts of provision of services, the law of the country or legal system of the habitual residence of the service provider shall apply. For contracts of franchise, the law of the country or legal system of the habitual residence of the franchisee shall apply. For contracts of distributorship, the law of the country or legal system of the habitual residence of the distributor shall apply.

For contracts of letter of credit, the main place of characteristic performance is given precision and clarity. It is the law of the country or legal system where the seller mainly receives payment against compliant documents. Given that a letter of credit is composed of several contractual arrangements, the law of the country or legal system where the seller mainly receives payment against compliant documents shall be used to govern the letter of credit transaction as a whole, so that there would be a coherent solution in determining the rights and obligation of the parties under the contract. The connecting factor of habitual residence of the characteristic performer has been deliberately omitted as a subsidiary connecting factor because a letter of credit contract which is composed of several contractual arrangements, is not susceptible to the connecting factor of the habitual residence of the characteristic performer. Thus, where the criteria of the place where the seller mainly receives payment against compliant documents does not work, the test of closest connection shall apply.

For contracts of intellectual property the main place of characteristic performance is given clarity and precision. It is the law of the country or legal system where the intellectual property right is mainly granted. The main place where the intellectual property right is mainly granted shall be ascertained from the agreement between the parties. If that is not possible, the main place where the intellectual property right was in fact exploited by the assignee or transferee of such right shall be the applicable law. In this connection, the habitual residence of the characteristic performer has been deliberately omitted as a subsidiary connecting factor because it does not fit properly in the context of a contract of intellectual property. Thus, where the criteria of the place where the intellectual property right is mainly granted does not work, the test of closest connection shall apply.

For contracts that do not fall into the category of contracts of sale, provision of services, franchise, distributorship, letters of credit, and intellectual property (etc), the criteria of the main place of characteristic performance shall be used to determine the law of the country or legal system that applies. In this connection, the connecting factor of the habitual residence of the characteristic performer shall be used as a subsidiary connecting factor, where the main place of characteristic performance cannot be identified by the decision maker.

B. Accompanying Recitals to the Principal Proposal

i. New Proposed Recital to Rome I Regulation

As far as the applicable law in the absence of choice is concerned, the concept of place of characteristic performance should as far as possible, and where the context so requires, be given a consistent interpretation with Article 7(1) of Brussels Ia (REGULATION (EU) No 1215/2012 of the European Parliament and of The Council of 12 December 2012).

a. Comment

In determining the applicable law in the absence of choice the concept of the place of characteristic performance should as far as possible, and where the context so requires, be given a consistent interpretation with Article 7(1) of Brussels Ia. The purpose of this recital is to enhance the coherence between jurisdiction and choice of law in commercial contracts. The aim is also to inspire the expansion of the scope of the current Article 7(1)(b) of Brussels Ia, so that the place of characteristic performance would apply generally to commercial contracts in a revised Article 7(1) of Brussels Ia.

ii. Another New Proposed Recital to Rome I Regulation

> *In determining the applicable law in the absence of choice, the parties shall be allowed to determine the place of the characteristic obligation under their contract. In order to verify whether the parties have agreed on a place of performance of the characteristic obligation under their contract, the court seised shall take into account all relevant terms and clauses of the parties' contract which are capable of clearly identifying the place.*
>
> *If that cannot be done, the court shall look to where the characteristic obligation has in fact for most part been carried out, provided this is not contrary to the parties' intention as it appears from the contract.*

a. Comment

The purpose of this new proposed recital is to enable the court to use the agreement of the parties on the place of characteristic performance in determining the applicable law in the absence of choice. This would also aid and simplify the determination of the applicable law in the absence of choice.

iii. Proposed Revision of Recital 19 to Rome I Regulation

> Where there has been no choice of law, the applicable law should be determined in accordance with the rule specified for the particular type of contract. Where the contract cannot be categorised as being one of the specified types or where its elements fall within more than one of the specified types, it should be governed *by the law of the country or legal system of the main place of characteristic performance of the contract.* ~~where the party required to effect the characteristic performance of the contract has his~~ habitual residence. In the case of a contract consisting of a bundle of rights and obligations capable of being categorised as falling within more than one of the specified types of contract, the *main place of characteristic performance of the contract shall be determined by inter alia ascertaining under the contract, the true professional that does the job that gives the contract its name and, which party does the relatively more important obligation.* ~~having regard to its centre of gravity.~~

a. Comment

Recital 19 to Rome I has been revised to apply the law of the country or legal system of the main place of characteristic performance, rather than the law of the habitual residence of the party required to effect the characteristic performance of the contract.

The criteria of 'centre of gravity', for determining the characteristic obligation of a commercial contract, has been revised to that of ascertaining the true professional that does the job that gives the contract its name, and what party does the relatively more important obligation. The criteria of 'which party does the relatively more important obligation' would work well for complex contracts where the parties perform mutual obligations, so that the decision maker shall weigh and compare the obligation of the parties, and in its view decide which obligation is relatively more important.

III. Alternative Proposal

A. Proposed Revised Recital 20 to Rome I Regulation

> Where the contract is manifestly more closely connected with a country other than that indicated in Article 4(1) or (2), an escape clause should provide that the law of that other country is to apply. In order to determine that country, account should be taken, inter alia, of whether the contract in question has a very close relationship with another contract or contracts; *and the place of characteristic performance of the contract.*

i. Comment

The alternative proposal is that the place of characteristic performance should be explicitly given special significance as a connecting factor that can displace Article 4(1) and (2) of Rome I. The alternative proposal is only to be utilised if the principal proposal is not accepted.

7

Conclusion

I. Summary of the Research Findings

This book has opined that the place of performance is of considerable importance in international commercial contracts. On this basis, the central proposal in this book is that the EU legislator should explicitly give the place of performance special significance under a revised Article 4 of Rome I.

First, in chapter two, it was demonstrated based on a historical analysis that the idea that the place of performance is of considerable significance in international commercial contracts is not new. Nineteenth century scholars such as Story and Savigny had already given special significance to the place of performance as a choice of law rule. Moreover, the significance of the place of performance in international commercial contracts was one of commercial common sense. The reason why the place of performance witnessed a steady decline in the twentieth century was because of some difficulties identified in applying it by the courts, such as in Germany and Switzerland. Schnitzer's doctrine of habitual residence of the characteristic performer was mainly a contrived solution to the problem of identifying the place of performance. But this shift from the place of performance to habitual residence was the most controversial aspect of his proposal.

Thus, Batiffol, the leading French scholar in the twentieth century, was on the right track when he proposed the place of characteristic performance as the principal choice of law rule in remedying the problems of the place of performance, which was later applied by the Paris Court of Appeal.

However, the European legislator under the Rome Convention, like the Swiss courts and legislators, preferred the criteria of habitual residence of the characteristic performer as the principal connecting factor for commercial contracts in determining the applicable law in the absence of choice. This criteria proved to be disappointing in practice in determining the relationship between Article 4(2) and (5) of the Rome Convention, because while some courts (such as Dutch and Scottish courts) applied Article 4(2) of the Rome Convention as a rigid rule, courts in England readily applied Article 4(5) of the Rome Convention by relying on the law of the place of performance.

There had been a proposal by the United Kingdom and some lobby groups for the place of performance to be given special significance under Article 4 of Rome I Proposal, but it was not accepted by the EU legislator.

In effect, what can be said is that the approach of the European legislator in not giving special significance to the place of performance lacked a historical basis because it did not fully consider or properly appreciate the criteria of place of characteristic performance as a connecting factor that can remedy the defect of the place of performance, or in the alternative give a better and more accurate guidance on when the escape clause can be invoked.

Second, in chapter three, it was opined that the place of characteristic performance should be the principal connecting factor under a revised Article 4 of Rome I, while the habitual residence of the characteristic performer is then made a subsidiary connecting factor. In the alternative, it was suggested that the place of performance should be explicitly given special significance in a revised recital stating that it should be taken into account in interpreting the escape clause.

Three main arguments were identified in favour of the doctrine of habitual residence of the characteristic performer: problems of classifying and identifying the place of performance, triumph of the law of the professional, and country-of-origin principle. It was then demonstrated that these arguments in favour of the doctrine of habitual residence of the characteristic performer as a better EU choice of law rule than the place of performance are not convincing.

Despite the proposal that the place of characteristic performance should be the principal connecting factor under a revised Article 4 of Rome I, it was opined that the escape clause should not be dispensed with because it is a necessity for the proper functioning of the EU choice of law rules conflicts-justice system. In the alternative, it was opined that the current rules could be retained and the place of performance explicitly given special significance under a revised Recital 20 to Rome I.

Given that it is mainly proposed that the place of characteristic performance should be the principal connecting factor under a revised Article 4 of Rome I, the determination of the concept of place of characteristic performance was further analysed, such as identifying the characteristic obligation, agreement on the place of performance, and determining what solution to utilise when the place of characteristic performance cannot be identified. It was then proposed that the determination of the concept of characteristic obligation should be reformulated by ascertaining under the contract who is the true professional that does the job that gives the contract its name, and the party who performs the relatively more important obligation. This formulation might also work in case of complex contracts where the parties perform mutual obligations. In addition, based on English case law under the Rome Convention and study by other scholars, one proposed the connecting factor that could be utilised for some complex contracts such as letters of credit and intellectual property under a revised Article 4 of Rome I.

It was opined that the court should give effect to the parties' agreement on the place of performance.

In situations where the place of characteristic obligations cannot be identified, it was proposed that the place of habitual residence of the characteristic performer should be utilised instead of an immediate resort to closest connection.

Third, in chapter four, it was opined that place of performance under Article 9(3) of Rome I is an expression of the principle of proximity. The argument was motivated by a historical analysis pre-Rome Convention, Article 7(1) of the Rome Convention and Article 8(3) of Rome I Proposal.

In pre-Rome Convention, it was opined that one of the reasons why the place of performance was of considerable significance in determining what was called foreign illegality at the time was because the place of performance usually had the closest or at least substantial connection to an international commercial contract, and thus would be interested in regulating an international commercial contract even though it is not the *lex causae*.

Under Article 7(1) of the Rome Convention, it was opined that though the place of performance was not expressly given special significance in determining what 'close connection' means, there was a vast consensus among scholars that the place of performance would best satisfy the requirement of 'close connection' when compared to any other connecting factor. Moreover, it was opined that the significance of the governmental interest analysis provision in Article 7(1) of the Rome Convention must not be overstated, as it only operates in the context of geographical and territorial connections that determine the concept of 'close connection'.

Under Article 8(3) of Rome I proposal, it was opined that what was at the heart of the negotiation process was how to make the concept of 'close connection' more precise. It was observed that there was a consensus among scholars such as Chong and Dickinson, and later representatives of Member States in the negotiation process, that the place of performance would best satisfy the criteria of 'close connection' when compared to other connecting factors.

Based on this historical analysis, it was opined that the place of performance under Article 9(3) of Rome I is an expression of the principle of proximity or 'close connection'. Again, it was opined that the concept of State or public interests must not be overstated in the context of Article 9(3) of Rome I because the substance and policies of the law of a country is only taken into account in applying foreign country overriding mandatory rules where it is the place of performance. It was however conceded that the place of performance would not always satisfy the requirement of proximity, especially in unusual cases where the place of performance takes place in many countries. It was then proposed that based on the principle of continuity, Article 9(3) should not be applied where the place of performance does not satisfy the requirement of 'close connection' as was the case under Article 7(1) of the Rome Convention.

Fourth, in chapter five, it was opined that based on the coherence between jurisdiction and choice of law in civil and commercial contracts, the place of performance should be given special significance under a revised Article 4 of Rome I. The coherence between jurisdiction and choice of law in the EU was classified into three categories: coherence of principles, coherence of connecting factors and coherence of interpretation. The historical connection between coherence of jurisdiction and choice of law in the context of the place of performance for contractual obligations was critically analysed, and the main lesson learnt was that if the EU legislator remedied the defect of place of performance of the contested obligation by moving to the concept of place of characteristic obligation for contracts of sale and provision of services, there is no good reason why the concept of place of characteristic performance should not be the main connecting factor under both a revised Article 4 of Rome I and Article 7(1) of Brussels Ia. In effect, if the reformulation made in this book on the concept of characteristic obligation was taken into account, the problems of determining the concept of characteristic obligation might be considerably reduced even in complex contracts.

Based on the ECJ jurisprudence of *Tessili*, it was opined that there is already a form of coherence between jurisdiction and choice of law in the context of the place of performance for commercial contracts, though it was admitted that the solution in *Tessili* was not a satisfactory one. At the expense of prolixity, it was again suggested that if the reformulation made in this book on the concept of characteristic obligation was taken into account, the problems of determining the concept of characteristic obligation might be considerably reduced even in complex contracts. In effect, this would make a revised Article 4 of Rome I and Article 7 of Brussels Ia apply to a wide variety of international commercial contracts.

The crucial contribution of chapter five was utilising the types of coherence between jurisdiction and choice of law in the EU to justify the central proposal in this book. It was argued that there was a coherence of the principle of proximity by using one connecting factor for both jurisdiction and choice of law in contracts of immovable property, employment contracts and non-contractual obligations. It was then opined by way of analogy that the same logic should apply to the place of performance as the principal connecting factor that determines proximity under a revised Article 4 of Rome I.

It was opined that based on a coherence of connecting factors, if the place of performance of the characteristic obligation was utilised under a revised Article 4 of Rome I, the designated court would apply its own law. It was then opined that this was a good thing, and international uniformity would not be threatened as well because in many cases it would be the 'home' of the client that would have jurisdiction. By way of analogy, it was opined that this was also the case with contracts of immovable property, contracts of employment and non-contractual obligations, where the coherence of connecting factors leads to a designated court applying its own law.

It was opined that based on a coherence of interpretation, the interpretation of the concept of place of performance of the characteristic obligation consistently in matters of jurisdiction and choice of law was a good thing because it would simplify the task of the court and lawyers. In order to facilitate the implementation of this proposal, it was considered at some length, when the coherence of interpretation can be invoked. In particular, the decisions of the CJEU, Opinion of Advocate Generals, Member State courts and scholars were considered. It was opined that these authorities had not articulated with precision what criteria or test to be used in utilising the coherence of interpretation. In essence, it was then proposed as a way forward that the coherence of interpretation should be utilised as a general rule in so far as the context of the case so requires, and reasons were provided to justify this proposal such as certainty, convenience, reduction of transaction costs and sound administration of justice.

More importantly, though the central proposal in this book is mainly targeted at the EU legislator, it is opined further that the proposed principal model of Article 4 of Rome I could be utilised as a guide in the form of an international solution, by legislators, judges, arbitrators, decision makers and other interested persons outside the EU, who are interested in reforming their choice of law rules on the law applicable in the absence of choice for international commercial contracts.

II. Transmission of the Model of the Revised Article 4 of Rome I Regulation to Other Countries or Legal Systems

In this section, it is suggested that the model of the revised Article 4 of Rome I (model statute) could be transmitted to other countries or legal systems outside the EU. In effect, the proposed model statute is the principal proposal in this book that makes the main place of characteristic performance the principal connecting factor for most international commercial contracts, while the habitual residence of the characteristic performer is given a subsidiary role. The escape clause is applied to maintain some flexibility, and the principle of closest connection resorted to in very limited cases where the characteristic obligation cannot be identified. In effect, the principle of closest connection would be strongly and appropriately ruled by the concept of place of characteristic performance.

At the expense of prolixity, the model statute which is proposed in this book could be utilised as a guide in the form of an international solution, by legislators, judges, arbitrators, decision makers and other interested persons outside the EU, who are interested in reforming their choice of law rules on the law applicable in the absence of choice for international commercial contracts. Indeed, some scholars rightly point out that 'the Rome I Regulation has inspired law reform recommendations outside of the European Union'.[1]

It must however be stated at the outset that there are different countries that have statutes or judge made laws or arbitral rules dealing with the determination of the applicable law in the absence of choice for international commercial contracts, so that this short conclusion does not make a detailed comparative analysis of the laws of such countries.[2] Moreover, this is not the focus of this book. Perhaps, another scholar

[1] B Hayward, *Conflict of Laws and Arbitral Discretion – The Closest Connection Test* (Oxford, Oxford University Press, 2017) 265 [6.113] citing inter alia M Keyes, 'Improving Australian Private International Law' in A Dickinson et al (eds), *Australian Private International Law for the 21st Century – Facing Outwards* (Oxford, Hart Publishing, 2014) 15, 43.

[2] See generally SC Symeonides, *Codifying Choice of Law Around the World: An International Comparative Analysis* (Oxford, Oxford University Press, 2017); Hayward (n 1).

could take up the challenge, and do a detailed study on the laws governing international commercial contracts worldwide and come up with a different solution.[3]

The contribution of this book, based on the research of the EU experience, is to propose a model statute that could be used as an international solution for determining the applicable law in the absence of choice for international commercial contracts. International uniformity in the area of international commercial contracts might not be a bad thing in the long run. International business persons conduct their business all over the world, and they do not always stipulate for a standard choice of law clause in their contracts. Given that it is argued that the proposed model statute generally enhances legal and commercial certainty in international commercial contracts, and also takes into account the expectation of such international commercial actors, applying the proposed model worldwide would be a good thing.

It might be counter-argued that an international solution for international commercial contracts is utopian. However, it is opined that as a starting point, countries around the world that apply the conflicts-justice system in whatever form might be attracted to the proposed model statute.[4]

Sections A and B below specifically (and briefly) focus on some countries or legal systems that might be receptive to the proposed model statute. The purpose of this analysis is to make the proposal and its implementation more concrete in the eye of the reader. Section C will consider whether the model statute can be utilised as an international solution for international commercial contracts.

A. Post United Kingdom Brexit

On 24 June 2016 the majority of the UK voted in a referendum to leave the EU (Brexit).[5] This aroused the attention of private international law scholars in the UK and other parts of the EU on the implication this development would have for private international law.[6] This section does not focus on what the general future implications might be as regards the relationship between the UK and the EU on

[3] cf Hayward (n 1).

[4] Symeonides (n 2) 171–218; SC Symeonides, 'Codification and Flexibility in Private International Law' – https://papers.ssrn.com/sol3/papers.cfm?abstract_id=1945924.

[5] Triggering Article 50 of the Treaty of the European Union.

[6] See for example A Dickinson, 'Back to the Future: the UK's EU Exit and the Conflict of Laws' (2016) 12 *Journal of Private International Law* 195; E Lein, 'Unchartered Territory? A Few Thoughts on Private International law Post Brexit' (2015/2016) XVII *Yearbook of Private International Law* 33; A Briggs, 'Secession from the European Union and Private International Law: the Cloud with a Silver Lining' – www.law.ox.ac.uk/sites/files/oxlaw/adrian_briggs_brexit_lecture.pdf; M Pilich, 'Brexit and EU Private International Law: May the EU Stay in?' (2017) *Maastricht Journal of European and Comparative Law* 1–17; J Fitchen, 'The Private International Law Consequences of Brexit' (2017) 35 *Nederlands Internationaal Privaatrecht* 411–32; G Rühl, 'Judicial Cooperation In Civil And Commercial Matters After Brexit: Which Way Forward?' (2018) 67 *International and Comparative Law Quarterly* 99; Z Tang, 'UK-EU Civil Judicial Co-operation after Brexit: Five Models' (2018) 43 *European Law Review* 648.

the Brexit. As Dickinson rightly submits, arguments or submissions on this issue are speculative.[7]

This section is focused on how the model statute might be applied when Brexit is fully actualised. The first proposed option is that in the event the EU negotiates the application of Rome I with UK, this might be a good opportunity to apply the model statute. One can confidently opine that based on the English approach taken under pre-Rome Convention, Article 4 of the Rome Convention, and UK's proposal in Article 4 of Rome I Proposal, which gave special significance to the place of performance, this model statute might be an attractive proposal the UK might make to the EU to adopt under a revised Article 4 of Rome I.

The possibility of reaching a compromise on a revised Article 4 of Rome I by adopting the model statute must not be regarded as idealistic. The UK in the past has played a critical role in reforming some aspects of EU private international law. The explicit utilisation of the doctrine of infection or accessory allocation under Recitals 20 and 21 to Rome I, and the revision of Article 7(1) of the Rome Convention into a new Article 9(3) of Rome I are examples of how the UK played a critical role in reaching a compromise with the EU on choice of law for contractual obligations.

If this compromise is reached with the UK and the EU on applying the model statute, in turn, the EU legislator might be attracted to the model statute, and accordingly revise Article 4 of Rome I as it applies to other Member States. The significance of this would be to enhance international uniformity so that international commercial actors in the EU and UK do not utilise divergent choice of law rules in determining the applicable law in the absence of choice. This would enhance confidence in business transactions as it relates to the relationship between the UK and the EU.

Second, assuming the EU and UK cannot reach a compromise on applying this model statute, or the UK decides to opt out of the EU completely (hard Brexit), this model statute can also be utilised by the UK legislator. In this connection, one is attracted to the pragmatic view of Briggs who submits that:

> When it comes to the rules which determine the applicable law for obligations, which is to say the Rome I and Rome II Regulations, the United Kingdom can if it wants to copy the text of the Regulations into its own private international law. Any state, from China to Peru, could do the same.[8]

He bases his submission on the common sense view that:

> it is hard to believe that there is a lawyer in full possession of his or her mind who would propose taking us back to these chapters of the common law. The main reason is the perfectly pragmatic one that the rules of private international law of the common law, to which one might otherwise return, are in significant parts so dreadful that they are simply unfit for purpose, at least without significant statutory repair.[9]

[7] Dickinson (n 6).
[8] Briggs (n 6) 6.
[9] ibid 7.

One would only qualify the acceptance of Brigg's submission to the extent that the UK or indeed any other country should not blindly copy Rome I. One does not think that Brigg's submission is that Rome I should be copied unthinkingly. This is where the model statute might be useful to the UK. The UK could amend Rome I to suit its interest and inter alia apply the model statute.

The UK could also enter into treaties based on an amended Rome I (that applies the model statute), with other countries, particularly the Commonwealth, with which it has close historical and political ties.

B. Commonwealth Countries

Commonwealth countries might also be receptive to the model statute. As stated in chapter two, English judges applied the concept of proper law of contract in the pre-Rome Convention period, and gave considerable significance to the place of performance in determining the test of closest and most real connection.[10] The only problem is that English common law was hostile to the use of presumptions in determining the applicable law, including the presumption of the place of performance.[11]

The Commonwealth approach as described above is generally applied by Commonwealth countries. For example, Oppong, who is a leading authority in African private international (and the academic godfather of private international law in Commonwealth Africa), submits that from the cases decided in Commonwealth African countries on the law applicable in the absence of choice for contractual obligations, 'it is evident that very considerable weight is given to the place of performance'.[12]

In Canada, the Ontario Court of Appeal in *Lilydale Cooperative Limited v Meyn Canada Inc*[13] applied the 'closest and most substantial connection test'[14] to the effect that '[t]he place of performance of the contract is related to its subject matter and, for determining the applicable law, is perhaps the most important criterion'.[15]

Also in Hong Kong, the Court of Final Appeal in *First Laser Ltd v Fujian Enterprises (Holdings) Co Ltd*[16] held that 'the intended place of performance has always been of great weight at common law',[17] and applied this choice of law criteria to an international commercial dispute before it.[18]

[10] See ch 2, s II.A.

[11] *Coast Lines Limited v Hudig and Veder Chartering NV* [1972] 2 QB 34, 44, 47.

[12] R Oppong, *Private International Law in Commonwealth Africa* (Cambridge, Cambridge University Press, 2013) 138.

[13] *Lilydale Cooperative Limited v Meyn Canada Inc* 2015 ONCA 281.

[14] First applied by the Canadian Supreme Court in *Imperial Life Assurance Co of Canada v Colmenares* [1967] SCR 443, 62 DLR (2d) 138, 1967 CarswellOnt 65 [14].

[15] *Lilydale* (n 13) [16].

[16] *First Laser Ltd v Fujian Enterprises (Holdings) Co Ltd* [2012] 15 HKCFAR 569.

[17] ibid [56].

[18] ibid.

Given that the place of performance is of considerable significance in determining the applicable law in the absence of choice for international commercial contracts in Commonwealth countries, it is submitted in this connection that the model statute might be attractive.

There are two main ways in which the model statute can be implemented by Commonwealth countries. First, the common law could be evolved to apply the criteria used in the model statute. This is a more pragmatic route, given that judge made law is a very significant source of law in the Commonwealth. A good reason for evolving the common law approach is that the test of closest connection in international commercial contract, without a connecting factor ruling (the test of closest connection) would likely lead to uncertainty, and it also gives the judge too much discretion in the determination of the applicable law. International commercial actors rely on certainty of the law to enhance the efficacy of their transactions. Moreover, the idea that the old English approach that use of presumptions (such as the presumption of the law of the place performance) or fixed connecting factors is not a good choice of law rule is now an outdated idea, given the significant number of private international law instruments that utilise presumptions or fixed rules in choice of law rules.[19]

It is submitted that judges in Commonwealth countries should not follow the English common law approach unthinkingly. They do not need to wait for a 'Lord Denning' to revolutionise private international law rules (as he did in the case of foreign currency obligations)[20] before they (judges in Commonwealth countries) make a shift.[21] Of course a uniform approach in the Commonwealth might be a good thing for international commercial actors who target their operations in those regions, but this does not mean judges in the Commonwealth should follow the English common law approach slavishly. This explains why Canada abandoned the traditional English common law approach on the recognition and enforcement of foreign judgment in favour of the 'real and substantial connection test'.[22]

In addition, and perhaps more important, England and the UK no longer applies the proper law of contract. In reality, the purity of English private international law has been adulterated by the Europeanisation of private international law, so that judges in Commonwealth countries should not apply English common law solutions in private international law unthinkingly. As Briggs aptly puts it:

> [W]e have had a wholly new version of our subject laid down and still being laid out. … It is no longer English law. Its civil and commercial core, in particular, has been taken over and is now found in European laws written in a mixture of black letters and invisible ink.

[19] See generally Symeonides (n 2).

[20] *Schorsch Meirer GMBH v Hennin* [1975] 1 All ER 152.

[21] See generally V Black, *Foreign Currency Claims in the Conflict of Laws* (Oxford, Hart Publishing, 2010).

[22] *Morguard Investment Ltd v De Savoye* [1990] 3 SCR 1077; *Beals v Saldanha* [2003] 3 SCR 416; *Club Resorts Ltd v Van Breda* [2012] SCC 17.

> Though the common law still controls some important parts of the subject, this territory is gradually being lost, and the common law rules of private international law are losing the universality which gave them their coherence. All this means that it no longer makes sense to think of our private international law as English. Its waters flow in two separate streams, but while one is in spate, the other is looking rather parched.[23]

Second, in the alternative legislators in Commonwealth countries could reform their choice of law rules in line with the model statute.

C. International Solution?

At the moment there is no international statute that provides a choice of law rule for determining the law applicable in the absence of choice for international commercial contracts.

The Hague Conference could have done it, but it didn't. The Hague Choice of Law Principles (Hague Principles) for international commercial contracts does not provide an international solution to determining the applicable law in the absence of choice for international commercial contracts.[24]

Article 4.17 of the commentary on the Hague Principles provides that:

> If the parties' intentions are neither expressed explicitly nor appear clearly from the provisions of the contract or from the particular circumstances of the case, there is no choice of law agreement. In such a case, the Principles do not determine the law governing the contract.

There is no official explanation why the Hague Principles do not provide an international solution for determining the applicable law in the absence of choice for international commercial contracts. In this connection, I consulted the academic commentaries of persons comprising the expert group that drafted the Hague Principles, but found no explanation.[25] I then consulted Oppong (who was a member of the expert group) by email, and he provided me with the following response:

> The only reason I recall is that it was not within the mandate of the Expert Group. We were tasked to focus on cases in which the parties have chosen the applicable law as it was thought that that is where there is enough common ground among states to make the principles viable.
>
> The ultimate goal was more about ensuring that there is harmony in respect of the limitations on freedom of choice – it was clear from our discussion that most countries

[23] Briggs (n 6).

[24] It is important to note that the Hague Principles are very influential. For example Australia may enact legislation to give effect to the Hague Principles. See generally M Douglas, and N Loadsman, 'The Impact of the Hague Principles on Choice of Law in International Commercial Contracts' (2018) 19 *Melbourne Journal of International Law* – https://papers.ssrn.com/sol3/papers.cfm?abstract_id=3230515.

[25] SC Symeonides, 'The Hague Principles on Choice of Law for International Contracts: Some Preliminary Comments' (2013) 61 *American Journal of Comparative Law* 1; D Girsberger and NB Cohen, 'Key Features of the Hague Principles on Choice of Law in International Commercial Contracts' (2017) 22 *Uniform Law Review* 315–35.

> allowed parties to choose the applicable law. The real issue was the limitations. We did not touch absence of choice at all.[26]

I also consulted Girsberger (Chairman of the expert group that drafted the Hague Principles), who offered the following explanation by email:

> Indeed, I believe that Richard Oppong is right. The Working Group was either instructed by the Council of the Hague Conference or itself decided quite early on to not include the fallback connecting factors in its proposal, because it was feared that this would delay the process inappropriately and may lead to failure due to the heavy differences between jurisdictions. Marta Pertegás was in charge of the instrument on the part of the Permanent Bureau of the Hague Conference at that time and may correct me if my recollection is wrong.[27]

I further contacted Pertegás, who offered me the following explanation by email:

> As Professors Oppong and Girsberger told you, the Working Group did not address the matter because the Group was not tasked to do so. In other words, there was no political mandate by the HCCH Organs (in particular, the Council on General Affairs and Policy) to consider rules in the absence of a choice of law by the parties. You can read more about it in the Conclusions and Recommendations of the Annual Meetings of that Council in the years 2008, 2009 or 2010. There is also an article published by the Permanent Bureau in the Uniform Law Review where, I believe, these circumstances are further documented.
>
> Having adopted the Rome I Regulation in prior years, the EU did not have much interest for further work in the area of the applicable law to contracts in the framework of the HCCH. On the other hand, other HCCH Members were keen to develop work on this area. The compromise was a limited mandate for the Working Group, focusing on the promotion of party autonomy.[28]

One opines that the expert group was not given a mandate to propose a solution for choice of law rules in determining the applicable law in the absence of choice for international commercial contracts because of the diverse approaches applied by various countries, particularly that of the United States and the EU, such that a uniform approach was not considered feasible.

As stated earlier in this conclusive chapter, a truly international solution to the determination of the applicable law in the absence of choice for international commercial contracts would be a good thing for businesspersons in the long run.

At first sight one might argue that the US would not be receptive to the model statute, given that many States in the US do not apply a blindfold conflicts justice

[26] Associate Professor Richard Frimpong Oppong of the Faculty of Law, Thompson Rivers University, Canada, V2C 0C8. Date of correspondence – 10 August 2018.

[27] Professor Daniel Girsberger of the Faculty of Law, University of Lucerne, Switzerland. Date of correspondence – 28 September 2018.

[28] Professor Marta Pertegás, Faculty of Law, University of Antwerp, Belgium. Date of correspondence – 7 October 2018.

system that does not look into the substance of the law.[29] Moreover the difference in thinking between EU scholars and American scholars in choice of law is well documented.[30] Unlike the US, the EU choice of law rules in determining the applicable law in the absence of choice for international commercial contracts prize certainty and uniformity over flexibility, does not generally apply issue-by-issue analysis, and governmental interest analysis. Moreover, the US has a diverse choice of law rules in its federation. This might explain why there has been no worldwide solution in the form of a truly international statute that determines the law applicable in the absence of choice for international commercial contracts.

It is opined that despite the differences between the US approach and EU approach, US legislators, judges, arbitrators and scholars might be receptive to the model statute if the idea in the model statute is dressed in another garb or repackaged. For States that are receptive to conflicts-justice principles, the place of performance could be proposed to such States as the principal connecting factor that should be utilised in determining the test of 'most significant relationship'[31] in international commercial contracts. For States that are not receptive to conflict-justice principles and prefer the governmental interest analysis theory, the place of performance could be proposed as the country or legal system that has the greatest interest in regulating an international commercial contract as a matter of policy, and should generally be the governing law. Such 'public law', 'sovereignty' and 'state interests' approach to the connecting factor of the place of performance might appeal to the eyes of a US judge, legislator, arbitrator or scholar. Inspiration may also be drawn comparatively from the European experience on Article 9(3) of Rome I.

III. Final Word

In this book, it was opined that the place of performance is of considerable importance in international commercial contracts, and then it was proposed that the EU legislator revises Article 4 of Rome I by explicitly giving special significance to the place of performance. Inspired by the EU experience, a model statute was proposed and drafted, which could be applied by legislators, judges, arbitrators and other decision makers outside the EU as an international solution for determining the applicable law in the absence of choice for international commercial contracts.

[29] P Hay, 'European Conflicts Law After the "American Revolution" – Comparative Notes' – https://illinoislawreview.org/wp-content/ilr-content/articles/2015/5/Hay.pdf, 2053–70; SC Symeonides, 'The American Evolution and the European Evolution in Choice of Law: Reciprocal Lessons' (2007–08) 82 *Tulane Law Review* 1471–760; O Lando, 'New American Choice-of-Law Principles and the European Conflict of Laws of Contract' (1982) 30 *American Journal of Comparative Law* 19–35; SC Symeonides, *An Outsider's View of the American Approach to Choice of Law: Comparative Observations on Current American and Continental Conflicts Doctrine* (Doctoral Dissertation, Harvard Law School, 1980).

[30] ibid (all).

[31] cf Restatement (Second) of Conflict of Laws s 188 (1969 Main Vol).

BIBLIOGRAPHY

I. Books

Ahern J and Binchy W (eds), *The Rome II Regulation on the Law Applicable to Non-Contractual-Obligations: A New International Litigation Regime* (The Hague, Martinus Nijhoff, 2009)

Ancel M-E, *La prestation caractéristique du contrat* (Paris, Economica, 2002)

Batiffol H, *Les Conflits de Lois en Matière de Contrats* (Paris, Rec Srirey, 1938)

Beale H et al, *Chitty on Contracts* 32nd edn (London, Sweet & Maxwell, 2015)

Beaumont PR and McEleavy PE, *Private International Law AE ANTON* 3rd edn (Edinburgh, W Green, 2011)

Beaumont P et al, *Cross-border Litigation in Europe* 1st edn (Oxford, Hart Publishing, 2017)

Beck G, *The Legal Reasoning of the Court of Justice of the EU* (Oxford, Hart Publishing, 2012)

Black V, *Foreign Currency Claims in the Conflict of Laws* (Oxford, Hart Publishing, 2010)

Briggs A, *Private International Law in English Courts* 1st edn (Oxford, Oxford University Press, 2014)

Briggs A and Rees P (P Rees as editor with no authorial role), *Civil Jurisdiction and Judgments* 4th edn (London, Informa/Lloyds of London Press, 2005)

Briggs A and Rees P, *Civil Jurisdiction and Judgments* 5th edn (London, Informa, 2009)

Cheshire GC, *International Contracts* 1st edn (London, Jackson, Son & Company, 1948)

——, *Private International Law* 4th edn (London; Oxford, Clarendon Press; Oxford University Press, 1952)

Cheshire GC and North PM, *Private International Law* 11th edn (Oxford, Oxford University Press, Oxford, 1987)

Collier J, *Conflict of Laws* 2nd edn (Cambridge, Cambridge University Press, 1994)

Collins L et al, *Dicey, Morris & Collins, The Conflict of Laws* 15th edn (London, Sweet & Maxwell, 2012)

Collins L, *Essays in International Litigation and the Conflict of Laws* (Oxford, Clarendon, corrected edn, 1996)

Corneloup S and Joubert N (eds), *Le Reglement communautaire Rome I' et le choix de loi dans les contrats internationaux* (Paris, LexisNexis Litec, 2011)

Cuniberti G, *Conflict of Laws: A Comparative Approach* (Cheltenham, Edward Elgar Publishing, 2017)

Dicey AV, *Introduction to the Study of the Law of the Constitution* 1st edn (New Yor, Macmillan and Company Limited, 1885)

——, *Conflict of Laws* 1st edn (London, Sweet & Maxwell, 1896)

——, *Conflict of Laws* 2nd edn (London, Sweet & Maxwell, 1908)

Collins L (ed), *Dicey and Morris, The Conflict of Laws* 8th edn (London, Sweet & Maxwell, 1967)

—— (ed), *Dicey and Morris, The Conflict of Laws* 11th edn (London, Sweet & Maxwell, 1987)

—— (ed), *Dicey and Morris, The Conflict of Laws* 12th edn (London, Sweet & Maxwell, 1993)

Dickinson A et al (eds), *Australian Private International Law for the 21st Century – Facing Outwards* (Oxford, Hart Publishing, 2014)

Everling U, *The Right of Establishment in the Common Market* (New York, Commerce Clearing House, 1964)

Falconbridge JD, *Essays on the Conflict of Laws* (Toronto, Canada Law Book Co, Ltd, 1947)

Fawcett J (ed), *Report and Development of Private International Law: Essays in Honour of Sir Peter North* (Oxford, Oxford University Press, 2002)

Fentiman R, *Foreign Law in English Courts* 1st edn (Oxford, Oxford University Press, 1998)

——, *International Commercial Litigation* (Oxford, Oxford University Press, 2015)

Ferrari F and Leible S (eds), *Rome I Regulation: the Law Applicable to Contractual Obligations in Europe* (Munich, Sellier European Law Publishers, 2009)

Fouchard G, *Goldman on International Commercial Arbitration* (E Gaillard and J Savage (eds), The Hague, Kluwer International, 1999)

Gutteridge HC and Megrah M, *The Law of Bankers' Commercial Credits* 5th edn (Abingdon, Taylor & Francis, 1976)

Hayward B, *Conflict of Laws and Arbitral Discretion – The Closest Connection Test* (Oxford, Oxford University Press, 2017)

Hill J and Chong A, *International Commercial Disputes: Commercial Conflict of Laws in English Courts* 4th edn (Oxford, Hart Publishing, 2010)

Hill J and Ni Shèilleabhain M, *Clarkson & Hill's Conflict of Laws* (Oxford, Oxford University Press, 2016)

Homberger A, *Die obligatorischen Vertrage im internationalen Privatrecht nach der Praxis des schweizerischen Bundesgerichts* (Unpublished PhD thesis, Berne, 1925)

Jennings R and Watts A (eds), *Oppenheim's International Law* vol I, 9th edn (Oxford, Oxford University Press, 1992)

Kaye P, *The New Private International Law of Contract of the European Community* 1st edn (Aldershot; Brookfield, Dartmouth Publishing Company, 1993)

Kegel G, *Internationales Privatrecht: Ein Studienbuch* 4th edn (Munich, Schwerpunktbereich, 1977)

Lando O et al (eds), *European Private International Law of Obligations: Acts and Documents of an International Colloquium on the European Preliminary Draft Convention on the Law Applicable to Contractual and Non-Contractual Obligations* 1st edn (Berlin, Mohr, 1975)

Lasok D and Stone P, *Conflict of Laws in the European Community* (London, Professional Books, 1987)

Lipstein K (ed), *International Encyclopedia of Comparative Law* vol III (Mouton, Brill/Nijhoff, 1976)

——, *Harmonization of Private International Law by the EEC* 1st edn (London, University of London Institute of Advanced Legal Studies, 1978)

Mann FA, *Foreign Affairs in English Courts* (Oxford, Oxford University Press, 1986)

——, *Further Studies in International Law* (Oxford, Oxford University Press, 1990)

Magnus U and Mankowski P (eds), *Brussels I Regulation* (Munich, Sellier European Law Publishers, 2007)

Magnus U and Mankowski P, *European Commentaries on Private International Law* vol II (Munich, Sellier European Law Publishers, 2017)

McParland M, *The Rome I Regulation on the Law Applicable to Contractual Obligations* (Oxford, Oxford University Press, 2015)

Mills A, *The Confluence of Public and Private International Law: Justice, Pluralism and Subsidiarity in the International Constitutional Ordering of Private Law* 1st edn (Cambridge, Cambridge University Press, 2009)

Morris JHC, *Dicey and Morris on the Conflict of Laws* 8th edn (London, Sweet & Maxwell, 1976)

——, *The Conflict of Laws* 2nd edn (London, Sweet & Maxwell, 1980)

Meeusen J et al (eds), *Enforcement of International Contracts in the European Union. Convergence and Divergence between Brussels I and Rome I* (Antwerp-Oxford-New York, Intersentia, 2004)

North PM, *Cheshire and North's Private International Law* 10th edn (Oxford, Oxford University Press, 1979)

North P (ed), *Contract Conflicts, The EEC Convention on the Law Applicable to Contractual Obligations: A Comparative Study* (Amsterdam, North-Holland Publishing Company, 1982)

Oppong R, *Private International Law in Commonwealth Africa* (Cambridge, Cambridge University Press, 2013)

Oser HL and Schönenberger W, *Kommentar zum schweizerischen Zivilgesetzbuch, Das Obligationenrecht, Allgemeine Einleitung* (Zurich, 1929)

Passarelli G, *Contract Law in Contemporary International Commerce* (Munich, Nomos, 2019)

Plender R and Wilderspin M, *European Private International Law of Obligations* 3rd edn (London, Sweet & Maxwell, 2009)

Plender R and Wilderspin M, *European Private International Law of Obligations* 4th edn (London, Sweet and Maxwell, 2014)

Rabel E, *The Conflict of Laws: A Comparative Study* Vol II, 2nd edn (Michigan, The University of Michigan Press, 1960)

Sarcevic P (ed), *International Contracts and Conflict of Laws: A Collection of Essays* (London, Graham & Trotman/Martinus Nijhoff, 1990)

Schnitzer AF, *Handbuch des Internationalen Privatrechts* 2nd edn (Zurich, 1944)

Schönenberger W, *Kommentar zum schweizerischen Zivilgesetzbuch, Das Obligationenrecht, Allgemeine Einleitung* (Zurich, 1929)

Seccombe M, and Weiler J (eds), *Integration through Law: Europe and the American Federal Experience Methods, Tools and Institutions* vol 1 (New York, Walter de Gruyter and Co, 1986)

Stone P and Farah Y (eds), *Research Handbook on EU Private International Law* (Cheltenham, Edward Elgar Publishing, 2015)

Story J, *Commentaries On The Conflict Of Laws, Foreign And Domestic* (Boston, CC Little and J Brown, 1834)

Symeonides SC, *Codifying Choice of Law around the World: An International Comparative Analysis* 1st edn (Oxford, Oxford University Press, 2014)

Torremans P et al, *Cheshire, North and Fawcett, Private International Law* 15th edn (Oxford, Oxford University Press, 2017)

Von Savigny FC, *Private International Law – A Treatise on the Conflict of Laws* (William Guthrie trans, London, T & T Law Publishers, 1869)

Westlake J, *A Treatise on Private International Law* (London, W Maxwell & Son, 1880)

II. Chapters in Books

Beaumont PR, 'The Brussels Convention Becomes a Regulation: Implications for Legal Basis, External Competence and Contract Jurisdiction' in J Fawcett (ed), *Report and Development of Private International Law: Essays in Honour of Sir Peter North* (Oxford, Oxford University Press, 2002)

Beaumont P and Yüksel B, 'Cross-border Civil and Commercial Disputes before the Court of Justice of the European Union' in P Beaumont et al, *Cross-border Litigation in Europe* 1st edn (Oxford, Hart Publishing, 2017)

Bonomi A, 'Article 9 of Rome I Regulation' in U Magnus and P Mankowski (eds), *European Commentaries on Private International Law* vol 1 (Munich, Sellier European Law Publishers, 2017)

Collins L, 'Practical Implications in England of the EEC Convention on the Law Applicable to Contractual Obligations' in P North (ed), *Contract Conflicts, The EEC Convention on the Law Applicable to Contractual Obligations: A Comparative Study* (Amsterdam, North-Holland Publishing Company, 1982)

Corneloup S, 'Choix de loi et contrats lies' in S Corneloup and N Joubert (eds), *Le reglèment communautaire 'Rome I' et le choix de loi dans les contrats internationaux* (Paris, Lexis Nexis, 2011), coll.du CREDIMI spec 285

Drobing U, 'Comments on Art. 7 of the Draft Convention' in O Lando et al (eds), *European Private International Law of Obligations Acts and Documents of an International Colloqium on the European Preliminary Draft Convention on the Law Applicable to Contractual and Non-Contractual Obligation* 1st edn (Berlin, Mohr, 1975)

Fentiman R, 'The Significance of Close Connection' in J Ahern and W Binchy (eds), *The Rome II Regulation on the Law Applicable to Non-Contractual-Obligations: A New International Litigation Regime* (The Hague, Martinus Nijhoff, 2009)

Ferrari F, 'Article 12 of Rome I Regulation' in U Magnus and P Mankowski (eds), *European Commentaries on Private International Law* vol II (Munich, Sellier European Law Publishers, 2017)

Güneysu-Güngör G, 'Article 4 of Rome I Regulation on the Applicable Law in the Absence of Choice – Methodological Analysis, Considerations' in P Stone and Y Farah (eds), *Research Handbook on EU Private International Law* (Cheltenham, Edward Elgar Publishing, 2015)

Harris J, 'Mandatory Rules and Public Policy under the Rome Convention' in F Ferrari and S Leible (eds), *The Law Applicable to Contractual Obligations in Europe* (Munich, Sellier European Law Publishers, 2009)

Hay P et al, 'Conflict of Laws as a Technique for Legal Integration' in M Seccombe, and J Weiler (eds), *Integration through Law: Europe and the American Federal Experience Methods, Tools and Institutions* Vol 1 (New York, Walter de Gruyter and Co, 1986, Volume 1)

Hoffmann BV, 'General Report on Contractual Obligations' in O Lando et al, *European Private International Law of Obligations: Acts and Documents of an International Colloquium on the European Preliminary Draft Convention on the Law Applicable to Contractual and Non-Contractual Obligations* 1st edn (Berlin, Mohr, 1975)

——, 'Assessment of the E.E.C. Convention from a German Point of View' in P North (ed), *Contract Conflicts: The EEC Convention on the Law Applicable to Contractual Obligations: A Comparative Study* (Amsterdam, North-Holland Publishing Company, 1982)

Jackson D, 'Mandatory Rules and Rules of "Ordre Public"' in P North (ed), *Contract Conflicts, The EEC Convention on the Law Applicable to Contractual Obligations: A Comparative Study* (Amsterdam, North-Holland Publishing Company, 1982)

Jaffey AJE, 'Choice of Law in Relation to Ius Dispositivum with Particular Reference to the EEC Convention on the Law Applicable to Contractual Obligations' in P North (ed), *Contract Conflicts, The EEC Convention on the Law Applicable to Contractual Obligations: A Comparative Study* (Amsterdam, North-Holland Company, 1982)

Jayme E, 'The Rome Convention on the Law Applicable to Contractual Obligations (1980)' in P Sarcevic (ed), *International Contracts and Conflict of Laws: A Collection of Essays* (London, Graham & Trotman/Martinus Nijhoff, 1990)

Juenger FK, 'The EEC Convention on the Law Applicable to Contractual Obligations: An American Assessment' in P North (ed), *Contract Conflicts, The EEC Convention on the Law Applicable to Contractual Obligations: A Comparative Study* (Amsterdam, North-Holland Publishing Company, Amsterdam, 1982)

Keyes M, 'Improving Australian Private International Law' in A Dickinson et al (eds), *Australian Private International Law for the 21st Century – Facing Outwards* (Oxford, Hart Publishing, 2014)

Lando O, 'Contracts' in K Lipstein (ed.), *International Encyclopedia of Comparative Law*, vol III, (Brill/ Nijhoff, Mouton, 1976)

——, 'The Law Applicable to the Merits of the Dispute' in P Sarcevic (ed), *Essays on International Commercial Arbitration* (Springer, Netherlands, 1989)

Largarde P, 'The Scope of the Applicable Law in the E.E.C Convention' in P North (ed), *Contract Conflicts: The EEC Convention on the Law Applicable to Contractual Obligations: A Comparative Study* 1st edn (Amsterdam, North-Holland Publishing Co 1982)

Lipstein P, 'Introduction: Conflicts Convention' in K Lipstein (ed), *Harmonization of Private International Law by the EEC* 1st edn (London, University of London Institute of Advanced Legal Studies, 1978)

Magnus U, 'Article 4 Rome I Regulation: the Applicable Law in the Absence of Choice' in F Ferrari and S Leible (eds), *Rome I Regulation: the Law Applicable to Contractual Obligations in Europe* (Munich, Sellier, 2009)

——, 'Article 4 of Rome I Regulation' in U Magnus and P Mankowski, *European Commentaries on Private International Law* vol II (Munich, Sellier European Law Publishers, 2017)

Mankowski P in U Magnus and P Mankowski (eds), *Brussels I Regulation* (Munich, Sellier European Law Publishers, 2007)

——, 'The Principle of Characterisitic Performance Visited Yet Again' in K Boele-Woelki et al (eds), *Convergence and Divergence in Private International Law: Liber Amicorum Kurt Siehr* (The Hague, Schultess and Eleven International Publising, 2010)

——, 'Article 3 of Rome I Regulation' in U Magnus and P Mankowski, *European Commentaries on Private International Law* vol II (Munich, Sellier European Law Publishers, 2017)

Mann FA, 'Effect of Mandatory Rules' in K Lipstein (ed), *Harmonisation of Private International Law by the EEC* (London, University of London Institute of Advanced Legal Studies, 1978)

——, 'Contracts: Effect of Mandatory Rules' in P North (ed), *Contract Conflicts: The E.E.C Convention on the Law Applicable to Contractual Obligations: A Comparative Study* (Amsterdam, North-Holland Publishing Company, 1982)

Mills A, 'The Application of Multiple Laws under the Rome II Regulation' in J Ahern and W Binchy (eds), *The Rome II Regulation on the Law Applicable to Non-Contractual-Obligations: A New International Litigation Regime* (The Hague, Martinus Nijhoff, 2009)

Morse CGJ, 'Contracts of Employment and the EEC Contractual Obligations Convention' in P North (ed), *Contract Conflicts: The EEC Convention on the Law Applicable to Contractual Obligations: A Comparative Study* (Amsterdam, North-Holland Publishing Company, 1982)

Nourrissat C, 'Le Dépeçage' in S Corneloup and N Joubert (eds), *Le règlement communautaire 'Rome I' et le choix de loi dans les contrats internationaux* (Paris, LexisNexis Litec, 2011)

Patocchi PM, 'Characteristic Performance: A New Myth in the Conflict of Laws? Some Comments on a Recent Concept in Swiss and European Private International Law', in MP Lalive (ed), *Études de droit international en l'honneur de Pierre Lalive* (Bâle/Francfort – sur-le-Main, Éditions Helbing & Lichtenhahn, 1993)

Philip A, 'Mandatory Rules, Public Law (Political Rules) and Choice of Law in the EEC Convention on the Law Applicable to Contractual Obligations' in P North (ed), *Contract Conflicts, The EEC Convention on the Law Applicable to Contractual Obligations: A Comparative Study* (Amsterdam, North-Holland Publishing Company, 1982)

Pocar F, 'Some Remarks on the Relationship between the Rome I and Brussels I Regulations' in S Ferrari and S Leible (eds), *The Law Applicable to Contractual Obligations in Europe* (Munich, Sellier European Law Publishers, 2009)

Sarcevic P (ed), 'The Law Applicable to the Merits of the Dispute' in *Essays on International Commercial Arbitration* (Amsterdam, Springer, 1989)

Vischer F, 'The Principle of the Typical Performance in International Contracts and the Draft Convention' in P North (ed), *Contract Conflicts, The EEC Convention on the Law Applicable to Contractual Obligations: A Comparative Study* (Amsterdam, North-Holland Publishing Company, 1982)

——, 'The Concept of the Characteristic Performance Reviewed' in *E Pluribus Unum, Liber Amicorum G Droz* (The Hague, Martinus Nijhoff Publishers, 1996)

——, 'Revolutionary Ideas and the Swiss Statute on Private International Law' in K Boele-Woelki et al (eds), *Convergence and Divergence in Private International Law: Liber Amicorum Kurt Siehr* (The Hague, Schultess and Eleven International Publising, 2010)

Von Overbeck AE, 'Contracts: The Swiss Draft Statute Compared with the EEC Convention' in P North (ed), *Contract Conflicts, The EEC Convention on the Law Applicable to Contractual Obligations: A Comparative Study* (Amsterdam, North-Holland Publishing Company, 1982)

III. Journal Articles

Alexander K, 'Civil Liability on the Periphery: Third Country Transactions in Violation of United States Economic Sanctions' (1999) 10 *European Business Law Review* 314

Ancel M-E, 'The Rome I Regulation and Distribution Contracts' (2008) 10 *Year Book of Private International Law* 221

Arzandeh A, 'The Law Governing International Contractual Disputes in the Absence of Express Choice by the Parties' (2015) *Lloyd's Maritime and Commercial Law Quarterly* 525

Atrill S, 'Choice of Law in Contract: the Missing Pieces of the Article 4 Jigsaw' (2004) 53 *International and Comparative Law Quarterly* 549

Baade HW, 'The Operation of Foreign Public Law' (1995) 30 *Texas International Law Journal* 431

Basedow J, 'A Common Contract Law for the Common Market' (1996) 33 *Common Market Law Review* 1169

Borum OA, 'Principles of the Private International Law on Contracts' (1940) 11 *Nordisk Tidsskrift for International Ret* 121

Badykov MR, 'The Russian Civil Code and the Rome Convention: Applicable Law in the Absence of Choice by the Parties' (2005) 1 *Journal of Private International Law* 269

Bagheri M, 'Conflict of Laws, Economic Regulations and Corrective/Distributive Justice' (2007) 28 *University of Pennsylvania Journal of International Law* 113

Baniassadi MR, 'Do Mandatory Rules of Public Law Limit Choice of Law in International Commercial Arbitration?' (1992–93) 10 *International Tax and Business Law* 59

Baxter IFG, 'International Business and Choice of Law' (1987) 36 *International and Comparative Law Quarterly* 92

Behr V, 'Rome I Regulation: A-Mostly-Unified Private International Law of Contractual Relationships within – most – of the European Union' (2011) *Journal of Law and Commerce* 233

Bleimaier JK, 'The Doctrine of Comity in Private International Law' (1978–79) 24 *Catholic Lawyer* 327

Blessing M, 'Mandatory Rules of Law *versus* Party Autonomy in International Arbitration' (1997) 14 *Journal of International Arbitration* 23

Blom J, 'Choice of Law Methods in Private International Law of Contract' (1978) 16 *Canadian Year Book of International Law* 230

Bonomi A., 'Note – Article 7(1) of the European Contracts Convention: Codifying the Practice of Applying Foreign Mandatory Rules' (2000–2001) 114 *Harvard Law Review* 2462

Borum OA, 'Principles of the Private International Law on Contracts' (1940) 11 *Nordisk Tidsskrift for International Ret* 121

Briggs A, 'Essay in International Litigation and the Conflict of Laws' (1995) 111 *Law Quarterly Review* 159

——, 'Principle of Comity in Private International Law' (2011) 354 *Recueil Des Cours* 77

Carruthers J, 'Party Autonomy in the Legal Regulation of Adult Relationships: what place for Party Choice in Private International Law?' (2012) 61 *International and Comparative Law Quarterly* 861

Childress DE, 'Comity as Conflict: Resituating International Comity as Conflict of Laws' (2010) 44 *UC Davis Law Review* 11

Chong A, 'The Public Policy and Mandatory Rules of Third Countries in International Contracts' (2006) 2 *Journal of Private International Law* 27

Chukwumerije O, 'Mandatory Rules of Law in International Commercial Arbitration' (1993) 5 *African Journal of International and Comparative Law* 561

Cohen S, 'The EEC Convention and U.S Law Governing Choice of Law for Contracts, with particular emphasis on the Restatement Second: A Comparative Study' (1988–89) 13 *Maryland Journal of International Law and Trade* 223

Collins L, 'Contractual Obligations – The EEC Preliminary Draft Convention on Private International Law' (1976) 25 *International and Comparative Law Quarterly* 35

Crawford EB and Carruthers JM, 'Connection and Coherence between and among European Instruments in the Private International Law of Obligations' (2014) 63 *International and Comparative Law Quarterly* 1

Cuniberti G, 'L'incertitude du lieu d'exécution sur la loi applicable au contrat. La difficile cohabitation des articles 4-2 et 4-5 de la Convention de Rome du 19 juin 1980' (2003) *Juris-Classeur Pèriodique* (general edn) 151

——, 'The International Market for Contracts – The Most Attractive Contract Laws' (2014) 34 *Northwestern Journal of International and Business* Law 455

——, 'The Laws of Asian International Business Transactions' (2016) 25 *Washington International Law* Journal (2016) 35
Daniel H, 'Choice of Law and Foreign Mandatory Rules in International Arbitration' (1994) 11 *Journal of International Arbitration* 57
David D, 'The Perils of Welfare Economics' (2002–03) 97 *Northwestern University Law Review* 351
Delaume GR, 'The European Convention on the Law Applicable to Contractual Obligations: Why a Convention' (1981) 22 *Virginia Journal of International Law* 105
De Lotbinière Mcdoughall A, 'International Arbitration and Money Laundering' (2004–05) 20 *American University International Law Review* 1021
De Miguel Asensio PA, 'Applicable Law in the Absence of Choice to Contracts Relating to Intellectual or Industrial Property Rights' (2008) 10 *Yearbook of Private International Law* 199
de Winter LL, 'Dwingend recht bij international overeenkomsten' (1964) 11 *Nederlandse Tijdschrift voor International Recht*, 329
Dickinson A, 'Third Country Mandatory Rules in the Law Applicable to Contractual Obligations: So Long Farewell, Auf Wiedersehen, Adieu?' (2007) 3 *Journal of Private International* 53
——, 'Rebuttable Assumptions (*ICF* v *Balkenende*)' (2010) *Lloyd's Maritime and Commercial Law Quarterly* 27
——, 'Fatal Accidents the Law Applicable to Claims by Family Members' (2016) 132 *Law Quarterly Review* 212
——, 'Back to the Future: the UK's EU Exit and the Conflict of Laws' (2016) 12 *Journal of Private International Law* 195
D'Oliviera HUJ, '"Characteristic Obligation" in the Draft EEC Obligation Convention' (1977) 25 *American Journal of Comparative Law* 303
Douglas M, and Loadsman N, 'The Impact of the Hague Principles on Choice of Law in International Commercial Contracts' (2018) 19 *Melbourne Journal of International Law* https://papers.ssrn.com/sol3/papers.cfm?abstract_id=3230515
Dutson S, 'A Dangerous Proposal: the European Commission's Attempt to Amend the law Applicable to Contractual Obligations' (2006) *Journal of Business Law* 608
Enonchong N, 'The Law Applicable to Demand Guarantees and Counter-Guarantees' (2015) *Lloyd's Maritime and Commercial Law Quarterly* 194
Erauw J, 'Observations about Mandatory Rules Imposed on Transatlantic Commercial Relationships' (2003–04) 26 *Houston Journal of International Law* 269
Fawcett JJ, 'Evasion of Law and Mandatory Rules in Private International Law' (1990) 49 *Cambridge Law Journal* 44
——, 'The Interrelationship of Jurisdiction and Choice of Law in Private International Law' (1991) 44 *Current Legal Problems* 39
Fentiman R, 'Commercial Expectations and the Rome Convention' (Case Comment) (2002) 61 *Cambridge Law Journal* 50
——, 'Choice of Law in Europe: Uniformity and Integration' (2007–08) 82 *Tulane Law Review* 2021
Fiorini A, 'The Codification of Private International Law: the Belgian Experience' (2005) 54 *International and Comparative Law Quarterly* 499
Fitchen J, 'The Private International Law Consequences of Brexit' (2017) 35 *Nederlands Internationaal Privaatrecht* 411
Fletcher JP, 'An Argument for Ratification: Some Basic Principles of the 1994 Inter-American Convention of the Law Applicable to International Contracts' (1999) 27 *Georgia Journal of International and Comparative Law* 477
Forsyth C and Moser P, 'The Impact of the Applicable Law of Contract on the Law of Jurisdiction under the European Convention' (1996) 45 *International and Comparative Law Quarterly* 190
Francescakis P, 'Quelques precisions sur les lois d'application immediate et leurs rapports avec les règles de conflit de lois' (1966) 55 *Revue critique de droit international privé* 1
Gabor FA, 'Private International Law Aspects of East-West Trade: A Synopsis of Recent Developments' (1989) 17 *International Journal of Legal Information* 144

Gibson CS, 'Arbitration, Civilisation and Public Policy: Seeking Counterpoise between Arbitral Autonomy and the Public Policy Defense in view of Foreign Mandatory Public Law' (2008–09) 113 *Penn State Law Review* 1227

Girsberger D and Cohen NB, 'Key Features of the Hague Principles on Choice of Law in International Commercial Contracts' (2017) 22 *Uniform Law Review* 315

Giuliano M et al, 'Draft Convention and Report' (1973) 9 *Revisita di diritto internazionale private e processuale* 189

Graziano TK, 'Jurisdiction under Article 7 No. 1 of the Recast Brussels I Regulation: Disconnecting the Procedural Place of Performance from its Counterpart in Substantive Law' (2015) 16 *Year Book of Private International Law* 167

Grusic U, 'Jurisdiction in Complex Contracts Under the Brussels I Regulation' (2011) 7 *Journal of Private International Law* 321

Guedj TG, 'The Theory of the Lois de Police, A Functional Trend in Continental Private International Law – A Comparative Analysis with Modern American Theories' (1991) 39 *American Journal of Comparative Law* 661

Gutierrez LG, 'Franchise Contracts and the Rome I Regulation on the Law Applicable to International Contracts' (2008) 10 *Year Book of Private International Law* 233

Hakki MM, 'Choice of Law, Contracts and The EC's 1980 Rome Convention: A Re-evaluation in the 21st Century' (2003) *Australian Law Journal* 156

Harris J, 'The Brussels I Regulation and the Re-emergence of the English Common Law' (2008) 4 *European Legal Forum* 181

——, 'Understanding the English Approach to the Europeanisation of Private International Law' (2008) 4 *Journal of Private International Law* 347

——, 'The Proposed EU Regulation on Succession and Wills: Prospects and Challenges' (2008) 22 *Trust Law International* 181

Hartley TC, 'Mandatory Rules in International Contracts: The Common Law Approach' (1997) 266 *Recueil des Cours* 341

——, 'The European Union and the Systematic Dismantling of the Common law of Conflict Laws' (2005) 54 *International and Comparative Law Quarterly* 813

Hay P, 'The Interrelation of Jurisdiction and Choice-of-law in United States Conflicts Law' (1979) 28 *International and Comparative Law Quarterly* 161

——, 'Comments on "Self-Limited Rules of Law" in Conflicts Methodology' (1982) 30 *American Journal of Comparative Law* 129

Hein JV, 'The Contribution of the Rome II Regulation to the Communitarisation of Private International Law' (2009) 73 *RabelsZ* 461

Hellner M, 'Third Country Overriding Mandatory Rules in the Rome I Regulation: Old Wine in New Bottles?' (2009) 5 *Journal of Private International Law* 447

Hill J, 'Jurisdiction in Matters Relating to a Contract under the Brussels Convention' (1995) 44 *International and Comparative Law Quarterly* 591

——, 'Some Private International Law Aspects of the Arbitration Act 1996' (1997) 46 *International and Comparative Law Quarterly* 274

——, 'Choice of Law in Contract under the Rome Convention: The Approach of the UK Courts' (2004) 53 *International and Comparative Law Quarterly* 325

Hook M, 'The Choice of Law Agreement as a Reason for Exercising Jurisdiction' (2014) 63 *International & Comparative Law Quarterly* 963

Horlacher HM, 'The Rome Convention and the German Paradigm: Forecasting the Demise of the European Treaty on the Law Applicable to Contractual Obligations' (1994) 27 *Cornell International Law Journal* 173

Jaffey AJE, 'Essential Validity of Contracts in the English Conflict of Laws' (1974) 23 *International and Comparative Law Quarterly* 1

——, 'The English Proper Law Doctrine and the EEC Convention' (1984) 22 *International and Comparative Law Quarterly* 531

Jamal F, 'The Law Governing the Validity of a Contract – A Reconsideration' (1983) 4 *Singapore Law Review* 111

James S, 'Rome I: Shall we Dance?' (2008) 2 *Law & Financial Market Review* 113

Juenger FK, 'The European Convention on the Law Applicable to Contractual Obligations: Some Critical Observations' (1981–82) 22 *Virginia Journal of International Law* 123

——, 'Two European Conflicts Conventions' (1998) 28 *Victoria Wellington Law Review* 527

Kaufmann-Kohler G, 'La prestation caractéristique en droit international privé et l'influence de la Suisse' (1989) XLV *Annuaire suisse de droit international* 195

Kegel G, 'Savigny and Story' (1989) 37 *American Journal of Comparative Law* 39

Lagarde P, 'The European Convention on the Law Applicable to Contractual Obligations: An Apologia' (1981) 22 *Virginia Journal of International Law* 91

——, 'Le Principle de Proximitè dans le Droit International Privè Contemporian' (1986) 196 *Recueil des Cours* 1

——, 'Le Nouveau Droit international des Contrats après l'entrée en vigueur de la Convention de Rome du Juin 1980' (1991) *Revue Critique de Droit International Privè* 286

——, 'Remarques sur la proposition de Règlement de la Commission Européene sur la Loi Applicable aux Obligations Contractulles' (2006) *Revue Critique de Droit International Privè* 331

Lando O, 'Scandinavian Conflict of Law Rules Respecting Contracts: Party Autonomy and Center of Gravity' (1957) 6 *American Journal of Comparative Law* 1

——, 'The Proper Law of the Contract' (1964) 8 *Scandinavian Studies in Law* 105

——, 'The EC Draft Convention on the Law Applicable to Contractual and Non-Contractual Obligations: Introduction and Contractual Obligations' (1974) 38 *Rabel Journal of Comparative and International Private Law* 6

——, 'New American Choice-of-Law Principles and the European Conflict of Laws of Contracts' (1982) 30 *American Journal of Comparative Law* 19

——, 'The EEC Convention on the Law Applicable to Contractual Obligations' (1987) 24 *Common Market Law Review* 159

——, 'Some issues Relating to the Law Applicable to Contractual Obligations' (1996–97) 7 *Kings College Journal* 66

——, 'Dicey and Morris: A Review' (1998) 47 *International and Comparative Law Quarterly* 394

Lando O and Nielsen PA, 'The Rome I Proposal' (2007) 3 *Journal of Private International Law* 29

Lando O and Nielsen PA, 'The Rome I Regulation' (2008) 45 *Common Market Law Review* 1687

Lein E, 'The New Rome I/Rome II/Brussels I Synergy' (2008) 10 *Yearbook of Private International Law* 177

Lei W, 'Mandatory Rules of the Rome I Regulation: Not "Old Wine in New Bottles"' (2011) 7 *Canadian Social Science* 166

Lipstein K, 'Characteristic Performance – A New Concept in the Conflict of Laws in Matters of Contract for the EEC' (1981) 3 *Northwestern Journal of International and Business* 402

Lorenzo SS, 'Choice of Law and Overriding Mandatory Rules in International Contracts after Rome I' (2010) 12 *Yearbook of Private International Law* 67

Maniruzzaman. AFM, 'Choice of Law in International Contracts – Some Fundamental Conflict of Laws Issues [article]' (1999) 16 *Journal of International Arbitration* 141

Mance J, 'Is Europe Aiming to Civilise the Common Law'? (2007) 18 *European Business Law Review* 77

Mann FA, 'Proper Law and Illegality in Private International Law' (1937) 18 *British Yearbook of International Law* 97

——, 'The Proper Law in the Conflict of Laws' (1987) 36 *International and Comparative Law Quarterly* 437

Marazopoulou V, 'Overriding Mandatory Provisions of Article 9(3) of Rome I Regulation' (2011) 64 *Revue Hellènique de Droit International* 779

Marshall BA, 'Reconsidering the Proper Law of Contract' (2012) 13 *Melbourne Journal of International Law'* 505

McGuiness GM, 'The Rome Convention: The Contracting Parties' (2000) *San Diego International Law Journal* 127
Meisel F, 'Harmonisation of Contracts, Jurisdiction and Conflicts of Laws in the European Community' (1988) 13 *Holdsworth Law Review* 46
Michaels R, 'EU Law as Private International Law? Reconceptualising the Country-of-Origin Principle as Vested-Rights Theory' (2006) 2 *Journal of Private International Law* 195
Mills A, 'The Dimensions of Public Policy in Private International Law' (2008) 4 *Journal of Private International Law* 201
Morris JHC, 'The Eclipse of the Lex Loci Solutionis – A Fallacy Exploded' (1952–53) 6 *Harvard Law Review* 505
Moss GC, 'Performance of Obligations as the Basis of Jurisdiction and Choice of Law (Lugano and Brussels Conventions Article 5(1) and Rome Convention Article 4) (1999) 4 *Nordic Journal of International Law* 379
Muir Watt H, 'Choice of Law in Integrated and Interconnected Markets: A Matter of Political Economy' (2003) 7 *Electronic Journal of Comparative Law* 1
O'Brian WE, 'Choice of Law under the Rome Convention: the Dancer or the Dance' (2004) *Lloyd's Maritime and Commercial Law Quarterly* 375
O'Connor G, 'When in Rome: An Examination of Article 4 of the Rome Regime on the Governing Law of International Contracts' (2010) 9 *Hibernian Law Journal* 39
Okoli CSA, 'The Significance of the Doctrine of Accessory Allocation as a Connecting Factor under Article 4 of Rome I Regulation' (2013) 9 *Journal of Private International Law* 449
——, 'Choice of law for Contract of Carriage of Goods in the European Union' (2015) 4 *Lloyds Maritime and Commercial Law Quarterly* 512
——, 'AASA: Locating the Central Administration of a Subsidiary Company which is part of a Group of Companies under Article 60 of Brussels I Regulation' (2015) *European Company Law* 13
Okoli CSA and Arishe GO, 'The Operation of the Escape Clauses in the Rome Convention, Rome I Regulation and Rome II Regulation' (2012) 8 *Journal of Private International Law* 513
Oppong RF and Niro LC, 'Enforcing Judgments of International Courts in National Courts' (2014) *Journal of International Dispute Settlement* 344
Parisot V, 'Note sous Civ 1ère 12 octobre 2011, no 10-19517' (2012) *Journal de Droit International*, Comm 20, 1335 (Convention de Rome du 19 juin 1980 sur la loi applicable aux obligations contractuelles – loi applicable au cautionnement)
Pavic V, 'Bribery and International Commercial Arbitration – The Role of Mandatory Rules and Public Policy' (2012) 43 *Victoria University Wellington Law Review* 661
Penadés MF, 'Commercial Choice of Law in Context: Looking Beyond Rome' (2015) 78 *Modern Law Review* 241
Pilich M, 'Brexit and EU Private International Law: May the EU Stay in?' (2017) 24 *Maastricht Journal of European and Comparative Law* 1
Prebble J, 'Choice of Law to Determine the Validity and Effect of Contracts: A Comparison of English and American Approaches to the Conflict of Laws' (1973) 58 *Cornell Law Review* 433
Punt B, 'Heading for a more Characteristic Jurisdiction?' (2009) *International Business Law Journal* 51
Reese WLM, 'Dépeçage: A Common Phenomenon in Choice of Law' (1973) 73 *Columbia Law Review* 58
Rammeloo S, '"From Rome to Rome" – Cross-border Employment Contract. European Private International Law: Intertemporal law and Foreign Overriding Mandatory Laws – Case C-135/15 *Greek Republic v. Grigorios Nikiforidis*, EU:C:2016:774' (2017) 24 *Maastricht Journal of European and Comparative Law* 298
Reimann M, 'Savigny's Triumph? Choice of Law in Contracts Cases at the Close of the Twentieth Century' (1999) 39 *Virginia Journal of International Law* 571
Reynolds FMB, 'The Enforcement of Contracts involving Corruption or Illegality in other Countries' (1997) *Singapore Journal of Legal Studies* 371

Richardson N, 'The Concept of Characteristic Performance and the Proper Law Doctrine' (1989) 1 *Bond Law Review* 284
Rogerson P, 'Habitual Residence: The New Domicile' (2000) 49 *International and Comparative Law Quarterly* 86
——, 'Conflict of Laws' (2009) *All England Annual Review* 5
——, 'Problems of the Applicable Law of the Contract in the English Common Law Jurisdiction Rules: The Good Arguable Case' (2013) 9 *Journal of Private International Law* 387
Rühl G, 'Methods and Approaches in Choice of Law: An Economic Perspective' (2006) 24 *Berkeley Journal of International Law* 801
——, 'Judicial Cooperation in Civil and Commercial Matters after Brexit: Which way forward?' (2018) 67 *International and Comparative Law Quarterly* 99
Schultsz J, 'Dutch Antecedents and Parallels to Article 7 of the EEC Contracts Convention of 1980' (1983) 47 *Rabels Zeitschrift* 267
Schu R, 'The Applicable Law to Consumer Contracts made over the Internet: Consumer Protection through Private International Law' (1997) 5 *International Journal of Law and Information Technology* 192
Shine P, 'The Problem of Place of Performance in Contract under Brussels I Regulation: Can One Size Fit All?' (2011) *International Company and Commercial Law Review* 20
Sian DCG, 'Contractual Illegality and Conflict of Laws' (1995) 7 *Singapore Academy of Law Journal* 303
Sinclair AM, 'Conflict of Law Problems in Admiralty' (1961) 15 *Southwestern Law Journal* 207
Smith H, 'Enforcement of Foreign Mandatory Rules' (2000) 1 *Hibernian Law Journal* 305
Siehr K, 'Private International Law and the difficult Problem to return illegally exported Cultural Property' (2015) 20 *Uniform Law Review* 503
Sing TK, 'Illegal Contracts in the Conflict of Laws: Some Recent Developments in Singapore' (1993) *Singapore Journal of Legal Studies* 214
Stein PL, 'Choice of Law: Defining the Place of Performance for General Contract Disputes in Oklahoma' (2011) 64 *Oklahoma Law Review* 17
Struycken THD, 'Some Dutch Reflections on the Rome Convention, Art 4(5)' (1996) *Lloyd's Maritime and Commercial Quarterly* 18
Symeonides SC, 'The American Evolution and the European Evolution in Choice of Law: Reciprocal Lessons' (2007–08) 82 *Tulane Law Review* 1471
——, 'Rome II and Tort Conflicts: A Missed Opportunity' (2008) 56 *American Journal of Comparative Law* 173
——, 'The Hague Principles on Choice of Law for International Contracts: Some Preliminary Comments' (2013) 61 *American Journal of Comparative Law* 1
Takahashi K, 'Jurisdiction in Matters Relating to Contract: Article 5(1) of the Brussels Convention' (2002) *European Law Review* 530
Tang Z, 'The Interrelationship of European Jurisdiction and Choice of Law in Contract' (2008) 4 *Journal of Private International Law* 35
——, 'Law Applicable in the Absence of Choice – The New Article 4 of the Rome I Regulation' (2008) 71 *Modern Law Review* 785
Tetley W, 'Evasion/*Fraude à la loi* and Avoidance of the Law' (1993–94) 39 *McGill Law Journal* 303
Tillman C, 'The Relationship between Party Autonomy and the Mandatory Rules in the Rome Convention' (2002) *Journal of Business Law* 45
Ubertazzi B, 'Licence Agreements Relating to IP Rights and the EC Regulation on Jurisdiction' (2009) 40 *International Review of Intellectual Property and Competition Law* 912
Untiedt KD, 'International Contracts under the Conflict of Laws Rules of Great Britain and Japan' (1984) 7 *Loyola of Los Angeles International and Comparative Law Journal* 193
Verhagen HLE, 'The Tension between Party Autonomy and European Union Law: Some Observations on *Ingmar GB LTD v. EATON LEONARD TECHNOLOGIES INC*' (2002) 51 *International and Comparative Law Quarterly* 135

Verschraegen B, 'Austrian Report' (2012) 20 *European Review of Private Law* 51
Viejobueno S, 'Private International Law Rules Relating to the Validity of International Sales Contracts' (1993) 26 *Comparative and International Law Journal of South Africa* 172
Villiers L, 'Breaking in the "Unruly Horse": The Status of Mandatory Rules of Law as a Public Policy Basis for the Non-Enforcement of Arbitral Awards' (2011) 18 *Australian International Law Journal* 155
Williams PR, 'The EEC Convention on the Law Applicable to Contractual Obligations' (1986) 35 *International and Comparative Law Quarterly* 1
Winnard S, 'Is it Mandatory? State Interests, General Words and International Contracts' (2014) 20 *New Zealand Business Law Quarterly* 244
Wojewoda M, 'Mandatory Rules in Private International Law' (2000) 7 *Maastricht Journal of European and Comparative Law* 183
Wolff LC, 'Flexible Choice-of-Law Rules: Panacea or Oxymoron?' (2014) 10 *Journal of Private International Law* 431
Yu H, 'Choice of the Proper Law Vs. Public Policy' (2008) 1 *Contemporary Asia Arbitration Journal* 107
Yuksel B, 'The Relevance of the Rome I Regulation to International Commercial Arbitration in the European Union' (2011) 7 *Journal of Private International Law* 149
Zebot CA, 'Efficiency and Equity in Welfare Economics' (1965) 88 *Monthly Labour Review* 528
Zweigert K, 'Some Reflections on the Sociological Dimensions of Private International Law or: What is Justice in the Conflict of Laws?' (1973) 44 *University of Colorado Law Review* 283

IV. Other Sources

Briggs A, Secession from the European Union and Private International Law: the Cloud with a Silver Lining – www.law.ox.ac.uk/sites/files/oxlaw/adrian_briggs_brexit_lecture.pdf
Carillo LF, *Contratos internacionales: la prestación caracteristica* (Bologne, 1994)
Financial Markets Law Committee, 'Legal Assessment of the Conversion of the Rome Convention to a Community Instrument and the Provisions of the Proposed Rome I Regulations' – European Commission Final Proposal for a Regulation on the Law Applicable to Contractual Obligations ('Rome I') (2006) 121(3) 12–14. www.fmlc.org/Documents/April06Issue121.pdf
Hay P, 'European Conflicts Law After the "American Revolution" – Comparative Notes' – https://illinoislawreview.org/wp-content/ilr-content/articles/2015/5/Hay.pdf
Hayward B, 'Is Arbitral Justice Blind? The Conflict of Law and International Commercial Arbitration' – http://afia.asia/2017/03/is-arbitral-justice-blind-the-conflict-of-law-and-international-commercial-arbitration/
www.abdn.ac.uk/law/research/eupillar.php
http://ec.europa.eu/justice/news/consulting_public/rome_i/contributions/university_hamburg_en.pdf
www.scotlawcom.gov.uk/files/4413/1739/0072/Private_International_Law__Consultative_Document_on_EEC_Preliminary_Draft_Convention_on_the_Law_applicable_to_Contractual_and_Non-Contractual_Obligations.pdf
Letter from Baroness Ashton of Upholland, Parliamentary under Secretary of State of State, to Lord Grenfell, Chairman of the HL Select Committee on European Union, 16 May 2006
Magnus U and Mankowski P, 'Joint Response to the Green Paper on the Conversion of the Rome Convention of 1980 on the Law Applicable to Contractual Obligations into a Community Instrument and Its Modernisation' COM(2002) 654 final
Ministry of Justice, 'Should the UK opt in?' *Response to Consultation* CP05/08CP(R), January 2009

Robitaille C, 'La doctrine de la prestation caractéristique en droit international privé des contrats' – www.memoireonline.com/a/fr/cart/download/t1TQK3lCZSqh

Summers A, 'Interpreting Article 4(3) of Rome' – www.academia.edu/1998215/Interpreting_Article_4_3_of_the_Rome_I_Regulation. P. 30

Symeonides SC, *An Outsider's View of the American Approach to Choice of Law:Comparative Observations on Current American and Continental Conflicts Doctrine* (Doctoral Dissertation, Harvard Law School, 1980)

——, 'Codification and Flexibility in Private International Law' – https://papers.ssrn.com/sol3/papers.cfm?abstract_id=1945924

INDEX